Israel and Surrounding Arab Countries in 1977

MEDITERRANEAN SEA

Alexandria

Port Said

Suez Canal

Ismailiya

Great
Bitter
Lake

★ Cairo

Suez

EGYPT

Nile

GULF OF SUEZ

Camp David

WILLIAM B. QUANDT

Camp David

PEACEMAKING
AND POLITICS

THE BROOKINGS INSTITUTION
Washington, D.C.

Copyright © 1986 by
THE BROOKINGS INSTITUTION
1775 Massachusetts Avenue, N.W., Washington, D.C. 20036

Library of Congress Cataloging in Publication data:

Quandt, William B.
  Camp David : peacemaking and politics.

  Bibliography: p.
  Includes index.
  1. Israel-Arab War, 1973—Peace. 2. Egypt,
Treaties, etc. Israel, 1979 Mar. 26. 3. United States—
Foreign relations—Near East. 4. Near East—Foreign
relations—United States. 5. United States—Foreign
relations—1977–1981. I. Title.
  DS128.183.Q36 1986   327.73056   85-48174
  ISBN 0-8157-7290-4
  ISBN 0-8157-7289-0 (pbk.)

1 2 3 4 5 6 7 8 9

Book design by Meadows & Wiser

THE BROOKINGS INSTITUTION is an independent organization devoted to nonpartisan research, education, and publication in economics, government, foreign policy, and the social sciences generally. Its principal purposes are to aid in the development of sound public policies and to promote public understanding of issues of national importance.

The Institution was founded on December 8, 1927, to merge the activities of the Institute for Government Research, founded in 1916, the Institute of Economics, founded in 1922, and the Robert Brookings Graduate School of Economics and Government, founded in 1924.

The Board of Trustees is responsible for the general administration of the Institution, while the immediate direction of the policies, program, and staff is vested in the President, assisted by an advisory committee of the officers and staff. The by-laws of the Institution state: "It is the function of the Trustees to make possible the conduct of scientific research, and publication, under the most favorable conditions, and to safeguard the independence of the research staff in the pursuit of their studies and in the publication of the results of such studies. It is not a part of their function to determine, control, or influence the conduct of particular investigations or the conclusions reached."

The President bears final responsibility for the decision to publish a manuscript as a Brookings book. In reaching his judgment on the competence, accuracy, and objectivity of each study, the President is advised by the director of the appropriate research program and weighs the views of a panel of expert outside readers who report to him in confidence on the quality of the work. Publication of a work signifies that it is deemed a competent treatment worthy of public consideration but does not imply endorsement of conclusions or recommendations.

The Institution maintains its position of neutrality on issues of public policy in order to safeguard the intellectual freedom of the staff. Hence interpretations or conclusions in Brookings publications should be understood to be solely those of the authors and should not be attributed to the Institution, to its trustees, officers, or other staff members, or to the organizations that support its research.

To Helena

Foreword

The Camp David Accords, signed by the President of Egypt and the Prime Minister of Israel on September 17, 1978, were an event of historic importance in the modern Middle East. These agreements, hammered out in lengthy negotiations over a period of some eighteen months, set the stage for the signing of a formal treaty of peace between Egypt and Israel on March 29, 1979. With these two states at peace, and both closely tied to the United States, the strategic map of the Middle East was fundamentally altered.

In the minds of most Americans, the Camp David Accords stand out as a signal achievement of U.S. foreign policy. But for many in the Middle East, the connotations are not so positive. Some Israelis feel they gave up too much for too little. Some Egyptians feel that their president should have got more for the Palestinians. And virtually everyone agrees that the Camp David formula for resolving the Palestinian question fell well short of the mark.

This study of the Camp David Accords and the diplomacy surrounding them is primarily a case study in U.S. foreign policy making. It is also an analysis of negotiations. And it tries to illustrate the close connections between the workings of the American political system and the president's capacity to conduct foreign policy.

William B. Quandt is a senior fellow in the Brookings Foreign Policy Studies program. Before coming to Brookings in 1979, he served on the staff of the National Security Council, where he was responsible for dealing with the Arab-Israeli conflict. He has the unique perspective, then, of having been a participant in, and an observer of, the events he describes. But this is not a memoir. It is political analysis based on unusually full access to the relevant documents and to most of the key players in the negotiations.

Many people helped the author in the course of his research. On the American side, President Jimmy Carter gave his permission for Quandt to consult classified documents held in Atlanta as part of the archive for his presidential library. He also agreed to be interviewed in Plains, Georgia. Among the other American participants in the Camp David negotiations, Quandt is especially grateful to Zbigniew Brzezinski, Hermann F. Eilts, William Kirby, Samuel W. Lewis, Jody Powell, Harold H. Saunders, Gary Sick, Cyrus R. Vance, Nicolas Veliotes, and Richard Viets. Saunders and Eilts, as well as David Shipler, John D. Steinbruner, and I. William Zartman, reviewed the manuscript in draft and made many useful comments.

In Egypt, Quandt was assisted by Muhammad Abdallah, Kamal Hassan Ali, Nabil al-Arabi, Usama al-Baz, Boutros Boutros Ghali, Ismail Fahmy, Ashraf Ghorbal, Mansur Hassan, Muhammad Ibrahim Kamil, Mustafa Khalil, Ahmed Maher, and Muhammad Shaker. In Israel, he was helped in his research by Aharon Barak, Hanan Bar-On, Simcha Dinitz, Ephraim Evron, Meir Rosenne, Elyakim Rubinstein, Eitan Ben Tsur, and Ezer Weizman. In Syria, he interviewed Abd al-Halim Khaddam and Faruk Sharaa. In Jordan, he had useful meetings with King Hussein, Crown Prince Hassan, Adnan Abu Audeh, Taher al-Masri, and Marwan Qasim.

In Atlanta, Don Shewe and Martin Elzy helped to make documents available from the Carter presidential archive. At the National Archives, Jill Merrill assisted in locating the first draft of the Egyptian-Israeli agreement at Camp David. Brenda Regar at the National Security Council expedited the security clearance of the manuscript. Steven M. Riskin and Margaret A. Siliciano provided invaluable research assistance. Caroline Lalire edited the manuscript; Alan G. Hoden and James E. McKee verified its factual content; Ruth E. Conrad cheerfully typed many drafts; and Susan L. Woollen helped in the final stages of preparing the manuscript for publication. The John D. and Catherine T. MacArthur Foundation and the Rockefeller Foundation provided funding for the project.

The views in this book are solely those of the author and should not be ascribed to the persons or foundations whose assistance is acknowledged above, or to the trustees, officers, or other staff members of the Brookings Institution.

Bruce K. MacLaury
President

February 1986
Washington, D.C.

Author's Preface

From January 1977 until July 1979, I was a member of the National Security Council staff, reporting directly to Zbigniew Brzezinski. My primary area of responsibility was the Arab-Israeli conflict. During those two and one-half years I participated in most of the meetings that President Jimmy Carter had with Middle East leaders. I traveled with Secretary of State Cyrus Vance on almost all his trips to the Middle East and worked closely with the able team he had assembled in the Near East Bureau. I participated in many of the policy deliberations on the Arab-Israeli conflict that took place in Washington. And I drafted endless numbers of policy memorandums. But I was primarily a witness and sometimes an adviser, not a policymaker.

Although I participated in the Camp David negotiations, I would not have hazarded to write about that complex diplomatic story based only on what I was able to observe. Fortunately, most of the other participants in the negotiations have been willing to share their recollections with me, and several of the principals in Egypt, Israel, and Washington have written their own accounts. All this has helped immeasurably.

Before deciding to undertake this project, I sought permission to consult the relevant documents on the American side. I knew that my own memory could easily fail me. Fortunately, President Carter was willing to grant me access to the papers held in Atlanta as part of his presidential library project. I was therefore able to consult the files that I had developed while on the staff of the National Security Council. Virtually all the records of presidential meetings were available, except for those restricted meetings for which personal notes of the participants are probably the only records. I was also able to consult cables to and from American embassies in the Middle East, messages sent to and from Carter, and many other fragments of the written record. Nowhere will the future historian ever find a complete documentary record, but the files I was able to examine were as good as any.

There are clearly advantages and disadvantages to writing about events in which one participated. The most obvious danger is tunnel vision, a tendency to see everything from one's own partial perspective. Lack of objectivity and apologetics can also enter in. Offsetting these potential problems are the advantages one gains from being there: a feel for the personalities and the way they dealt with one another, a sense of context, and an understanding, at least in part, of why policies were adopted.

Because of my role as a middle-level participant on the American side, and my special access to U.S. documentation, this study is primarily about how U.S. policy toward the Arab-Israeli conflict was formulated at a particular time. The rules governing my access to highly classified material should be explained. I was allowed to take notes, but not to make actual copies of documents. The manuscript was submitted to a review by the National Security Council to ensure that no sensitive information that could harm the security of the United States was included. Only two very minor deletions were made in the course of this review.

The reader will note that I quote directly more often from American officials than from Egyptians or Israelis. There is a reason for this. The U.S. government is able to declassify the comments of its own officials, but has no right to do so when the communications of other governments are involved. I have respected this rule.

When quotation marks are used, the reader can be assured that the words appear that way in some document. Verbatim accounts of presidential meetings, however, do not exist. No tape recordings were made, and stenographers were never present. Usually a notetaker, often myself, would try to reconstruct the conversation from notes immediately after the meeting. This method usually captured the substance, and often the tone, of the discussion, but in this case the use of quotation marks simply shows what the memorandum of conversation reports, not exactly what was said.

When the positions of foreign leaders are characterized in my account of events, the reader can assume that I have consulted the written record where possible, even if quotation marks are not used. I have tried not to rely much on memory alone. Obviously, when I speculate about why some action was taken, I am on my own and do not pretend to have unique sources that allowed me to get inside the minds of Carter, Begin, and Sadat. I try to tell what happened and what was said, and sometimes I make a guess as to why. I hope that the factual material is given credence even by those who dispute my interpretations.

Ideally, an account of the Camp David Accords should deal as much with the decision processes in Israel and Egypt, and perhaps in Syria and Jordan and among the Palestinians, as it does with those in Washington. But my comparative advantage is that I know the American side of the story in considerable detail. Where possible, I have included information about the positions of other parties. But the task of rounding out the story, of completing the picture of the negotiating process, will have to await the efforts of others with access to information that I did not have.

This account is also centered on the presidency. By chance, I was able to observe much of the unfolding of American policy toward the Middle East in 1977–79 from a position of near proximity to the White House, literally from an office in the Old Executive Office Building overlooking the Oval Office. I saw much less of how Congress went about its business and how the various interest groups tried to influence events. I happen to believe that the presidential perspective is a valuable one, but it cannot tell the whole story. Once again, I hope that others will complement this account by concentrating on the roles of Congress, the press, the lobbies, and public opinion. I have tried to assess their influence when I felt it necessary to do so, but much more could, and should, be said on that topic.

W.B.Q.

Contents

1. *Introduction*   1

2. *American Politics and Foreign Policy*   6
   The Role of Congress—The Electoral Cycle—The President and His Role—The
   Pattern of the First Year—The Pattern of the Second Year—The Pattern of the
   Third Year—The Pattern of the Fourth Year—Conclusion

3. *Getting Started, Getting Acquainted*   30
   The Arab-Israeli Conflict in Early 1977—The Middle East Team—Received Wisdom
   on the Middle East—Setting the Course—On-the-Job Education—Rabin's Visit and
   Adventures in Public Diplomacy—Carter Meets the Arabs—Conclusion

4. *Meeting Menachem Begin*   63
   Who Is Begin?—Fahd's Visit—Preparing for Begin—Carter Meets Begin—Vance to
   the Middle East, August 1977—Conclusion

5. *The Unraveling of the Grand Design*   96
   The Search for an Opening—Lebanon, Settlements, and the PLO—Preparing for
   Geneva—Secret Channels—Carter's Second Round of Personal Diplomacy—Pro-
   cedures and Politics—Politics to the Fore—Conclusion

6. *Changing Course*   135
   Clinging to Geneva—Sadat's Road to Jerusalem—Washington Reassesses—Begin's
   Plan for Home Rule—Negotiations in Ismailiya and Jerusalem—Conclusion

7. *Inching toward Camp David*   168
   Outline of an American Strategy—Sadat and Carter at Camp David—To Link or
   Not to Link—Pressure on Israel—Begin's Six Noes—A Partial Retreat—Proposals,
   Planes, and Pleas—Marking Time at Leeds Castle—Carter Decides on a Summit
   Meeting—Conclusion

8. *The First Ten Days*   206
   Preparations for the Summit—The President's Briefing Book—At the Summit—
   Conclusion

9. *Success* 237

End Game: Day Eleven, September 15, 1978—Waffling on the West Bank: Day Twelve, September 16, 1978—The Settlements Flap—The Finale: Day Thirteen, September 17, 1978—The Scorecard

10. *Interpretations* 259

Post-Summit Strategies—Preparing for the Next Round—The Blair House Talks—Opening Bids—Mounting Pressures—Vance to the Middle East—Conclusion

11. *The Treaty* 291

Talks Resume—Camp David II—Carter and Begin in Washington—Carter to the Middle East—Finale—Signing the Peace Treaty—Conclusion

12. *Conclusion* 320

Camp David and the Palestinian Question—Assessing Carter's Role—Developments since Camp David—Camp David: Model or Obstacle?—A Realistic Approach to Peace—The American Role

Appendixes

A. *U.N. Resolutions 242 and 338*   341
B. *Joint Communiqué by the Governments of the United States and the Union of Soviet Socialist Republics, October 1, 1977*   343
C. *President Anwar Sadat's Address to the Israeli Knesset, November 20, 1977*   345
D. *Egyptian Proposal at Camp David*   356
E. *First Draft of the American Proposal at Camp David, September 10, 1978*   361
F. *President Carter's First Draft of the Sinai Proposal*   369
G. *The Camp David Accords, September 17, 1978*   376
H. *American Answers to Jordanian Questions, October 1978*   388
I. *Egyptian-Israeli Peace Treaty, March 26, 1979*   397

Chronology 407

Bibliography 413

Index 415

Camp David

CHAPTER ONE

Introduction

The Camp David Accords, signed by Egyptian President Anwar Sadat and Israeli Prime Minister Menachem Begin on September 17, 1978, were a significant turning point in recent Middle East history. Praised by some for laying the foundations for peace between Egypt and Israel, the accords have also been criticized for failing to achieve a comprehensive settlement, including a resolution of the Palestinian question. But supporters and critics alike recognize the importance of what happened at Camp David, and both groups acknowledge the vital role played by the United States in reaching an agreement.

As time passes it becomes easier to assess the legacy of Camp David, though no final verdict can be rendered. For example, the essence of the peace treaty between Egypt and Israel has been respected by both sides, but the full promise of peace and normal relations has not been achieved. A cold peace best describes Egyptian-Israeli relations in the mid-1980s, and some still fear that a resumption of a cold war cannot be precluded.

It is also clear that Camp David had a profound effect on inter-Arab relations, resulting in strains between Cairo and many Arab capitals. But Egypt cannot be isolated from the mainstream of Arab politics for long, and by the mid-1980s Egypt had resumed diplomatic relations with some Arab countries and had expanded its informal ties with others, without having to renounce the peace with Israel.

With hindsight, one can also see that the Camp David Accords were successful only in resolving the bilateral dispute between Egypt and Israel, and even there some minor problems remained unsettled. The elaborate formula for addressing the Palestinian question through the establishment of an autonomous regime for the West Bank and Gaza has remained a dead letter, even though the general principle of establishing transitional arrangements that would allow Palestinians to join in negotiating a final agreement with Israel has been widely accepted.

At the time of Camp David it was generally believed that Egypt was the key to war and peace in the Middle East. If Egypt chose peace, other

Arab states would eventually follow. If they did not, at least there would be no further wars. But the Israeli invasion of Lebanon in June 1982 showed the limits of the slogan of "no more wars" that had grown out of Anwar Sadat's dramatic visit to Jerusalem in November 1977.

Futhermore, the three main architects of the Camp David Accords, Anwar Sadat, Menachem Begin, and Jimmy Carter, all became disillusioned by some of the events that took place after the signing of the Egyptian-Israeli peace treaty. Sadat was frustrated by the lack of progress in carrying out the provisions of Camp David concerning the Palestinians. He also confronted staggering domestic problems for which peace was supposed to have been a solvent. On October 6, 1981, while commemorating the 1973 war with Israel, Sadat was gunned down by Islamic extremists. Among their many charges against him were the Camp David Accords. Sadat's successor was considerably less enthusiastic about peace with Israel.

Menachem Begin had every reason to believe in 1981 that his vision of a powerful Israel, in permanent control of Jerusalem, the West Bank, and Gaza, would be the historical legacy of Camp David. But the Lebanon war of 1982 created great controversy within Israel and raised questions about Begin's leadership and his dream. The casualties were high, and the effect on the fragile economy was devastating. Political cleavages deepened. Begin's health was poor; his wife, and lifetime companion, died; and in late 1983 Begin announced that he felt obliged to relinquish the office of prime minister.

The once proud and feisty Israeli leader, who had fought for every word of the Camp David Accords as if his country's survival depended upon it, retreated into seclusion, making no effort even to ensure the victory of his party in the 1984 elections. In the end the Labor party returned to power on a platform that rejected much of what Begin had fought so hard to achieve. Although Prime Minister Shimon Peres presided over an awkward coalition that included many Begin supporters from the Likud bloc, clearly Labor, if able to rule without Likud, would be willing to cede control over some of the West Bank in return for peace with Jordan.

Jimmy Carter's fate was less dramatic than that of the other two Camp David protagonists. Carter received wide praise for his achievement in promoting peace between Egypt and Israel.[1] Even his harshest domestic

1. A *New York Times* poll conducted in February 1985 found that the Camp David peace negotiations were viewed as the most successful American foreign policy initiative in

critics gave him high marks for Camp David, and history will probably remember his role in promoting peace between Israel and Egypt as his finest achievement. But this apparent success was not enough to ensure his reelection in 1980, nor was it sufficient to maintain a strong bipartisan commitment to the Camp David Accords. By the mid-1980s few Americans seemed to feel that a solution to the Palestinian problem was either possible or necessary, and few showed concern that the Egyptian-Israeli peace might unravel.

American indifference to the Middle East may not, of course, mean that progress toward peace in the region is impossible. It may be that Israel and its Arab neighbors can reach agreements without help from the United States. Indeed, this would be a welcome development in Washington. But the experience of Camp David provides little evidence that the American role can be diminished without jeopardizing the prospects for peace. A review of the past may offer some thoughts about the prospects for future negotiations.

Looking at the Camp David record, some have argued that by 1977 Egypt and Israel were well on their way to making peace without the assistance of the United States. They cite as evidence secret meetings between Egyptians and Israelis that the Americans did not participate in and supposedly knew nothing about. And they also point out that both parties periodically ignored American advice.

Others maintain, however, that peace between Egypt and Israel was only possible because of the role played by the United States. Of the four agreements negotiated between Egypt and Israel from 1974 to 1979, each involved intense participation by the United States at the highest levels. No formal agreements were reached in this period or subsequently through any other means.

Neither of these perspectives is adequate. Successful Arab-Israeli negotiations clearly require more than an act of American will. Certain preconditions are needed, especially a predisposition on the part of the Middle East parties to settle their differences through negotiations. At the same time there apparently needs to be an intermediary between Israel and its neighbors to help overcome deep distrust and historically rooted antagonism. And the United States, with its vast economic and military resources, can help to change the calculus of benefit and risk for the parties to the conflict by making bilateral commitments to them.

recent years. Both Democrats and Republicans gave Camp David a high rating. See Adam Clymer, "Camp David at Top in U.S. Policy Poll," *New York Times*, April 1, 1985.

For Egypt and Israel, it is fair to say that peace was possible, but not inevitable, after the October 1973 war. Each party saw merit in resolving the dispute through negotiations under American auspices. But the two sides still had fundamentally different approaches to peace. Left to themselves, they would probably not have found their way to agreement.

The U.S. role became crucial because both Egypt and Israel wanted American involvement and hoped to win Washington to their point of view. Neither wanted the United States to be an entirely neutral intermediary. Neither expected the Americans to content themselves with the role of postman. Both hoped that the United States would advocate their views in their adversary's capital and would be generous in rewarding any of their concessions made in the course of negotiations. This expectation gave the United States considerable influence, but Washington was never in a position to impose terms of settlement on either Egypt or Israel.

In the course of the negotiations that led first to the Camp David Accords in September 1978 and then to the Egyptian-Israeli peace treaty of March 1979, the United States did not resort to heavy-handed pressure on either side. Threats were rarely uttered. On most issues the United States did not have clear preferences. Whatever the parties could agree on would generally be acceptable to Washington. But the Americans did have judgments about what might be acceptable to each side, what trade-offs were possible, and what the reactions of other regional parties might be. As a result, the Americans were not shy about putting forward ideas of their own, though they were rarely wedded to them as matters of principle.

The Camp David negotiations involved the president and his secretary of state, Cyrus R. Vance, to an almost unprecedented degree. The closest comparison was former Secretary of State Henry A. Kissinger's shuttle diplomacy in 1974–75, also in pursuit of a Middle East accord. Why the Americans were prepared to devote so much time and energy to this issue is still something of a mystery, but the memories of the October 1973 war, the threats of Soviet intervention, and the oil price shock of that year were still vivid in 1977. Although Carter did not have to deal with the Arab-Israeli conflict as an actual crisis, he was aware it could quickly become one.

The United States found itself in an unusual role as a broker for an Egyptian-Israeli agreement. Only on rare occasions was Carter called on to commit the United States to a specific course of action. Mostly he was trying to urge two very strong-minded men, Anwar Sadat and Menachem Begin, to make commitments to each other. To this end, Carter found himself in the role of psychotherapist, gently trying to explain to each man the problems of the other in the hope of overcoming fears and distrust. He also acted as messenger, conveying positions and impressions back and forth. On other occasions he was more the arbitrator, pressing for agreement along lines that he had determined were fair. In the end Carter tried to persuade Sadat and Begin, and through them their respective political systems, to reach a peace agreement.

All the while Carter had to pay heed to the effect his Middle East diplomacy was having on his own political position. Perhaps more than any other foreign policy issue, the Arab-Israeli conflict can take its toll on the standing of a president. Domestic politics quickly becomes intertwined with strategic analysis. Presidents rarely tackle Middle East issues with much enthusiasm, knowing they will invariably be controversial, and often intractable as well.

The record of the Camp David negotiations shows much about the power of the United States as a mediator in complex international disputes. But it also reveals serious limits on that power, limits that are deeply rooted in the nature of the American political system. Both these themes—of presidential power and the constraints on it—will be seen as the Camp David story unfolds. Central to this analysis is the idea that presidents must function within boundaries set by the electoral cycle. In practice, these political realities limit the time that a president can devote to any foreign policy issue.

By looking at American foreign policy toward the Arab-Israeli conflict with domestic political realities clearly in mind, I hope to paint a convincing picture of how a president makes decisions on fateful and usually controversial matters. After setting the stage with an analysis of the American political cycle and its characteristic impact on policymaking, I turn to a detailed reconstruction of the events that led to the Camp David summit in September 1978, and eventually to the negotiated peace between Egypt and Israel the following spring.

CHAPTER TWO

American Politics and Foreign Policy

The conduct of American foreign policy can be viewed from many different perspectives, each of which may shed some light on a remarkably intricate process. Some analysts, for example, concentrate on the output—the formal positions, the documents, the presidential statements—then work back from that to deduce motives and causes. This deductive method assumes a high degree of rationality in the formulation of policy.

A second approach much in vogue among one-time practitioners of foreign policy is to focus on the politics of decisionmaking. This view assumes that what becomes foreign policy is the result of a complex game of bargaining in which the important players usually represent bureaucratic interests. A variant of this school of thought focuses more on the interplay of individuals, especially the president and his chief advisers, and tries to understand the conceptual frame of reference of top decisionmakers. Once that is understood, and once the relations among key actors are identified, policy outcomes can be inferred.[1]

A weakness of both the bureaucratic politics perspective and the focus on presidential leadership is the relative neglect of the workings of the American political system as it influences the conduct of foreign policy. Congress, public opinion, interest groups, the press, and especially the electoral cycle all play a major part in the way in which foreign policy issues are handled by presidents and their advisers. Domestic political considerations must always be taken into account if a president wishes to use his influence effectively. This does not mean that any given course of action is necessarily precluded by domestic political realities, but some seem to entail high costs. A president may decide that the stakes do not

1. These alternative models are discussed at greater length in William B. Quandt, *Decade of Decisions*, pp. 3–36. See also Steven L. Spiegel, *The Other Arab-Israeli Conflict*, pp. 1–15, for the thesis that the role of the president and his views are the key to understanding policymaking. Full references to the works cited appear in the bibliography.

warrant drawing down on his political capital by his taking a controversial position on the Middle East.

THE ROLE OF CONGRESS

The role of Congress is especially important in the shaping of Middle East policy. Congress cannot determine the American position on such issues as the future borders between Israel and Jordan, the best approach to negotiations, or even the legal status of Jerusalem. Those remain prerogatives of the executive. But many of the instruments for implementing policy lie with Congress, primarily because of its control over the budget.

Congress, for example, must approve aid levels to Egypt and Israel. By the mid-1980s the amounts involved exceeded $5 billion annually, dwarfing all other aid programs. Congress can also review major arms sales and may seek to block them by legislative action. The executive usually is able to get its way on those issues, but sometimes the prospect of a fight is enough to inhibit action. And because of the War Powers Act, Congress is in a position to veto the deployment of American troops in combat situations beyond an initial sixty-day period.

Apart from these specific powers, Congress also plays an important role in influencing public opinion. Administration officials are frequently called to testify, and congressmen and senators can use those occasions to mobilize sentiment for or against the administration's policy, as can the various interest groups. Leading congressmen can attract attention to their views through speeches, press conferences, and well-timed leaks. Generally, Congress takes a predictably pro-Israeli stance, so that any administration will be sensitive to the possibility of adverse congressional reactions if it seeks to pressure Israel.

These domestic political constraints are not, however, constants. Strong presidential leadership can sometimes offset congressional opposition. Public opinion can change. Interest groups rise and fall in their influence and control over resources. Partisan alignments are not always stable, especially on Middle East issues.

In a crisis a president can often appeal successfully to the American public for support. He can speak of threats to vital national interests, and if issues of war and peace or national survival seem to be at stake, domestic political considerations lose much of their usual importance in decision-making. If, however, the crisis drags on for long, if the costs are high, and if American casualties are taken, the scope for freedom of action for a president begins to narrow.[2] As happened in both Vietnam and Lebanon, Congress may take the lead in pressing for disengagement.

THE ELECTORAL CYCLE

One feature of the American political system is constant; yet its influence on foreign policy is often ignored. Every four years, with absolute regularity, presidential elections take place. Every two years, congressional elections occur. These are major political events, and successful presidents inevitably gear many of their moves to this electoral cycle.

Whatever his values or his personality, a president will feel freer to try new initiatives in the first year of his first term than he will in his fourth year. Midway through a term, most presidents begin to want a visible success in foreign policy, or at least they want to limit the damage that might be done by clinging to an unpopular course. These are not political absolutes, but they are regular features of the foreign policy process and help to account for the often observed inconsistencies in the formulation and conduct of American foreign policy.

Several aspects of the Arab-Israeli conflict as an issue in U.S. foreign policy make the electoral cycle even more important in this area than it might be in others. Because the issues are controversial, because public interest is great, because the stakes are high, and because U.S.-Soviet relations are involved, policy toward the Arab-Israeli conflict is typically made at the highest level. Deep presidential involvement ensures that political considerations permeate the conduct of Middle East policy.

While responsibility for Middle East policy is lodged at the White House, expertise and knowledge are not. No president has ever come to office with a deep understanding of the complexities of the Middle East. Usually foreign policy as a whole is far from what the president best understands. Presidents reach the top by mastering the arts of domestic politics, concentrating on local issues, the economy, and the party. Farm subsidies and school busing may be issues that they understand from firsthand experience, but rarely do presidents have much background in international affairs. Dwight D. Eisenhower and Richard M. Nixon were partial exceptions, but even then their experience was most relevant to managing relations with European allies and dealing with the Soviet Union.

2. A recent example was President Reagan's policy in Lebanon from 1982 through 1984. For a critique, see William B. Quandt, "Reagan's Lebanon Policy."

If presidents cannot be expected to know much about the Middle East, where do they get their information and their cues? To some extent, especially as candidates for office, they rely on information provided by interest groups, personal friends, or party professionals. Later, as presidents, they encounter a massive bureaucracy, capable of providing vast amounts of information on any topic. Bureaucrats, however, are often suspect, especially if they have been working loyally for the previous administration. It often takes a long time for presidents to overcome their distrust of the "professionals," and during this period they are likely to operate from premises that are more clearly shaped by domestic politics than by strategic analysis.

Presidents do not, of course, rely entirely on amateurs for their views on international affairs. As candidates, they usually surround themselves with advisers, often professors and former officials, and from those ranks they make many key appointments once in office. The positions of secretary of state, national security adviser, secretary of defense, and director of Central Intelligence are all likely to be filled by trusted political appointees who will reflect the president's views to the bureaucracy as much as channel the bureaucracy's perspective to the president. At the outset of an administration, these political appointees may clash with the career bureaucrats, but as time goes on they usually reach a modus vivendi.

Still, the point remains that there is little continuity in personnel at the highest levels of government. Every four years, or at most every eight years, a large turnover in top jobs is likely. The frequency of personnel changes makes it difficult for entrenched bureaucratic views on foreign policy to prevail in presidential decisionmaking, since they are generally filtered through political appointees who owe their loyalty to the president and whose careers rise and fall with his. There are both advantages and disadvantages associated with this feature of the system. At best, innovation may be possible. At worst, inconsistency and confusion result.

THE PRESIDENT AND HIS ROLE

Jimmy Carter's involvement in the formulation of Middle East policy provides an excellent case for studying the role of the president and the influence of the broader political system in the shaping of foreign policy. Unlike many other presidents, Carter was an "outsider," relatively new to Washington and its ways. Most national and international issues were beyond the direct experience of this former governor of the state of

Georgia. But Carter did have plans, ambitions, and a steely determination to tackle tough issues early on in his presidency. He definitely intended to be an activist president.

During his four years in office, Carter learned much about Washington and the world, as does every president. But Carter never felt comfortable in the role of a deal-making politician. He acted as if he felt that by taking the correct position he could count on public and congressional support. This apolitical, even naive, stance cost him dearly. And yet, as this study will show, Carter was aware of, and responsive to, the pressures of the domestic political scene as he grappled with Middle East issues. If this was true for an unconventional politician like Carter, one can assume that most other incumbents of the Oval Office will be even more attuned to domestic politics as they think about foreign policy.

The analysis in this book concentrates on the president and his top advisers, their views, predispositions, and preferences. They are seen as dealing with complicated issues that they imperfectly understand, trying to lay down sound guidelines that will protect the national interest while simultaneously watching how their moves play out within the domestic arena.

The interplay among these key people, the often intractable issues of the Middle East, and the dynamics of the American political system, which is hardly designed to simplify the task of conducting foreign policy, is analyzed. Special attention is paid to the position in which the president finds himself at any given moment in the political cycle, that is to say how he calculates his moves in terms of their effect on his political standing and his prospects for reelection. This approach has most merit, of course, for a first-term president, but with suitable adjustments it could be adapted to a second term as well.

The president and his top advisers are seen as involved in a contest as they struggle with Middle East issues. They are trying to use the resources at their disposal to get others to change their positions, often at great cost and risk. They are engaged in a game of influence, and to be successful they need a strategy, a sense of timing. In brief, they must think politically.

Above all else, a president must try to develop, and then preserve, his base of power. He must constantly monitor both the international and the home-front reactions to his moves. Periodically, he may realize that he is on a track that is not working, or one that entails high costs, or one that is simply not geared to the realities either of the Middle East or of

Washington. Midcourse corrections are then made, a new approach may be tried, and once again the reaction of others will be watched.

Success and failure are often hard to judge in foreign policy. Few objective indicators exist. Subjective judgments, often shaped by the debate in the domestic political arena, come to play a significant role in determining whether to stay the course or try something else. Ideology usually has less of a role in all this than political pragmatism. Presidents want to know if their policies are working and whether they are popular. If so, they can be made to fit whatever ideological mold is currently in fashion.

A president's assessment of costs and opportunities is generally a product of his experience in office and of his position in the electoral cycle. For analytical purposes, and at the risk of some distortion of a more complex reality, it is helpful to distinguish among typical patterns in the first year of a presidential term, the second year, the third, and the fourth. These categories are useful for understanding the typical evolution of policy over a four-year cycle. They alert the observer to the changing weight of domestic political considerations as a presidential term unfolds. The timing of a president's decisions will be heavily influenced by this cycle unless he is reacting to a foreign policy crisis.

Learning about the Middle East

During a normal four-year presidential term, a president engages in two learning processes that affect Middle East policymaking. The first, learning about Middle East issues in their regional and global setting, takes place through meeting with advisers and foreign leaders, through reading diplomatic cables and intelligence reports, through newspapers and television, and sometimes through travel to the region. Abstract issues come to be associated with real people; foreign leaders are seen as friends or adversaries; the connections among issues begin to appear; complexity and nuance are increasingly recognized.

Often the result of this experience with Middle East issues and personalities is to instill a degree of caution and realism in presidential thinking. Grand designs seem to crumble in the face of Middle East unpredictability; even the smallest initiatives take time to produce results; the domestic constraints operating on foreign leaders come to be appreciated as a part of the Middle East scene; the gap between rhetoric and action is understood, and words alone are given less credence than at the outset of a presidential term. With experience, presidents also tend to shy away from public diplomacy in the Middle East. Ideological zeal and preconceptions are overtaken by more immediate experiences.

As a president moves toward a better understanding of the Middle East, his capacity for making informed decisions improves. Mistakes are still made, but there is less self-delusion, less wishful thinking, and less anger when plans unravel. As the president and the bureaucracy begin to see eye-to-eye, a more consistent policy line also emerges.

Learning about Washington

The second learning process involves understanding the domestic political environment in which Middle East policy debates take place. Even the most seasoned Washington insider cannot appreciate the special pressures exerted on the White House when Middle East issues become controversial. On-the-job training is the only way to learn about the problems of dealing with the press, Congress, and the pro-Israeli lobby when U.S. policy is seen as tilting too far toward the Arabs.

Presidents often deny that they allow domestic political considerations to influence their views of the national interest. But of course they do and they should. After all, foreign policy cannot be conducted in a vacuum. Presidents need public and congressional support. If they lose it, they cannot achieve their goals and they may fail to be reelected.

The result of this second learning process is to make a president careful about what he says and does on the Middle East. His political advisers will be tempted to push the State Department to the fore on controversial issues, protecting the president from possible criticism. Even a popular president will worry about losing the support of the Jewish community as elections approach. For a weak president, especially a Democrat, this can be a significant consideration.

The two learning processes result in greater presidential realism about the Middle East as a region and about the domestic scene. They both encourage caution instead of bold moves, unless a compelling crisis forces a president to act.

Striking a Balance

On the substance of the Arab-Israeli dispute, however, the two processes tend to work at odds. The result of learning about the Middle East tends to move a president toward what might be called an evenhanded position, in which support for Israel is balanced by some concern for the Arab point of view. This has been true for presidents as different as Eisenhower, Nixon, Gerald R. Ford, Carter, and Ronald Reagan.

By contrast, the result of gaining experience with the realities of domestic politics is to reinforce a president's tendency to emphasize one-sided support for Israel—particularly in election years and in public statements. A gap often appears between what a president thinks and says in private and what he says for domestic political effect. This causes confusion in the Middle East and in Washington and creates cynicism about presidential statements made on the Middle East in election years.

With a four-year presidential term, the effect of these two learning processes is to make the second and third years the best time for steady policymaking on the Middle East. During the first year a president is still learning the basic ingredients of the Middle East game and is likely to misjudge what can be accomplished. He may also be inattentive to the domestic political scene, with the result that he may pay a high price for little gain. During the fourth year a president is better informed about the Middle East but is not inclined to do much because of the preoccupation with the reelection campaign.

A Second-Term President

For a president in his second term, the pattern changes significantly. The first year and a half may be the best time for taking foreign policy initiatives. The president probably knows as much about substance as he ever will. The reelection has provided the proof he may feel he needed that the public is behind him. The danger here is that a president will think his mandate makes him omnipotent, and that can lead to costly mistakes.[3] Late in the second year congressional elections may assume particular importance, since any significant loss in the House or Senate can erode presidential power and signal to the president's party that it must begin to take its distance from him if it hopes to do well in the next presidential election.

The danger of the third and fourth years in a second term is that the president is becoming a lame duck. Because he cannot run for reelection, his power begins to slip. The succession struggle within his own party can be debilitating, and during the last year the president may find Congress in an assertive mood. The idea that a president who does not

3. See Arthur Schlesinger, Jr., "Curse of the Second Term," *Wall Street Journal*, May 9, 1985.

have to face reelection can act free of domestic political concerns misses the point. He may be free, but he is not taken seriously as he reaches the end of his second term.

Managing the Electoral Cycle

A skillful president will learn how to make use of the political cycle to enhance the chances of success in his foreign policy; a careless one will probably pay a high price for ignoring domestic realities. Events, of course, can get out of control, as they did for Jimmy Carter with the Iranian hostage crisis in 1979. It was particularly bad luck for him that the crisis happened just as an election year was beginning. By contrast, Ronald Reagan managed to terminate the controversial American military presence in Lebanon before his reelection campaign began in 1984, and the issue seemed to do him no political harm at the polls. Luck and skill go hand in hand in successful political careers.

If American presidents can gain from the intelligent manipulation of the political cycle, timing their moves for maximum effect, the same is true for foreign leaders who deal with the United States. If they understand the workings of the American political system, they can seek to turn it to their advantage, asking for aid when a president is most able to respond, helping him through an election year by deferring action on controversial arms requests, or delaying a response to a demand from Washington in anticipation of American preoccupation with the domestic agenda. Both Sadat and Begin tried on occasion to take these political realities into account, and they became effective at manipulating American politics to their own advantage.

Looking back on their time in office, presidents and their advisers usually decry such heavy intrusion of domestic politics into the foreign policy arena. Some have argued that the only solution to the problem is to elect a president for one term of six years. For example, former Secretary of State Cyrus Vance wrote:

From experience in the making of foreign policy in several administrations, I have concluded that a four-year presidential term has serious drawbacks, especially when it comes to foreign affairs. It takes each new president from six to nine months to learn his job and to feel comfortable in the formulation and execution of foreign policy. For the next eighteen months the president can operate with assurance. But during the last year or so, he is running for reelection and is forced to divert much of his attention to campaigning. As a result, many issues are ignored and important decisions are deferred. Sometimes bad decisions are made under the pressures of months of primary elections. And at home and overseas, we are frequently seen as inconsistent and unstable.

We should, I believe, change the current four-year term to a single six-year term in which the president would be free of the pressures of campaigning and would have more time to carry forward the public business.[4]

Others have tried to address the problem by pleading for bipartisanship, the removal of foreign policy from the domestic political agenda. Carter's national security adviser, Zbigniew Brzezinski, wrote:

Every Administration goes through a period of an ecstatic emancipation from the past, then a discovery of continuity, and finally a growing preoccupation with Presidential reelection. As a result, the learning curve in the area of foreign policy tends to be highly compressed. Each Administration tends to expend an enormous amount of energy coping with the unintended, untoward consequences of its initial, sometimes excessive, impulses to innovate, to redeem promises, and to harbor illusions. In time, preconceptions give way to reality, disjointedness to intellectual coherence, and vision to pragmatism. But by the time this happens, the Presidential cycle is usually coming to an end. That the four-year election process has a pernicious influence on foreign policy is evident, but it is also clear that this structural handicap is not likely to be undone.

The four-year Presidential cycle makes the need for bipartisanship even greater. Bipartisanship could compensate for Presidential discontinuity, but in fact bipartisanship faded coincidentally with the beginning of the period of frequent changes of Presidents.[5]

Finally, some have accepted the situation as it is and have urged presidents to use the brief windows of opportunity that do exist by asserting strong leadership. Former President Nixon, for example, said:

The only time you have a window of opportunity to come up with anything responsible in the Middle East is non-election years. In 1986, there's no way you can do anything in the Middle East that won't be tilted too far in the direction of Israel.[6]

THE PATTERN OF THE FIRST YEAR

A president and his advisers often begin their term with relatively little understanding of foreign policy issues. This is particularly true of the Middle East problem, where the complexity of the Arab-Israeli conflict is often lost in the midst of campaign slogans. This lack of background

---

4. Cyrus Vance, *Hard Choices*, p. 13.
5. Zbigniew Brzezinski, *Power and Principle*, p. 544.
6. Karen Elliott House, "Nixon Advises Reagan to Move Quickly on Foreign Policy, Focus on Few Issues," *Wall Street Journal*, November 13, 1984.

is especially important if the president has been a Washington outsider and if there has been a change of administration. But even for a Washington insider, such as a senator with experience on the Foreign Relations Committee or a vice president moving up to the presidency, there is little reason to expect more than a faint familiarity with Middle East issues.

Presidents are not allowed the luxury of taking no position on issues until they have learned enough to make sensible judgments. Instead, on issues that evoke strong public interest, such as the Middle East, candidates for the presidency are expected to have a position and may even devote a speech to the topic.

These first definitions of a president's position, often taken in the midst of the campaign, are usually important in setting the administration's initial course. They are likely to reflect general foreign policy predispositions—a tough policy toward the Soviets, for example—and will generally imply that the previous administration was on the wrong track and that things will soon be put straight. (This, of course, assumes that the presidency is passing from one party to the other.) Besides defining a course of action by contrasting it with that of his predecessor in office, a newly elected president will have to decide what priority to attach to the Middle East. Not all issues can be dealt with at once, and a signal of presidential interest or disinterest may be more important in setting the administration's policy than the substantive position papers that inevitably begin to flow to the White House.

If Middle East issues are treated as matters of importance, and if presidential predispositions are reflected in the charting of the initial course, the early months of the new term are likely to be marked by activism. Having just won a national election, the president will probably be optimistic about his ability to use the office to achieve great results in foreign and domestic policy. If initiatives are decided on for dealing with Middle East problems, they tend to be ambitious. The common feeling is that much catching up needs to be done after the policy drift of the preceding election year. It takes time to recognize what will work and what will not.

It also takes time for a president and his advisers to develop a comfortable working style. Confusion is not unusual in the early days. Public statements may have to be retracted, and people have to learn who really speaks for the president among the many claimants to the role. Time is needed, too, for the president and the new secretary of state to develop contacts with the various Middle East leaders. These contacts will eventually add to their education, but at the outset there is usually only a slight understanding of the Middle East players, their agendas, and their strengths and weaknesses. They, after all, also have domestic political realities that need to be understood and taken into account.

What this adds up to is a somewhat experimental first year: policy objectives are set in lofty terms; predispositions, ideology, and campaign rhetoric still count; and Middle East realities are only dimly appreciated. Usually toward the end of the first year, the administration becomes aware that the policy agreed upon in January or February has lost momentum or is on the wrong track. Reassessments are then likely, but not until considerable time and energy have been invested in pursuing false leads and indulging in wishful thinking.

Since the June 1967 Arab-Israeli war, elements of this pattern are easily found in 1969, 1977, and 1981. Only with President Nixon's second inauguration in 1973 was the pattern somewhat broken, partly because the Watergate crisis erupted in the spring of that year and prevented Nixon from concentrating on the Middle East until he was forced to do so by the outbreak of the October 1973 war. Nixon's first year as president, by contrast, fitted the pattern nicely.

Nixon, 1969

In 1969 Nixon and Secretary of State William P. Rogers attached high priority to creating a framework for resolving the Arab-Israeli conflict. To this end, a series of discussions took place, some involving the Soviet Union and some the British and French as well. Contacts with Arabs and Israelis were less important. In this period it was widely believed that the key to stability in the Middle East lay in finding an agreement between Washington and Moscow. This was, after all, the beginning of the era of détente, when most international issues were seen as influenced by the state of U.S.-Soviet relations.

By fall 1969 the United States began to press for a common U.S.-Soviet statement of principles for settling the Arab-Israeli dispute. The Soviets were reticent. They seemed unwilling to be put in a position of accepting anything that President Gamal Abd al-Nasser of Egypt might reject. Unable to get full Soviet agreement, the Americans finally presented their views to the parties and then went public with what came to be known as the Rogers Plan. Within days it was rejected by Egypt, Israel, and the Soviet Union. Even earlier, Henry Kissinger, working from his position as national security adviser to the president, was doing his best to challenge the viability of this approach. With the failure of the Rogers Plan, the stage was set for a policy reassessment, and for the emergence of Kissinger as Nixon's most important adviser on the Middle East.

Carter, 1977

President Carter in 1977 followed a somewhat similar path. His aim was to promote a comprehensive Middle East peace, to be achieved through a series of negotiations that would conclude with the convening of a peace conference at Geneva. An effort was made to work out common principles in advance of the conference; inevitably this caused controversy both within the region and within the United States. By fall the United States and the Soviet Union issued a joint statement on the Middle East, similar in its thrust to the Rogers Plan. Again, the reaction of the Israelis was negative and the Arab response was mixed. Domestically, Carter came in for acute criticism, and by late October he was beginning to conclude that he had reached the end of the road. At that point President Sadat decided to break the stalemate by traveling to Jerusalem, thereby forcing Washington to reassess its policy.

Reagan, 1981

President Ronald Reagan, who in so many ways seemed to be different from his predecessors, nonetheless fell into the same pattern as Nixon and Carter in his first year. Reflecting his general view of foreign policy, Reagan placed primary emphasis on the Soviet threat to the Middle East, not on the Arab-Israeli dispute. With the assistance of Secretary of State Alexander M. Haig, Jr., he articulated a policy aimed at consolidating a "strategic consensus" among the "moderate" states of the region. In theory, the common preoccupation with the Soviet threat on the part of countries like Israel, Egypt, and Saudi Arabia would create the conditions for a loosely structured U.S.-led regional alliance.

Ignoring the history of the last regional defense effort in the mid-1950s—first-termers often ignore history—the Reagan administration set about building the infrastructure for the strategic consensus through a series of arms sales to pro-American regimes. If the premises of policy were valid, the anti-Soviet forces in the region would recognize that arms sold to their rivals could help form a shield against Soviet aggression, and they would therefore withhold their objections. The test case for this theory came with the decision to sell a sophisticated aerial surveillance aircraft, the AWACS (airborne warning and control system), to Saudi Arabia.

Israel, which had been led by Reagan's rhetoric to expect that it enjoyed a privileged place among U.S. friends in the area, decided to launch a major campaign to block congressional approval of the sale. In the end Reagan won the fight, but at considerable cost and only after many months. In the meantime regional issues were bubbling, especially in Lebanon, a further challenge to the idea that a concentration on the Soviet threat could bring stability to the Middle East region.

Added to this were the predictable divisions within the administration, with Secretary of Defense Caspar W. Weinberger opposing a strategic cooperation agreement with Israel that was being promoted by the secretary of state. By the late fall of 1981, the "strategic consensus" rhetoric was being abandoned, and the stage was set for a policy reassessment.

THE PATTERN OF THE SECOND YEAR

Despite the disappointments of dealing with the Middle East in the first year, presidents rarely decide to drop the issue in their second year. Either by design or as a result of crises, the region has a way of staying near the top of the foreign policy agenda. But if recent experience is a guide, the second year is likely to be marked by more success for American diplomacy, either in promoting agreement through negotiations or in the skillful management of a crisis.

The difference between the first and the second year shows that experience can be a good teacher. Policies in the second year are often more in tune with reality. There is less of an ideological overlay in policy deliberations. At the same time goals are usually less ambitious. Plans for comprehensive solutions may be replaced by attempts at more modest partial agreements.

By the second year some of the intrabureaucratic feuding and backbiting is likely to have subsided, or at least the president has had the chance to put an end to it if he so chooses. The gap between the political appointees and the foreign service professionals has also narrowed, and more regional expertise is typically being taken into account during policy discussions. If a senior bureaucrat has survived into the second year, he is no longer seen as the enemy and has often been judged a team player. In any case, the failures of year one tend to make the president's men less contemptuous of the knowledge of the professionals.

During the second year presidents also begin to realize that mishandling Middle East policy can be costly. Congressional elections are scheduled for November, and usually the party in power has to expect some losses. The president needs to keep Congress with him, if at all possible, and thus he has a strong interest in minimizing those losses. This is no time for controversial initiatives in the Middle East that may be strongly rejected by Israel and its friends in the United States.

If action must be taken on Middle East issues, there is a high premium on success. The mood is much less experimental than in the first year. Practical criteria come to the fore. Success may require compromises with principle. This is the year in which presidents realize that the dictum "politics is the art of the possible" applies to foreign as well as domestic policy.

Nixon, 1970 and 1974

During each of the last four presidential terms, the most noteworthy achievements in Middle East policy have come in the second year. In 1970, for example, Secretary Rogers was able to succeed with a modest proposal to bring the "war of attrition" to a close. Instead of the comprehensive plan he had outlined in December 1969, in June 1970 he proposed that the Egyptians and Israelis "stop shooting and start talking." With many inducements and pressures on both sides, he and Nixon succeeded in arranging a cease-fire.

The Nixon administration also confronted a crisis in September 1970, with the hijacking of three international airliners to Jordan, coupled with an attempt by the Palestine Liberation Organization (PLO) to bring down, or at a minimum gravely weaken, King Hussein's regime. The crisis had the potential of erupting into a major regional conflict involving both Syria and Israel. With some risky brinkmanship, Nixon and Kissinger helped to bolster King Hussein enough to enable him to prevail against the PLO, and the Syrian-Israeli confrontation never took place. The management of the crisis showed considerable skill, though the lessons drawn in its aftermath were questionable.[7]

Even in Nixon's second term, the second year was unusually successful in the Middle East, despite the closing vise of the Watergate fiasco. Two sets of complex negotiations over the disengagement of military forces

7. William B. Quandt, "U.S. Policy in the Jordan Crisis, 1970," in Barry M. Blechman and Stephen S. Kaplan, eds., *Force without War*, pp. 257–88.

took place under the direction of Secretary of State Kissinger. Egypt and Israel agreed on a separation of their armies along the Suez Canal in an agreement that had great significance for the ultimate achievement of peace between the two countries. A few months later Syria and Israel concluded a similar agreement on the Golan Heights. And even though it was not followed by other agreements, the accord between Israel and Syria remained intact as of the mid-1980s.

Carter, 1978, and Reagan, 1982

For Carter, his second year was dominated by the effort to reach a peace agreement between Egypt and Israel. The Camp David Accords, which marked the high point of this process, are analyzed in detail in later chapters.

For President Reagan, his second year was mixed. Some of the shortcomings of the first year came back to haunt him, especially in the careless encouragement given to the Israelis to believe that the United States would favor a war against the PLO in Lebanon as part of a grand anti-Soviet strategy.[8] Had the war launched by Israel in June 1982 been fairly short and low in costs, both human and material, the Reagan administration might have condoned it. The publicly declared goal of the Israelis was not what the Americans opposed. Rather, it was the way the war was conducted, the mounting pressure of domestic and international opinion, and the anguished reactions of friendly Arab regimes which convinced the administration that it should intervene to end the fighting. In the midst of the crisis, Secretary of State Haig was fired and was replaced by George P. Shultz, which meant that Israel's staunchest friend in the top echelons of the Reagan administration was replaced by someone with a different outlook.

As the Lebanon war came to a close, in part through the efforts of presidential envoy Philip Habib, Shultz began to work with a small group of Middle East specialists to design a framework for postwar Middle East peace efforts. The result was a speech delivered by President Reagan on September 1, 1982. Although immediately rejected by Israeli Prime Minister Begin, it won broad American support, even within the Jewish community, and it evoked considerable interest within the Arab world and in Israel. As a statement of policy, it remains an important document, even though the follow-up to the speech was so hesitant that it produced

8. Ze'ev Schiff and Ehud Ya'ari, *Israel's Lebanon War*, pp. 62–77.

no concrete results. Still, U.S. policy in the last six months of 1982 showed much more sophistication and realism than it had in the preceding year and a half.

THE PATTERN OF THE THIRD YEAR

During the third year of a typical presidential term, the Middle East is often seen as an arena that can damage a president's political prospects. The tendency, therefore, is to try for the appearance of success if negotiations are under way, even if the result leaves something to be desired. The administration will be prepared to pay heavily in promises of aid and arms to get an agreement.

If the prospects for an agreement do not look good during the third year, the tendency is to cut one's losses and to disengage the president from the diplomatic effort. Above all, he does not want to be seen as responsible for a failure as the election year approaches. And certainly by the end of the third year, if not considerably earlier, the preelection season is likely to have begun.

The rush for success, along with the tendency to abandon controversial and costly policies, means that mistakes are often made in the third year. Opportunities may be lost through carelessness. The price of agreement may become very high as the parties to the conflict realize how badly Washington wants a success. Political considerations tend to override the requirements of steady, purposeful diplomacy. Nonetheless, this is sometimes a year in which genuine achievements are possible, especially if the groundwork in the second year has been good.

Nixon, 1971

Looking at the recent past for examples, one finds that in 1971 the Nixon administration toyed with a promising idea planted by Egyptian President Sadat. In February of that year, Sadat had talked of the possibility of a limited agreement to reopen the Suez Canal. This would have been accompanied by a disengagement of military forces. For several months American diplomats pursued the idea with varying degrees of enthusiasm. By August, however, it became clear that the White House was not ready to put its weight behind a serious effort, and the initiative died.[9] In

---

9. Referring to this period in his memoirs, Kissinger later wrote: "What finally got me involved in the execution of Middle East diplomacy was that Nixon did not believe he could risk recurrent crisis in the Middle East in an election year. He therefore asked me to step in, if only to keep things quiet." Henry A. Kissinger, *White House Years*, p. 1285.

retrospect it seems as if Sadat's idea might have been one way to prevent the October 1973 war. But such strategic thinking was not in the minds of those who were in charge of American policy at that time.

Ford, 1975

Four years later, in 1975, Gerald Ford had succeeded Nixon to the presidency and was beginning to plan for his own election in 1976. The Arab-Israeli conflict was still on the agenda, with President Sadat particularly anxious for further progress before the American election year arrived. At Ford's instruction, Kissinger tried to broker an agreement between Egypt and Israel in the spring, but this effort failed. A period of reassessment followed, and Ford even decided to withhold some military supplies from Israel. By early summer, however, the political pressures on Ford were mounting, especially from the Senate, to lift the arms embargo on Israel.

In this atmosphere Kissinger resumed his diplomatic efforts, and on September 1, 1975, a series of agreements were signed that came to be known as Sinai II. Israel undertook to withdraw from a significant portion of Sinai, in return for which the United States made a remarkable number of bilateral commitments, many of which had to do with the future conduct of negotiations. In retrospect it seemed as if Ford had paid a very high price for little more than keeping the negotiating process alive. In later years American officials spoke of Sinai II as a model to be avoided.

Carter, 1979

Carter's third year was mixed. At considerable political risk the president traveled to the Middle East in March 1979 to bring the Egyptian-Israeli peace treaty negotiations to a close. For him personally this was a signal achievement, and the results have stood the test of time fairly well. Like Ford four years earlier, Carter was willing to make extensive promises to both parties in order to reach agreement. Both Sadat and Begin knew that Carter wanted an agreement and that they could expect to receive some commitments from the United States as the price for it.

If the treaty represented the best that could be achieved early in the third year, the fate of the negotiations on Palestinian autonomy was more typical of the political caution that sets in as elections approach. The United States, Egypt, and Israel were all pledged to begin negotiations on a transitional regime for the West Bank and Gaza shortly after the signing of the peace treaty. Carter had promised that he would continue to take an active personal part in the negotiations.[10]

By mid-1979, however, Carter was beginning to be worried that Senator Edward M. Kennedy would challenge him in the Democratic party primaries in 1980. Moreover, the Iranian revolution had sparked an increase in the price of oil, and lines were forming at gas stations throughout the country. Carter reacted by retreating to Camp David to consult with his advisers and experts, then emerged to give a speech that became best known for his reference to a sense of "malaise" among the American people. Carter's political fortunes were already slipping when in November 1979 an angry mob of Iranians seized the U.S. embassy in Tehran and held American diplomats hostage. Three days later Senator Kennedy formally announced his candidacy for president. And in late December the Soviets invaded Afghanistan.

In short, Carter was unable to capitalize politically on his one genuine success in 1979, the Egyptian-Israeli peace treaty; instead he saw his political fortunes take a sudden turn for the worse. Not surprisingly, Carter turned his attention away from the Arab-Israeli issue and the autonomy talks.

Secretary of State Vance was eager to get on with the second part of the Camp David negotiations, but Carter succumbed to the recommendation of Vice President Walter F. Mondale to appoint a special negotiator. Carter chose Robert S. Strauss, a man of remarkable domestic political skills, but one with little background for dealing with the complexities of the Middle East.[11] By fall Strauss concluded that there was little he could hope to accomplish, and he left the Middle East job to return to the reelection campaign. He was succeeded as special negotiator by Sol Linowitz, a skilled diplomat who was new to Middle East issues. Some headway was made in dealing with technical matters, but without Carter's direct involvement it was difficult to break the stalemate.

As a result, the autonomy negotiations faltered during the latter part of the president's third year, but Carter was not blamed. He, after all, was the architect of the Egyptian-Israeli peace treaty, and that would be the issue he would hold out before the voters in 1980 to bolster his claim of foreign policy accomplishments.

10. See Carter's answers to King Hussein in appendix H.

11. See Jimmy Carter, *Keeping Faith*, p. 491, on his political reasons for selecting Strauss and on Vance's objections.

Reagan, 1983

President Reagan's third year was also mixed in terms of Middle East diplomacy. At the outset Reagan seemed to be trying to entice King Hussein of Jordan into negotiations by making far-reaching promises. When these failed to overcome the king's reticence, Reagan and Secretary Shultz turned their efforts to working out an agreement between Israel and Lebanon. But the agreement, reached on May 17, 1983, was made contingent on Syria's willingness to withdraw its troops from Lebanon. Most of the American diplomats in the region knew that this condemned the agreement to failure, but Reagan and Shultz were adamant in insisting that it could not be modified.

Pressure then mounted to force the Syrians to comply. The Syrians reacted by demonstrating that they could not so easily be taken for granted or pushed, and by the fall of 1983 the United States and Syria were on the verge of open hostilities. On October 23 a massive explosion destroyed the Marine barracks near the Beirut airport, killing 241 Americans and wounding many more. Early in December two U.S. aircraft were shot down while bombing Syrian military positions within Lebanon. By year's end it was clear to nearly everyone, especially in Congress, that something had gone fundamentally wrong with U.S. policy in Lebanon. The much heralded May 17 agreement was canceled by the Lebanese government a few months later, a further reminder of the misjudgments made in Washington during 1983. Rarely has U.S. policy been more dramatically repudiated.

THE PATTERN OF THE FOURTH YEAR

Most presidents go to great lengths to deny that electoral considerations influence their conduct of foreign policy. But as political realists, they all know they must take politics into account. If nothing else, the extraordinary demands on a presidential candidate mean that little time is left for consideration of complex foreign policy problems, for meeting with visiting heads of state, or for fighting great battles with Congress over aid or arms sales. Added to this is the desire not to lose the support of the Jewish community, for many of whom Israel is of special concern. This support is important not only because of votes but perhaps more so because of financial contributions to the party and congressional candidates.

The guidelines for the fourth year with respect to the Middle East are thus fairly simple. Try to avoid controversy. Steer clear of new initiatives. Try to defer arms sales to the Arabs, while appearing generous to Israel. Speak of Israel as a strategic asset, even if you have not previously used this term. If crises are forced upon you, they must of course be dealt with; even in election years presidents have considerable authority in emergencies, as Eisenhower showed in his handling of the Suez crisis on the eve of the 1956 elections.

Not surprisingly, the fourth year of presidential terms is not noted for many achievements in the Middle East. In 1972 Nixon scored several other foreign policy spectaculars, including the opening to China and the conclusion of the SALT (strategic arms limitation talks) treaty. But the Middle East was too risky, or the time was seen as inappropriate for new initiatives. Even when Sadat expelled some 15,000 Soviet advisers in July, the American response was lukewarm. Secret talks were held on the Middle East with the Soviets, but they seemed to be aimed more at bolstering the atmosphere of détente than at producing results in the region.

In 1976, too, the United States did little in the Middle East. Lebanon was in turmoil, and the Americans seemed to be giving their blessing to the entry of Syrian forces into that country as a way of bringing about a modicum of stability. The entry of Syrian forces made the Israelis nervous, but tacit understandings between Syria and Israel were reached in order to prevent direct clashes. Damage limitation was achieved, but the more fundamental problems of Lebanon, to say nothing of those of the broader region, had no place on Ford's election-year agenda.

The year 1980 was an unhappy one for Jimmy Carter. In the Middle East, it brought nothing but bad news. Americans were held hostage in Iran. The Soviet Union was in occupation of Afghanistan. The Palestinian autonomy talks were going nowhere. And the president's own political fortunes were in doubt. Illustrative of the intense concern that Middle East issues not cause further damage to an already weakened president was the decision shortly before the New York primary election to change the American vote from yes to no on a U.N. resolution critical of Israel.[12]

12. See Hamilton Jordan, *Crisis*, pp. 200, 228, and 234, for the judgment that the U.N. vote hurt Carter in the New York primary. See also Rosalynn Carter, *First Lady from Plains*, pp. 321–22. Mrs. Carter blamed Vance for reviving the flap over the U.N. vote just before the New York primary in which she was actively campaigning. In her words: "Heaven knows, Cy Vance doesn't have a political bone in his body. . . . I went straight to the telephone to call Jimmy. 'Doesn't Cy know we're in a campaign?' I asked. 'It was bad enough in New York already, but I may as well come home now. We're finished.'"

But the damage was already done, and Carter lost the primary to Senator Edward Kennedy.

Reagan's fourth year was likewise devoid of accomplishments in the Middle East. The most dramatic development came in early February 1984, when the president suddenly decided, against the advice of his secretary of state, to remove the U.S. Marines from Beirut. The marines had been an issue of mounting concern to Congress and the public. Once American lives were no longer threatened, public attention tended to turn away from the horrors of Lebanon. As the election campaign gained momentum, the Middle East never became a serious issue.

In brief, most presidents recognize that they can achieve little in the Middle East in the midst of an election campaign. But even if they were willing to take the risks, the Middle East parties would be unlikely to make concessions to an American president who might not be in office the following January. Arabs and Israelis alike want to know who will be in the White House for the next four years before they make major decisions. This situation weakens the influence of the president in his fourth year even when he is not up for reelection.

CONCLUSION

The American political system was not designed with the conduct of foreign policy in mind. Checks and balances, frequent elections, and the concept of popular sovereignty were all meant to limit abuses of power, not to make it easy for a president to govern. In foreign policy the constraints are often less than in the domestic arena. But in modern times even foreign policy has become controversial, and thus subject to all the political forces that limit the power of a president. Nowhere is this more true than in dealing with the Arab-Israeli conflict.

To understand how U.S. Middle East policy is made, one needs to look carefully at the views of key decisionmakers, especially the president and his top advisers. The individuals do matter. But they operate within a political context that has some regular features. Therefore, if these powerful individuals are to leave their imprint on policy, they will have to understand what the broader political system allows. And they will have to learn much about the political realities of the Middle East as well. The interaction of these two learning experiences shapes the context in which presidents make policy toward the Middle East.

Presidents do have great power at their disposal. It is often most usable in the midst of crises, when the normal restraints of political life are suspended, at least for a little while. Presidents can also usually count on a fairly wide latitude in the conduct of foreign policy in their first one or two years. But in time the need to appeal to the electorate, to have congressional support, and to prepare for reelection comes to dominate thinking at the White House, regardless of who the incumbent is.

Those conditions mean that the United States is structurally at a disadvantage in trying to develop and sustain policies for regions like the Middle East. It is hard to look beyond the next few months. Consistency is often sacrificed for political expediency. Turnover of personnel in top positions erodes the prospects for continuity.

At the same time the United States, for these very reasons, rarely pursues a strongly ideological foreign policy for long. There is pressure to follow a course that has broad popular support and avoids extremes of left or right. Pragmatic criteria are a common part of policy debates: if one course of action has clearly failed, another can be tried. These shifts may be hard on the nerves of leaders in the Middle East, but sometimes the experimental approach is needed if a workable policy is to be found.

Given that every president must operate within certain constraints set by the nature of the American political system, is it inevitable that foreign policy must suffer as a result? The answer, based on this study, is that there is considerable scope for improvement even without a fundamental change in the system.

To take an example, each president when coming to office has a tendency to believe that he can reshape the realities of the Middle East. In time he learns otherwise. This learning period seems to take much of the first year. But it need not always be a wasted year. Even if a president cannot be expected to master the nuances of the Arab-Israeli conflict immediately, he can begin with a modest agenda until he feels more secure in his knowledge, and he can rely more heavily on the advice of those who have had experience.

Similarly, the typical errors of the third year, the rush for success and the corollary tendency to miss opportunities, might be curtailed if there was greater awareness of the dangers. The domestic political gains and losses associated with the conduct of Middle East diplomacy in the third year have probably been overestimated. There is no evidence that Ford and Carter were helped by their successes, nor were Nixon and Reagan punished for their third-year fumbles. Although little can be done to prevent the distortions brought on by the election year, presidents need not act as if the election has already begun by the middle of their third year. There might well be a good case for acting presidential instead.

The role that Jimmy Carter played in the Camp David Accords and the Egyptian-Israeli peace treaty shows that determined presidential leadership can help to resolve complex international disputes. But Carter had hoped to do even more, especially on the sensitive Palestinian issue. That he was unable to achieve his more ambitious goals was not only due to the intractability of the problem; he was also weakened by the normal workings of the American political system, which force a first-term president to devote enormous time and energy to his reelection campaign. This study therefore shows both the power of the presidency in foreign policy and its limitations.

CHAPTER THREE

Getting Started, Getting Acquainted

When President Jimmy Carter was sworn into office on January 20, 1977, the Middle East was already on his foreign policy agenda and very much on his mind. This did not mean, however, that Carter came to power with a clear strategy for dealing with the Arab-Israeli conflict, or that the elements of an American peace plan were already developed.

What the president carried with him were perceptions of the problem and a predisposition to be an activist in trying to find a solution. What he had to learn would come from an endless stream of reporting about the events in the Middle East, meetings with leaders from the area, and consultations with his chief advisers. In addition, at crucial moments he would be obliged to make political judgments about what Congress and the American public would support and what would best advance his prospects for accomplishing the wide range of objectives he had for his presidency.

It was far from inevitable that the Middle East would become one of Carter's main preoccupations in the months ahead; yet that is precisely what happened. To some degree, the president's religious orientation led him to a concern with the lands he had read so much about in the Bible.[1] The idealist in him also seemed to believe that real peace between Arabs and Israelis could be achieved, and he clearly wanted to play a role in bringing that about if possible. Finally, his commitment to the theme of human rights entailed a genuine concern for the homelessness of the Palestinians.

Carter came to office with comparatively little experience in politics. He had served one term as governor of Georgia from 1971 to 1974, but by law could not run for reelection. As governor, Carter had shown a clear commitment to civil rights and had adopted an administrative style characterized by great attention to detail.

On a personal level, Carter identified himself as a born-again southern

---

1. Jimmy Carter, *Keeping Faith*, pp. 273–74.

Baptist, but he was not shrill in trying to impose his religious beliefs on others. Nor did he belong to the most conservative wing of the church. His religion was important to him, but it was a very personal matter. It did mean, however, that he had a great interest in the Holy Land.

As governor, Carter had traveled to Israel in 1973, but apart from that experience he had little direct knowledge of the Middle East. His sister Gloria had married a Jew, and he had heard about Zionism from that branch of the family. He had never met an Arab before becoming president, except once socially at a racetrack in Florida. But those who knew Carter best sensed that he saw in the Palestinian question parallels with the situation of American blacks. As president, he placed a high priority on human rights and saw the Palestinian issue through that lens.

During the campaign for president, Carter spent time reading about foreign policy issues. He also was an active participant in the meetings of the Trilateral Commission, then headed by Zbigniew Brzezinski, who became something of a foreign policy tutor for him. It was before a meeting of the Trilateral Commission in Tokyo in late 1975 that Carter gave his first speech on the Middle East.

Carter also brought to the job of being president a background as an engineer. He wanted to understand issues in detail. When confronted with a problem, he immediately tried to learn as much as possible so that he could begin to work on a solution. He was a believer in the maxim that hard work could produce results, and he hated to admit defeat. Some of his advisers felt that he took special pleasure in tackling problems that no one else had been able to solve.

Carter was most impressive in small groups. Indeed, he built his campaign for president around a series of such meetings. He was less skillful in handling television or in giving speeches to large audiences. His delivery was wooden, the rhetoric was stilted, and he often seemed uncomfortable. His inability to sway large numbers of people through the media became a liability for him as president when he sought to build support for his programs.

Moreover, Carter was not the normal horse-trading, back-slapping kind of politician.[2] He had little flair for making deals to win the support of a reluctant congressman. His view was that he should do what was right and that others would have to support him because of this.[3] Needless

2. For a useful analysis of Carter's "enigmatic" style and personality, see Hedley Donovan, *Roosevelt to Reagan*, pp. 230–46.

3. Carter's press secretary, Jody Powell, in an interview with me on June 11, 1985,

to say, his relations with party politicos and Congress were not always smooth.

Besides these influences from his own background, President Carter carried with him the memory of the 1973 Arab-Israeli war. It had contributed to an enormous increase in the world price of oil, which in turn had stimulated inflation and a slowing of economic growth.[4] Not surprisingly, Carter was determined to avoid a recurrence of such a crisis if at all possible.

By 1977 the price of oil had stabilized somewhat, but the widespread belief was that further turmoil in the Middle East could renew the price spiral. Stable oil prices required Middle East stability, and that meant progress toward defusing the explosive Arab-Israeli conflict. High on Carter's domestic agenda was the development of a comprehensive energy policy, and his concern for energy reinforced his belief that progress must be made in the Middle East soon.

THE ARAB-ISRAELI CONFLICT IN EARLY 1977

The energy crisis and the Arab-Israeli conflict were closely associated in Carter's mind. And it was the latter that he was determined to tackle as a matter of high priority.

Since the Arab-Israeli war of June 1967, Israel had been in occupation of territory seized from Egypt, Jordan, and Syria. A second round of war had followed in October 1973, leaving Israel in control of most of the Sinai Peninsula and all of the West Bank, Gaza, East Jerusalem, and the Golan Heights. (See the map in the front of the book.)

U.S. policy toward the Arab-Israeli conflict since the 1967 war had

---

distinguished between Carter's willingness to act like a normal politician during an election campaign and his feeling once in office that he no longer needed to do so. It was almost as if he were atoning for his campaign behavior once elected, said Powell. The best example was his election as governor of Georgia in 1970. During the primary campaign Carter ran to the right of former governor Carl Sanders on the race issue. But on inauguration day Carter publicly called for an end to racial segregation.

4. Carter explicitly noted these concerns in his speech before the United Nations General Assembly on October 4, 1977: "Of all the regional conflicts in the world, none holds more menace than the Middle East. War there has already carried the world to the edge of nuclear confrontation. It has already disrupted the world economy and imposed severe hardships on the people in the developed and the developing nations alike. So, true peace—peace embodied in binding treaties—is essential." "United Nations: Address before the General Assembly, October 4, 1977," *Public Papers: Carter, 1977*, vol. 2, p. 1720. Carter's earliest public statement as president in which he associated the vulnerability of oil supplies and the need for Middle East peace came in his spontaneous remarks at Clinton, Massachusetts, on March 16, 1977. Ibid., vol. 1, p. 387.

been based on U.N. Resolution 242, which called on the Arabs to recognize Israel's "right to live in peace within secure and recognized boundaries free from threats or acts of force" and enjoined Israel to withdraw its armed forces from "territories occupied in the recent conflict." In shorthand, this came to be known as the "territory for peace" formula. After the 1973 war U.N. Resolution 338 had been adopted; it called on the parties to the conflict to begin negotiations "under appropriate auspices aimed at establishing a just and durable peace in the Middle East." (See appendix A for the texts of Resolutions 242 and 338.)

By 1977 the question confronting the new president was whether it was possible to resume a negotiating process between Israel and its Arab neighbors that could yield agreement along the lines of "territory for peace." Fortunately for Carter, the United States had established a record after 1973 as a negotiator of limited agreements between Israel and its Arab neighbors. Former Secretary of State Henry Kissinger had perfected the art of "shuttle diplomacy," moving in step-by-step fashion to work out partial agreements between the combatants. By September 1975 Egypt had signed two disengagement agreements with Israel and had recovered a portion of its territory in Sinai. Syria had reached a limited agreement on the Golan Heights in 1974. Along the way the United States had acquired both a reputation as the only party that could bring the Arabs and Israelis together and a bundle of commitments to the two sides of the conflict.

Notably lacking, however, was any success in grappling with the Palestinian problem or in bringing Jordan into the negotiating framework. Nonetheless, a model did exist against which to measure possible future moves. And when Carter came to office, the United States enjoyed tolerably good relations with all the principal states, especially Israel, Egypt, Jordan, Saudi Arabia, and Syria.[5]

What was missing in early 1977 was any sense of American leadership. During the 1976 election year the Middle East had received little attention. Lebanon was in crisis, the Arabs seemed badly divided, and the administration of President Gerald Ford was content to rest on its laurels with the Sinai II agreement of the previous year. There were no ongoing negotiations. There was no momentum to keep up. President Ford had gone so far as to inform President Sadat that the United States could do nothing on the Middle East in an election year.[6]

5. See William B. Quandt, *Decade of Decisions*, passim.
6. Author's interview with Ambassador Hermann F. Eilts, Boston, November 30, 1984.

But there were expectations, especially among the Arabs, that the Americans, once done with their quadrennial binge of electioneering, would turn again to the question of Middle East peacemaking. In anticipation of this, the Saudis, who at the time were riding the crest of their petrodollar wealth, had tried to patch up the quarrel between Egyptian President Anwar Sadat and Syrian President Hafiz al-Asad. By late 1976 a semblance of Arab solidarity had been created. The Saudis had also conveyed to the new administration that they would try to keep oil prices from rising, but that they would be able to do so only if progress were made toward resolving the Arab-Israeli conflict.

THE MIDDLE EAST TEAM

Carter's personal inclinations thus meshed well with perceived Middle East realities. In addition, his chief Middle East advisers, Secretary of State Cyrus Vance and National Security Adviser Zbigniew Brzezinski, were both proponents of an active American role in the search for Middle East peace.[7]

Carter had selected as secretary of state a man whom he did not know particularly well but who came to the office with impressive credentials. Vance was a lawyer with a special interest in international issues. He had served in the Lyndon Johnson years as deputy secretary of defense, and in that capacity had witnessed the evolution of U.S. policy at the time of the 1967 Arab-Israeli war.

Vance had also gained experience as a mediator and negotiator. He had participated in the initial Paris talks on Vietnam in 1968 and had tried to work out an agreement on Cyprus in 1967. During these frustrating experiences he had learned that negotiations had their ups and downs, and he came to realize the need for patience. These were qualities that served him well when he took on the Arab-Israeli dossier.

The new secretary of state was not an academic. He had not written extensively about foreign affairs like his predecessor, Kissinger, and therefore his views were not well known to the public. But it soon became clear that he had been marked by the Vietnam War and was dubious about sending U.S. troops into third-world conflicts. He also attached great importance to the management of U.S.-Soviet relations, at the center of which were arms control negotiations. Finally, Vance had an

---

7. Cyrus Vance, *Hard Choices*, pp. 447–48. Brzezinski had participated in the Brookings study group that produced a 1975 report called *Toward Peace in the Middle East* and had also spelled out his views on the Arab-Israeli conflict in an article "Peace in an International Framework," written by Brzezinski, François Duchêne, and Kiichi Saeki.

attachment to the United Nations and genuinely believed that it could play a helpful role in reducing international tensions.

Vance's colleagues came to see in his approach something that they called principled pragmatism. And it was certainly true that foreign leaders came to respect Vance for his directness and honesty. Of all the Americans who dealt extensively with both Arabs and Israelis, he was the one who best retained the confidence of both sides, though with Sadat it took some time for the two men to develop a close relationship.

Carter's national security adviser, Brzezinski, was from a different world than Vance. An immigrant from Poland, he had received his doctorate at Harvard and had been a professor of international politics at Columbia. His prolific academic writing had focused on the Soviet Union and Eastern Europe but had also included studies of Japan and Africa. Apart from a brief period on the Policy Planning Staff of the State Department, Brzezinski had had little direct experience in government. But he did know Carter personally and had been active in his campaign.

If Vance was the steady, patient negotiator, Brzezinski was the theoretician and the manipulator. He operated on two distinct levels. More than anyone else in Carter's entourage, he had a talent for providing a general frame of reference for policy debates. Formulations came easily to him, and Carter found this useful in integrating all the discrete pieces of information that flowed in his direction. At the other end of the intellectual spectrum, Brzezinski was fascinated by the interplay of personalities. He liked the game of political maneuver and was often frustrated by Vance's legalistic views and Carter's apolitical approach to problems. He was above all else an activist. Ideas flowed freely from his office; in the first months of the Carter presidency he was the chief foreign policy innovator.

Although Vance and Brzezinski came to differ on how best to deal with the Soviet Union, they basically saw eye-to-eye on the Arab-Israeli conflict. Both felt that Carter should treat it as a high priority. They favored a comprehensive settlement, if at all possible, and took the Palestinian issue seriously. Neither was anti-Israeli, but both were prepared to argue that Israel should make substantial territorial concessions as the price of peace.

RECEIVED WISDOM ON THE MIDDLE EAST

Two important developments took place in the Middle East in January 1977 that influenced the new administration's perceptions of the timing and urgency of any new initiative. First, the Israeli government decided to hold early elections in May, which meant that a strong Israeli government could be in place by midyear. It had previously been thought that elections might not take place until much later in the year. Second, riots broke out in Cairo in reaction to sudden food price increases. The Sadat regime, on which the Americans were counting so heavily, seemed to be in serious trouble. Lack of progress on the peace front could further weaken Sadat's position.

The outgoing Ford administration left behind a number of transition papers on the Middle East written by State Department and National Security Council specialists. The judgments they contain reflected a widely shared view of the situation facing the new Carter team. It would be a mistake to think that the papers had a direct influence on policy, but they did capture the closest thing to a consensus that one could find in official Washington circles. As such, they merit attention.[8]

One important judgment in the papers was that the status quo in the Arab-Israeli area was inherently unstable. Either there would be progress toward a settlement or there would be a slide toward confrontation. A temporizing American policy might succeed in buying some time, but the weight of the analysis was that the administration should use its full influence for a settlement.

Having raised the danger of an Arab-Israeli war, the analysts went on to speak of the opportunity for progress in negotiations. A move in that direction would inevitably cause some strain in U.S.-Israeli relations, which might be offset somewhat by pressing the Arabs hard on the question of peace. The analysts viewed a revival of the 1973 Geneva formula, a multilateral conference of all the parties under the cochairmanship of the United States and the Soviet Union, as unavoidable in light of the Arab refusal to consider further partial agreements. But they noted that Geneva might be primarily "symbolic, a cover for serious negotiations which would take place elsewhere." This was essentially the way in which the Geneva conference of 1973–74 had functioned. As for the Soviets, they "do not seem essential to the negotiating process itself." The analysts observed, however, that the United States would still have to decide whether to aim for partial or comprehensive agreements, how to handle the Palestinian representation question, how to take into account

8. The three documents consulted were "Arab Peace Offensive," January 4, 1977; a paper on the Arab-Israeli dispute dated January 14, 1977; and an undated paper "Inter-Arab Politics and a Peace Settlement."

the upcoming Israeli elections, and how to develop contacts with the negotiating parties.

Much of the optimism in these transition papers stemmed from a perception of a comparatively moderate Arab coalition of which Egypt, Syria, Jordan, and Saudi Arabia were the core members. Indeed, Saudi influence was thought to be especially strong. Egypt's temptation to go it alone was acknowledged, as was Syria's fear of precisely that possibility, but it was agreed that there was "no likelihood that Egypt, Syria, or Jordan will break ranks to attempt separate negotiations with the U.S. and Israel." Saudi Arabia, it was noted, would probably raise the price of oil if no progress was made in negotiations.

Concerning Geneva, the analysts concluded that Egypt would reluctantly accept the Syrian idea of a joint Arab delegation. As for the Palestinians, the point was made that they could be brought into negotiations only if Egypt, Syria, and Saudi Arabia were in agreement. When inter-Arab divisions existed, the analysts said, Arab radicalism would flourish and undercut Saudi influence.

Regarding the Israeli front, the analysts expressed the view that the Israeli elections in May would prove to be the most important development in the Middle East in the next six months. Prime Minister Yitzhak Rabin would seek to use his consultations with Carter to bolster his position. The analysts thought there might be a national unity government led by Shimon Peres or even Menachem Begin, the leader of the Likud bloc opposition. Such a government, it was felt, would be more rigid, especially on the West Bank question.

Taken as a whole, these views suggested that the professionals in the bureaucracy were inclined to support an active American role. Great importance was attached to the momentary emergence of a moderate Arab coalition. Most of the problems that were to be encountered in coming months were anticipated to some degree, though the possibility of a change in the Israeli government was only mentioned in passing. And the pressures, primarily from Saudi Arabia, on Sadat not to break with Syria were overstated. Still, Carter could expect to find a bureaucracy that would happily follow him in the activist course he had already decided on and that would be well able to keep him abreast of the complex twists and turns of Middle East politics.

A rare degree of consensus therefore existed among the president, his top advisers, and the bureaucracy. If only the Middle Easterners could be convinced, and if only the American political system would be supportive, the president might expect to make a good start on his ambitious search for peace between Arabs and Israelis. Yet the question arose of how to translate the general commitment to an active American role into a strategy for negotiations. Here details and nuance would take on more importance than the broad judgments that led to the initial view that the Middle East deserved top priority on the Carter foreign policy agenda.

A lengthy learning process was about to begin, as is always true in a presidential first year, and mistakes along the way were inevitable. Nonetheless, an important decision had been made at the very outset of the administration, without much debate: the Arab-Israeli conflict would be dealt with as a matter of high priority by the president, and American influence would be committed to achieving a negotiated peace settlement.[9]

SETTING THE COURSE

One of the first directives to be issued by Brzezinski in his capacity as national security adviser was to order a review of Middle East policy for early February. On February 4, 1977, the Policy Review Committee met for the first time under the chairmanship of Secretary Vance to discuss three Middle East topics: aid to Israel; legislation aimed at the Arab boycott of Israel, which had become a controversial issue during the campaign; and, most important, the general strategy for promoting Arab-Israeli negotiations.

A large crowd was assembled in the situation room in the basement of the White House for this first strategy session. In time the number of cabinet-level participants in such discussions would be pared down to Vance, Secretary of Defense Harold Brown, and Brzezinski, along with Vice President Walter Mondale and often the president's political adviser, Hamilton Jordan. But this committee meeting was attended by the secretary of commerce, the director of the Office of Management and Budget, and many junior officials. Remarkable amounts of bureaucratic energy were spent to gain entry to these meetings, because no one wanted to have the precedent set that he could be excluded.

Topic one on the agenda was aid to Israel. In fiscal year 1977 Israel had received $1.785 billion in loans and grants to cover economic and military requirements. The specialists in the Ford administration who had studied the Israeli economic situation felt that only $1.5 billion should

9. Vance, *Hard Choices*, p. 164.

be requested of Congress in fiscal year 1978. But the Policy Review Committee quickly made the recommendation to stay at the former level to help create a positive political climate for Vance's first trip to Israel. The vice president urged that in return for increasing the level of aid to Israel Carter should seek a promise from the Israelis not to lobby Congress for an even larger increase. The president subsequently approved these recommendations, adding that they should be linked to the cancellation of a controversial Israeli program to sell the Kfir aircraft to Ecuador.[10]

After an inconclusive discussion of antiboycott legislation, the committee turned to the main topic of the day. Brzezinski dominated the discussion, arguing that the Arab-Israeli conflict required urgent attention and that Secretary Vance should use his upcoming trip to discuss both substance and procedures. Drawing on his own previous thinking on the topic, Brzezinski contended that the United States should seek a consensus on broad principles, which could then be implemented in stages. From the Arab side, the United States should seek explicit commitments to peace. Formal recognition of Israel and an end to the state of war would not be enough. More tangible actions, such as diplomatic relations and a willingness to engage in normal peaceful relations, like trade and tourism, would have to be part of the package. Brzezinski also urged that the United States try to make a distinction between recognized borders, which would approximate the 1967 lines, and security arrangements, which might entail demilitarized zones and even for a period the stationing of Israeli troops beyond the recognized borders. This was the distinction between sovereignty and security that Kissinger had tried to establish as early as 1973, with some success. Little was said in this session about the Palestinian question, though everyone acknowledged that it too would have to be dealt with in due course.

The committee participants all agreed that there should not be a rush to Geneva. Some degree of prior agreement should be sought through bilateral American diplomatic contacts with each of the parties. Reference was made to a pre-Geneva round of meetings, to which President Carter reacted in writing by noting that his own meetings with Middle East leaders could help fill this need.

Brzezinski and Vance placed different emphasis on two points con-

10. The decision not to approve the Kfir sale provoked the first organized protest from the pro-Israeli lobby and the Jewish community in general. For a useful discussion of Carter's problems with American Jews, see Peter Evan Bass, "The Anti-Politics of Presidential Leadership."

cerning Geneva: Brzezinski felt that the administration should use Geneva only to complete an agreement and that the Soviets should not be included in the discussions at the outset; Vance, by contrast, felt that it would be an error to put Geneva off too long and that at some point the Soviets would have to be brought into the talks. Despite their differences, both men agreed that 1977 was a propitious year to work for Middle East peace and that the United States should aim for a comprehensive agreement on general principles rather than concentrate only on small steps as Kissinger had done.[11] Brzezinski believed that the president would have maximum leverage in his first year because of the nature of the domestic political system. Vance no doubt agreed but recognized that even a powerful president could not necessarily get his way in the Middle East. As he later wrote: "Attempting to reach a comprehensive peace would not, of course, rule out falling back to additional partial agreements if that was all that appeared possible."[12]

ON-THE-JOB EDUCATION

By the time Secretary of State Vance left for the Middle East on February 14, the president had already decided to try to reconvene the Geneva conference by the end of 1977. He attached great importance to making progress in the first year of his presidency. It remained to be seen, however, how the Arabs and Israelis would react to the ideas of the new administration.

At this early stage U.S. policy was aimed at exploring two central questions. Were the parties to the conflict disposed to negotiate with one another, directly or indirectly? And was there common ground in the form of certain key principles that could guide the talks? No one expected an early breakthrough or detailed formulations of position.[13]

Vance used his first round of meetings to sound out each of the leaders on his attitude and position, but the secretary did not begin to put forward American ideas at that stage. During his initial meeting with Prime Minister Rabin in Jerusalem, the Israeli leader identified three important issues that would have to be resolved in negotiations: the nature of peace, the boundaries of peace, and the Palestinian problem. He spoke of the need for normal relations as the principal element of peace. Regarding

---

11. Zbigniew Brzezinski, *Power and Principle*, pp. 86–87.

12. Vance, *Hard Choices*, p. 166.

13. See I. William Zartman and Maureen R. Berman, *The Practical Negotiator*, p. 9, for an outline of these analytically distinct stages of negotiations.

borders, he said that for real peace Israel would make territorial compromises in all sectors. Arrangements for security and sovereignty would all be open for negotiation.

Turning to the Palestinian problem, Rabin said that it was not the crux of the conflict, but that for any peace to be durable a solution must be found. There should be two states: Israel and a Jordanian-Palestinian state. Any agreement would be with Jordan, and the Palestine Liberation Organization (PLO) would not be an acceptable partner in negotiations. He added that Israel was prepared to try either for a comprehensive settlement or for a partial agreement. The role of the United States, he urged, should be to concentrate at this time on procedures for negotiations, not on substance. He mentioned the Rogers Plan of October 1969 (formulated by Secretary of State William Rogers), which had called on Israel to withdraw from all of Sinai in return for peace with Egypt, as a premature American effort to engage in substance that had not been acceptable to either party.

Turning to other matters, Rabin asked for additional U.S. military assistance, saying that Israel was stronger than it had been two years earlier but that it must remain strong in order to negotiate. On Lebanon, Rabin made it clear that he did not want Syrian troops moving into south Lebanon even if that might bring some stability to the area. The PLO was preferable to the Syrians in the south, said the Israelis, presumably because Israel could strike at PLO targets without risking an all-out war with Syria.

In a separate meeting with Foreign Minister Yigal Allon, Vance pressed for clarification of the Israeli view on Palestinian participation in the negotiations along with Jordan. Would it make any difference, Vance asked, if the PLO were to accept U.N. Resolutions 242 and 338 and change its charter that called for Israel's destruction? Allon answered that "a PLO that accepts 242 would no longer be the PLO."[14] The American side saw this as an invitation to try to get the PLO to accept 242, and over the next several months this idea was pursued through a variety of channels.

Vance had one bit of bad news for the Israelis: Carter, primarily as part of his genuine commitment to arms control, and not for reasons of Middle East policy, had decided not to approve the sale to Israel of a particularly lethal kind of cluster bomb. This issue had arisen at his first

14. Vance, *Hard Choices,* p. 171.

press conference, on February 8, and he had promised to make a decision within one week. An intense lobbying effort had been launched, but Carter had held his ground. To show that the decision was not aimed at Israel, he eventually ordered that this type of "fuel-air explosive" would not be included in the American arsenal either.[15]

Vance also informed the Israelis that the United States would not approve the sale of Kfir jets, which included American-made engines, to Ecuador. Once again, this was a decision that caused some friction in U.S.-Israeli relations but had little to do, in Carter's view, with the Middle East. Quite simply, the United States, as a matter of policy, would not allow its own aircraft companies to sell sophisticated jet fighters to Latin America and so would not approve the sale of a comparable Israeli fighter that included American components. Nonetheless, the reaction of Israel's friends in Congress was such that Carter was put on notice that political costs were involved in saying no to Israel.

When Secretary Vance visited the Arab capitals—Cairo, Damascus, Amman, and Riyadh—he found a generally positive, if guarded, attitude and a sense of urgency. President Sadat, in particular, was anxious to see a negotiating process resumed with active American involvement. As always, he wanted to see an American plan. In an effort to get around the tricky issue of Palestinian participation in the negotiations, Sadat said he would try to get the PLO to recognize Israel, in which case it should be invited to the Geneva conference. If this proved impossible, the Egyptian minister of defense would represent the Palestinians. Although this alternative seemed a bit implausible, it indicated that Sadat was anxious to find a way around procedural hurdles. Sadat also told Vance that he had never meant to say there was no possibility of peace until the next generation. On the whole, Sadat sought to give the impression of being a flexible negotiator, but he did not want to get into details at that point.[16]

After Vance returned to Washington, the president chaired a full session of the National Security Council to hear his report. A memorandum had been prepared for the participants laying out the positions of each of the countries on the key issues of peace, borders, the Palestinian question, and procedural matters. Areas of agreement and disagreement were noted. In general, the picture seemed hopeful. All the leaders accepted the idea

15. The formal decision not to produce the CBU-72, as it was called, was made by Carter on April 16, 1977.

16. See Vance, *Hard Choices*, pp. 168–71, for a summary of Vance's impressions.

of a Geneva conference and were ready to work closely with the United States to prepare the way for it. They all agreed to try for substantial agreement before the actual conference, and they all agreed that the issues of peace, borders, and the Palestinians were central.

Secretary Vance told the National Security Council that the Arabs differed on how they should be represented at Geneva. The Syrians and the Jordanians favored a single Arab delegation, presumably to reduce the chance that Sadat would try to make a separate agreement. Sadat was unhappy with this idea, and Vance implied that the Arabs would have to get their house in order on the question of Palestinian representation. He anticipated that the most difficult issue would prove to be the question of territory, including Jerusalem. With considerable foresight, Vance noted that Rabin was in political trouble and that the upcoming elections could bring change in Israel. Somewhat cryptically, President Carter stated that Israel's recognition of the PLO might be the determining factor in whether the Geneva conference would take place in 1977. (During this period Carter frequently used the terms PLO and Palestinians almost interchangeably.)

By the end of this meeting, Brzezinski believed that all the participants were much on the same wavelength and that Vance, in particular, felt a sense of urgency.[17] In a memorandum to the president written after the meeting, Brzezinski cautioned against the rush to Geneva, arguing that going to the conference would be a concession to the Soviets for which the United States should get something in return. Carter noted his agreement. Brzezinski also warned that if the United States pressed the PLO role too hard, the moderate Arabs might be undercut. Once again the president indicated his agreement.

Despite his sense of urgency, Secretary Vance felt that until the visit by Prime Minister Rabin in early March, the United States should proceed cautiously so as not to arouse Congress or the American Jewish community, which was beginning to show anxiety about possible pressure on Israel.[18] Carter seemed to share this view. In a question-and-answer session at the Department of the Interior on February 18, he spoke of 1977 as the year for reconvening the Geneva conference and defined the U.S. role as that of a mediator, placing the primary responsibility for peace on the countries in the region. He noted that the United States wanted to avoid an

17. Brzezinski, *Power and Principle*, pp. 88–89.
18. Vance, *Hard Choices*, p. 172.

explosion in the Middle East and that the hope for peace was the brightest he could remember.[19]

RABIN'S VISIT AND ADVENTURES IN PUBLIC DIPLOMACY

President Carter's first direct involvement in Arab-Israeli peacemaking came in his meeting on March 7, 1977, with Prime Minister Rabin. Carter was eager to get off to a fast start and begin to grapple with the hard substantive issues. Rabin, by comparison, was cautious, as befitted a man who would soon face elections and who had seen the restlessness of previous American administrations lead to plans and proposals that put pressure on Israel. Still, the initial encounter was cordial, and Carter gave full vent to his sentimental and biblical commitment to the idea of a Jewish state.

In his welcoming remarks on the White House lawn, he referred somewhat carelessly to Israel's need for "defensible borders," a slight difference from the language of U.N. Resolution 242, which spoke of "secure and recognized" borders. The Israelis were pleased, since this was one of their favorite expressions and generally implied that significant territorial adjustments would have to be made in the 1967 lines. Carter, who had little patience for such codewords, had not intended to signal any change in U.S. policy. Nonetheless, the Israelis put out the word to the press that this should be seen as a significant development, and the Arabs reacted sharply and requested clarifications. Secretary Vance immediately stated that the president had meant "no change in position by the use of the words 'defensible borders.'"[20]

Meetings with Rabin

The first meeting between Carter and Rabin covered all the key issues of peace, borders, and the Palestinians.[21] On the sensitive issue of territory, Rabin said that "the bulk of Sinai" could be given back to Egypt in return for peace. Concerning the outpost of Sharm al-Sheikh at the tip of the Sinai Peninsula, Rabin said Israel had no need for sovereignty but did need control, plus a land connection and some changes in the old border.

19. "Department of the Interior: Remarks and a Question-and-Answer Session with Department Employees, February 18, 1977," *Public Papers: Carter, 1977*, vol. 1, pp. 203–04.

20. Bernard Gwertzman, "Carter Causes Stir by Seeming to Back Israel on Frontiers," *New York Times*, March 8, 1977.

21. Yitzhak Rabin, *The Rabin Memoirs*, pp. 292–99, gives a generally accurate, though selective, account of the meeting.

Pressed by Carter on the difference between control and sovereignty, Rabin said this issue could be explored further, but presumably not until after the Israeli elections. The American side saw this as a hopeful sign.

Turning to the other territories, Rabin said Israel did not want to come down from the Golan Heights. Terming the West Bank the most delicate issue, he said that he would not draw lines but that Israel would not agree to total withdrawal.[22] Rabin went on to say that this question of territorial compromise in the West Bank would figure in the upcoming Israeli elections.

Rabin then held forth on the Palestinian issue, again saying that it was not the heart of the matter but that it should be solved in an honorable way and that Israel no longer ignored the problem. Referring to a Jordanian-Palestinian state, Rabin said that how the Palestinian identity might be worked out within that state was not Israel's business. When Carter evoked the model of the American federation of states, Rabin again replied that any agreement would have to be reached with Jordan. How Jordan solved the problem of Palestinian self-expression was up to the Jordanians, but there could be no third state. He then urged the United States not to press the idea of a unified Arab delegation at Geneva, referring to the bilateral Rhodes negotiations in 1949 as a positive precedent. Geneva, he said, should be carefully prepared, especially the questions of peace and borders.

After further talks with Rabin over dinner and in a private session upstairs in the White House, Carter concluded that the Israeli leader was "very timid, very stubborn, and also somewhat ill at ease."[23] Obviously in a somber mood, Carter opened the next day's session with a rather harsh injunction to Rabin to forget about the past and to adopt a fresh perspective. For the first time the president raised the question of Israeli settlements in occupied territory, which he termed illegal. "Your control over territory in the occupied regions will have to be modified substantially in my view. The amount of territory to be kept ultimately by you would

22. In February the Israeli chief of staff had told one of the Americans accompanying Vance that Israel's security requirements in the West Bank could be met by demilitarization, a few Israeli-manned strong points along the roads leading up from the Jordan Valley, and several radar sites on the high ground. This comment had been reported to Carter and may have left the impression that Israeli security problems could be dealt with fairly easily.

23. Carter, *Keeping Faith*, p. 280; and Brzezinski, *Power and Principle*, p. 90, where he recounts the story of Rabin incurring Carter's anger by turning down an offer to see the president's daughter, Amy, during their private meeting upstairs in the White House.

only, in my judgment, involve minor modifications in the 1967 borders."[24]
As a consolation prize of sorts, the president said he thought some security
arrangements beyond those borders would be possible.

As if the atmosphere were not already chilly enough after his reference
to the 1967 borders, Carter turned to the PLO issue. The previous
evening Congressman Thomas P. O'Neill had urged Rabin to deal with
the PLO. Carter returned to that theme, saying that he deplored terrorism
but that the United States had been obliged to talk to the North Koreans
and the French had dealt with the Algerian National Liberation Front.
"We see a possibility that Palestinian leaders can be absorbed in an Arab
delegation. And we don't know any Palestinian leaders other than the
PLO. We hoped you could accept such an arrangement. It would be a
blow to U.S. support for Israel if you refused to participate in the Geneva
talks over the technicality of the PLO being in the negotiations." Carter
added that Rabin's position seemed more inflexible now than when Vance
had seen the prime minister in February.

Rabin responded by urging the president not to take clear substantive
positions before negotiations. Vance probed to see if Rabin would agree
to deal with the PLO if it accepted U.N. Resolution 242. Rabin said no.
In any case, he maintained, the United States and Israel should not argue
over hypothetical issues. Showing his frustration, Carter replied: "I have
never met an Arab leader, but I need to be in a position to talk to them.
. . . We cannot maintain the commitment of a large portion of our
resources and capital to work for peace in the Middle East if we lose this
year's chance. If we lose 1977 as an opportunity for peace, it will be hard
to marshal such efforts again." As the meeting came to a close, Rabin
once again pleaded with Carter not to reveal the differences of opinion
between them over borders and the Palestinian question. Carter responded
by noting that the United States and Israel agreed on the concept of full
peace. He ended the session by saying he believed Israel was the fulfillment
of biblical prophecy.

Carter, Vance, and Brzezinski have all portrayed this meeting with
Rabin in negative terms.[25] The Israeli prime minister was also disap-

---

24. This quotation, and subsequent ones from presidential meetings, are taken from
the official memorandums of conversation prepared after the meetings. These are not
verbatim records, but rather reconstructions of the conversation from notes taken during
the meetings.

25. Carter, *Keeping Faith*, p. 280; Vance, *Hard Choices*, p. 173; and Brzezinski, *Power
and Principle*, pp. 90–91.

pointed, though he recognized that Carter's views on peace were the most favorable Israel had ever heard.[26] In retrospect, these meetings stand out for the seriousness and the intelligence of the discussion on both sides. Difficult issues were being raised and debated. No attempt was made to gloss over differences. And compared with the disagreements between Carter and Rabin's successor, Menachem Begin, the differences were not profound. Still, the subjective feeling on each side was what counted, and the verdict was that the meetings had not been successful. This judgment led both leaders to a round of public diplomacy that probably complicated this early phase of peacemaking and turned it quickly into a Washington spectator sport played out under the glare of publicity.

Public Comments

Rabin made the first move in comments to the press on the afternoon of the second meeting. Picking up on Carter's public reference to "defensible borders," he defined it as meaning that Israel should never be expected to return to the 1967 lines, implying, of course, that Carter agreed with him. Off the record, Israelis began to say they preferred Kissinger's step-by-step approach to Carter's search for a comprehensive settlement at Geneva—even though Rabin had told Carter in private that Israel was prepared to try for a comprehensive settlement and would be ready to go to Geneva.[27]

In a press conference held the same day that Rabin's comments appeared in the press, Carter was asked if he agreed that "defensible borders" for Israel meant that Israel should be able to keep some of the land occupied in 1967. Carter dismissed this as a debate over semantics. Then he floated the idea of "defense lines" that might be different from legal borders. "There may be extensions of Israeli defense capability beyond the permanent and recognized borders," an idea the Arabs would not like. He added the thought that some of these arrangements might just be for an interim period of up to eight years. After observing that he could not predict the lines to which Israel might withdraw as part of a final peace, he went on to say: "I would guess it would be some minor adjustments in the 1967 borders. But that still remains to be negotiated." Somewhat wistfully, and not for the last time, he said it looked as if

26. Rabin, *Rabin Memoirs*, p. 298.

27. Rabin's remarks on "defensible borders" were carried in Bernard Gwertzman, "Rabin, after Carter Talks, Urges a Goal of 'Real Peace' in Mideast," *New York Times*, March 9, 1977.

peacemaking between Israel and her Arab neighbors would be a long, tedious process.[28]

Returning to his basic point, Carter added that there were three related elements: peace, border delineations, and dealing with the Palestinian question. A moment later he gave examples of security arrangements that might protect Israel, such as demilitarized zones and electronic watch stations. On each of these points except the Palestinian question, Carter had now broken fresh ground in his public comments, and in the process had raised concern among both Arabs and Israelis.[29] And he had probably weakened Rabin and his party in the upcoming elections.

A few days later, on March 16, President Carter spoke at a town meeting in Clinton, Massachusetts. In response to a question on the Middle East, he further fleshed out his views, with strong emphasis on the need for concrete Arab commitments to peace, including normal relations. As for borders, he did not repeat his view on the 1967 lines, merely saying the two sides would have to negotiate. Then came the blockbuster: "And the third ultimate requirement for peace is to deal with the Palestinian problem. . . . There has to be a homeland provided for the Palestinian refugees who have suffered for many, many years."[30] In closing, he noted that the U.S. role was to be a catalyst. With these comments he had certainly helped set off a chemical reaction in Israel.

Vance and Brzezinski were both taken by surprise by the president's remarks on a Palestinian homeland.[31] They were not the only ones. The PLO leadership was holding a meeting of its National Congress in Cairo at precisely this time, and Yasir Arafat's initial reaction to the homeland remark was cautiously positive. Carter was not, however, deliberately trying to send Arafat a signal by his remarks.[32]

As one looks back at the public and private record, it appears as if President Carter deliberately ventured into public diplomacy in the hope

28. "The President's News Conference of March 9, 1977," *Public Papers: Carter, 1977,* vol. 1, pp. 342–43.

29. See Carter, *Keeping Faith,* pp. 280–81, where he says he decided to "plow some new ground."

30. "Clinton, Massachusetts: Remarks and a Question-and-Answer Session at the Clinton Town Meeting, March 16, 1977," *Public Papers: Carter, 1977,* vol. 1, p. 387.

31. Carter makes no mention of his Clinton remarks in his memoir, nor does Vance; Brzezinski says he was surprised by the reference to a "Palestinian homeland," but was ordered by Carter not to issue any clarifications. Brzezinski nonetheless called Israeli Ambassador Simcha Dinitz to say he did not think it meant anything new. Brzezinski, *Power and Principle,* p. 91; and interview with Vance in New York, March 1, 1984.

32. Interview with President Carter, Plains, Georgia, May 22, 1985.

of shaking things up and accelerating the negotiating process. As a newcomer to international politics, he was impatient with fine diplomatic distinctions, with the taboos surrounding certain "buzzwords," and with the unimaginative and repetitive nature of many of the discussions of the topic. As a politician, he also seemed to recognize that his power to influence events would be greatest in his first year. Thus, in a pattern typical of a new incumbent of the Oval Office, he was impatient to get on with the task.[33]

There is little evidence that Carter sympathized with Rabin's political problems or realized how his own comments could affect Israeli public opinion in the preelection period. For Carter, this was a time for bold action. He had trouble understanding that Rabin's political imperatives were to play it safe. The U.S. and Israeli political cycles were out of phase.

Nor does Carter seem to have been concerned about raising Arab expectations that might subsequently be disappointed. Instead, he seemed to take pride in putting the United States on record with positions he felt he could defend to both sides. In retrospect, it was probably a mistake for Carter to get into discussion of details of a peace settlement at this early stage. But he was a detail man and had a hard time holding his tongue in public, even when his secretary of state and political aides urged him to do so.

The idealist in Carter spoke of mobilizing "world public opinion" against any intransigent party, and this way of seeing things helped him to justify the openness of his diplomacy. In time the political costs of adopting such a high profile would begin to sink in, as would the extraordinary complexity of the issues, but as of mid-March President Carter felt he was off to a good, even if controversial, start.[34]

CARTER MEETS THE ARABS

Until April 1977 President Carter had never met any Arab leaders. Nonetheless, he seemed to be well disposed toward them, as his comments

33. See Jody Powell, *The Other Side of the Story*, p. 56, where he says Carter understood that his leverage at home and abroad "would never be greater than during his first year in office, and he was determined to waste no time in using it."

34. The president's political advisers, however, were beginning to worry about the growing criticism of Carter's Middle East policy by the American Jewish community. Mark Siegal, an aide to Hamilton Jordan, was therefore named as liaison with the Jewish community, a post he held until his resignation in the aftermath of the sale of F-15 aircraft to Saudi Arabia in the spring of 1978.

to journalists in late March indicated: "We have strong indications that the Arab leaders want to reach a substantial agreement." He went on to term them "very moderate."[35] In the same session he defended himself against the charge of being too frank in his public statements, a theme that was beginning to be aired in the press after his burst of public diplomacy in early March.

Sadat

Egyptian President Sadat's reputation preceded him to Washington. He had become something of a media star, and former Secretary of State Kissinger had lavished praise on him as a statesman and man of vision. In 1974 and 1975 Sadat had shown a willingness to negotiate partial agreements with Israel under U.S. auspices. It was generally assumed in Washington that Sadat was ready to resume the peace process, though it was not clear how far he was prepared to go, or how far out of step with the other Arab parties he was prepared to get. No one expected Sadat to be the main obstacle along the road to Middle East peace.

Carter's welcoming remarks on April 4, the day of his first meeting with Sadat, were warm and generous, in contrast to his frosty demeanor toward Rabin a few weeks earlier. No doubt, the personal chemistry between the two men was good, and Carter immediately considered Sadat a friend and a man of rare courage. This did not mean, however, that their first exchanges were entirely cordial.

Carter opened their talks by making it clear that the United States would be active in promoting a settlement but that the parties to the conflict would also have to do their share. Sadat responded by asking for an American proposal, as he had done during the first disengagement negotiations in late 1973. He pleaded that there was no mutual confidence between Israel and the Arabs and that, in any case, the United States held 99 percent of the cards.

Early in the discussion Sadat adopted a technique he was to use repeatedly in the coming months. He would tell Carter what concessions he was prepared to make but would then urge the president to use them to extract comparable concessions from the Israelis. For example, Sadat quickly acknowledged that there could be some slight modifications in the 1967 lines—at least in the West Bank, but not in Sinai. He also said

35. "Interview with the President: Remarks and a Question-and-Answer Session with a Group of Publishers, Editors, and Broadcasters, March 25, 1977," *Public Papers: Carter, 1977*, vol. 1, p. 513.

he would have no objection if the United States offered Israel a defense pact. Then, while expressing his support for the idea of a Palestinian homeland, he said that such a Palestinian state should have some link to Jordan. But he held firm on two points: there could be no Israeli soldiers remaining on Egyptian territory, and the matter of open borders and diplomatic relations involved state sovereignty and could not be part of the bargaining.

Turning to the idea of a Geneva conference, Sadat maintained that peace in the Middle East should be made under American auspices. If, before Geneva, the United States could produce some proposals, they would be accepted, and Egypt would go to Geneva simply to sign the agreements. Or Sadat could go to negotiate with Israel at Geneva; that process would take ten years and Egypt would get nothing. Sadat clearly shared Carter's own sense of urgency, saying that an agreement should be reached in 1977 and implemented before the "expiration" of the second disengagement agreement in October 1978.[36]

Sadat reiterated the impossibility of opening borders to free movement of people and goods, which brought a sharp objection from Carter, who argued that Israel should get peace and open borders in return for withdrawal. Concerning the exchange of ambassadors, Sadat insisted that peace could not be imposed. This was a matter of sovereignty. After all, the United States did not have diplomatic relations with the Soviet Union for sixteen years. The main point, he said, was to end the state of belligerency, to normalize the situation, and then to guarantee the settlement.

Carter's response was frosty: "Well, this has not been very productive to this point. You don't see any time when it could be done." Sadat hesitated, then played his card, saying that he did not know if in a peace agreement he could add a clause on normalization of relations in five years or so. Or perhaps the United States could guarantee the normalization. When peace was achieved, and there were guarantees, this issue should not be a problem. But the United States should be there as a witness. It would be very difficult.[37]

36. Sadat frequently spoke of October 1978 as the end date for the Sinai II agreement, even though that agreement had explicitly said that it could be superseded only by another agreement and that all disputes between the two countries should be settled by peaceful means. Sadat's sense of urgency must have been in part due to his difficult domestic situation as reflected earlier in the year by riots, student strikes, and the arrest of Libyan agents.

37. Carter places this exchange in his after-dinner meeting with Sadat, along with

The American side immediately recognized that Sadat had hinted at flexibility on the crucial issue of normal relations with Israel. From there he moved on to show an open attitude toward the procedural question of how the Arabs should be represented at Geneva. He noted that Syrian President Hafiz al-Asad insisted on a single Arab delegation as a way to reduce Sadat's room for maneuver. Sadat clearly did not like the idea but said that if Carter found it necessary for him to make concessions, and if Carter could convince him that Israel wanted peace, Sadat would agree to it. But one delegation would reduce his flexibility.

Even though Sadat had gone quite far in this first conversation, Carter was still impatient. Reflecting on his own political calendar, he said that if progress was not made in 1977, it would be even more difficult in 1978 and 1979. As an incentive, however, he said to Sadat: "I can see the possibility that ten years from now our ties to you in the economic, military, and political spheres will be just as strong as the ties we now have with Israel." But, he cautioned, this would require a strong Egyptian-Israeli relationship.

The first day's talks concluded with a discussion of the Horn of Africa and Soviet intentions there. That evening, Sadat was entertained at the White House, after which he and Carter had a warm private conversation. The contrast with the Rabin visit was once again apparent.

The next day, April 5, the two presidents concentrated on military assistance issues. Sadat displayed political sophistication in saying he did not want to link the peace issues and the question of arms supply. He said he preferred not to raise battles that Egypt might lose in Congress while he was trying to concentrate on the main issue of peace. Expressing his sympathy with Carter, he said all these efforts with Congress would try the president's patience. Carter responded by offering some help to Sadat to keep his Soviet-built air force from deteriorating.

Carter then raised the possibility of meeting with the PLO leader Yasir Arafat. In Carter's mind, this might be a vital issue. He concluded the meeting, saying: "If we can get your advice and support at the crucial moments, I think we might be able to go to Geneva only for the signing ceremony. That would be the best possible outcome. If we go to Geneva with lots of loose ends and with the Soviets present, there is little chance of reaching harmony there." Sadat agreed, noting that the parties could talk about procedures for years.

Sadat's willingness to consider some minor changes in the 1967 lines. Carter, *Keeping Faith*, pp. 283–84.

From these talks it seemed as if Sadat and Carter saw the situation in similar terms. They were both anxious for quick results. They both wanted substantial agreement before Geneva and hoped to limit the role of the Soviets in the negotiating process. Sadat showed sensitivity to Carter's political problems and was willing to reveal some of the cards he would be prepared to play as negotiations unfolded.

As Sadat left Washington, Carter and his aides had little doubt that Sadat was ready for another round of negotiations. On substance, he seemed adamant that all Egyptian territory be returned by Israel. On other issues, including procedural questions, he seemed more flexible. His views on the Palestinian question were the most puzzling, and the Americans were never quite sure how strongly committed to the Palestinians Sadat was. At this stage, however, he had said nothing to indicate that he was prepared for a separate agreement with Israel that offered nothing to the Palestinians.

Post-Sadat Assessment

No doubt the Americans were fond of Sadat, but they also found him difficult to read. Vance noted this later when he said of Sadat: "Strong on principles, weak on implementation, he appeared to expect concrete solutions to flow automatically from political level agreement on the essentials."[38] Brzezinski worried about Sadat's ability to distinguish fact from fiction.[39] Still, the American side had reason to feel satisfied following Sadat's visit. After three intensive months of working on the Middle East, some progress was being made, and Sadat's attitude suggested that further movement could be expected.

Within days, however, a new element entered the equation: Israeli Prime Minister Rabin was forced to resign from office, to be replaced on an interim basis by Shimon Peres. Few tears were shed in Washington, at least not by Carter.

After his meetings with Sadat, President Carter turned his attention to his other passion, the energy problem. During the third week of April he made two major speeches on this topic. In his mind, a comprehensive energy policy was a corollary of a comprehensive Middle East policy. Both were ambitious goals, but this was still the initial phase of the administration's political cycle, when one could afford to aim high and

38. Vance, *Hard Choices*, p. 174.
39. Brzezinski, *Power and Principle*, p. 93.

hope to succeed. Harsh realities, both domestic and international, would assert themselves soon enough.

On April 19, 1977, Secretary Vance chaired another meeting of the Policy Review Committee to take stock and to prepare for the next round of meetings. In brief, the committee felt that reconvening Geneva in 1977 remained a high priority to prevent political deterioration on the Arab side. The United States would seek as much agreement as possible on general principles before Geneva, but the questions of final borders and the Palestinians were certain to be the most difficult issues. After June the administration would consider the option of direct contacts with the PLO. With respect to the Soviets, the committee maintained a cautious attitude: the administration would begin to talk to them about the Middle East but would not bring them into the process in a significant way. The committee also felt that the new Israeli prime minister, presumably Shimon Peres, should be invited to Washington in June, after which Vance would make another trip to the area to try to flesh out basic principles of agreement. Secretary of Defense Brown cautioned that it would not be possible to go to Geneva in 1977 just to sign an agreement.

During the meeting two new ideas came up: first, the possibility of a referendum to determine the future of the West Bank, an idea favored by Vance; and second, the possibility of getting the PLO to accept U.N. Resolution 242, with a reservation to the effect that the reference in the resolution to solving the refugee problem was not an adequate basis for dealing with the Palestinian question. The second suggestion was made by Brzezinski, who also reiterated the importance of separating security arrangements from the question of borders.

Already one could see that Vance, in particular, was looking for a way to deal differently with the West Bank than with the other occupied territories, and that efforts were being made to figure out how to get the Palestinians into the negotiating process, either by pressing for a change in the PLO position or by calling for a referendum in which West Bank and Gaza Palestinians would be able to express their views.[40] The meeting ended with a reminder from Vance that the United States wanted to avoid a "Rogers Plan" that might be rejected by all parties. He also noted

40. I attended this meeting as a member of the National Security Council staff and was asked to prepare an analytical paper on the idea of a referendum. In my view, the idea sounded appealing, but in fact would not help solve the problem. If a referendum was held under Israeli auspices, the results would lack legitimacy; if a genuine referendum produced results that were unpalatable to Israel, it would lead nowhere. I argued instead for consideration of the Algerian model, whereby an agreement was first negotiated in detail, then submitted to the population in question for ratification.

that the administration needed to evaluate how much leverage it had with Israel and that for the moment no further arms agreements should be made.

In the week following the Policy Review Committee meeting, President Carter met with Syrian Foreign Minister Abd al-Halim Khaddam; and then on April 25 with King Hussein of Jordan. During his talks with the Syrian envoy, Carter agreed to meet with President Hafiz al-Asad in Geneva the following month. Otherwise, during this period Carter limited his public comments to a reiteration of the importance of dealing with the three core issues of peace, borders, and the future of the Palestinians. He also formally approved a recommendation to send an air force team to Egypt to discuss Sadat's request for F-5E aircraft and a maintenance program for the Soviet-supplied MIGs.[41] At this point the administration was still not prepared to provide lethal equipment to Egypt.[42]

King Hussein

Carter's first meeting with King Hussein on April 25 was cordial but broke little new ground. The king made it clear that his willingness to participate in any negotiations with Israel would depend on Israel's willingness to return the West Bank and East Jerusalem. He acknowledged that some minor border rectifications could take place, but argued that security was less a matter of geography and borders than a state of mind and a feeling of wanting to live in peace. He went on to say that if Israel were to withdraw from the West Bank, that area could be placed under an international authority for a transitional period, allowing the Palestinians there to exercise their right of self-determination.

Carter said he thought international public opinion could be mobilized behind a fair proposal, but went on to warn: "If there is no possibility of common agreement, it might be an error to meet in Geneva. But if there is a chance of progress, we will consider taking a strong position of advocating a comprehensive settlement, or we might judge that it would be better to refrain from doing so." Hussein urged the president to stay with his present course of talking to all the parties and then coming up with U.S. ideas. To go to Geneva without a previously agreed plan, the king said, would be a disaster that would have serious implications for

41. On April 29, 1977, the president made another formal decision on an arms package for Egypt. He approved the sale of fourteen C-130 transports, twelve remotely piloted vehicles, five reconnaissance pods, and the MIG maintenance program.

42. Brzezinski, *Power and Principle*, p. 94, terms these decisions a reward for Egypt's moderation.

the future.[43] Carter said that he agreed.[44] He added that he did not want the Soviets to play more than a minimal role in the process. Vance demurred slightly, noting that so far the Soviets had been constructive and that at some point they would want a more active role. Hussein concluded with an important point: the Arabs might be able to agree on principles, but the initiative would have to come from the American side.[45]

Asad

Carter's meeting with Syrian President Asad in Geneva on May 9, 1977, was remarkable for several reasons.[46] First, Asad was the only leader to meet Carter on neutral turf, so to speak, rather than in Washington. Sadat was reported to be resentful that Asad received such special treatment from the American president. Second, Carter's welcoming comments were particularly effusive, referring to Asad as the "great leader" of Syria and to his "close friendship" with him only minutes after the two leaders had met for the first time. Third, Carter reiterated publicly his support for a Palestinian homeland in Asad's presence. Fourth, the two men, in some ways similar in their origins but very different in their political values and careers, seemed to get along remarkably well during their nearly seven hours together in talks and over dinner.

The talks began in the late afternoon with the president reiterating his now familiar line that unless substantial agreement could be reached before the Geneva conference it might be better not to go at all. Asad nodded his agreement as Carter spoke of the need for progress in 1977. Asad then took the floor for most of the next hour with his obligatory

43. On April 27, 1977, the *New York Times* quoted King Hussein, in remarks at Blair House after meeting with Carter, as saying: "My own feeling has been that Geneva would be a disaster without prior planning and without a realistic appraisal of all the difficulties and possibilities toward making progress in advance of holding the meeting." See Bernard Gwertzman, "Carter Cautions on Geneva Talks; Consults Hussein."

44. While seeing King Hussein off on April 26, Carter said offhandedly to reporters: "And I think unless we see some strong possibility for substantial achievements before a Geneva conference can be convened, unless we see that prospect, then I think it would be better not to have the Geneva conference at all." "Visit of King Hussein I of Jordan: Remarks to Reporters Following King Hussein's Departure, April 26, 1977," *Public Papers: Carter, 1977*, vol. 1, p. 723.

45. In his meeting with Hussein the following day, Carter said he had some concern that a Palestinian entity might be pro-Soviet. This was the first time Carter had raised this issue in one of his high-level meetings.

46. See Jimmy Carter, *The Blood of Abraham*, pp. 67–73, for an account of this meeting.

speech on the history of Arab nationalism and Israeli expansionism. Carter listened somewhat impatiently, trying to indicate that this was already familiar to him or somewhat beside the point. Then Asad stopped abruptly, saying it was time to talk of the present. He agreed that the three key issues were borders, Palestinian rights, and the prerequisites of peace.

Expanding on Syria's position, Asad said there must be full evacuation of occupied territory. Otherwise the seeds of future conflict would remain. Time was on Syria's side, but why should time be allowed to pass while there was so much bloodshed? Syria was ready to talk of peace, but not if territory were to be lost. Secure borders did not exist with modern weapons. In response to a question from Carter, Asad implied that demilitarized zones on both sides of the borders could be accepted if they did not involve huge armies close to Damascus. Asad added that he would agree to an end of the state of belligerency as well as to certain security measures. That was all that would be needed for peace.

Turning to the Palestinian question, Asad proved himself to be wily and elusive, while at the same time showing the American side that it had nothing to teach him on this topic. But he resolutely refused to state his own preferred outcome. He placed emphasis on the need to include something for the refugees outside the occupied territories. He was not necessarily opposed to the idea of a Jordanian-Palestinian federation, but he expressed skepticism, asking what would be in it for the Palestinians. And would King Hussein really favor it? In a passing comment about Lebanon, Asad said Lebanon was a burden on Syria because of its contradictions, its lack of authority, and its confusion.

Carter then asked Asad if he thought the PLO would agree to accept U.N. Resolution 242, except for the part that treated the Palestinians only as refugees. Asad said the answer would depend on what the PLO would get in return. What was the importance of such a step before Geneva? Carter replied that many American Jews believed the PLO intended to destroy Israel; the PLO's acceptance of the resolution would remove that argument. "I need to have American Jewish leaders trust me before I can make progress," said Carter. Asad replied by saying he could not predict the PLO's response, but he could sound its leaders out. Carter asked him to do so, adding that it might be important to talk to Arafat directly at some point and that this was now impossible because of the PLO's position on 242.[47]

---

47. Vance, *Hard Choices*, p. 177, notes this point.

Returning to the question of peace, Carter spoke hopefully of regional economic development. Asad replied by saying it was important to prevent a new round of war. Ending the state of belligerency would lead automatically to peace. There was no intermediate stage. An end to belligerency by itself would solve many psychological problems. Security measures could be added to buy time. Economic development would help. But one could not say what else might take place in the future. Commerce required two partners, and no one in Syria would now be prepared to trade with Israel. In conclusion, he added that East Jerusalem would have to be returned to the Arabs, though the Holy Places could be given a special status.[48]

CONCLUSION

Having met with Asad in Geneva, Carter had completed his initial round of talks with the leaders of all the states that were slated to attend a future Geneva peace conference. Meetings with Saudi Arabia's Crown Prince Fahd and with the soon-to-be-elected Israeli prime minister were still in the offing, but the basic groundwork had been laid by mid-May.

Carter's views on the Arab-Israeli conflict had come into fairly clear focus after only four months on the job. The president was openly committed to an active American role in trying to break the deadlock in Arab-Israeli peace negotiations. He saw the Middle East dispute as closely related to both the energy crisis and the danger of superpower confrontation. He was also convinced that progress must be made in 1977, or the chance for peace might be lost. On these points it would be hard to fault Carter's judgment.

On substantive issues Carter had accepted the idea that he should try to break new ground, that the stale, old formulations should not be treated as sacred. He therefore deliberately—though sometimes awkwardly—spoke publicly of three basic requirements for Middle East peace. First, peace should entail normal relations, such as exchange of ambassadors, trade, open borders, tourism, and regional economic cooperation. An end to the state of belligerency would not be enough in his view to convince the Israelis to make concessions. He was sensitive to the Israeli argument that there was an asymmetry in asking the Arabs to make peace and the Israelis to give up territory.

48. Carter, *Blood of Abraham*, p. 72, recounts this part of the discussion. In *Keeping Faith*, p. 286, Carter termed Asad "very constructive in his attitude and somewhat flexible."

By spelling out the contents of peaceful relations, Carter hoped to overcome Israeli fears and to induce the Arabs to accept Israel's existence in a positive spirit. The idealist in him believed this would be possible if only political leaders would listen to the deep yearning for peace of their own people. His meeting with Rabin convinced him the Israelis valued such a concept of peace. His meetings with Sadat and Hussein convinced him peace might be possible. Here again Carter seemed to be on fairly solid ground.

Second on the president's agenda was the need for borders that would be recognized and arrangements for security that might go beyond the borders. From what Carter knew of the Arab position, he had no reason to believe that any significant changes in the 1967 lines would be recognized, but he did sense more flexibility among the Arabs when it came to demilitarization, peacekeeping forces, early warning stations, and perhaps even some form of Israeli military presence beyond Israeli borders for a transitional period. He thus tried to meet Israel's concern for security by placing heavy emphasis on these technical arrangements, which in any case appealed to the engineer in him. In this area, as in the area of peace, he felt the Arabs would have to make concessions.

Carter was also prepared to consider how the United States could bolster Israeli security, up to and including a U.S.-Israeli defense pact as part of an overall settlement. But in return, he felt—and was prepared to say in public—Israel should eventually return to the 1967 lines, with only minor modifications. This last point was unpalatable to Israeli politicians, though the Israeli chief of staff had confidently told the Americans that he could ensure Israel's security from within the 1967 lines if he could count on demilitarization of sensitive areas and a few early warning stations.

In spelling out his views on peace, borders, and security, Carter was admittedly going beyond the language of U.N. Resolution 242. He felt, however, that he was clearly within its spirit and that his views were consistent with previous U.S. policy.[49] Carter was no doubt correct to try to encourage fresh thinking on these topics, but he was politically insensitive in the way he spoke in public about the 1967 borders, especially

---

49. Previous American presidents had said that the final borders "should not reflect the weight of conquest" and should be "mutually agreed." In September 1975, however, as part of the Sinai II agreement, President Ford wrote a letter to the Israelis saying that in any future negotiations over the Golan Heights, the United States would take into account Israel's position that it should not return to the 1967 borders.

just before the Israeli elections. In private, all former presidents had talked of the 1967 borders, with only minor modifications, as the likely basis for any negotiated agreement, and Carter gained nothing by injecting this idea into his public rhetoric at such an early date.

It was on the Palestinian question, however, that Carter was most innovative and controversial. Presidents Nixon and Ford had limited themselves to saying the Palestinians had legitimate interests that should be dealt with in a future peace settlement. They had nonetheless felt that Jordan should be the negotiator on behalf of the Palestinians. After September 1975 the United States had been bound by a pledge to Israel not to "recognize or negotiate with the Palestine Liberation Organization so long as the Palestine Liberation Organization does not recognize Israel's right to exist and does not accept U.N. Resolutions 242 and 338." Carter's advisers felt the Palestinian issue deserved higher priority than it had been previously accorded, but they were still not prepared to urge the president to launch a dramatic initiative on the issue.

Carter took the lead in articulating a new position for the United States on the Palestinian question, calling for the creation of a "homeland" for the refugees. It was not entirely clear what he had in mind, and he often seemed to equate the PLO and the Palestinians. The humanitarian question of refugees and the demands of highly politicized Palestinian nationalists engaged in armed struggle were not sharply differentiated in his mind. Nor had he foreseen the political costs of injecting this theme into his public statements at such an early date. But if he spoke out publicly in favor of real peace for Israel, his instinct for fairness seemed to tell him that some nod toward Palestinian rights was also warranted.

It was not surprising, given his views, that Carter sought some way to establish direct communications with the Palestinians. To this end, he floated the idea with several Arab leaders that the PLO should accept U.N. Resolution 242, with a statement of reservation, as a way of opening direct contacts. Before long, however, Carter was beginning to feel the political heat, and his statements on the Palestinians became more circumspect, first stressing his preference for a link between a Palestinian homeland and Jordan, then dropping all reference to a homeland, and eventually conveying his opposition to an independent Palestinian state. In this early period, however, his idealistic impulse, his concern for human rights, seemed to propel him into these uncharted waters.

Looking back, one could say that Carter would have been better off politically to have talked less in public about the Palestinians and to have been more consistent on this sensitive issue. But Carter was not a conventional politician, and he deliberately sought to inject controversial ideas into the debate over the Middle East. It took some time for him to realize that the cost of sticking to those positions in his public statements was high. So he pulled back, giving the impression to Arabs and Israelis alike that he could be made to back down under pressure. Backing down was costly, a mistake that could have been avoided, but also one that is common for first-term presidents in their first year.

In this phase of his Middle East diplomacy, Carter showed considerable skepticism toward the idea of a Geneva conference as an end in itself. He frequently talked of the need for prior agreement on general principles before convening such a conference. He went so far as to say that Geneva should not be held unless significant progress was made in advance. To some extent, this pronouncement may have been meant as a form of pressure on the Arabs, who were thought to favor a Geneva meeting more than the Israelis. But all the Arab leaders agreed with Carter about Geneva, even Asad. What they really wanted was an American plan that the United States would impose on Israel, not lengthy and open-ended negotiations at Geneva.

Carter never quite seemed to grasp this point, and in particular he misread Sadat's deep skepticism about a Geneva conference that was not well prepared in advance. Sadat was not entirely consistent in his views about Geneva, but he generally seemed to believe that such an international conference should be primarily a signing ceremony after an agreement had been worked out in secret bilateral talks. Geneva was to be a facade, but it could also become a trap if treated too seriously. More than any other single element, it was this concern that later seems to have prompted Sadat to go to Jerusalem.

Carter's initial doubts about Geneva also reflected a skeptical attitude about the role of the Soviets in the negotiating process. The president was willing to go through the motions of consulting with them, acknowledging that eventually they would have to be given some role at Geneva, but he did not want to include them in the substantive discussions. On this point, all the Middle East leaders seemed to agree with him.

From this overview of Carter's thinking as of mid-May 1977, it appears as if his views were somewhat more in harmony with those of his national security adviser, Brzezinski, than with Secretary of State Vance. Although on the whole there was a rare degree of congruence in the views of all the top officials and their staffs, Brzezinski was more skeptical of Geneva and of the Soviet role than Vance was. On these points, they tilted in opposite directions, though no sharp disagreement occurred and Carter was never asked to make a concrete choice between these two tendencies. On all the other matters of substance, Carter, Vance, and Brzezinski were in agreement. Brzezinski, however, seemed to enjoy the president's penchant for public diplomacy and confrontation with Israel, whereas Vance was a more conventional practitioner of quiet diplomacy, though equally tough minded in his attitude toward Israel.

Despite a few missteps and false starts, and his questionable handling of the visit by Prime Minister Rabin, Carter was about where he wanted to be with his Middle East policy after his first four months. He had reestablished American leadership in the peace process. He had shaken things up, and in so doing had put some pressure on both Arabs and Israelis. He had laid the basis for personal relationships with the key leaders in the area.

Carter had paid an unnecessarily high price in domestic political terms to get to that point. At this early stage in his presidency he was not particularly concerned. Later, however, he found that many in the Jewish community and in Congress were very critical of his initial moves in the Middle East, with the result that they were unwilling to give him the benefit of the doubt in his confrontations with Menachem Begin. Even more damaging, his early penchant for speaking out against Israel on some points may have marginally contributed to undermining the Labor party in the May elections.

If Carter's approach to the Arab-Israeli conflict had any chance of success, it required an Israeli partner willing to accept the concept of "territory for peace" with each of its neighbors. With a Labor-led government, Carter might have had a chance of moving toward agreement on such principles and the eventual reconvening of the Geneva conference. But Carter was not sufficiently political in his thinking to consider how his statements and actions might affect the Israeli domestic political scene.

As Carter was soon to learn, the best formulated of plans cannot stand up to the vagaries of Middle East politics. On May 17, 1977, Israelis went to the polls and voted in the Likud bloc, headed by Menachem Begin. This meant that Carter's initial strategy was in need of review and adjustment, since it had largely been predicated on an understanding of what Israel's Labor party leadership might be persuaded to accept. Menachem Begin was another matter altogether. Carter's next challenge would be to deal with this veteran politician, an unknown quantity with a hard-line reputation.

CHAPTER FOUR

Meeting Menachem Begin

When Menachem Begin, leader of the Likud coalition, became Israel's prime minister, on June 21, 1977, the Carter administration was obliged to reassess its Middle East strategy. Until then, it was assumed that peace negotiations could proceed based on the "territory for peace" formula embodied in U.N. Resolution 242. According to this view, Israel should return most, if not all, of the territory occupied in the 1967 war, and in exchange should be recognized by its Arab neighbors. All parties—Egypt, Israel, Jordan, Syria—would be expected to agree to security arrangements along the borders. Somehow the Palestinian voice should be expressed in the negotiations, and some solution to the refugee problem should be found.

President Carter had made a few original, and controversial, suggestions on how a peace settlement might be achieved, but his underlying approach to the Arab-Israeli conflict was very much within the mainstream of U.S. official thinking since the 1967 war. It took the election of Menachem Begin to convince the Americans they needed to adjust their strategy.

When events do not fit expectations, policymakers react in several different ways. Some may deny that anything has gone wrong. Others try to make minimal adjustments to accommodate the new realities. A few may suspend previous beliefs and try to reassess the new situation. Others see in the changed circumstances an even stronger rationale for pursuing the previous policy. Wishful thinking, denial, confusion, rationalization, as well as genuine rethinking and analysis—all are part of the reassessment that periodically takes place in the top levels of foreign policy officialdom when the world outside refuses to fit the perceptions and expectations held in Washington. And once policies are set, inertia also plays a large part.

These moments of reassessment can be valuable to an administration, since some degree of adjustment to reality is essential if policy is to have a chance of succeeding. A new administration in its first year can profit from having its initial assumptions questioned. Mid-course corrections can help keep policies on target. In this sense, Begin's election might have helped refocus the somewhat general approach of the administration as it moved from articulating broad principles to the more difficult task of trying to shape actual agreements between Israel and its Arab neighbors.

President Carter has said he was "shocked" by Begin's election.[1] If so, the reason must have been Begin's militant defense of Israel's claim, grounded in history and the Bible, to hold onto all the land of Eretz Israel—including, of course, the West Bank and Gaza—and his fierce commitment to additional Israeli settlements in occupied territories. These were the two issues on which Begin seemed to differ most from his predecessors.

WHO IS BEGIN?

Menachem Begin was virtually unknown to American officialdom. Since Israel's creation in 1948, the United States had dealt with a succession of Israeli governments led by the Labor party. Prime ministers such as David Ben-Gurion and Golda Meir had developed deep ties to the American Jewish community and to the power centers of Washington. By contrast, Begin was known primarily as the fiery leader of the preindependence Irgun movement, associated with such bloody acts as the massacre of Palestinian villagers at Deir Yassin and the bombing of the King David Hotel.

After independence, Begin had led the Herut party, with an emblem and an ideology that laid claim to all of Eretz Israel, defined as both Palestine and Transjordan. For the next twenty years Begin fought for his beliefs from within the Israeli parliament, or Knesset, where his debating skills and intelligence came to be recognized, if not always appreciated, by his adversaries.

From 1967 to 1970 Begin had been a member of a national unity government. He resigned, however, in mid-1970, when the cabinet, led by Golda Meir, agreed to accept U.N. Resolution 242 with the understanding that its withdrawal provision applied to all fronts, including the West Bank.

Few Americans who followed Israeli affairs ever expected Menachem Begin to succeed in his bid to become prime minister. Labor seemed to have a firm grip on power. But voters in Israel, as elsewhere, are capable

---

1. Jimmy Carter, *Keeping Faith*, p. 284. Carter also said that he found a replay of Begin's interview on ABC's "Issues and Answers" to be "frightening" (p. 288).

of surprising the pundits. Faced with scandals within the Labor party, mounting internal problems, and strains in relations with the United States, many Israelis turned to Begin's Likud bloc in the hope it could provide strong leadership in troubled times.

Begin was a puzzle to the Americans who met him. His Polish origin showed through in his courtly manner, his formal dress, and his historical frame of reference. His terrible personal trauma as a Jew in central Europe at the time of Hitler's rise to power seemed never far from his mind. Nearly all his immediate family had been killed in the Holocaust. The depth of his feelings about the tragedy that had befallen his people seemed to make him incapable of having much empathy for others with grievances, especially for Palestinians who expressed their anger and frustration in attacks on Jews.

To many Americans, Begin came across as self-righteous and self-confident, a fighter for his beliefs. But he also had a sense of humor he could use to good effect, and he had an impressive memory from which he drew endless, if not always apt, historical analysis.

It should have been obvious to Carter and his colleagues that Begin was absolutely serious about his commitment to retaining control over Judea and Samaria, as he always insisted on calling the West Bank. In early encounters with Carter and his team, Begin brought maps with which to illustrate his standard lecture on Judea and Samaria. History and religion were at the heart of his claim to these areas, not just security. A rough kind of logic was also at work: if Israel had no valid claim to Judea and Samaria, which had been the center of the ancient Jewish kingdoms, what right did Israel have to Tel Aviv and the coastal strip, with which the historical ties were tenuous at best?

Begin had derived his beliefs from the revisionist wing of the Zionist movement, Betar, led by Vladimir Ze'ev Jabotinsky. He had devoted himself to the revisionist cause and had looked to Jabotinsky as a mentor and something of a father figure. It is not so clear that Jabotinsky was particularly fond of Begin; nonetheless the disciple was shattered by his leader's death in 1940.[2]

Begin was imprisoned in the Soviet Union shortly after Jabotinsky's death, and then in early 1942 was allowed to go to Palestine as part of a Polish army unit. Eventually he joined the anti-British underground and led the Irgun fight for Israel's independence.

2. See Eric Silver, *Begin*, pp. 10–20.

But it was Ben-Gurion, not Begin, who won the credit for forging the modern Jewish state, and in many quarters, including the American Jewish community, Begin was treated as a dangerous extremist in the years after Israel's statehood.

Ben-Gurion and Labor had agreed to a Jewish state in only part of Eretz Israel, which left Begin with an unfulfilled cause—the liberation of the remainder of the Jewish homeland. This had been Jabotinsky's dream, and his disciple was equally wedded to it. It gave a raison d'être to his political career.

None of these points was immediately apparent to Carter and his associates. They found it hard even to find a good account of Begin's life.[3] Although they quickly perused some of Begin's own writings, they tended to think Begin had mellowed in the course of the past thirty years. His tough campaign-style rhetoric about Judea and Samaria was seen as little more than a move to stake out a tough bargaining position.

It would take Carter more than a year to understand that Begin was as adamant in refusing to relinquish Judea and Samaria as Sadat was in refusing to give up any of Sinai. In time, both these positions came to be seen as near absolute, beyond the reach of negotiations. But that was not at all clear in mid-1977.

Begin's election coincided with a sense of mounting irritation within the administration over the attacks on the president's policies in the Middle East launched by friends of Israel.[4] Carter's national security adviser, Zbigniew Brzezinski, sensed that Begin's extremism might help Carter to mobilize American Jewish opinion to his side. But he also felt that the president should not be identified as the only spokesman on Middle East policy, and he urged that Vice President Walter Mondale be given more of a role.[5] On balance, Brzezinski seemed to think that Begin's election would ultimately be helpful to the administration's strategy, if only because it would be easier to pressure a government led by Begin than one in which Begin was leader of the opposition. In Brzezinski's analysis, the president should be able to count on the support of the Israeli opposition, as well as the bulk of the American Jewish community, if he ever faced a showdown with Begin.

Whether Carter's shock or Brzezinski's optimism would prove to be

3. The most widely read book about Begin in the White House was J. Bowyer Bell, *Terror Out of Zion.*

4. Carter, *Keeping Faith,* p. 288.

5. Zbigniew Brzezinski, *Power and Principle,* p. 96.

warranted remained to be seen. For the moment the United States could do little but wait until Begin had formed a cabinet and paid his first call on Carter. Meanwhile, one more Arab leader, Crown Prince Fahd of Saudi Arabia, was scheduled to visit Washington, and the administration had to give him a fair hearing before turning to reassess its policies.

FAHD'S VISIT

Although Saudi Arabia was not a direct participant in the conflict with Israel, Carter and his advisers attached great importance to the Saudi Kingdom as they developed their Middle East strategy. The Saudis, of course, were seen as pivotal in keeping the price of oil from rising. They were also viewed as a moderating force in inter-Arab politics. And their wealth was believed to be a potential resource to be used on behalf of regional economic development. Not surprisingly, Carter's words of welcome for Crown Prince Fahd on May 24 were particularly warm.

Carter opened the private discussion by saying that some of Begin's remarks had caused him concern. He implied, however, that his own views had not changed. Fahd responded by noting that on the Arab side there was a deep desire for peace. He had recently met with Anwar Sadat and Hafiz al-Asad in Riyadh after Begin's election, and they had all agreed that they must control their nerves. Fahd added that progress toward peace in 1977 was essential if the moderate Arab coalition was to hold together. Israel was now accepted as a state by the Arabs, he said, but the Palestinians also needed a state. Such a state should be independent first; then it would probably develop links to Jordan.

If the Palestinians got their state, said Fahd, they would breathe more easily, they would gain their self-respect, and, in the main, they would be satisfied. That in itself would help remove the complexes they had acquired in the past. They would be less vulnerable to outside influences. They would regain their pride, and they would be at peace and be able to look for some kind of relationship with Jordan. Carter replied by stressing that the PLO should accept U.N. Resolution 242. Doing so, he explained, would have a positive effect on American public opinion. Using a theme that he was frequently to repeat to Arab leaders, Carter said he had to have public opinion with him, as well as support from Congress and the American Jewish community.

The following morning, May 25, Carter and Fahd met alone and talked primarily about economics and oil. Fahd said he could not commit

Saudi Arabia to a "Marshall Plan" for the Middle East in present circumstances. (Some Americans had hoped that Saudi money could be used to launch a massive economic development plan for the Middle East as an adjunct to U.S. diplomatic efforts to resolve the Arab-Israeli conflict.) On oil prices, he urged Carter to work on Iran and Venezuela to prevent prices from rising during 1978. On political issues, Fahd agreed to try to convince the PLO to accept 242 so that a U.S.-PLO dialogue could begin.[6]

During the Fahd visit, the administration floated an ambitious idea on energy security. The concept was that Saudi Arabia should supply one billion barrels of oil for the U.S. Strategic Petroleum Reserve, but the oil would not be paid for until it was consumed. The one-billion-barrel level would be maintained indefinitely by periodic replenishments, and Saudi Arabia would receive credits for purchases in the United States as the oil was actually used. Another ten billion barrels of oil would be dedicated for American use in Saudi Arabia, to be drawn on by the United States in the event of future embargoes. Not surprisingly, Fahd's reaction was negative, and Carter concluded that the whole idea was doubtful. Apparently the idea originated with James R. Schlesinger, who was soon to become Carter's secretary of energy, and who could at least not be blamed for thinking in modest terms. The unanswered question is what would have been in it for the Saudis had they accepted such a fantastic proposition.

Although Fahd's visit produced few concrete results, Carter still hoped the Arabs would be able to stick to a comparatively moderate posture. In any event, the visit had been pleasant on a personal level and left a feeling of goodwill. This feeling could not be savored for long, however, because the time for readjusting the initial strategy had come. June became the month for preparing a new position. The redoubtable Menachem Begin would arrive in Washington in mid-July, and Carter's

---

6. "The President's News Conference of May 26, 1977," *Public Papers: Carter, 1977,* vol. 1, p. 1019. Carter said that he still stood by the views he had spelled out in March, including the right of the Palestinians to a homeland. He incorrectly noted that U.N. Security Council Resolutions had recognized this right. The subsequent attempt to clarify his remarks by citing the U.N. General Assembly Resolution of 1947, which called for the partition of the Palestine mandate into a Jewish state and an Arab state, did little to reassure the president's critics. They were quick to point out that his remarks could be viewed as a call for Israel to return to the 1947 partition lines, not just the 1967 lines, which were already bad enough from their point of view. This was one more bit of evidence for the friends of Israel that Carter was pro-Palestinian.

skills as statesman and negotiator, perhaps even as theologian and psychologist, would all be put to the test.

PREPARING FOR BEGIN

To deal with the new Begin government, Carter first had to understand in depth where Begin stood on the issues. This involved a careful study of Begin's positions and some reading about his historical role. Carter also felt the need to strengthen his domestic base. Early in June he met with Mondale; Hamilton Jordan, the assistant to the president; Stuart Eizenstat, the assistant for domestic policy; and Brzezinski to discuss a campaign led by the American Israel Public Affairs Committee against Carter's policies.[7]

Initial Assessment

Carter's staff first summarized Begin's views in early June in a memorandum to the president outlining a fifteen-point program of the Likud bloc. Carter quickly reacted to the memo. Several points stood out: number three, highlighted by the president, called for an increase in "setting up of defensive and permanent settlements, rural and urban, on the soil of the homeland"; five and six stated that the government would participate in the Geneva conference, but that negotiations should be direct, without preconditions, and without any formula being imposed from outside.

Shortly after this exposure to Begin's views, Carter received a memorandum on a conversation between Brzezinski and Shmuel Katz, one of Begin's close associates who had come to Washington to explain the soon-to-be prime minister's ideas. Katz spoke of the right of the Jewish people to "Western Palestine as a whole," by which he meant all the territory west of the Jordan River. On the touchy question of settlements, he said that refraining from settlement would prejudge the outcome of negotiations, which Israel wanted to avoid. (Carter underlined this last point and added an exclamation point in the margin.) Another point noted by Carter was Katz's assertion that if an Arab entity of any kind was formed west of the Jordan River, it would be a threat to Israel. Katz went on to say he did not much care about Arab recognition of Israel. He understood the Arabs perfectly. Whatever they might say, they believed that Israel must be eliminated. Carter noted sternly on the memo: "I see no moderation here. J."

---

7. Brzezinski, *Power and Principle*, p. 97. Carter told the group that he felt he was carrying too much of the burden himself in defending his Middle East policies.

Vance Takes Charge

While Carter absorbed the harshness of Begin's vision, the Middle East team, increasingly under Secretary of State Vance's leadership, began to develop concrete ideas for moving the "peace process" forward. Meeting on June 10, the Policy Review Committee felt Begin should be invited to Washington as soon as possible. The United States should begin to emphasize the importance of reconvening the Geneva conference, with as much prior agreement as possible, even though Israel was likely to stand fast by the slogan of "Geneva without preconditions." The question of arms supplies to Israel came up, and the view was expressed that some requests should be granted immediately, some should be granted during the visit, and some should be related to subsequent progress in negotiations.

On the procedural side, the committee recommended that Vance should make a trip to the Middle East in August, and then arrange for informal meetings in the United States with foreign ministers before convening Geneva. For the moment the PLO question would be left aside, and the Soviets would not be brought into the talks.[8]

During this meeting Vance, developing ideas that had been on his mind, spoke of the possibility of a trusteeship for the West Bank and Gaza as well as a referendum. The ideas were deemed worthy of further study. Already the administration was beginning to seek ways of injecting the concept of a transitional phase into the negotiation over the West Bank and to get around the question of PLO participation by holding out the possibility of a referendum.

Mondale's Speech

Vice President Mondale was more concerned with a speech he was scheduled to make in San Francisco the following week. He felt that the Jewish community was becoming restive, and he wanted to be in a position to mention that new decisions on arms for Israel had been made. He was also worried about the adverse effect that arms sales to Egypt and Saudi Arabia might have.

The vice president's speech to the World Affairs Council of Northern

---

8. Vance had, however, agreed with Gromyko on May 21 that there would be monthly consultations on the Middle East at the ambassadorial level. Testimony by Assistant Secretary of State Alfred L. Atherton, Jr., before the Subcommittee on Europe and the Middle East of the House Committee on International Relations, June 8, 1977, "Department Discusses U.S. Efforts in Search for Middle East Peace," *Department of State Bulletin*, vol. 77 (July 4, 1977), p. 27.

California on June 17, 1977, turned out to be a good summary of official administration thinking on the Middle East on the eve of Begin's arrival in Washington. Repeating Carter's three elements of a comprehensive peace, Mondale mentioned "some arrangement for a Palestinian homeland or entity—preferably in association with Jordan." The details, Mondale said, should be worked out by the parties in negotiations. Geneva could provide the forum for face-to-face negotiations. Although he did not announce any new arms deals, he did make the following important statement, which thereafter was part of official policy: "We do not intend to use our military aid as pressure on Israel. If we have differences over military aid—and we may have some—it will be on military grounds or economic grounds but not political grounds. If we have differences over diplomatic strategy—and that could happen—we will work this out on a political level. We will not alter our commitment to Israel's military security."[9]

Over the ensuing months, which were often filled with strong U.S.-Israeli disagreements, the administration never suspended military aid. Although Mondale had not specifically excluded the use of economic aid, that also was never used as a form of heavy-handed pressure on Israel. Carter did not hesitate to argue with the Israelis in public, at least during his first year in office, but he was unwilling to touch economic or military assistance.

The Visit Approaches

One week after Mondale's speech, the Policy Review Committee met again to consider arms sales to Israel, Egypt, and Saudi Arabia. The recommendation was made to sell Israel a modest package of 200 TOW antitank missiles, 700 armored personnel carriers, and 15 combat engineering vehicles. (Carter immediately approved this recommendation.) Several items previously considered were turned down on technical grounds, and a second package of F-16 aircraft and AH-1 helicopters was to be held until the Begin visit. A number of nonlethal items were also recommended for Egypt, and the Saudi request for F-15 aircraft was put on hold for the moment.

9. "A Framework for Middle East Peace: Shaping a More Stable World," *Department of State Bulletin*, vol. 77 (July 11, 1977), p. 45. The American side interpreted the pledge on military aid to mean that existing programs and levels of assistance would not be cut. It was not meant as a blank check and was not inconsistent with the notion that future arms commitments might be related to progress in the peace talks.

The discussion then turned to the Begin visit, now set for July 19, just three weeks off. Vance favored quiet diplomacy, though he acknowledged the need for a public relations strategy and a press campaign. Brzezinski focused on the two issues that were to become central in the U.S.-Israeli debate over the coming months: first, the need to get from Begin an interpretation of U.N. Resolution 242 that would not be seen by the Arabs as precluding a priori the return of the West Bank; and second, some understanding on the question of settlements in occupied territories. In other words, the United States should try to get Begin to reaffirm Israel's commitment to the exchange of "territory for peace" on all fronts of the conflict, and to agree to suspend settlement activity because it would prejudge the outcome of negotiations. In posing the issues in this way, Brzezinski was taking direct aim at Begin's most cherished beliefs. A clash was bound to result, a prospect that Brzezinski accepted more readily than most of the president's other advisers.

Brzezinski was also concerned that Begin might look reasonable by saying he would go to Geneva without preconditions, while continuing to build settlements and to reject Israel's long-standing interpretation of 242, which had accepted the principle of territorial compromise with each of Israel's neighbors. Then, if Geneva failed, the blame would be placed on the Arabs, who were insisting on "preconditions." Begin's apparent reasonableness was in fact a mask for a hard position on substance. For the first, but not last, time, Brzezinski raised the possibility of getting the Arabs, especially Sadat, to help the United States put pressure on Begin by adopting a very forthcoming position on normalization of relations with Israel. American officials felt that a moderate Arab position was a prerequisite, especially in domestic political terms, for any effective move to put pressure on Begin.

As the meeting came to a close, Secretary Vance said that regardless of the outcome of the Begin visit, he planned to return to the Middle East to put forward American ideas to establish a framework for negotiations before Geneva. He noted, however, that if the United States pushed Begin too hard, he would become more intransigent and would even strengthen his standing in Israel. In that case, quipped Secretary of Defense Harold Brown, "We have him just where he wants us."

Staking Out Positions

The public campaign against Begin's interpretation of U.N. Resolution 242 picked up in late June, when the State Department spokesman released a full text of American views on the elements of a comprehensive peace settlement.[10] Not only did this release mark the opening shot in what came to be a prolonged struggle with Begin over the interpretation of 242, but it also reflected a conscious decision, urged especially by Brzezinski, to put the State Department, rather than Carter, in the forefront of the debate. The key elements of this statement were as follows:

The United States policy since 1967 has consistently sought to apply the principles agreed upon in that resolution [242] through the process of negotiations called for in Security Council Resolution 338 of October 1973, which all the parties have also accepted.

The peace foreseen in these resolutions requires both sides to the dispute to make difficult compromises. We are not asking for any one-sided concessions from anyone. The Arab states will have to agree to implement a kind of peace which produces confidence in its durability.

In our view, that means security arrangements on all fronts satisfactory to all parties to guarantee established borders. It also involves steps toward the normalization of relations with Israel.

The peace, to be durable, must also deal with the Palestinian issue. In this connection, the President has spoken of the need for a homeland for the Palestinians whose exact nature should be negotiated between the parties.

Clearly, whatever arrangements were made would have to take into account the security requirements of all parties involved.

Within the terms of Resolution 242, in return for this kind of peace, Israel clearly should withdraw from occupied territories. We consider that this resolution means *withdrawal from all three fronts in the Middle East dispute—that is, Sinai, Golan, West Bank and Gaza*—the exact borders and security arrangements being agreed in the negotiations.

Further, these negotiations must start without any preconditions from any side. This means, *no territories, including the West Bank, are automatically excluded from the items to be negotiated*. To automatically exclude any territories strikes us as contradictory to the principle of negotiations without preconditions.

Nor does it conform to the spirit of Resolution 242, which forms the framework for these negotiations.

Every administration since 1967 has consistently supported Resolution 242 and it has the widest international support as well.[11]

10. See "U.S. Statement on the Middle East," *New York Times*, June 28, 1977. In part this statement was a response to highly publicized criticism by Senator Jacob Javits of New York delivered in the Senate on June 27, the same day as the State Department release. Javits focused his criticism on Mondale's speech in San Francisco, arguing that the Carter administration was asking for more concessions from Israel than from the Arabs. An article discussing the advance text of the Javits speech is Wolfgang Saxon, "Mideast Peace Plan Attacked by Javits," *New York Times*, June 27, 1977.
11. "U.S. Statement on the Middle East" (emphasis added).

During the first two weeks of July, the State Department took the lead in developing a set of principles designed to govern a comprehensive settlement of the Arab-Israeli conflict and a set of procedural ideas to solve the problem of Palestinian representation at Geneva. On July 5 Secretary Vance chaired a meeting of the Policy Review Committee, and for the first time he took a strong and assertive role in guiding the discussions.[12] He came prepared with seven draft principles and four procedural alternatives. Ideas that had previously been discussed were now put on paper and refined. Vance thought these principles and procedural alternatives should be reviewed with Begin during his Washington visit, and then discussed with the key Arab leaders during the secretary's August trip to the Middle East. With luck, some degree of prior agreement on general principles could then be forged in talks at the foreign minister level in September. If the question of Palestinian representation could also be resolved, Geneva could be convened sometime in the fall. The U.S. role, as Vance saw it, was moving from the "prenegotiation" stage of testing the intentions of each party to the search for a formula for actual talks.

The most controversial of the principles had to do with Israeli withdrawal from occupied territories and the creation of a Palestinian entity. In the original formulation, point four read as follows: "It is understood that the withdrawal called for in Resolution 242 will be to mutually agreed and recognized borders which will approximate the 1967 lines, with minor modifications." Point five included the following sentence: "Means shall be sought to permit self-determination by the Palestinians in deciding on their future status, as through a transitional international trusteeship during which their desires can be formulated and expressed." During the July 5 discussion the committee members generally felt that Carter should stick to his position on the 1967 lines, despite heavy opposition from Israel and its supporters. Carter's own view, expressed in a note on the minutes of the meeting, was that point five should be revised to express a preference for "Palestinian-Jordanian affiliation."

Turning to procedural matters, Vance outlined four ways in which the Palestinians might be included in the negotiations. One—and the method clearly preferred by Vance—Palestinian representatives, including some PLO members, could be part of a unified Arab delegation. Two, if the PLO were to accept 242, it could go to Geneva as a separate

---

12. Brzezinski, *Power and Principle*, p. 99.

delegation. Three, Palestinians could be included in one of the other national Arab delegations. Four, prior agreement could be sought that Palestinians would join the conference later, when the Palestinian issue came up on the agenda.

Vance's preference for a single Arab delegation was largely dictated by his desire to get Syria to the conference. He readily acknowledged that working groups could be established with separate national delegations and that ultimately Israel would sign separate agreements with each state. But a single Arab delegation, at least to get the conference started, had the advantage of getting both Syria and some Palestinians into the game. Sadat would not be pleased, but he had told Carter he would accept such an arrangement if necessary. Israel's objection could also be anticipated, especially to the idea that the PLO in some form could be included in negotiations.

During this same meeting there was some discussion of selling F-16s to Israel and allowing the Israelis to use military assistance credits to build the Chariot tank in Israel. This was the primary topic of discussion one week later, on July 12, at another Policy Review Committee meeting. Vance argued that there was no urgent military necessity for agreeing to Israel's requests, but that there were political reasons for considering a favorable response. In something of a reversal of his previous position, he now maintained that security considerations should be decoupled from the peace talks. Brzezinski disagreed, saying that decisions on arms should be used as positive incentives for a settlement. If Begin was moderate and if he made concessions, Brzezinski thought, he should be rewarded, perhaps even with the offer of a full-fledged military alliance. Secretary Brown weighed in on Vance's side, emphasizing the importance of the attitude in Congress.

Discussion then turned to the Begin visit and the way to make use of the draft principles. Vance felt it was no longer enough to say that the United States stood by U.N. Resolutions 242 and 338. It was time to "bite the bullet" and begin to put forward ideas on substance. Vance would therefore review the principles with Begin, leaving the more general strategic overview to the president. Concern was expressed that Begin might think the United States was trying to impose a plan of its own. Vance replied that the United States could not be just a mediator. Brzezinski tended to agree, and Brown added the thought that the principles should be put forward as a judgment of what was attainable, not as a blueprint.

One of the participants in the meeting raised the question whether the

1967 lines should be mentioned in writing. The consensus seemed to be that some revisions in the principles could be made, and that Vance could orally amplify on them in his talks with Middle East leaders. Assistant Secretary Alfred L. Atherton, Jr., warned there would be an explosion in Israel if the United States talked to the Arabs about those principles.

Clearly, political considerations were on everyone's mind. Aware of the difficulty of devising principles acceptable to both Arabs and Israelis, the administration was beginning to adjust its sights. The consensus was that pre-Geneva talks at the foreign minister level should take place in September, but that there was little hope of making headway on substance. Some fuzziness would remain by the time Geneva was held. By contrast, an agreement on procedural matters might be possible. Without much debate, the drift away from substance and toward procedure was beginning. Unfortunately, procedures were also controversial, since they involved the sensitive question of how to involve the Palestinians in the negotiations.[13]

By the end of the meeting it was decided that Vance would discuss a revised set of five principles with Begin, but would make no mention of either the 1967 lines or a Palestinian-Jordanian link. He would, however, be prepared to tell Arab leaders that the United States still favored those positions.

That same day, July 12, President Carter held a news conference in which he stated that his previously expressed views on the 1967 borders and a Palestinian homeland had not changed, but that he did not favor an independent Palestinian entity, preferring that it be linked to Jordan. He then announced that he had been in recent contact with Sadat about some alleged Egyptian violations of the Sinai II agreement, which were going to be cleared up. He also announced that Egypt had agreed to return the bodies of nineteen Israeli soldiers killed in the 1973 war. In

13. My own view, spelled out in a memorandum written on July 11, 1977, was that the time had come for adjustments in our strategy. Geneva did not look promising. Changes in the Israeli position made the West Bank "negotiable," but not "returnable." At the same time the Arabs were waiting expectantly for the United States to pressure Israel, but did not agree among themselves. "Meanwhile, the PLO waits in the wings, working energetically to retain its relevance, doing nothing to revise its policies. Arafat repeatedly says in private that he has only one card to play—recognition of Israel—and that will not be done unless he is assured in advance that Israel will recognize the PLO and accept a Palestinian state. In short, a total impasse looms on this front, with little prospect for change in the near future." Meanwhile, Sadat seems to see Geneva as only for signing an agreement, not for real negotiations. As a result, "there is serious reason to question whether a Geneva conference should be reconvened this year."

concluding, he said the United States was not putting forward ideas with the attitude that the parties had to accept them as a precondition for going to Geneva. It was up to the Israelis and Arabs to work out their own agreement.[14] With these remarks Carter hoped to create a good atmosphere for his talks the following week with Begin.

Domestic Politics

On the eve of the Begin visit, it was clear that domestic political considerations were beginning to affect U.S. policy deliberations. Carter was spending time, in his own words, repairing his damaged political base among Israel's American friends.[15] He was gradually watering down the strong public statements of March, especially with respect to the "Palestinian homeland." Since substantive issues were proving so intractable, he also tended to concentrate on procedural concerns. Geneva, which had been a somewhat remote notion at first, was beginning to become more concrete, and with that came a need to grapple with the question of Palestinian representation in negotiations.

One could sense some frustration on Carter's part that the Middle East was taking so much of his time, with so little to show for it. Nonetheless, the United States was still holding firm to its role as catalyst in the negotiating process and was beginning to move from publicly espoused generalities to fairly specific formulations that were to be discussed in private. Public diplomacy had been costly for Carter, and though he continued to speak out on Middle East issues, he did so with greater caution and reluctance than before. In these circumstances Vance, the professional negotiator who abhorred public diplomacy, was well positioned to carry the talks forward.

CARTER MEETS BEGIN

All the preparations for Begin's visit should have put the president on guard. He knew that the Israeli prime minister had a reputation as a hard-liner, a partisan of the view that the Jewish state must encompass all the land from the Mediterranean Sea to the Jordan River and that within this area the right of Jews to settle the land could not be denied. Begin's attitude toward the United States and its role was also markedly different from that of his predecessors. Whereas other Israeli prime

14. "The President's News Conference of July 12, 1977," *Public Papers: Carter, 1977,* vol. 2, p. 1236.
15. Carter, *Keeping Faith*, p. 290.

ministers had firmly believed policy should be coordinated with Washington, Begin strongly resisted the idea of an active American diplomatic role, for fear that an "externally devised formula" might be imposed on Israel.[16] The U.S. role, in Begin's view, was to help bring the parties to the negotiating table. Then Israel would work out the terms of peace treaties with each of its adversaries, with the United States serving as little more than an observer. If Begin held to these views, it seemed to the Americans that a confrontation would be inevitable.

Despite his reputation for extremism, Begin was also known to be an exceedingly courteous, if formal, person. If dealt with in polite terms, he would reciprocate. He was also a stickler for words and had a penchant for legalistic argumentation. Nonetheless, behind this somewhat menacing exterior lurked a man of obvious intelligence and a kind of integrity. Begin honestly told his listeners what he believed and what he meant to do. It was not his fault if they did not always listen.

Carter and his associates took longer to realize that Begin was also a superb politician, carefully calculating his moves, with a masterly sense of timing and a remarkable capacity for brinkmanship. They took even longer to recognize that Begin's views on Judea and Samaria were rock hard, not subject to the normal bargaining expected of most politicians.

For reasons that are still not clear, Carter apparently concluded that the best way to deal with Begin was to avoid sharp controversy and be very polite on the personal level. Perhaps the adverse reaction to his meeting with Yitzhak Rabin in March had left its mark. Perhaps the political costs of constant bickering with the Israelis were beginning to make themselves felt. Or perhaps the president felt he could have more influence with Begin if he first succeeded in winning his trust and confidence. In any event, Carter's first meetings with Begin were remarkably cordial and conciliatory and left Carter with the impression that Begin might be more flexible on substantive issues than had been supposed.

First Encounter

The president opened his talks with Prime Minister Begin on July 19 by reiterating his commitment to a comprehensive peace settlement. But he quickly added that the United States had no plan and no preconditions. No outsider could impose peace. While repeating his views on peace,

16. Yitzhak Rabin, *The Rabin Memoirs*, p. 317.

territory, and a Palestinian homeland, Carter said these were all issues that would have to be resolved ultimately through direct negotiations. "We have no desire to be intermediaries."

Begin's first words were of praise for the U.S. ambassador to Israel, Samuel W. Lewis. Next he noted worrisome developments in southern Lebanon, but promised that Israel would never take the United States by surprise there. Then he raised a request from Ethiopia for help against the Muslim rebels in Eritrea. Finally, he said: "Now to our problems," and he launched into a lengthy review of the history of the Arab-Israeli conflict. When he spoke of the danger to Israel if it should ever return to the 1967 lines, tears almost came to his eyes. Men would not be able to defend women and children, he said.

In answer to a question from Carter, Begin affirmed that Israel was ready to negotiate on the basis of U.N. Resolutions 242 and 338. He then outlined his proposal for convening the Geneva conference with an opening session, followed by the establishment of "mixed commissions" that would negotiate peace treaties. When the peace treaties were ready for signature, the Geneva conference would be reconvened. If this plan did not work out, Israel was ready for negotiations through "mixed commissions" without Geneva, or for "proximity talks," relying on the good offices of the United States.

Carter then said that Begin's attitude toward setting up new settlements in Israeli-occupied territory could jeopardize any prospect for negotiations. He implied that Rabin had agreed the PLO could participate in negotiations as members of the Jordanian delegation. Begin denied this, saying that Palestinians could participate along with the Jordanians, and that Israel would not inspect their credentials, but they could not be PLO. At this point Begin asked his friend Shmuel Katz to talk about the history of the Palestinian Arabs, the thrust of which was that the Palestinians already had their homeland on the east bank of the Jordan. The meeting ended with a request from Carter that the Israelis stop overflying Saudi territory. Begin promised to look into the matter.[17]

Later that same day, July 19, Secretary of State Vance met with Begin and the Israeli delegation to review the five principles the American side had developed. First, however, Vance and Begin discussed the procedural ideas brought by the prime minister. Vance asked about a single Arab

17. Foreign Minister Dayan was not invited by Begin to accompany him to Washington, but he gives an account of the meeting in his book based on the cabled report. Dayan was pleased with Carter's emphasis on "full peace." Moshe Dayan, *Breakthrough*, pp. 18–25.

delegation at Geneva. Begin said it was illogical. Vance then suggested that one Arab delegation might be formed just for the purpose of convening Geneva, after which the negotiations would take place in bilateral groups. Begin replied that when the issue arose, Israel would try to find a way. He would consider Vance's suggestion. With this minor victory behind him, Vance turned to the five principles.

The first point was simply a call for a comprehensive peace settlement. Begin's only comment was that the goal should be defined as "peace treaties" between Israel and her neighbors. Point two reaffirmed U.N. Resolutions 242 and 338 as the bases of negotiations, to which Begin posed no objection. The third point called for normal relations and an end of belligerency as part of the peace settlement. Begin said, rather stiffly, that this was redundant once peace treaties were mentioned. The American side agreed to a revision calling for an end to the state of war and the establishment of relationships of peace. So far, Vance and Begin had managed to find common ground.

Points four and five were the difficult ones for the Israelis. Point four called for Israeli withdrawal to "mutually agreed and recognized borders on all fronts, phased over years in synchronized steps, and with security arrangements and guarantees." Begin reacted negatively to the idea of external guarantees, noting in a phrase he became particularly fond of: "In the whole world, there is no guarantee that can guarantee a guarantee." Begin did not react to the point calling for withdrawal "on all fronts," saying simply he would inform the president in their private talk about his views on borders.[18]

Vance then read out the fifth point: "A settlement must include provisions for a Palestinian entity and for means of assuring Palestinian adherence to the terms of the peace agreement. The Palestinian entity will not be militarized, and there will be provisions for an open economic and social relationship with Israel. Means should be sought to permit self-determination by the Palestinians in deciding on their future status."

Begin, in another of his often used phrases, said he would have to agree to differ. He would present the idea to the cabinet, but he would oppose it. Accepting it would lead to a Palestinian state, a "mortal danger"

18. Secretary Vance was left with the impression that Begin had accepted this point, and says in his book that "this turned out to be only the first of many misunderstandings with Begin on exactly what had been agreed in our discussions." Cyrus Vance, *Hard Choices*, p. 183.

for Israel. Such a state would become a Soviet base, with planes arriving from Odessa and Soviet generals in the West Bank. Jerusalem would be under crossfire from three directions. Vance tried to temper this adverse reaction by putting forward his idea of a trusteeship for the Palestinian state. Israel could even be one of the trustees, along with Jordan. At the end of the trusteeship, there should be a plebiscite and self-determination. The United States would favor a link between the Palestinian entity and Jordan. Begin was unimpressed, and indeed Vance had not made a compelling case for his ideas. He seemed to be grasping at straws rather than exploring useful principles to guide the negotiations.

Returning to procedural matters, however, the two men found common ground. Vance would meet with the foreign ministers of Israel, Egypt, Jordan, and Syria in New York before the convening of the Geneva conference. Begin termed this a sound idea.

Carter and Begin Alone

Begin had doubtless heard that part of the normal visit with President Carter included a private meeting after the formal dinner. Rabin's meeting in March had been chilly, and Begin must have hoped for a more positive encounter as he went upstairs alone with Carter on the evening of July 19. During the meeting Begin told the president that he was making tentative plans to meet directly with Sadat.[19] And he also presented to Carter a lengthy document detailing all the strategic benefits that the United States gained from its ties to Israel. Always a proud man, Begin was making the point that aid to Israel was not charity, but a sound investment for which good value was given in return. (Much of the document consisted of items of captured Soviet military equipment that Israel had turned over to the United States.) The discussion also turned to the prospects for peace; here Carter sought to be conciliatory. He urged Begin to stop settlements at least until the Geneva conference began. The president noted the following on a memorandum that Brzezinski had prepared for him before the meeting:

On point 4, [Begin] thinks UN 242/338 adherence is adequate prior to Geneva— asks that we not use phrase "minor adjustments" without prior notice to him—I agreed.—He will try to accommodate us on settlements. Wants to carry out Mapai Plan at least. Will give us prior notice. I suggested that they wait until

19. Carter, *Keeping Faith*, p. 291.

after Geneva talks and restrict new settlers to existing settlements. This is difficult for him.—Will stay on Golan. I told him Syria won't agree—W Bank, Gaza—Jerusalem. "No foreign sovereignty." Sinai—"Substantial withdrawals."[20]

The Second Day

The president had argued with Begin that security was not based on control of territory alone, but he noted to his advisers that Begin could not yet see this. After this meeting with Begin, the president had no reason to doubt the Israeli leader's determination to keep control over the West Bank, Gaza, and Jerusalem. Nonetheless, Carter concluded that Begin had accepted the first four of the five U.S. principles, including point four, which referred to withdrawal on all fronts. Perhaps the president interpreted what Begin had told him in their private meeting as an opening position, something like the campaign promises that American candidates are often obliged to make and then seek to water down once in office. In any event, the meeting between the two delegations the next day in the cabinet room was cordial. Carter outlined areas of agreement and disagreement, and seemed to imply that Begin would accept a single Arab delegation at Geneva for the plenary session.

Turning to substance, the president noted that there were major differences between Israel and the Arabs. The United States would offer its good offices to bridge the gap. In a revealing comment that reflected his approach to these negotiations, he said, "As you get to know each other, maybe we'll get some reconciliation." This optimistic view stayed with Carter through the next year and finally helped convince him that Sadat and Begin should be brought together at Camp David.

Carter went on to develop his idea that the United States could only be effective in the negotiations if it had the trust of all parties. As the meeting came to an end, Begin made a brief appeal for military assistance, but in a welcome change from the past this was not an issue that took much time. Begin seemed to want to keep the diplomatic talks separate from questions of aid for fear the two might be linked. Differences over matters of substance clearly remained, but both leaders were prepared for a "political truce."[21]

---

20. Handwritten note on page 2 of a memorandum from Brzezinski to Carter, dated July 19, 1977. Dayan, *Breakthrough*, pp. 19–20, gives more detail on Begin's views on borders as presented to Carter in their private meeting on July 19, 1977.

21. Carter, *Keeping Faith*, p. 290. Carter noted in his diary that after the first day of talks he felt that Begin would prove to be a "strong leader, quite different from Rabin."

Assessing the Visit

Begin left Washington in good spirits. In his public comments about Carter he was extremely positive, mentioning him on one occasion in the same context as his mentor and idol, Ze'ev Jabotinsky.[22] But the era of good feeling was to be short-lived. The day after Begin returned home, the Israeli cabinet conferred legal status on three settlements established under the previous government. The State Department was quick to express its disappointment, but under persistent questioning Carter acknowledged that Begin had not violated the letter of any promises made. Carter had talked about the importance of not building new settlements, and the possibility of sending new settlers to already established settlements, but he had said nothing about legalizing settlements already in existence. Not for the last time, Begin was to slip through a crack left by imprecise language on the American side. In public Carter chose not to react, but in private he was extremely annoyed, especially since he had just approved a significant arms sale to Israel in which, for the first time, Israel was allowed to use American credits to build its own tanks.[23] While showing some understanding of Begin's actions, he nonetheless reiterated that the United States believed such settlements were illegal and that in no circumstances should they be considered permanent.[24]

Begin's visit left the American side with no doubt that the gap between Israel and the most moderate of the Arabs remained large. Nonetheless, there were some positive elements in the equation. Begin did seem ready for negotiations with the Arabs at Geneva, and he did not object strongly to the face-saving concept of a unified Arab delegation for purposes of convening the conference. While negative on the PLO, he had repeated the statement that Palestinians could be present in the negotiations and

22. "Press Conference with Prime Minister Begin upon His Return from the U.S., July 25, 1977," in Meron Medzini, ed., *Israel's Foreign Relations*, vol. 4, p. 51. Through other sources, however, American officials heard that Begin's privately expressed view was that Carter was soft. According to one source, Begin had described the president as a "cream puff."

23. On July 22, 1977, Carter approved the use of $107 million in foreign military sales credits for the Chariot tank. This was part of a package that included eighteen AH-1S helicopters and two hydrofoils and some miscellaneous ammunition. Carter had personally added the Chariot tank financing to the package.

24. "The President's News Conference of July 28, 1977," *Public Papers: Carter, 1977*, vol. 2, pp. 1366–70; and "Interview with the President: Question-and-Answer Session with a Group of Editors and News Directors, July 29, 1977," ibid., pp. 1393–94.

that Israel would not inspect their credentials. With respect to Egyptian territory he had promised substantial withdrawals. On Lebanon he had promised prior consultation with Washington before taking any actions. And he had seemed ready to lower the rhetorical level before Geneva.

On the negative side, Begin's views on the West Bank and Gaza were much more adamant than his predecessors'. Instead of placing primary emphasis on Israeli security needs when discussing territory, Begin infused his presentations with a heavy dose of history and ideology, a sharp contrast to the comparatively pragmatic presentations of the Labor party leaders when discussing the same issues. On the question of settlements in occupied territories, Begin soon made clear that he would pay little heed to Carter's pleas for restraint.

Finally, one could detect in Begin's remarks a fundamental reinterpretation of U.N. Resolution 242, which had previously been understood as implying some degree of Israeli withdrawal on each front of the conflict in return for Arab commitments to peace, recognition, and security. Later his views became even more clear, but Begin's reluctance to accept the phrase "on all fronts" should have been ample evidence that he had no intention of withdrawing Israeli forces under any circumstances from the West Bank. He had told Carter in private that he would accept "no foreign sovereignty" over Judea and Samaria. But he had also said that he did accept 242, and Foreign Minister Moshe Dayan had artfully suggested that the Arabs could always raise the issue of withdrawal even if Israel had a different approach to solving the problem of the West Bank.

Begin's stubbornness on this point became increasingly apparent to the Americans, but in July 1977 his remarks were glossed over, dismissed as rhetoric and the residue of campaign sloganeering. The Americans were not used to dealing with men of deep ideological convictions. They took some time to realize that Begin meant exactly what he said on the Palestinian question.

VANCE TO THE MIDDLE EAST, AUGUST 1977

As Secretary of State Vance was preparing to leave for the Middle East in late July, any ambiguity about Begin's attitude toward withdrawal from the West Bank should have been removed. Israeli Ambassador Simcha Dinitz came to see Vance with a message from Begin on July 27. The prime minister wanted to make clear that in saying that U.N. Resolution 242 applied to each front, he had not meant that withdrawal was required on each front. Vance was furious, viewing Begin as backsliding from an agreement that had been reached.[25] Begin also objected to any reference to the PLO in the formulations being considered by the American side on Palestinian representation. Vance explained to the ambassador that he thought it might be possible to find a formula that would allow PLO members who were not "well known" to be at Geneva.

On July 30 Begin wrote directly to Carter, pleading that Vance not be allowed to talk to Arab leaders about the 1967 lines with minor modifications. What would there be left to negotiate about, he asked? Turning to the fourth and fifth of the American draft principles, Begin archly noted that it was his duty to say that, whatever the odds, the Israeli delegation would unflinchingly stand by the principles he had outlined in the course of his "unforgettable nocturnal conversation" with the president in the White House.

The president replied that Vance would discuss all five points with the Arabs, and, if asked, would repeat in private the well-known American views on principles governing a settlement. Begin, after all, had not earned much credit with Carter by his handling of the settlements issue after his visit to Washington. The president was not inclined to reward Begin by yielding to his request, and by so doing giving the Arabs the impression that under Israeli pressure the United States was beginning to back away from its publicly espoused positions. Carter had agreed not to talk in public, but he was not ready to muzzle Vance in private on the eve of an important diplomatic effort.

On the same day that Dinitz came to see Vance to discuss his trip, July 26, a message reached the White House from the PLO. The message indicated that the PLO was prepared to live in peace with Israel and there would be "no possibility of two meanings." Yasir Arafat would make this clear in a public statement, as well as in a private commitment to Carter. In return, however, the PLO wanted the United States to make a commitment to an independent Palestinian "state unit entity," which could be linked to Jordan. Carter's reaction was to note on the message: "If PLO publicly and privately meets minimum requirement of Kissinger-Israeli commitment, we will begin discussions with them. Get message to them. J."

Vance's Instructions

On the eve of Vance's departure, Carter still felt that Begin's views were predicated on PLO intransigence and that PLO acceptance of 242 would

25. Vance, *Hard Choices*, p. 186.

open the way for a U.S.-PLO dialogue that would "break the ice."[26] Thus began a new phase, lasting almost two months, of trying to devise some formula that the PLO would accept so that direct talks could begin.

At this time American thinking on the Palestinian issue was still somewhat tentative, but on several points consensus was taking shape. All the foreign policy advisers seemed to agree that some form of Palestinian participation in the negotiations would be essential. After all, each of the Arab parties was emphasizing this, even if with varying degrees of enthusiasm. The American side also widely believed that the viewpoint expressed by former Israeli Foreign Minister Yigal Allon, to the effect that Israel would be interested in any move by the PLO toward acceptance of 242 and Israel's right to exist, should be taken seriously. The depth of Begin's hostility to the PLO had not yet been fully absorbed in Washington. Finally, the American side thought PLO acceptance of 242 would have a considerable effect on the Arab world, eliminating any remaining basis for Arab objections to dealing with Israel. If the PLO was prepared to talk with Israel, why should any of the other Arab parties be more adamant? Sadat could then get on with negotiations with Israel, without feeling constrained by the opinion of the Syrians in particular.

What the American side misunderstood was not only the intensity of Begin's feelings, but also the struggle among Egypt, Syria, and Saudi Arabia over who would broker the U.S.-PLO relationship. There were also serious divisions within the PLO, and the private messages of moderation from PLO Chairman Yasir Arafat did not ensure that he could deliver his own Fatah organization, to say nothing of the PLO as a whole. Nonetheless, Vance left for the Middle East with the goal of trying to find a formula for U.S.-PLO talks.

Just before Vance's departure, the president wrote out in hand the guidelines for the trip. The full text of these instructions was the following:

You have a difficult trip and we wish you well. I hope that the parties will: (a) accept our five principles. If not, we need enough public support so that, with the USSR, we can marshall world opinion against the recalcitrant nations; (b) agree to pre-Geneva discussion, perhaps in September in N.Y.; (c) adopt general delegate configuration and similar arrangements for Geneva; and (d) arrange for the PLO to attend, together with Arab nations, on the basis of U.N. Resolutions 242 and 338 (with "refugee" exception only), with the understanding that the Palestinian question will be on the agenda.

26. Note by President Carter on a draft reply to a message from the PLO, dated July 26, 1977.

We should keep the Soviets informed, be completely frank with all parties, and be prepared to move strongly (and probably publicly) after you return.

If the PLO will meet our requirement of recognizing Israel's right to exist, you may wish to arrange for early discussions with them—either in private or publicly acknowledged. Best wishes, *Jimmy*[27]

This note to Vance indicates that a subtle shift was beginning to take place in the president's thinking. Only a few months earlier Carter had been insistent that Geneva would make sense only if there was careful preparation. Now he was thinking of Geneva in more concrete terms, as a forum in which negotiations would take place. The reason was simple: Begin would not budge on substance in the pre-Geneva period, thus undercutting the idea of a "well-prepared" conference. So Carter was gambling that Begin would prove more flexible once talks were actually under way. Carter's new position on Geneva was not identical to Sadat's concept and became the source of growing doubts about American strategy in the Egyptian president's mind.

For Geneva to take place with full Arab participation, it was important to find a solution to the question of Palestinian representation—note the emphasis on the role of the PLO in Carter's instructions to Vance—and it would eventually be important to coordinate with the cochairman of the Geneva conference, the Soviet Union. Moving in those directions set Carter at odds with Israel, and was thus fraught with political consequences on the domestic front. Nonetheless, Carter seemed to be prepared to head down this path, convinced that Middle East peace was a worthy goal and that time was running out on making further headway through quiet diplomacy.

Vance in Egypt

Vance's first stop was in Alexandria. He found Sadat impatient, rather uninterested in hearing about Begin's ideas, and full of thoughts of his own that he wanted to try out. Nevertheless, Vance methodically reviewed the U.S. draft principles and the procedural arrangements for Palestinian participation in the negotiations. Sadat gravely asked Vance what the American position was on final borders and was relieved to hear that it had not changed. The borders would have to be agreed upon in talks among the parties, but the United States thought they should approximate the 1967 lines with only minor modifications. Sadat said: "Marvelous.

27. Letter from President Carter to Secretary of State Vance, dated July 30, 1977.

Very good." He was less charitable toward Begin's views on territory, accusing the prime minister of favoring expansionism and not genuinely wanting peace. Vance presented Begin's procedural suggestions, but Foreign Minister Ismail Fahmy dismissed them as unacceptable.

Turning to the question of Palestinian representation, Sadat said the PLO should not be included in the Jordanian delegation. Instead, he proposed that the Palestinians be represented by the military assistant to the secretary general of the Arab League, who just happened to be Egyptian. Sadat said he thought he could convince the Palestinians, but, answering Vance's question about Syria's attitude, he said Asad would be furious. Fahmy added that this would mean a delegation from the Arab League representing the Palestinians, within which there would be Palestinians but no prominent PLO members.

Sadat then stated that he could not accept a single Arab delegation at Geneva. If there is one delegation, "we shall explode." Each party would have a veto over the others. Sadat did not want anyone else dictating Egypt's position. Returning to the question of minor border rectifications, Sadat said these could apply only to the West Bank. On Golan and in Sinai, where there had been internationally recognized borders, there could be no minor rectifications at all. Jabbing again at the Syrians, Sadat asserted that once he signed with Israel, Asad would follow suit. As for the Soviets, Sadat said, they should have nothing to do with the actual negotiations. They should be allowed only to save face, but the United States should get the credit.

Sadat went on to say that Egypt and Israel were incapable of reaching anything together. Too much distrust existed on both sides. Sadat then suggested that "working groups" under Secretary Vance be formed to prepare everything before Geneva, an idea he had vaguely floated in public a few weeks earlier. This preparation should be done discreetly, not openly. The model should be the first disengagement agreement that Kissinger negotiated. Turning again to the Soviets, Sadat said they wanted to strangle him. Syria, and maybe Jordan, were also against Egypt. There was no problem with the Palestinians, but King Hussein still wanted the West Bank. In the end, the result would be something like the king's idea of a United Arab Kingdom, linking Jordan and the West Bank, but that should not be mentioned now.

Sadat then said he would agree that PLO leaders need not take part in the negotiations. But the United States must be very active. If asked to choose between a Geneva conference with a unified Arab delegation or three separate national delegations holding bilateral talks with Israel, Sadat would prefer the second alternative. He added that this was not yet his decision, but that he needed to be convinced Geneva could be made to work.

Sadat's views on normal relations with Israel also seemed to be somewhat harsher than they had been during his talks with Carter in April. Only after complete Israeli withdrawal would he agree to talk about normal relations. Otherwise Israel would be using the occupation of Egyptian land to pressure Sadat. He would not end the state of belligerency until the last Israeli soldier had left Egypt. Somewhat surprisingly, Fahmy proved to be more forthcoming, saying the Israelis could be given assurances that normalization would take place after full withdrawal.

Vance tried to move the discussion into more productive channels by mentioning his idea of a trusteeship for the West Bank and Gaza. Israel and Jordan might be joint trustees, he said. Sadat refused to consider the idea; Israel must be excluded. The Arab states might serve as trustees, but, Sadat noted, the West Bank was not part of Jordan any more than Gaza was part of Egypt. Reverting to his constant concern, he urged Vance to get on with the job of developing general principles of agreement. Then the details could be worked out by the parties.

None of this seemed encouraging, but Sadat had another surprise in store for Vance—a statement from the PLO leaders of what they would be willing to say with regard to Resolution 242. Since it did not include a clear acceptance of 242, Vance was not particularly impressed.

Over lunch Vance, Fahmy, and U.S. Ambassador Hermann F. Eilts discussed further the question of how the PLO could state its acceptance of the U.N. resolution. They finally agreed on the language:

The PLO accepts United Nations Security Council Resolution 242, with the reservation that it considers that the resolution does not make adequate reference to the question of the Palestinians since it fails to make any reference to a homeland for the Palestinian people. It is recognized that the language of Resolution 242 relates to the right of all states in the Middle East to live in peace.[28]

To Eilts's surprise, Vance was willing to drop the words "including Israel" from the end of the last sentence.[29]

Before Vance's departure, Sadat made one more unexpected move.

28. Vance, *Hard Choices*, p. 188. In his book Vance does not say that this formulation was worked out in Alexandria, but does note that he passed it to the Saudis.

29. Communication from Ambassador Hermann F. Eilts, June 10, 1985.

Taking Vance aside, he pulled from his pocket the text of a draft peace treaty he said Egypt would be prepared to sign. He urged Vance not to tell anyone other than the president about this document. His idea was that Vance should get comparable drafts from the Israelis, Jordanians, and Syrians, and should then come up with a U.S. compromise version. As an added incentive, Sadat had written into the margin in his own handwriting the fallback positions he would agree to. Most of these were not very important, but Sadat was putting his cards almost face up on the table, ingratiating himself with the American side by giving them in advance some room for bargaining.

The idea for a draft peace treaty may have been stimulated by Vance. Earlier he had told the parties to the conflict that he was anxious to move from agreed principles to draft texts of treaties over the next several months. But he was totally surprised by Sadat's decision to hand him such a document during their meeting in Alexandria.[30] Because of this Egyptian initiative, Vance pressed all the other leaders he met on his trip to give him similar draft peace treaties.

At a news conference after these talks, Sadat implied that he and Vance had agreed to form working groups before Geneva. Vance was still not sure what Sadat had in mind, and when asked at subsequent stops what had been agreed to, he responded by mentioning the meetings he hoped to have with foreign ministers in New York in September. It was clear, however, that the Syrians in particular were suspicious of Sadat's moves and that Asad and Sadat were making no efforts to coordinate their positions before Geneva.

Sadat's own comments in private with Vance should have dispelled the idea that it would be easy to forge a common Arab position on anything, but for the moment Vance persisted in trying to pin down the notion of convening Geneva with a single Arab delegation, as the easiest way to get the Palestinians into the talks. Once the negotiations were under way, each national delegation could operate on its own. What Vance was not yet prepared to endorse was the Kissinger approach of proceeding on only one front at a time. But that was precisely what Sadat was telling the Americans he favored.

30. Interview with Cyrus Vance, New York, March 1, 1984. Ismail Fahmy claims that Vance raised the idea of draft peace treaties during this first visit and that the Egyptians agreed to give him such a document upon his return some ten days later. Ismail Fahmy, *Negotiating for Peace in the Middle East*, pp. 216–19. Fahmy accurately summarizes the content of the Egyptian draft on pp. 217–19.

On to Damascus, Amman, and Taif

Vance's talks in Syria and Jordan did not open any new avenues. Asad was flatly opposed to Sadat's idea of working groups before Geneva. But in Saudi Arabia things began to pick up. PLO leader Arafat had just been in the kingdom and had left with the Saudis a new formulation on 242. Carter tried to help move the process from Plains, Georgia, by saying publicly on August 8 that if the Palestinians would recognize 242, the United States would start discussions with them and the way would be open for Palestinians to participate in the Geneva conference. He also confirmed that the PLO was free to add a reservation to their acceptance of 242 to the effect that it was inadequate because it dealt with the Palestinians only as refugees.[31]

Secretary Vance also tried to clarify the U.S. position at a news conference as he left Taif for Tel Aviv. Asked about his former statement in February that the PLO should accept 242 and also amend its charter calling for Israel's destruction, he said that acceptance of 242 would be adequate. These modifications in the U.S. position, however, were not enough to secure PLO acceptance of 242, and the Saudis, who thought they had such assurances from Arafat, were perturbed.[32] Vance therefore left empty-handed, having received nothing from the PLO for his efforts, but having assured himself a very hostile reception in Israel.

A Blast from Begin

Begin's meeting with Vance on August 9 in Jerusalem did much to dispel the lingering good feelings from July. In public and in private Begin was extremely critical of the United States for offering to deal with the PLO on any terms whatsoever. He implied that Vance's offer to talk with the PLO if it accepted 242 was comparable to Neville Chamberlain's appeasement of Hitler. After reading to Vance from the PLO charter, Begin commented that it was a sad day for free men when the United States agreed to talk to an organization that held such views. He stated that

31. "Plains, Georgia: Exchanges with Reporters at Carter's Warehouse, August 8, 1977," *Public Papers: Carter, 1977*, vol. 2, pp. 1459–60.

32. The PLO apparently got mixed signals from the Egyptians and Saudis, the effect of which was to make it seem as if the U.S. position on what the PLO would get in return for accepting 242 was hardening. Also, the PLO began to hear distorted and alarming versions of Vance's trusteeship idea. In this atmosphere the PLO Executive Committee voted heavily against adopting the U.S.-proposed language on 242. Syrian pressure was probably also one of the reasons for the PLO action.

Israel would not go to Geneva if the PLO was there. If Palestinian Arabs were in the Jordanian delegation, Israel "would not search their pockets," but if they were from the PLO, Israel would say no. "We will not, we cannot, give our acceptance. We can't and we shan't," said Begin, intoning the phrase for maximum dramatic effect. Hardening his former position, he ruled out entirely Israel's acceptance of a single Arab delegation at Geneva.

On substantive issues Begin was somewhat encouraged by the idea of preparing draft peace treaties, quoting Hersch Lauterpacht, an authority on international law, to the effect that peace treaties automatically entailed full diplomatic relations. The next day Begin raised for the first time his idea of offering "our Arab neighbors in Judea, Samaria, and Gaza full cultural autonomy" and choice of Israeli citizenship with full voting rights.[33] Begin reiterated his request that the Carter administration not repeat in public or private its views on the 1967 lines. What would there be left to negotiate? Only "one-half of minor modifications" could be discussed with the Arabs.

Return to Egypt

After leaving Israel, Vance made a brief stop to see Sadat again near Alexandria. He reviewed the results of the trip and discussed the meetings of the foreign ministers in New York in September. All the parties had been asked to provide draft peace treaties. Vance repeated his belief that it would be easiest to get Palestinians to Geneva as part of a single Arab delegation.

Sadat wanted to get Vance's judgment on whether Begin was seriously interested in peace or was just maneuvering. Vance, despite his recent frustrations with Begin, said he thought Begin was sincere in wanting peace. Fahmy intervened to urge the United States to put forward a proposal of its own. Sadat added that there was no rush with respect to Geneva. It could be later in the year, or "whenever we are really ready." He dismissed Asad's reticence, saying that once Egypt had signed, then Asad would come along. One Egyptian official suggested that "we should give him trouble in Lebanon." He added that Israel might also be planning to strike at the PLO in Lebanon to ensure that the moderate tendency in the PLO would be put on the defensive.

---

33. Dayan, *Breakthrough*, p. 25, gives a brief summary of this meeting, but does not mention the idea of autonomy.

Before the talks concluded, Sadat returned to the topic of why the Israelis were taking such a hard line. Was it tactical or strategic? Vance again offered the judgment that much of the Israeli leader's toughness was tactical, though his opposition to the PLO seemed fundamental. Despite the American attempt to be optimistic, Sadat was reportedly disappointed by Vance's report of Begin's views.

The Balance Sheet

The results of Vance's trip to the Middle East in August were mixed. On the positive side, some headway had been made in getting all the parties to begin to develop their substantive ideas. All had agreed to convey their views to Washington in one form or another, and Egypt and Israel had specifically committed themselves to draft peace treaties. Vance even had the Egyptian copy in hand, with Sadat's fallback position already spelled out in the margins. The idea was taking root that the United States would begin to develop "negotiating drafts" based on the views of the parties themselves and on some of the concepts that Carter and Vance had been discussing for several months. These could then be raised with the foreign ministers in September.

Also on the hopeful side were the attitudes toward peace expressed by Sadat and Israeli Foreign Minister Moshe Dayan. Vance came away from his talks particularly impressed by Dayan, which helped to offset his chilly feelings toward Begin. Sadat was harder to read, but he seemed to be trying to figure out the position of his Israeli adversaries, which was more than the other Arab leaders did. Their preferred stance was to wait for the United States to deliver Israeli concessions. By contrast, Sadat was involved in the game, capable of taking initiatives, such as the draft peace treaty, and eager to win the confidence of the Americans by making some concessions in advance, thus establishing an aura of collusion between Washington and Cairo.

On the negative side, Vance's trip had not advanced the procedural arrangements for negotiations or the PLO acceptance of U.N. Resolution 242. If anything, both Egypt and Israel were more adamantly opposed to the idea of a single Arab delegation at Geneva than they had been in earlier talks. And Syria and Jordan were just as unwilling to go on any other basis. The effort to get the PLO on record in support of 242 had apparently almost worked, but in the end Arafat had not been able to deliver. The result had been to heighten Israeli suspicions of U.S. moves, while at the same time causing considerable confusion within the PLO as different Arab emissaries conveyed conflicting versions of the American position to Arafat. In this context, Begin's refusal to consider a strengthening of the U.N. Truce Supervision Organization in southern Lebanon, as proposed by Vance, was cause for alarm, since it raised the suspicion in American minds that Begin might be planning to strike against the PLO in Lebanon.

Vance's idea of a trusteeship for the West Bank and Gaza, to be followed by a plebiscite and self-determination for the Palestinians, had not been well received by either the Arabs or the Israelis.[34] The Arabs had disliked the patronizing overtones of a trusteeship, which implied that the Palestinians were not yet ready for statehood. (Syrian Foreign Minister Abd al-Halim Khaddam had quipped that the Palestinians were capable of running all twenty Arab states.) The idea that Israel and Jordan might be the trustees had evoked strongly negative responses, especially from the PLO when it heard that the United States was planning to put the PLO's two greatest adversaries in charge of the West Bank and Gaza for an indefinite period. For Begin, of course, the idea of ceding control over Judea and Samaria was anathema. His own view was that the Arabs of Eretz Israel, as he called them, should be offered "cultural autonomy," essentially placing them in the same category as the Arabs who had remained within Israel's borders from 1949 to 1967, though Israeli citizenship would not be automatically accorded them.

CONCLUSION

In summary, the period since Begin's election had seen some progress but also a noticeable shift in the terms of reference. Already the West Bank and Gaza were being discussed in a different context from that of the other occupied territories. The Carter administration recognized the importance of the change, but was unsure how to interpret it or what to do about it. The previous emphasis on a well-prepared Geneva conference was giving way, in the face of Israeli firmness and Begin's slogan of "negotiations without preconditions," to a belief that little more could be achieved until actual negotiations had begun. And Carter was showing

---

34. Vance, *Hard Choices*, pp. 189–90. Vance notes that the trusteeship idea, while ultimately rejected, may have helped stimulate the idea of a transitional period for dealing with the West Bank and Gaza, a point that was ultimately incorporated into the Camp David Accords and thereafter became part of the conventional wisdom on how to deal with this disputed area.

by his public comments that he was tiring of the role of public advocate of controversial ideas. The diplomatic moves were increasingly being carried out by the State Department, in particular by Secretary Vance. Quiet diplomacy had replaced public pronouncements. Several tracks were being pursued simultaneously by the Carter administration, with the result that on occasion the separate tracks got entangled with one another.

Still, even if the picture in mid-August was mixed, and there was little cause for great optimism, movement was occurring and all the parties were focusing on Washington. American leadership of the peace process was accepted, though with reservations. But time was also working against the original concept of a comprehensive negotiated settlement, especially as divisions emerged among the Arabs and the Israeli attitude hardened. Time was now of the essence if further progress was to be made.

The Vance trip had pretty much convinced the Carter administration that little more progress could be achieved in the absence of actual negotiations in which all the parties took part. Otherwise the Arabs would wait indefinitely for an American plan, while Israel would rally its supporters to resist an American-imposed peace. For the United States to continue to play a substantive role, it was judged, Geneva must first be convened. Only then could Washington begin to push its views on the content of a settlement without being accused of prejudging the outcome of talks by prematurely introducing an American blueprint. If the United States was to be a mediator, first the parties themselves would have to become more engaged in the process.

This judgment meant that the next phase of discussions would have to concentrate on how to get negotiations started, with Geneva increasingly seen as the vehicle for doing this. At least all the parties continued to pay lip service to the idea of a Geneva conference. Procedures would henceforth get more attention than substance, which meant finding a basis for involving the Palestinians in the process and for bringing in the Soviets because of their role as cochairman. On both counts the administration underestimated the domestic political costs of pursuing such a strategy. But it would not be long before Carter felt the consequences.

CHAPTER FIVE

The Unraveling of the Grand Design

One concrete result of Secretary of State Vance's trip to the Middle East in August 1977 was to accelerate the prenegotiation maneuvering by all parties to the conflict. Everyone knew the moment of truth was approaching. All the preliminary rounds of contacts had been made. Generalities had been discussed. Procedural issues were being slowly resolved. Pressure was building to make decisions on matters of substance and to begin the process of negotiating. To say the least, discomfort reigned in all the major Middle East capitals.

The Israelis were clearly unhappy with the drift of American thinking on the substance of a peace settlement. While welcoming the emphasis on normal relations of peace, Prime Minister Begin and Foreign Minister Dayan were uneasy about the American commitment to the 1967 lines as the eventual "secure and recognized borders" of Israel. Moreover, Washington kept pressing the Palestinian issue and seemed to be eager to bring the PLO into the picture. Geneva was beginning to look more and more like a trap rather than a forum for the long-sought opportunity to negotiate directly with the Arabs. Begin had told Carter during his first meeting that he was seeking ways of establishing contact with various Arab leaders; after Vance's trip he began to pursue the idea with fresh enthusiasm.

President Sadat was also uncomfortable with the American strategy. His preference all along had been for an American plan that would be worked out through secret discussions. He had no appetite for real give-and-take negotiations with Israel. He wistfully recalled Henry Kissinger's shuttle diplomacy as a model worthy of emulation. But this time the goal should be a comprehensive peace settlement, not another interim agreement.

At this stage Sadat was not prepared to make a separate peace with Israel. He continued to insist that a broader framework be established first. Only then could he move forward to a bilateral agreement. Sadat was eager to take credit for opening the way to a solution of the Palestinian problem and was in touch with the PLO to figure out some means of bringing Palestinians into the picture. Americans who talked to Sadat were not certain exactly what the Egyptian leader would insist on for the Palestinians. Some thought he would settle for principles alone, leaving it up to the Palestinians to decide whether they were prepared to begin talks with the Israelis. Others felt Sadat would need tangible movement in the direction of a Palestinian settlement before he would make full peace with Israel. All recognized that the stronger the principles, the more willing Sadat would be to say that he had done his duty to the Palestinians and would proceed on his own.

In contrast to his attitude toward the Palestinians, Sadat had little regard for King Hussein of Jordan and much contempt for President Hafiz al-Asad of Syria. He was obviously alarmed by the American emphasis on Geneva as a real venue for negotiating, fearing Asad would gain a veto power over his moves. Sadat had always argued that Geneva must be well prepared, meaning that the United States should work out most of the details before any negotiations began. Geneva would essentially be for signing, not for bargaining.

Sadat's strategy was to press the Americans to put forward a plan of their own. That was the purpose behind the draft treaty he had given to Vance in Alexandria. Sadat generally liked the substance of the American position as he understood it, but he had little patience for the idea that at some point the parties would really have to sit down together and negotiate.

The other parties to the conflict, primarily Syria, Jordan, and the PLO, were almost like spectators. They took predictable stands, but little action. They followed the American moves carefully, noted the contradictions in American policy, and imagined that complex plots were being hatched against their interests. They knew Sadat was quite capable of moving off on his own, and they distrusted Begin. These sentiments produced a passivity, a tentativeness on their part. They wanted to be part of the game, but they were not in a position to take initiatives. They could react, reject, observe. They were not yet ready to take steps aimed at shaping the process. That was left to the United States, Egypt, and Israel.

THE SEARCH FOR AN OPENING

The two months following Secretary of State Vance's Middle East trip were a time of political testing. The stakes were high for everyone.

Judgments were being made about fundamental positions. The credibility of the new American president was on the line. In this atmosphere every nuance in the American position was scrutinized for meaning. The Carter administration could no longer explain away some of its positions or statements as lack of experience. That may have worked in the first few months, but by fall the administration was being held to a higher standard: it was being taken seriously. Not surprisingly, this meant that the potential for considerable misunderstanding existed. In retrospect, one can see that during this period Washington had serious problems of communication with each of the parties to the negotiating process.

Washington officialdom was not entirely aware of how edgy the parties were becoming as the moment of truth seemed to be approaching. Instead, the tendency was to continue pushing on several fronts in the hope that something would open up. The American initiatives at this stage had a scattershot quality about them rather than constituting elements of a tightly controlled strategy that was internally consistent. The reason for this was quite simple: Carter and Vance were not sure how things would work out. They recognized that the Arabs were divided; they knew that Israel was suspicious; they felt the erosion of domestic support; they sensed that time was running out. So it seemed reasonable to pursue almost any promising opening to get negotiations started. That would at least establish a floor of sorts, and once the process had begun the United States could again take stock and figure out how to press forward with substantive proposals.

The somewhat eclectic nature of the American effort was reflected in the different initiatives being pursued in August and September. First were the draft peace treaties Vance had requested. One part of the Vance team began to develop compromise versions that could be presented to the parties at the appropriate moment. Second was another attempt to open a dialogue with the PLO. While the last serious effort was being made on this front, the Arab states were beginning to tell Washington that the United States should come out in favor of self-determination for the Palestinians rather than try so hard to get the PLO to accept U.N. Resolution 242. Palestinian rights, they said, should take priority over who represented the Palestinians.

Third—and this was where public attention was focused—was the overt goal of reconvening the Geneva conference. To this end, the United States began to talk to the cochairman of the conference, the Soviet

Union, about a statement of principles that could be issued jointly. These discussions went on during much of September, with little reference to the first two initiatives. The administration also held specific discussions with each of the parties about procedural arrangements for Geneva, focusing primarily on how the Arab parties would be represented and how the Palestinians would be included.

During all these maneuvers the U.S.-Israeli relationship was undergoing strain. The Carter-Begin honeymoon had not lasted long. Begin's attitude on settlements, and the American belief that the Israeli prime minister had hardened his position, created ill feelings. Washington became suspicious that the Israelis might strike at the PLO in southern Lebanon to ensure that nothing would come of the U.S.-PLO dialogue. To retain some credibility with the Arabs on the eve of negotiations, the United State could not be indifferent to new Israeli settlements or to threats of military action in Lebanon. But Carter by now preferred to pursue these issues in private, not in public.

In the hope of offsetting some of the unpleasantness in U.S.-Israeli relations, the Carter administration decided to introduce the idea of a formal U.S. security commitment to Israel as part of a general settlement. Dayan found the concept appealing; Begin shrewdly refused to show much interest, implying that Israel would be doing the United States a favor in any such security relationship, not the other way around.

As a backdrop to this activity, the president and Secretary Vance were vaguely aware that Israel was seeking direct contacts with Jordan and Egypt. Such action was not unprecedented and did not set off alarm bells in Washington. The administration seemed to feel that if the concerned parties could work something out on their own, more power to them. After all, Carter was not eager to play the role of mediator indefinitely. He kept saying that his patience was wearing thin, that the negotiating process was tedious, and that other issues demanded his attention. His level of frustration visibly increased during September and October, conveying an important message to the Middle East players. Sadat and Begin correctly concluded that Carter would not object to secret Egyptian-Israeli contacts, even if the consequence of these might be to compromise the chance of holding the Geneva conference.[1]

---

1. In a memorandum I drafted for Brzezinski on August 22, 1977, I raised the question whether we should encourage a secret meeting between Dayan and Sadat. I also noted that

LEBANON, SETTLEMENTS, AND THE PLO

The administration spent much of August and September quarreling with Israel over Lebanon and settlements and pursuing the PLO. On August 14 Carter sent Begin a blunt note expressing his concern about possible military action in south Lebanon against the PLO. Carter warned that such action would have the "gravest consequences" for Israel. While sharing Begin's concern for the Christian population in south Lebanon, Carter said he did not believe that their long-term position would be helped by Israeli military action. On August 16 Begin sent his reply, promising that he would take no action in southern Lebanon against Carter's wishes and without prior consultation. He also repeated his position that the PLO could not be at Geneva and promised that he would send a draft peace treaty to Washington, as requested, after his return from Romania in the last week of August.

Carter responded to Begin on August 18 in an oral message to be delivered by Ambassador Lewis. The president welcomed the news on Lebanon, but added that he still viewed Israeli settlements in occupied territory as illegal. (The Israeli cabinet had approved three new settlements the previous day.) Lewis's instructions continued: "These illegal, unilateral acts in territory presently under Israeli occupation create obstacles to constructive negotiations. . . . You should inform Prime Minister Begin that the repetition of these acts will make it difficult for the president not to reaffirm publicly the U.S. position regarding 1967 borders with minor modifications." To make sure the point was not lost, the Department of State spokesman criticized both the settlements and the Israeli decision a few days earlier to extend social services to the Palestinians of the West Bank, a move that seemed to imply a permanency to the Israeli presence there.[2]

In the midst of the dispute with Israel over Lebanon and settlements, the administration received a message in the last week of August from the PLO. Sent on the eve of the PLO's Central Committee meeting in Damascus, it implied that PLO leader Yasir Arafat had softened his conditions for accepting 242. He would agree to 242 if the United States

we should consider shifting our effort away from a dialogue with the PLO and toward support for the concept of Palestinian self-determination.

2. Bernard Gwertzman, "U.S. Assails Israelis on New Settlements in West Bank Region," *New York Times*, August 19, 1977, carries the text of the State Department's condemnation of the settlements, using essentially the same language as the president's letter but omitting the threat to refer to the 1967 borders if such acts continued.

would make certain private commitments concerning the role of the PLO in future negotiations. Carter was cautious, noting on the message that the United States could not certify that the PLO represented the Palestinian people as Arafat had requested.

A few days later, the PLO Central Committee concluded its meeting in Damascus by issuing a communiqué that was widely interpreted as a rebuff to the United States. Nonetheless, Carter was prepared for one more round of talks. Landrum Bolling, a private American who knew Arafat and was trusted by Carter, came to see National Security Adviser Brzezinski on September 6. He was given a message for Arafat, the gist of which was that the United States would offer to talk to the PLO— but could not go beyond that—if the PLO accepted 242 with a statement of its reservation about the inadequacy of the resolution's treatment of the Palestinian question. Brzezinski warned that time was running out. If Arafat held out too long, events might pass him by. The administration suggested specific language for the PLO to use in accepting 242 with a reservation, and made a promise to issue a public declaration in favor of Palestinian representation at Geneva in the near future.[3]

The talks between Bolling and Arafat took place on September 9 and 11. Arafat insisted that the PLO had not rejected 242 in its recent Damascus communiqué. He explained at length the convoluted politics within the PLO. He then reviewed recent developments, stating that on August 3 he had received a hopeful message, apparently from the Egyptians who had just met with Vance, that implied the United States would recognize the PLO, talk to it, and invite it to Geneva in return for PLO acceptance of 242. Then on August 9 the PLO had received another message, this time from the Saudis, that took all these promises back. The United States would only agree to talk to the PLO, nothing more, in exchange for acceptance of 242. On top of that, someone had conveyed to Arafat a distorted version of the five points that Vance had taken with him to the Middle East in August. The idea of a trusteeship for the West Bank and Gaza, possibly including Israel and Jordan as trustees, had also been brought to Arafat's attention. Such a plan would be a disaster for the Palestinians, Arafat said, and the news of it strengthened the hard-liners at the Central Committee meeting in Damascus.

Arafat explained at length the pressure he was under from the various Arab states. At one point he said he was subject to "Arab blackmail" on the issue of 242. He reviewed the positions of the Arab leaders, remarking

3. Zbigniew Brzezinski, *Power and Principle*, p. 105. In a talk with me on April 6, 1984, Bolling said he had no objection to being named as the emissary.

that there was a danger they might sell out the Palestinian cause, but he also produced a copy of a note from Sadat that he had just received pledging not to betray the Palestinians. After further lengthy discussions, Arafat promised to come up with a new statement on 242. Several days passed with no further word. Meanwhile, on September 13, the Department of State spelled out the American position on Geneva:

> Along with the issues of the nature of peace, recognition, security, and borders, the status of the Palestinians must be settled in a comprehensive Arab-Israeli peace agreement. This issue cannot be ignored if the others are to be solved.
>
> Moreover, to be lasting, a peace agreement must be positively supported by all of the parties to the conflict, including the Palestinians. This means that the Palestinians must be involved in the peacemaking process. Their representatives will have to be at Geneva for the Palestinian question to be solved.[4]

On September 18 Syrian Foreign Minister Abd al-Halim Khaddam handed the American ambassador in Damascus a proposed statement that the PLO would be prepared to make. It read: "The reservation of the PLO regarding Resolution 242 is that it does not establish a complete basis for the Palestinian issue and the national rights of the Palestinians. It also fails to refer in any manner to a national homeland for the Palestinian people."

The next day the Americans replied that a positive acceptance of 242 was still needed, which could be combined with this statement of reservation. Several days later Bolling, who had seen Arafat the previous week, went to Brzezinski to say that Arafat could not accept 242, even with the reservation, unless the United States would guarantee that a Palestinian state would result from the negotiations and that the PLO would lead the state.

These new conditions were so far from what Carter was prepared to accept that the search for a formula for starting a U.S.-PLO dialogue came to an abrupt halt. From then on, the Carter administration would shift its attention to the question of Palestinian representation at Geneva without trying to get prior PLO acceptance of 242. Carter no doubt felt he had taken considerable political heat in pursuit of the PLO, only to have the effort lead nowhere. What he and his colleagues had not understood, in part because they had not been listening carefully, was that some of the other Arabs, especially the Syrians, did not want the United States to deal directly with the PLO. After all, one of their

---

4. "Status of Palestinians in Peace Negotiations," *Department of State Bulletin*, vol. 77 (October 10, 1977), p. 463.

sources of leverage was their claim to be able to speak on behalf of the Palestinians, and they were loathe to give that up.[5]

While the PLO was engaged in an intense internal debate over whether the American conditions for opening a dialogue were worth considering, tensions began to rise again in south Lebanon. Israeli-backed Christian militiamen opened attacks on Palestinian-held areas. Within days, Washington received reports of Israeli intervention in the fighting. Begin had not lived up to his promise to Carter of the previous month to take no action in Lebanon without prior consultation. The president was concerned that if he appeared to be acquiescing in Israel's attacks on the PLO, he would undermine his credibility with Arab leaders.

According to the Arms Export Control Act of 1976, American arms sold to Israel could be used only for "legitimate self-defense." When Carter learned that some armored personnel carriers of the Israeli defense forces were inside Lebanon to support the Christian militiamen, he informed the Israelis that they were violating the terms under which the equipment had been provided. He was told that the reports were inaccurate and that all American-supplied equipment had been removed. By resorting to new and exotic technology, the Americans were immediately able to determine that this was not true. Concrete evidence was shown to the president that several armored personnel carriers were located in a Lebanese village. Carter was furious, both because of what the Israelis had done and because of their attempt to mislead him.

On September 24, 1977, Carter sent an urgent message to Begin. The key sentence in this long missive read: "I must point out that current Israeli military actions in Lebanon are a violation of our agreement covering the provision of American military equipment and that, as a consequence, if these actions are not immediately halted, Congress will have to be informed of this fact, and that further deliveries will have to be terminated."

Begin argued that Israel's actions had been defensive and had therefore not violated any agreement. But at the end of his discussion with the American deputy chief of mission who had delivered Carter's letter, he opened a cabinet, took out a bottle of whiskey, and poured two glasses.

5. Jimmy Carter, *Keeping Faith*, p. 292. Carter noted in his diary on August 29 that Asad had made the constructive suggestion that the Arab League might substitute for the PLO at Geneva. Asad had also said in an interview that Palestinian rights were far more important than the question of who represented the Palestinians. In the interview and elsewhere, Asad dismissed the idea of normal relations with Israel and said the failure of the Geneva conference might not be such a bad thing. John B. Oakes, "Assad Favors Peace with Israel, but Rejects Any Closer Relations," *New York Times*, August 29, 1977.

Raising his glass as if to acknowledge that the United States had won this round, he said Israel would withdraw its forces from Lebanon within twenty-four hours.[6] A few days later Begin sent a letter to Carter saying he was eternally grateful for American efforts to arrange a cease-fire in south Lebanon.

For the moment, the danger that an explosion in Lebanon might derail the broader diplomatic effort had ended, without any overt sign of struggle between the United States and Israel. Quiet and firm diplomacy had produced results without adverse domestic political fallout. What the Americans may have failed to understand, however, was that Begin was prepared to show flexibility on issues that were not central to his ideology, such as Lebanon. But this did not mean that Carter could hope for comparable success in pressing for concessions on the West Bank.

PREPARING FOR GENEVA

In the second week of August, while Vance was returning from the Middle East, Arthur J. Goldberg, the former Supreme Court justice and ambassador to the United Nations, came to see Carter. He brought with him a memorandum supporting the idea of getting talks started at Geneva, even without much prior agreement. Once talks began, he argued, they could evolve into "proximity talks," such as those successfully conducted by Ralph Bunche in 1949 at Rhodes which led to the armistice agreements. (In Rhodes the delegations had ostensibly negotiated through a third party, but in fact there were direct informal talks as well.) Carter was impressed by Goldberg's argument, and that may have reinforced the trend toward treating Geneva as a desirable end in itself.[7]

Vance also felt it was time to concentrate on convening the conference, since his talks had convinced him that little more could be accomplished until Israel and the Arab parties themselves began to engage in some form of negotiations. They were still by and large watching and waiting to see what the United States might do next. Sadat was something of an exception in that he was actively putting forward Egyptian ideas, but these were still general and were largely designed to get the United States to come forward with its own proposals.

With an Egyptian draft treaty in hand, and an Israeli draft on its way,

---

6. Brzezinski, *Power and Principle*, p. 107, refers to this incident, but gives the date of Carter's letter as September 25.

7. Carter, *Keeping Faith*, pp. 291–92.

Vance decided to start work on a U.S. compromise proposal. The work would have to be handled with utmost care and secrecy, since the Carter administration had said repeatedly that it would not try to impose a blueprint of its own. The draft would take the form of "suggestions" designed to help move the negotiations toward concreteness. Crucial issues, such as the exact location of final borders, might be left undetermined in these first drafts. During the last part of August a small team began work on these documents, producing models for an Egyptian-Israeli treaty, as well as ones between Israel and its two other neighbors, Jordan and Syria. A draft for an interim regime on the West Bank and Gaza was also produced.

On August 28 Carter met with his senior advisers—Vice President Mondale, Vance, Secretary of Defense Brown, Brzezinski, and press spokesman Jody Powell—to discuss Middle East strategy. The president and Vance were both angry at Begin for his recent decision to set up more settlements, and Brzezinski felt they were both in a mood for a showdown with Israel.[8]

Shortly after this meeting, on August 30, Vance sent a strategy memorandum to the president on the upcoming round of talks that would take place in September with the Middle East foreign ministers. Vance stressed the need for agreement on Palestinian representation, as well as more concreteness from the Israelis about their territorial aims on the Egyptian and Syrian fronts. He also recommended that the president discuss with Foreign Minister Dayan the idea of a transitional regime for the West Bank. Dayan had reportedly told Vance that a transitional regime would not necessarily be in conflict with what he was seeking. Vance also noted that the Soviets were eager for Geneva and wanted to talk about a date for the conference and a joint invitation.

Attached to Vance's memo were drafts of proposed Egyptian-Israeli and Syrian-Israeli agreements. Article two stated: "The permanent border between Egypt (Syria) and Israel, conforming except as otherwise agreed between them to the 1949 Armistice Demarcation Lines, is shown on the annexed map (Annex 1)." No map was provided.

Brzezinski also weighed in with his thoughts on Middle East strategy in a memorandum to the president on September 2. (Since Carter was an insatiable reader of memos, much of the policy debate among his advisers was put on paper for him to consider.) While Vance was most

8. Brzezinski, *Power and Principle*, pp. 105–06.

concerned with getting the process of drafting agreements started, Brzezinski was looking for ways to change the political context among the Middle East states. His focus in this memo was on the Syrians, the PLO, and the Soviets. He recommended that Carter write to President Asad to try to induce greater flexibility in his position. He also recommended a public statement, to be issued by Vance's spokesman, calling for Palestinian participation in the negotiations. This move was aimed at adding credibility to the efforts of the American emissary to Arafat that were about to begin. Agreement with the Soviets on setting a date for Geneva was also part of the strategy that Brzezinski recommended. Finally, he urged Carter to develop a plan for dealing with Israeli settlements on the West Bank.[9]

The next day, September 3, Brzezinski forwarded to the president a copy of the Israeli draft treaty that Begin had promised to send after his return from Romania.[10] The treaty text itself consisted of some forty articles, many of them dealing with minor details. The draft, not surprisingly, was long on demands for Arab concessions and short on what Israel would give in return. Territory, the most sensitive topic, was not addressed in the draft at all.

Instead, Dayan wrote a letter to Vance dated September 2 in which he reiterated Israel's position on withdrawal, as presented by Begin to Carter during their first private meeting. Dayan specifically said Israel would seek to retain territorial control in Sinai from Sharm al-Sheikh in the south to just west of Gaza. He also outlined the need for security zones, but repeated that Israel was prepared for substantial withdrawals.

On the Syrian front, Dayan stated that Israel would be prepared to negotiate a new boundary to replace the cease-fire line, but that the boundary should take into account the security of Israel's water sources and its northern areas. Turning to the Jordanian front, Dayan said that in the West Bank Israel would support equal rights for Arabs and Jews, but that there should be no foreign rule or sovereignty. The Jordan River should be the basis for the security of Israel's eastern border, in Dayan's somewhat convoluted phrase. Other proposals, however, could be put

9. Ibid., p. 106.

10. Ismail Fahmy, *Negotiating for Peace in the Middle East*, pp. 223–28. Fahmy summarizes the Israeli draft, but mistakenly says that Dayan gave it to Vance on September 19. In fact, a copy was provided to the American embassy in Tel Aviv on September 2. It was somewhat unpolished, however, and contained many errors and repetitions, showing evidence of being hastily assembled. A cleaner copy was indeed brought by Dayan to Washington, and this was the draft shown to Fahmy that he accurately, if tendentiously, summarizes.

forward and would be received by Israel with an open mind. All subjects, he said, were open for negotiations.

The American reaction to the Israeli draft treaty and Dayan's letter was less than euphoric. The documents still presented the maximal Israeli position and showed no hint of any give on the territorial issue. Nor did they say anything about settlements, another issue the Americans found especially vexing. Much of the detail in the treaty seemed irrelevant, or perhaps even designed to drive Sadat, who hated to deal with details, to distraction. Still, the United States now had in hand two drafts and could begin to elaborate on its own version as a reasonable compromise.

Carter next turned his attention to Asad and tried to enlist his help with the PLO. On September 6 Carter sent a letter to the Syrian leader stressing that the time was coming to move from generalities toward greater concreteness. "This will help initiate a negotiating process and will create a context in which American influence can be used constructively. We cannot, of course, guarantee precisely how Palestinian concerns will be met in the negotiations, but I can assure that my government does believe that Palestinians should be represented at Geneva and should participate in shaping their future in conformity with the principles of U.N. Resolution 242 and of self-determination." Carter went on to urge Asad to get the PLO to accept 242 with a reservation. That would allow for a full hearing of PLO views at Geneva.

Asad, who was always slow to respond, sent a letter on September 12, ostensibly replying to Carter's letter of August 14 in which the president had requested that each party send him a statement of its views on a settlement. After an opening critique of Israel's policy, Asad spelled out the Syrian position on Geneva, borders, Palestinian self-determination, refugees, and "ending the state of war," which would mean peace. Demilitarized zones on both sides of the border could be accepted, and the agreement should be based on 242 and 338. The letter was not encouraging, nor did Asad depart from his well-known views, but at least he was still in the game. A few days later, on September 18, his foreign minister also conveyed a statement from the PLO on its reservation to 242. This fell far short of what the Americans wanted, but again it reinforced the impression that the Syrians were not closing any doors.

SECRET CHANNELS

As Geneva appeared to be approaching, the diplomacy became extraordinarily complicated. On one level, all parties were making public statements, most of which added to the confusion and tension. On a more businesslike level, positions were being committed to paper in typical prenegotiation fashion. From the perspective of the diplomats, the fact that these documents were often extreme and unrealistic was less important than that they existed at all. Procedural issues were being wrestled with even more intently than substance. And at the deepest level of all, secret contacts were taking place, including those between Israel and two of its neighbors.

Jordanian-Israeli contacts had a long history, and the United States had usually been kept informed of them. They often proved to be useful in working out tacit understandings, but they had never produced a breakthrough. The mere fact they had to be kept secret indicated the pressures operating on the Jordanian side. Still, the United States had consistently supported the idea of direct contacts between Israel and its Arab neighbors. The only time the United States had intervened to thwart direct talks had been early on in the Egyptian-Israeli disengagement negotiations in November 1973. At that time the rationale had been that the United States was trying to build its own credibility as a mediator.[11]

During their initial talks at the White House, Begin had told Carter that he was planning to meet with some top Arab leaders, in particular Sadat.[12] Sadat had told Vance in August that he wanted to meet the Israeli prime minister, and this information had been passed along to Begin.[13] Talks between Egypt and Israel were not viewed as antithetical to Geneva. The Americans had always assumed that Geneva would in large part be a facade behind which quiet contacts of that kind could be promoted to do the real job of bargaining.

In the last half of August the Begin government began its first direct talks with an Arab leader—King Hussein of Jordan. On August 22 Foreign Minister Dayan met with Hussein in London. Dayan concluded from these discussions that Hussein was not prepared to break with the Rabat summit consensus, which had designated the PLO as the sole legitimate representative of the Palestinians. Jordan would take no initiatives, and the king flatly rejected the division of the West Bank as a basis for agreement with Israel. He continued to insist on full Israeli withdrawal from all occupied Arab territory, including East Jerusalem.[14]

11. William B. Quandt, *Decade of Decisions*, pp. 218–20.

12. Brzezinski, *Power and Principle*, p. 100; and Carter, *Keeping Faith*, p. 291.

13. Carter, *Keeping Faith*, p. 296. Prime Minister Begin, in a letter sent to Carter on November 15, 1977, on the eve of Sadat's arrival in Israel, referred to Vance's telling him of Sadat's interest during the secretary's visit to Jerusalem in August 1977.

14. Moshe Dayan, *Breakthrough*, pp. 35–37.

Shortly after Dayan's return from London with his pessimistic assessment of Jordan's position, Prime Minister Begin flew to Romania for talks with President Nicolae Ceauşescu, the leader of the only communist state that maintained full diplomatic relations with Israel. According to Israeli sources, Begin took the initiative to go to Romania. His main message was that he wanted to meet with Sadat.[15]

Begin returned from Romania on August 30. Five days later Dayan left for a secret trip to Morocco to discuss with King Hassan the possibility of arranging meetings with the Egyptians. Such an encounter was not unprecedented. Late in 1976 Israeli Prime Minister Rabin had reportedly gone to Morocco on a similar mission. Now, however, the trip assumed a special importance: it showed Israel's desire to deal directly with Sadat and to avoid total reliance on the American mediation effort. In his talks with King Hassan, Dayan suggested secret meetings between Egypt and Israel aimed at informal understandings. The Americans would be brought in as guarantors of the understandings once the parties had met and worked out the essential elements. Hassan offered to try to set up a meeting between Begin and Sadat. Dayan left for home with the hope that something might come of these efforts. So far, secrecy had been maintained, and the Americans had not been informed.[16]

With unprecedented speed, the Moroccans conveyed the Egyptian answer to Dayan several days later. Sadat would send an emissary, Hassan Tuhamy, to meet with Dayan in Morocco on September 16. At this point both Israel and Egypt were hedging their bets. They had not decided against Geneva, but they did not want to rely primarily on such an unwieldy forum. And they were eager to see how far they could go toward agreement without American involvement. For the Israelis, the American emphasis on a comprehensive settlement, and especially the flirtation with the PLO, had raised danger signals.

For the Egyptians, the American insistence that Syria and the Palestinians be in the game from the outset and that Geneva be the forum for at least some of the bargaining reduced Sadat's room for maneuver. Perhaps the secret channel could be used to open up new options. In any case, Egypt and Israel had already negotiated two disengagement agreements in 1973 and 1975, so that it was not surprising that they would establish some direct channel before, or even at the same time as, Geneva. Sadat must have assumed, however, that the Syrians might learn of these meetings and would become even more suspicious than they already were

15. Eitan Haber, Ze'ev Schiff, and Ehud Ya'ari, *The Year of the Dove*, pp. 3–4.
16. Dayan, *Breakthrough*, pp. 38–54.

of Sadat's intentions. Clearly, Sadat cared little for Asad's concerns. Nor did he choose to inform his foreign minister, Ismail Fahmy, who would doubtless have raised questions.

Sadat's choice of Tuhamy for this sensitive mission seemed peculiar because he had no previous experience of negotiating with the Israelis and was known to be close to religious conservatives and the Saudis. But he did have fairly good credentials as an early member of the revolutionary movement that had toppled the Egyptian monarchy in 1952. Perhaps most important, he had a history of involvement in clandestine activities.

Dayan's trip to Morocco was, of course, secret, but it was widely noted at the time that he had dropped out of sight while in Europe and had returned to Israel instead of proceeding to the United States as planned. The actual meeting between Tuhamy and Dayan took place on September 16. Tuhamy said the Americans should not be informed, though once the parties reached agreement the Americans should be allowed to take the credit. Tuhamy confirmed that Ceauşescu had suggested to Sadat that he should meet Begin. Sadat was ready, provided Israel gave a prior commitment to full withdrawal from all Arab land. He said Egypt was ready for a package deal to be negotiated in secret, not in Geneva.

Dayan was eager to know how far Sadat would go without the other Arab leaders. Would Sadat be ready to sign an agreement even if Asad did not? Did Israel have to agree to withdraw from all the territories, or just Egyptian territory, to meet Sadat's condition for talking to Begin? These were questions to which Dayan would return over and over in later months, always looking for an opening for a separate agreement with Egypt. From the talks with Tuhamy, Dayan could be reasonably sure that an agreement with Egypt was possible if Israel agreed to a full withdrawal from Sinai. But he was not sure how much more Israel would have to put into the equation, and it would take most of the next year to get an answer. Still, he knew that Sadat was interested in a deal, that he was prepared for secret talks, and that Geneva was a secondary matter. That was quite a bit to learn from one encounter.[17]

CARTER'S SECOND ROUND OF PERSONAL DIPLOMACY

After meeting with Begin in July, Carter had not talked directly with any of the Arab or Israeli leaders for two months. By mid-September,

17. Ibid., pp. 43–53.

however, he was preparing for a new round of intensive discussions with the foreign ministers of Israel, Egypt, Syria, and Jordan. His frame of mind as he entered this second round of personal diplomacy was one of considerable impatience and irritation with the slow pace of the bargaining. The Israelis had earned his wrath by their settlements policy; Carter was especially angry with a statement by Minister of Agriculture Ariel Sharon in early September claiming that he had a plan to settle two million Jews in a security belt from Golan, through the West Bank, and into Sinai.

Carter was also sensitive to criticism that he was paying too much attention to the PLO. In comments to news editors on September 16, he sounded defensive when answering a question about why he had embraced the PLO. He said he had never called on the PLO to be part of the negotiations; he had asked only that the Palestinians be represented. He also denied that he favored a Palestinian state, expressing his preference for an entity associated with Jordan. Finally, he reminded the questioners that the United States was not just an idle bystander or an uninterested intermediary. The United States, he said, had a direct, substantial interest in a permanent peace in the Middle East.[18]

Dayan in Washington

Carter expected his meeting with Dayan on September 19 to be difficult.[19] It was preceded, however, by a cordial meeting between Vance and Dayan. Despite Tuhamy's request that his meeting with Dayan be kept a secret from the Americans, the Israeli foreign minister told Vance about his trip to Morocco.[20] He did not go into great detail but referred several times to his recent attempts to determine the position of the Arab parties. Vance was glad to be informed, but no alarm bells went off. After all, he had conveyed to Begin a month earlier Sadat's interest in meeting with the Israeli prime minister.

18. "Interview with the President: Remarks and a Question-and-Answer Session with a Group of Editors and News Directors, September 16, 1977," *Public Papers: Carter, 1977*, vol. 2, pp. 1623–24.

19. Carter, *Keeping Faith*, p. 292.

20. Interview with Cyrus Vance in New York, March 1, 1984. An aide to President Sadat had also informed the American ambassador to Cairo, Hermann Eilts, whose reaction was that if the meeting had been serious Tuhamy would not have been sent. On January 23, 1985, Usama al-Baz told me that the Tuhamy-Dayan meeting was meant to find out if the Israelis were serious about peace. Sadat was not then thinking of a bilateral Egyptian-Israeli agreement only. Martin Indyk, *"To the Ends of the Earth,"* p. 36, sees the Tuhamy-Dayan meetings in the context of preparing for Geneva.

Most of Vance's session with Dayan concentrated instead on the Israeli draft treaty. Dayan said he had concluded that neither Egypt nor Jordan was prepared for diplomatic relations. By comparison, this issue was of highest priority for Israel. He also asked Vance what the United States would be prepared to guarantee in a settlement. He even hinted that U.N. forces might be useful in Sinai.

Softening the Israeli position on territory considerably, Dayan said a U.N. force might be able to help ensure free navigation through the Strait of Tiran. The best alternative, he said, would be for Israel to retain sovereignty at Sharm al-Sheikh, but the goal was free navigation, and maybe Israel could retain control without sovereignty—this from the man who months earlier had said openly that he would rather have Sharm than peace with Egypt! He did add, however, that even though there was nothing sacred about al-Arish on the north coast of Sinai near Gaza, Israel would want arrangements to allow Israeli settlers to remain there even if Egypt were to have sovereignty.[21]

Dayan then went to the White House, where he met first with only Carter and Mondale. According to Dayan, it was an extremely unpleasant encounter, with the American side, especially Mondale, making accusations against Israel.[22] The most contentious topics were Israeli actions in Lebanon and settlements in the occupied territories. When the larger meeting began at 3:30 p.m., Carter reiterated his grievances against Israel, claiming that the Arabs had been more flexible than Begin. He termed the Israeli position on Palestinian representation as too intransigent. Begin had initially told him that Palestinians could be at Geneva if they were not well-known PLO members and that their credentials would not be examined. Begin subsequently hardened his position, saying no PLO members at all could be there.

Carter specifically asked Dayan to accept a unified Arab delegation, including Palestinians who would not be well-known PLO members, for the opening session of Geneva. Thereafter, negotiations could take place bilaterally, except on the Palestinian question. Dayan said this plan would probably be acceptable. He added that a committee to discuss the Palestinians could be formed, but not to discuss territory, only the refugee question. In response to a question from Carter, he rejected the idea of a referendum for the Palestinians after a short transitional period. He then reiterated that Palestinians at Geneva would have to be part of a

21. Dayan, *Breakthrough*, pp. 55–58, gives a detailed account of this meeting but leaves out his indications of flexibility.

22. Ibid., pp. 59–60.

Jordanian delegation. Dayan made clear that his idea was to have an opening session at Geneva and then negotiations with the heads of state. The latter talks would not take place at Geneva. If agreement was reached in these secret talks, the parties could return to Geneva to sign. Somewhat surprisingly, Secretary Vance expressed his general agreement with this point of view.

Carter began to soften a bit, assuring Dayan that the United States would not support the Syrian view, which would have the Arabs negotiating as a collective whole. Dayan responded by saying the United States should not rule out the idea of some West Bank mayors joining with King Hussein in a Jordanian delegation. If everything else was all right, said Dayan, the talks would not break down over a Palestinian saying he was with the PLO. Israel would agree to negotiate with anyone from the West Bank, provided he had not carried out military operations against Israel.

After a review by Secretary Vance of the fundamentals of the U.S. position, including some further discussion of U.S. guarantees, Dayan spelled out a new Israeli policy on settlements. For one year there would be no new civilian settlements. At six sites that were former military camps, Israeli settlers could establish homes, but only if they put on uniforms and served in the military. Families would only come later. No land would be expropriated. These *nahal* settlements would not be turned into civilian outposts for at least one year. In any case the location of the settlements would not determine future borders. If there was an agreement with the Arabs, Israel would either remove the settlements or work out their status.[23]

Dayan said he would recommend this plan to his government if Carter felt it would help the negotiations. The same was true for the idea of a unified Arab delegation for the plenary session at Geneva. Dayan urged, however, that the United States should force this idea on Israel. Begin would object, so it should be clear it was an American idea. Finally, Dayan also urged the Americans not to deal seriously with Fahmy. Instead, talks should be with Sadat. Dayan was once again referring indirectly to his recent meeting in Morocco.

Despite the occasional unpleasantness that accompanied these talks,

23. Uzi Benziman, *Prime Minister under Siege* (in Hebrew), p. 22, quotes Dayan as saying in this meeting: "Settlements are not an obstacle to peace; the borders will not be fixed as a result of settlements. We settled areas in which we intend to stay, but if in negotiations other borders are decided upon, we will not block achievement of a settlement because of the existence of settlements."

the American side had inched forward toward finding some common ground with Israel. Although Carter was still not entirely satisfied with the Israeli position on settlements, he felt that progress had been made by limiting the numbers and types of settlements for the next year. On Palestinian representation, Dayan was willing to accept Palestinians, including some who might identify themselves with the PLO, and was even prepared to accept a multinational grouping to discuss refugee claims, though he continued to insist that the West Bank would be negotiated only with Jordan. Finally, Dayan had also agreed to the idea of a unified Arab delegation at the Geneva plenary session, which was little more than a device for finessing the question of Palestinian representation, and he had shown more than passing interest in the question of U.S. guarantees as part of a settlement.

Carter, who had been genuinely irritated with the Israelis, came away from the meeting feeling that Dayan had shown considerable flexibility.[24] What the president did not know was that some of what Dayan had said was well beyond what Begin would accept. And in the end, it was the prime minister, not the foreign minister, who would sway the cabinet on most crucial issues.

Dayan's own feelings toward Carter were less generous after this meeting. The foreign minister was angry, and was not reluctant to make his views known to the American press. Hamilton Jordan tried to persuade the Israelis to put a more positive gloss on their accounts of the session. Domestic politics were obviously still an important consideration, and Carter's advisers were anxious to shield the president from the continuing criticism that he was too tough on the Israelis and too soft on the PLO.[25]

Fahmy in Washington

If Carter had been intent on demonstrating his toughness to Dayan, he was more inclined to tell his next visitor, Egyptian Foreign Minister Fahmy, of the limits of American influence. Fahmy has attached great significance to his meetings with Carter on September 21, implying that Sadat's decision to go to Jerusalem stemmed from the loss of confidence

24. Carter, *Keeping Faith*, pp. 292–93. See also Dayan's account, *Breakthrough*, pp. 59–63, which is generally accurate but somewhat selective. Vance details the understanding with Israel on settlements in *Hard Choices*, p. 191; and Brzezinski in *Power and Principle*, p. 107, notes that Dayan urged Carter to extract the concession on the unified Arab delegation from Israel.

25. Dayan, *Breakthrough*, pp. 63–64, tells of Hamilton Jordan's efforts.

the Egyptian president had in Carter after reading the reports of these meetings. During a private session with Fahmy, Carter apparently said he could not put pressure on Israel. To do so would be "political suicide." He also informed Fahmy that he would have to bring the Soviets into the picture.[26]

Fahmy brought with him an eight-page letter from Sadat to Carter. Sadat was very tough on the Israelis, arguing that time was running out. The two key issues were now withdrawal and the Palestinian state. The moderate Arabs were under great pressure. It had become imperative to convene the Geneva Conference in 1977, and the parties should stop haggling over procedures.

When the larger meeting between Carter and Fahmy began, differences of basic approach quickly surfaced. The president explicitly said he did not think that much more progress could be made before Geneva. To get negotiations started, the United States favored a unified Arab delegation, including Palestinians other than Arafat. The actual negotiations would take place in bilateral groups, except the refugee question, in which the PLO could be included. The Soviet Union would be cochairman, and the United States would work things out with it.

Fahmy replied by saying that Egypt was not in a hurry for Geneva. (Sadat's letter had said just the opposite.) The only remaining problem was Palestinian representation, and talks should not begin until that was resolved in a clear way. Fahmy raised the possibility of a new U.N. resolution and was told by Carter that the United States would veto it. Egypt's position, according to Fahmy, was that the PLO had to be given the chance to go to Geneva. If it chose not to do so, Egypt would go anyway and would even sign a peace treaty with Israel. But the PLO had to have the choice.

Showing considerable exasperation, Carter said he had gone about as far as he intended to go. He reviewed the U.S. position on substance, and then observed that Egypt wanted to go to Geneva only to sign, whereas the United States felt Geneva was important to get a negotiating process started. Carter appealed to Fahmy to accept the idea of a unified

26. Fahmy, *Negotiating for Peace*, pp. 195–96. Carter was fond of using the phrase "political suicide." On October 22, 1977, for example, before a Democratic fund-raising dinner he said that if he ever hurt Israel, it would "almost automatically" result in his "political suicide." See "Los Angeles, California: Remarks at a Democratic National Committee Fundraising Dinner, October 22, 1977," *Weekly Compilation of Presidential Documents*, vol. 13 (October 31, 1977), p. 1651.

Arab delegation. "Let me worry about Asad and Hussein," the president said, adding that the Soviets should neither be excluded nor given a major role. As differences were narrowed, the United States would put forward ideas of its own. But Carter could not simply impose his own views. He needed the support of the American Jewish community, of Congress, and of the public. Fahmy reportedly felt that Carter was advertising his weakness by making that statement, and was also hinting at some type of sinister dealings with Syria and Jordan behind Egypt's back.[27]

Khaddam in Washington

Carter's offhand remark about dealing with the Syrians was put to the test on September 28, 1977, when the president met with Syrian Foreign Minister Khaddam. Following his regular practice, Carter met alone with Khaddam, with only an interpreter present, for one-half hour. Looking back on this private session, Khaddam indicated that Carter had gone quite far in promising that the PLO would be included at Geneva. When the issue arose in the broader meeting, Khaddam claimed that Carter backed down somewhat, raising doubts about his true position.[28] The record of the larger meeting shows, however, that Carter forthrightly outlined the American position, expressing his preference for a unified Arab delegation at Geneva, including PLO members, the only caveat being that they should not be "well known or famous."

Carter also told Khaddam that the United States and the Soviet Union were in the process of working on a joint invitation to Geneva. Khaddam referred to the reservation to 242 that the PLO had forwarded to the United States through Syria, adding that perhaps a new U.N. resolution should be considered that would deal directly with the Palestinian question, which 242 did not do.

The president also tried to address Syria's fear that Egypt would use Geneva as a cover for negotiating a separate peace with Israel. He correctly

27. See Fahmy, *Negotiating for Peace*, pp. 197–214, for a full account of the meeting and its significance. A careful checking of Fahmy's version against the American transcript shows several discrepancies, but his account is essentially accurate. No verbatim record exists, for both sides had only notetakers present who subsequently tried to reconstruct as much of the conversation as possible while concentrating on getting the substantive points down correctly. This was true at all presidential meetings and accounted sometimes for the different interpretations the parties to the talks gave later. The one clear mistake Fahmy makes is in his characterization of his exchanges with Brzezinski, some of which seem to come from a private meeting between them the following day.

28. Interview with Abd al-Halim Khaddam, Damascus, December 28, 1982.

pointed out that it was up to the Arabs to decide on how much they wanted to coordinate their positions at Geneva. No one could prevent them from adopting the position that no Arab party would sign an agreement until all issues had been resolved.

Then Carter said he envisaged a series of bilateral agreements at Geneva, and that if Syria was dissatisfied with the results, it could withhold its agreement. This missed the point and may have even aroused Syrian fears. Khaddam wanted a veto over a separate Egyptian-Israeli agreement, not the right to stand aside and watch one be concluded, as Carter was suggesting. True, he was asking for something that Sadat was determined to refuse, and the Americans were unwilling to pressure Sadat into accepting a Syrian veto. Carter was being frank in acknowledging that this was an issue for the Arab side to solve. The United States would not go beyond supporting the idea of a single Arab delegation for the plenary session of Geneva as a way of getting Palestinians into the negotiations.

In the end, this meeting apparently reinforced Syria's suspicions, and something about the private talk with Carter stuck in Khaddam's mind years later as showing weakness on Carter's part. Whether this conclusion was justified is impossible to determine, but it is worth noting that both Fahmy and Khaddam drew similar conclusions from their private meetings with Carter. Dayan also had been disturbed by his private talk with Carter.

Each party seemed to be grasping at small signs to judge U.S. intentions. Something that Carter might have said in March 1977 without causing a ripple would now be endowed with great significance as everyone awaited Washington's next move and tried to figure out how to deflect it, maneuver around it, or turn it to good advantage.

Carter and Vance may have been aware of how sensitive everyone had become to the nuances of U.S. policy, and on the whole they projected a consistent line. But more care was probably needed to avoid the impression of American vacillation in the eyes of the Arabs, or of unfair pressure as seen by the Israelis. The Americans had to tread a fine line, and it was not surprising that there were some stumbles along the way. But the missteps of September were minor compared to what lay ahead.

PROCEDURES AND POLITICS

In the course of the September 1977 consultations, Carter and Vance had come to an explicit conclusion: further progress on substantive issues could be made only when a negotiating process that directly involved the parties to the conflict had begun. Further rounds of U.S. shuttle diplomacy or mediation would produce little and would continue to erode the president's political base of support at home. To pressure Israel on such issues as settlements and Palestinian rights, the Carter administration felt the need to have the Arab parties actively involved in direct negotiations with Israel. Otherwise the process was coming to resemble a U.S.-Israeli dialogue, with the Arabs as onlookers. The prenegotiations phase had to be brought to a close soon.

Procedures for Geneva

To get to Geneva, as a step toward genuine negotiations, Carter tried to find common ground not only between Israel and the Arabs but also among the Arabs themselves. The administration knew by now that Egypt and Israel were capable of dealing directly with each other and that each preferred bilateral negotiations to a broader multinational forum. It wanted the Geneva setting because no one in Washington thought Sadat was prepared to go all the way in concluding a final agreement with Israel unless some progress was being made on the Palestinian question. Sadat himself was the authority on this point, as was his foreign minister.

Geneva, then, was to be the umbrella under which Sadat and Begin could move forward at whatever pace they could sustain, pulling in their wake, if possible, Jordan, the Palestinians, and perhaps even the Syrians. The problem was that the umbrella could not be raised until the most skeptical of the parties, the Syrians and the Palestinians, were satisfied. Insofar as they thought Geneva would to be little more than a figleaf for another separate Egyptian-Israeli agreement—a Sinai III—they had little reason to go along. Yet if their demands for a virtual veto over Egyptian moves were accepted, no progress could be made in negotiations.

To resolve this dilemma, the United States tried to resort to some constructive obfuscation, giving each party the impression that its concerns were being met. The Egyptians and Israelis were assured that the actual negotiations would be conducted bilaterally. The Syrians, Jordanians, and Palestinians were told that there would be a single Arab delegation and that they would have to work out their own negotiating strategy to prevent bilateral deals at the expense of a comprehensive agreement.[29]

---

29. Indyk, *"To the Ends of the Earth,"* p. 43, misinterprets this as meaning that the

The Arabs were told that the PLO could be present within the Arab delegation, provided the actual delegates not be well-known officials. At the same time the Israelis were told that they would have the right to object to any new participants, as agreed on at the first session of the Geneva conference in 1973.

Given the difficulty of working all this out smoothly without agreement among the Arabs themselves, the Carter administration was tempted to go over the heads of the regional parties, who seemed hopelessly mired in procedural arguments, and work out a joint invitation to Geneva with the cochairman, the Soviet Union.

Involving the Soviets

Vance had always felt the Soviets would have to be brought into the discussions at some point, if only to limit their potential for troublemaking. And he hoped that a joint U.S.-Soviet invitation would help to resolve the procedural issues and would put pressure on Syria and the PLO in particular. He had urged Soviet Ambassador Anatoly Dobrynin on August 29 to ask Foreign Minister Andrei Gromyko to send him ideas for a joint communiqué on the Middle East.[30]

On September 9 Dobrynin handed Vance a draft called "Joint Soviet-U.S. Statement on the Middle East." In several respects it was a more moderate document than might have been expected. It did not call for direct PLO participation in the talks, nor did it mention a Palestinian state. No call was made on Israel to return to the borders of 1967 or to abandon East Jerusalem. Much of the language of the document came from U.N. Resolution 242, with the significant addition of the words "Palestinian national rights." Vance reacted with interest and assigned Assistant Secretary Alfred L. Atherton, Jr., to pursue talks with a Soviet diplomat named Mikhail Sytenko.

The day after receiving the Soviet draft, on Saturday, September 10, Secretary Vance chaired a strategy meeting at the State Department. No mention was made of the draft. Instead the emphasis was on Israeli settlements and Palestinian representation at Geneva. One group felt that

---

Syrians would be able to veto any agreement reached between Egypt and Israel. He says that the plenary at Geneva was to have the power to approve any agreement reached in the bilateral subcommittees. In fact, all the United States ever suggested was that the working groups might report to the plenary, and even this point was omitted from subsequent versions of the working paper.

30. Vance, *Hard Choices*, pp. 191–92.

the time had come for a showdown with Israel on these two issues, as well as on borders and a Palestinian entity. The possibility of a U.N. resolution on the illegality of Israeli settlements was raised. Another group, somewhat surprisingly represented by the Middle East specialists, felt that the president could not afford to be drawn into a prolonged confrontation with the Israelis before Geneva. Instead, the emphasis should be on starting negotiations and then turning attention to the substantive issues. (The second view may have been reinforced by a comment by Carter to a journalist to the effect that if no progress was made in the next few weeks, he would suspend his efforts. This was hardly the attitude with which to start a showdown with Begin, for it would encourage the Israeli leader to resist, hoping Carter would back down.)

On September 23 Gromyko met with Carter and indicated that the Soviets wanted to be brought into the negotiating process. That same day Begin sent the president a message saying that two Soviet representatives had called on him with this information: the Soviet Union would restore diplomatic relations with Israel on the day Geneva was convened. Begin made no comment on this point other than that the Soviets obviously wanted Geneva to take place and wanted to share in the diplomatic process.

By September 27 Atherton was able to report to Vance that he was close to having worked out an acceptable draft with Sytenko. The Soviets were holding out for the phrase "legitimate national rights" of the Palestinians and were unwilling to endorse the concept of "normal peaceful relations." Over the next several days the Soviets changed their stance, agreeing to drop the word "national," settling for "legitimate rights" and accepting "normal peaceful relations." For the United States, the only new formulation was that referring to "legitimate rights of the Palestinian people." Previously the Americans had spoken only of "legitimate interests" of the Palestinians. No one was quite sure what these subtle differences meant, but they had acquired great symbolic significance.

Another Round with the Foreign Ministers

Besides their talks with the Soviets, Vance and Carter continued to discuss procedural matters with the Middle East parties. Vance met with Dayan on September 26. The Israeli foreign minister was somewhat uneasy about the idea of "not well-known" PLO members being at Geneva. It mattered, he said, how well known they were, and in any case they would have to be identified as members of the Jordanian delegation. Dayan seemed to be backing up a bit, and the Americans assumed that Begin was pulling on the reins.

Atherton and the U.S. ambassador to Egypt, Hermann F. Eilts, also met with Fahmy on two occasions to review the American draft of an Egyptian-Israeli peace treaty. Fahmy convinced the Americans to refer specifically to the internationally recognized border that had existed before 1967 as the final boundary between Egypt and Israel.[31]

Although much of the focus in late September was on Israel, Egypt, and the Soviet Union, Vance and Carter also met with Jordan's able foreign minister, Abd al-Hamid Sharaf. His advice was for the Americans to concentrate more on Palestinian rights than on who should represent the Palestinians. He flatly ruled out the possibility of including the PLO in Jordan's delegation to Geneva, which reinforced the American view that only a unified Arab delegation that included Palestinians in their own right could overcome the problem of Palestinian representation.

On September 28 Carter held a cordial meeting with Sharaf in which the Jordanian clearly spelled out his ideas on substance and procedures. The Palestinian question should be dealt with at Geneva by all the parties. Jordan favored a transitional arrangement under international authority, leading to a referendum in which the Palestinians could choose independence or association with Jordan. Autonomy under Israeli occupation, as proposed by Begin, was rejected outright.

Carter expressed sympathy with Sharaf's views, but said that Geneva would help to mobilize international opinion against the intransigent parties. Although he was sometimes tempted to say "to hell with it," he thought all parties should now go to Geneva and hope for the best. Letting his irritation show more than usual, Carter said the Arabs had to find some solution among themselves for the question of Palestinian representation, subject only to the constraint that Israel would not sit down with well-known PLO figures. The president then stated that some issues would have to be negotiated bilaterally, such as borders, and that if the Arabs insisted on the whole delegation dealing with such matters, "that would cause me to be completely frustrated and I wouldn't want to spend more time on it." Only the Palestinian question was an appropriate one for multilateral negotiations.

---

31. Fahmy, *Negotiating for Peace*, pp. 229–31, accurately summarizes the American draft but gets the date wrong. He received the draft on September 23, not September 25.

As the meeting came to an end, Carter showed Sharaf a draft of the U.S.-Soviet communiqué that was nearing completion. Fahmy and Dayan were also shown drafts at about the same time.[32]

Just as the U.S.-Soviet declaration was reaching completion, the United States also circulated a draft statement on procedures for Geneva.[33] This document called for a unified Arab delegation, including Palestinians who might be "not well-known members of the PLO," for purposes of convening the Geneva conference. After the plenary session, talks would take place bilaterally, except discussions about the West Bank and Gaza, which would be dealt with by a committee consisting of Israel, Jordan, Egypt, and the representatives of the Palestinians.

In the midst of all this diplomatic activity, the United States gave little thought to how it might make use of the nearly completed U.S.-Soviet communiqué. On technical grounds the draft was acceptable to Carter and Vance, both of whom felt the United States should be prepared to go on record in support of Palestinian rights if the Soviets would agree to normal peaceful relations as the goal of the negotiations. The Americans did not think of the communiqué as a complete statement of the U.S. position, but rather as a document codifying those points on which the United States and the Soviet Union agreed on the eve of the Geneva conference. Insofar as the document had a strategic purpose, it was designed to squeeze the Syrians and PLO, both of whom were quibbling over procedures.

The October 1, 1977, U.S.-Soviet Communiqué

With these points in mind, Carter authorized the release of the document on October 1, 1977. The key paragraph read as follows:

The United States and the Soviet Union believe that, within the framework of a comprehensive settlement of the Middle East problem, all specific questions of

32. In a memorandum I wrote to Brzezinski on September 29, I warned that we were planning to show Dayan the draft of the U.S.-Soviet statement before reaching full agreement with the Soviets. This would magnify the importance of any changes that might subsequently be made. For example, we were considering a change of language from Palestinian "interests" to "rights." "I'm afraid it may be too late to do much about this, but you may be hearing more about this later, so I wanted you to know what is happening."

33. In another memorandum to Brzezinski, dated October 1, 1977, I urged that we drop the formulation "not well-known PLO members" from our draft working paper on procedures for the Geneva conference. No one liked it. I also reported that Dayan had again said that Geneva was mostly a facade and that our main effort should be to promote secret contacts with Sadat, while freezing Fahmy out of the picture. Egypt would not be able to sign a separate peace, according to Dayan, but progress could be made in secret talks.

the settlement should be resolved, including such key issues as withdrawal of Israeli Armed Forces from territories occupied in the 1967 conflict; the resolution of the Palestinian question, including insuring the legitimate rights of the Palestinian people; termination of the state of war and establishment of normal peaceful relations on the basis of mutual recognition of the principles of sovereignty, territorial integrity, and political independence.[See appendix B for the full text.]

Neither Carter nor Vance had done much to cover the president's political flanks in advance of this statement. Congress had not been fully consulted. The press had not been given background briefings. The American Jewish leadership had not been contacted. Dayan, however, had been given a draft on September 29, and therefore the Israelis knew what was coming and had time to put their friends on notice. As a result, an otherwise peaceful Saturday erupted into controversy, accusations, and recriminations. It seemed to be less the words in the document that offended the friends of Israel than the fact the Soviets had been brought so prominently into the picture. Neoconservatives, which included Republicans and Democrats, were both pro-Israeli and anti-Soviet, and they took the lead in attacking the communiqué. Carter's moves were just what they opposed. Liberal Democrats were also against the statement, primarily because of its appearance of pressing Israel too hard on the Palestinian issue.[34]

Sadat's Reaction

If there was any consolation for the president after October 1, it came from the fact that the Syrians, and not only the Israelis, were squirming, and that President Sadat was reported to have termed the statement a "brilliant maneuver."[35] Presumably Sadat was reacting positively to what he saw as an attempt to pressure the Syrians, who at that point were his main nemesis. He had at times shown some concern about a Soviet role, though always saying the Soviets should be allowed to save face. But his real fear was that the Syrians would be in a position to impede his talks with the Israelis.

By the time of the October 1 statement, Sadat had already set up a secret channel to the Israelis and was certain that talks could take place

---

34. Brzezinski, *Power and Principle*, p. 110, does admit that more could have been done to prepare the way domestically for the statement. Carter and Vance defend the statement on substance and say little about the adverse political fallout. See Carter, *Keeping Faith*, p. 293; and Vance, *Hard Choices*, pp. 191–92.

35. See the letter written by Ambassador Hermann Eilts to the *New York Times*, January 12, 1982.

directly if necessary. But he still wanted the PLO to endorse the negotiating process, since that would relieve him of any charge that he was abandoning the Palestinian issue. So he was pleased to see in the U.S.-Soviet statement a strong statement on Palestinian rights and a call for Palestinian participation in the Geneva conference.[36]

It has often been said that Sadat's decision to go to Jerusalem was a direct response to the U.S.-Soviet communiqué. Such comments usually come from Israeli sources, and probably Sadat at some time gave that explanation to the Israelis. But he makes no such statement in his autobiography, and other Egyptians who were involved in the talks at the time have denied it.[37]

Sadat's concerns at the time of the U.S.-Soviet communiqué were perhaps best captured in two highly sensitive oral communications that he conveyed to President Carter. On October 1, before seeing the final text of the communiqué but after receiving Fahmy's preliminary report, Sadat said he was generally pleased with what Fahmy had told him of his talks in Washington. He did say, however, that he sensed that Carter was modifying his view on how Geneva should function. Instead of going to Geneva just to sign, Carter now was talking of a certain phase of the negotiations actually taking place there. Sadat again urged a phase of preparatory talks before going to Geneva to complete the details.

Sadat's message then acknowledged the American procedural proposals for Geneva, indicating that Sadat was ready to agree with them. But if the question of Palestinian representation could not be solved as the United States was proposing, Egypt would agree to include Palestinians in the Egyptian delegation. Syria and Jordan would protest, but Sadat would handle the situation provided Carter took into account the need to establish a Palestinian state, which should be linked to Jordan. As an alternative, Sadat repeated his suggestion that the assistant to the secretary general of the Arab League could represent the Palestinians at Geneva. Finally, Sadat said that negotiations in New York modeled on the Rhodes talks of 1949 would be suitable for the pre-Geneva phase.

Two days later Sadat sent another private oral message to Carter, this time in full knowledge of the U.S.-Soviet communiqué. He stated simply that Yasir Arafat had just agreed that the head of the Palestinian delegation

---

36. Fahmy, *Negotiating for Peace*, pp. 234–36, details his generally positive reaction to the communiqué.

37. See Indyk, *"To the Ends of the Earth,"* pp. 41–43, for a review of the evidence.

in the unified Arab delegation to the Geneva conference would be an American professor of Palestinian origin.[38]

These messages strongly suggest that Sadat was not alarmed by the U.S.-Soviet communiqué per se. He was, however, still uneasy about any Geneva conference at which actual negotiations would take place before agreement had been reached on a generally accepted framework. He had always insisted that a prior phase of talks should take place so that Geneva would be used largely for signing. Insofar as Geneva had value, it was to bring the Palestinians into the peace process, forcing them to assume some responsibility for their own fate and releasing Egypt from the charge of making a separate peace with Israel. The question of Palestinian representation was uppermost in Sadat's mind as he communicated with Carter in the first days of October. And he had reason to believe he had found a formula for Palestinian representation at Geneva that would be acceptable to the PLO, to the United States, and to Israel.

Whatever doubts Sadat may have had about the American strategy in early October were greatly increased by Carter's apparent backing down in the face of Israeli pressure after the dispute over the U.S.-Soviet communiqué. The immediate cause for this perception was the apparent outcome of a lengthy talk between Carter and Dayan in New York on October 4.

POLITICS TO THE FORE

On October 4, 1977, President Carter spent most of the day dealing with the aftermath of the U.S.-Soviet communiqué. As previously scheduled, he addressed the U.N. General Assembly, using the occasion to reassure Israel that there had been no change in basic policy. He also met with Egyptian Foreign Minister Fahmy, and then spent most of the evening with Israeli Foreign Minister Dayan. In retrospect, October 4 stands out as an important day in the evolution of the American strategy aimed at comprehensive peace negotiations. On that day domestic political considerations came explicitly to the fore and clearly affected the public expression of U.S. policy, with consequences unforeseen by the American side.

Carter's speech to the United Nations said little that was new, but it did serve to reassure the Israelis and their friends that the fundamentals

38. Fahmy, *Negotiating for Peace*, p. 252. Fahmy says Arafat had told Sadat that Edward Said, a professor at Columbia University and a member of the Palestine National Council, could represent the Palestinians at Geneva.

of U.S. policy had not changed. When he spoke of the Middle East, Carter emphasized the need for "binding peace treaties" reached through negotiations based on U.N. Resolutions 242 and 338. He maintained that the American commitment to Israel's security was unquestionable, and he put his concern for Palestinian "legitimate rights" in the context of his broader commitment to human rights. Then he added, much to the pleasure of the Israelis, that how these rights were to be defined was up to the parties to decide in negotiations, not for the United States to dictate. The United States would not try to impose its views on the parties.[39]

At noon Carter met for an hour with Fahmy for talks that were described publicly in positive terms. Carter noted in his diary that Fahmy brought a letter from Sadat "urging that nothing be done to prevent Israel and Egypt from negotiating directly, with our serving as an intermediary either before or after the Geneva Conference is convened."[40]

Carter's most important meeting of the day took place with Dayan at 7 p.m. For more than three hours the two men argued and debated and negotiated. Even then, it took two more hours of talks between Vance and Dayan in the early morning hours to reach agreement on a number of points.

The American objective in these talks was to overcome the apparent obstacle raised by the U.S.-Soviet communiqué and to secure Israeli agreement to proposals on procedures for the Geneva conference. At this point the formal Israeli position was that Palestinians could be at Geneva only as members of the Jordanian delegation. The issue of the West Bank would be discussed with Jordan alone, and the issue of Gaza would be discussed with Egypt. Israel would accept a unified Arab delegation only for the opening sessions of Geneva. Unless the Israelis made some changes in these positions, Geneva would never be held with Arab participation.

---

39. "United Nations: Address before the General Assembly, October 4, 1977," *Public Papers: Carter, 1977*, vol. 2, pp. 1720–21.

40. Carter, *Keeping Faith*, p. 294. Carter appears to be referring to the two oral messages Sadat sent him, dated October 1 and October 3. In them Sadat does talk of the United States playing the role of intermediary. In an interview with me on May 22, 1985, President Carter said he could not recall if Sadat's message specifically mentioned the importance of not preventing direct negotiations, or if Fahmy made the point orally, or if Carter inferred it from the message. Fahmy makes no mention of this meeting, but goes into considerable detail about a meeting on October 5, 1977, when he claims Carter urged him to meet secretly with Dayan. There is no American record of such a meeting. See Fahmy, *Negotiating for Peace*, pp. 236–38.

Jordan would not agree that the Palestinians be represented inside their delegation; the Syrians would not agree to any of the Israeli conditions.

When the talks with Dayan began, procedural issues were not at the top of the agenda. Instead, Carter said he wanted to restore harmony to the U.S.-Israeli relationship. Dayan agreed that this was the moment to seek a breakthrough in negotiations, especially with Egypt, but that it could not be done on the basis of the U.S.-Soviet communiqué, which was totally unacceptable to Israel. If Israel was not obliged to approve it, the joint statement need not block the way to Geneva.

Dayan then turned to the politics of the problem. He described the mood in Israel as terrible. He asked Carter if the president could say publicly that all past agreements between the United States and Israel would be kept. He hinted that Israel might publish these agreements to help reassure Israeli public opinion. He also asked Carter to say that 242 did not require Israel to withdraw to the 1967 borders or accept a Palestinian state. Elaborating on this point, Dayan asked Carter for assurances that the United States would not pressure Israel to accept a Palestinian state, even in federation with Jordan.

Carter hesitated, saying he had no intention of using pressure but did not want to make such a statement. Dayan responded that he would have to say that he had asked for such reassurances and that the president had refused.[41]

Carter turned the discussion to the question of Palestinian representation, maintaining that the Israeli position was too rigid. Here Dayan began to show some flexibility, no doubt going beyond what Begin had authorized. In effect, he said that Israel would accept Palestinians at Geneva who were not members of the Jordanian delegation, and that they could include PLO sympathizers and even PLO members from the West Bank and Gaza, provided Israel was now dealing with them. He also modified the Israeli position by saying that the future of the West Bank and Gaza could be discussed in a multilateral setting that included Israel, Jordan, Egypt, and the Palestinians.

Carter left for a previously scheduled dinner after about an hour. Vance continued the discussion, and Dayan showed imagination in dealing with the question of Palestinian representation. A secret understanding was reached that Israel would be informed in advance who the Palestinians at Geneva would be and could use "reasonable screening" to ensure that

41. Brzezinski, *Power and Principle*, p. 108, gives details of the meeting and uses the word "blackmail" in relation to this tactic of Dayan's.

known PLO members were not included. With this sensitive point nearly agreed upon, Dayan had ceded on the issue of having Palestinians at Geneva as part of a unified delegation with essentially the same status as the other Arab participants. In particular, he had agreed for the first time that the future of the West Bank and Gaza could be discussed with Palestinian representatives, not just with Egypt and Jordan.[42]

Having shown some flexibility on Palestinian representation, Dayan returned to the question of U.S. pressure. Vance assured him that the president would say the United States would not use military or economic aid as a form of pressure on Israel.

At this point Carter rejoined the talks. Vance summarized his understanding with Dayan on Palestinian representation. Carter replied that Israel could not have a veto over who the Palestinians would be, but that the United States would inform Israel in advance, and if the names were not acceptable, Israel could always refuse to participate. Dayan specifically said that Palestinians from the West Bank, such as the mayors, some of whom were members of the PLO, could participate without causing any problem for Israel.

Dayan added that Israel did not want to miss a chance of peace with Egypt because of possible objections from Syria. He also warned that the United States should be open to the idea of less than a full peace agreement. It would be hard for Sadat to sign a treaty with Israel, he said, while Syria was out of the picture. A three-quarters peace might be attainable. Carter should not hold out for all or nothing. The Soviets should not be part of the process, and the United States should try to help get secret negotiations going at the head-of-state level.

The discussion turned to the Syrian position, and Dayan expressed his long-standing pessimism about progress on that front. For Sadat, recovery of Sinai would be a major achievement, whereas Asad would need to point to a Palestinian state to justify his participation in peace talks with Israel. Carter replied that he would do what he could to help get either an overall agreement or individual agreements. Dayan replied that the future was with Egypt. The other parties were not ready.

42. Dayan, *Breakthrough*, p. 71, notes that this was a change of position and that Begin was not happy to learn about it. Some have even maintained that Begin, who was in the hospital at the time, suffered a relapse on reading Dayan's report of the meeting. See Benziman, *Prime Minister under Siege*, pp. 27–32, for a detailed account of the October 4 meeting. Benziman observes that Dayan felt he had neutralized the U.S.-Soviet communiqué, but at the price of accepting the Palestinians as a full party to the negotiations. The Palestinian genie, says Benziman, was out of the bottle and Dayan knew it.

Besides, if one wheel of a car was removed, it could not be driven. If Egypt was out of the conflict, there would be no war. Carter asked about the Golan Heights, and Dayan hinted it might be possible for Israel to make a distinction between sovereignty and security needs, implying that Israel could forgo the first if it achieved the second. Carter raised the possibility of guarantees, and Dayan responded that Israel would be interested in being treated like a NATO ally and would even offer the United States bases in Israel.

At that point Carter must have felt encouraged by the direction of the talks. He abruptly shifted from the substance of the Arab-Israeli conflict to the other major problem that had been on his mind for some time. "Let's talk politics," he said to Dayan. Carter felt he was in a difficult spot because of the attacks on his policies by American Jews and Congress. He said that because he did not want to counterattack, he was vulnerable. It was important for the world to see that the United States and Israel were working together.

Dayan seemed to sense an opening. He replied that it was possible to reach an agreement. Israel could go along with the procedures that Carter and Vance had outlined. In return, Carter should say that all previous agreements with Israel remained in force and that there would be no imposed settlement and no pressure in the form of cuts in economic or military aid. Israel should be free to object to a Palestinian state, and the United States should say that Israel did not have to withdraw to the 1967 lines or accept the U.S.-Soviet joint communiqué. Dayan could then tell the American Jews that there was an agreement and they would be happy. But if he was obliged to say that Israel would have to deal with the PLO or a Palestinian state, then there would be screaming in the United States and in Israel. Carter saw the thrust of Dayan's remarks and said a confrontation would not be good for Israel either.[43]

Dayan again said that unless an agreement was reached, he would have to be very critical of the U.S.-Soviet communiqué. Carter asked how this should be handled in public. Should there be a joint statement or separate statements? Secretary Vance argued that Israel should issue its own statement, but the United States should not be directly associated with it. Dayan was unhappy with this suggestion, observing that it would be bad if the United States did not say something that night. Carter hesitated, and then sided with Dayan. Vance was told to work out a joint

43. Brzezinski, *Power and Principle*, p. 109, gives the text of this part of the exchange.

statement with Dayan. Having made this essentially political judgment, Carter left. Two hours later a joint statement was issued:

The U.S. and Israel agree that Security Council Resolutions 242 and 338 remain the agreed basis for the resumption of the Geneva Peace Conference and that all the understandings and agreements between them on this subject remain in force.

Proposals for removing remaining obstacles to reconvening the Geneva Conference were developed. Foreign Minister Dayan will consult his Government on the results of these discussions. Secretary Vance will discuss these proposals with the other parties to the Geneva Conference.

Acceptance of the Joint U.S.-U.S.S.R. Statement of October 1, 1977, by the parties is not a prerequisite for the reconvening and conduct of the Geneva Conference.[44]

Besides this joint statement, the United States and Israel had reached agreement, subject to formal approval by both governments, on the text of a working paper to settle the procedural issues in the way of convening the Geneva conference.[45] This document was not published at the time, since Vance wanted to consult with the Arab parties on it, but it quickly became known as the U.S.-Israeli Working Paper, even though the Israeli cabinet did not formally approve it until October 11. Dayan and Vance also reached agreement on a "minute" that summarized their discussion on how Israel would exercise the right to screen names of Palestinian representatives to the conference and could withhold its participation in the conference if persons to whom it objected were present in the Palestinian delegation.

In one sense, the Carter-Vance-Dayan marathon meeting could be seen as moving the process of negotiations forward. Several sticky procedural issues were resolved, by and large on terms that should have been acceptable to the Arab parties. The revised working paper contained a provision for Palestinian participation both in a unified Arab delegation and in the working group on the future of the West Bank and Gaza. But the October 4 session could not be judged by such criteria, not in light of the highly charged political atmosphere in which the talks took place.

The simple fact was that the United States and Israel entered the talks that night on the verge of a major confrontation and emerged seven hours later with an agreement in hand. This was the message both to the

44. "Geneva Peace Conference on the Middle East: United States-Israel Joint Statement Issued following a Meeting between the President and Israeli Foreign Minister Moshe Dayan, October 5, 1977," *Public Papers: Carter, 1977*, vol. 2, p. 1728.

45. Dayan, *Breakthrough*, pp. 70–71.

Israelis, and their American friends, and to the Arabs. Both sensed that something important had happened and that Carter had backed down in the face of domestic and Israeli pressures. Carter's retreat, if that in fact is an appropriate term in the circumstances, was not so much on substantive issues as on the highly charged matter of the meaning of the U.S.-Soviet communiqué. Although Carter never wavered in thinking that he had held firm, the widespread perception, caused by the joint statement with Israel, was that the United States had abandoned the position it had just worked out with the Soviets.

Brzezinski at the time worried about the impression left with the Israelis that the president was susceptible to pressure.[46] According to informed Egyptian sources, Sadat drew the same conclusion from the meeting and soon began his search for alternatives to heavy reliance on the United States to produce the breakthrough he was seeking.

CONCLUSION

In the two months after Vance's return from the Middle East in August 1977, the Carter administration was trying to pursue its broad objective of promoting Arab-Israeli negotiations through a series of increasingly complex diplomatic moves. The American side seemed to feel the need to knock on almost every door in the hope that one would be opened. Draft peace treaties were being drawn up. Positive signals were being given to Egyptians and Israelis about their secret meetings. Detailed discussions of procedural matters were being held with all parties. Contacts were taking place with the PLO through intermediaries. And moves were under way to develop a basis for a joint U.S.-Soviet invitation to Geneva as a way of cutting through much of the seeming irrelevancy of the procedural debate. Not surprisingly some of these steps got tangled up with others, thus giving off signals to the Middle East parties of confusion and a loss of stamina on the part of the United States.

During this critical period Carter made two major misjudgments. First, he paid little attention to ensuring that domestic support for his Middle East initiative could be sustained. Carter had sensed during the summer that the American Jewish community was growing fearful of his approach, whatever its feelings about the Begin government might have been. He had taken steps to shore up his base of support and had gone to great lengths to be cordial to Begin in their first meeting. But at the same time

---

46. Brzezinski, *Power and Principle*, p. 109.

he was willing to authorize sensitive efforts to woo the PLO and to involve the Soviets in the negotiations, both of which were anathema to Israel and its supporters. To make these moves without having covered his political flanks was risky indeed. Carter seemed surprisingly unaware of the problem until it hit him full force on October 1. By then he felt he needed overt Israeli help to deal with his own domestic problem, a situation that gave Dayan great leverage in the negotiations. For the first time Carter gave clear priority to domestic political concerns by ordering Vance to issue a joint statement with Dayan as a way of quelling domestic political opposition.

Second, Carter misjudged Sadat's relations with the other Arab parties. From their very first meeting Sadat had indicated his skepticism about Geneva as a forum for actual negotiations. His main concern seemed to be that the Israelis would drag out the talks endlessly unless there was some prior understanding on a framework. He was also outspoken in his warnings that the Syrians, in particular, would seek to limit his freedom of maneuver. In August he tried to steer the United States away from Geneva as an end in itself by giving Vance a draft of a peace treaty. In September he opened a secret channel to the Israelis without telling Carter about it. Then in early October Sadat sent two important messages to Carter. He was still in favor of Geneva as a way of getting the Palestinians into the negotiations, but he insisted on a preparatory phase of talks under U.S. auspices.

Sadat's frustrations were only partly appreciated by the American side. To have accepted his position would have meant delaying Geneva, perhaps indefinitely, leaving Carter with little to show for his intensive involvement with the Middle East crisis. So Geneva became more of an end in itself, to get negotiations into a new phase in which the parties themselves would carry more of the burden. Once this shift in emphasis was made in August, it meant that several procedural problems would have to be resolved and the most intractable parties to the Geneva conference would have to be accommodated, at least to some extent. Otherwise the talks would never get off the ground. The Americans therefore tried to get the PLO to accept 242 and emphasized Palestinian participation in the Geneva conference.

In the end, a formula was in fact found on Palestinian participation that could have been acceptable to everyone, but in the process Carter took a beating on the home front. At nearly every press conference he had to defend himself against the charge that he was breaking U.S.

commitments to Israel not to deal with the PLO. In reality, he was adhering to the letter of those agreements and probably interpreted them more rigidly than others would have done. But he got blamed for chasing after the PLO anyway, and had little to show for it. The domestic costs were not offset by any visible gain. He would probably have done as well in Arab eyes to have advocated Palestinian rights, as he did in the joint U.S.-Soviet communiqué, without at that stage showing such an intense interest in getting the PLO to accept 242.

The PLO's acceptance of 242 might have meant something to an Israeli Labor party government, as former Foreign Minister Yigal Allon had earlier indicated, but to Begin it had no significance at all. After all, Begin's goal was to keep the West Bank, not to find a moderate Arab partner, whether Jordanian or Palestinian, with which to share it. In some ways a PLO wedded to a radical policy was preferable to a moderate PLO. At least Arafat would then not be dealing directly with Carter.

In hindsight, the U.S.-Soviet communiqué was also a mistake, especially in the way it was handled. The substance of the document was not exceptional and might have even served a useful purpose with the Syrians and PLO; Carter and Vance have defended it on those grounds. But it was a political document, and the administration should have recognized that it would not be judged by its content alone. The fact of the joint statement was more important than its words, and yet that point was not well understood within the administration. There was a curiously apolitical attitude toward the document. It was not even taken seriously until it became an issue of domestic political debate. It was just one more of the doors on which the United States was knocking, and little concern was expressed about its likely consequences.

Several lessons can be drawn from this phase of the negotiations. First, as strategies evolve in the face of new realities, there is a danger of losing control of the diplomatic process. Eclecticism creeps in as new ideas are suggested before old ones have exhausted themselves. For example, the U.S.-Soviet communiqué complicated the quiet discussions that had been under way for some time, aimed at devising acceptable procedures for convening Geneva. But administrations rarely sense until it is too late that one strand of policy is getting in the way of another. It requires the tightest discipline from the top on down not to let things get out of hand as the negotiations move toward the moment of truth, when parties have to make concrete decisions.

Second, the parties to negotiations will be anxious to test the United

States on its diplomatic skill, toughness, and resolve as the time of decision approaches. The right position on substance or procedures is not enough to win the confidence of the parties. From the evidence now available, each of the Middle East players drew conclusions about the American position in September and early October primarily based on perceptions of Carter's strength and determination. His private admissions to Arab leaders that he had to take American Jewish opinion into account were seen not as admirable signs of candor, but as expressions of weakness. Statements that would have passed unnoticed earlier in the year were parsed for subtle meanings. Everyone was testing the positions of the other parties, especially of Washington, before making final commitments to Geneva or to anything else. This fact was not adequately appreciated by Carter. Had it been, the president and his advisers would have been more careful about what they said and how they said it.

Third, because any initiative in the Middle East is bound to be controversial, it makes little sense to launch initiatives that cannot be sustained. But having taken the flak for adopting controversial postions, a president gains nothing by backing down. This simply conveys an impression of vulnerability and vacillation, which in itself is destructive to presidential authority. It is bad enough to make mistakes that have costly political consequences, but it does little good to try to recoup public esteem by appearing to cave in under pressure.

Finally, and perhaps most important, a president should be careful about asking a foreign leader to help him solve a domestic political problem. That gives the other party enormous leverage and legitimizes its intervention in American political affairs. Inviting Dayan to "talk politics" on October 4 signaled a weakness in Carter's position. Dayan exploited the opportunity brilliantly and succeeded simultaneously in winning Carter's gratitude and in sowing suspicions between the United States and the Arabs at a crucial moment. Although Dayan could not guess what the result of his efforts would be, he must have known on the morning of October 5 that he had played a weak hand with consummate political skill. Having done so, he was easing the United States away from center stage and giving Sadat strong reasons to deal directly with the Israelis.

CHAPTER SIX

Changing Course

The first week of October 1977 proved to be a crucial turning point in Carter's approach to Arab-Israeli peace. What began as an attempt to override procedural obstacles and to put some pressure on the Syrians to drop their objections to Geneva ended with a "working paper" that was widely seen by the Arabs as a retreat from previously held American positions under pressure of domestic pro-Israeli opinion.

The U.S.-Soviet communiqué of October 1, while encouraging to some of the Arab parties, had alarmed the Israelis and their supporters and had led directly to the Carter-Dayan reconciliation on October 4. At that meeting Foreign Minister Dayan made an important tactical concession on Palestinian representation at Geneva, to restore the impression of U.S.-Israeli harmony and thereby nullify the adverse reaction in Israel to the U.S.-Soviet communiqué. It proved to be a brilliant move. Carter credited Dayan with flexibility and began to vent his frustrations on the Arab parties, especially the Syrians.

To make sense as a multinational forum, Geneva had to include both Syrian and Palestinian representatives. Somewhat surprisingly, the Palestinian part of the procedural puzzle seemed closer to resolution than ever in early October. The Israelis, or at least Dayan, had agreed that there could be a single Arab delegation at Geneva, which would include Palestinians, some of whom might be PLO supporters from the West Bank and Gaza. Sadat, claiming to speak for Yasir Arafat, said the Palestinians could be represented by an American professor of Palestinian origin, an idea that Dayan had found intriguing.

If the Palestinian role at Geneva was taking form, the same could not be said of the Syrian role. President Asad had insisted all along on a joint Arab front to do the actual negotiating with Israel, so that Syria would have an effective veto over any separate Egyptian moves. Syria also wanted to be involved in any discussions on the Palestinian problem. In late September the American side had tried to assuage some of the Syrian doubts by noting that nothing could keep the Arab parties from coordinating their positions at Geneva if they chose to do so and that the various working groups could periodically report back to the plenary session. In the working paper that emerged from the Carter-Dayan meeting of October 4, however, no mention was made of a role for the plenary other than to convene the conference. Reference to the PLO was dropped. And most galling to the Syrians, they were the only party left out of the discussion of the future of the West Bank and Gaza.

Sadat also had his doubts about the drift of events, but it was not so much the U.S.-Soviet communiqué or the working paper that concerned him. Rather, it was the rush to Geneva as an end in itself, coupled with the realization that Carter was under intense domestic pressure. Until this time Sadat had counted heavily on U.S. efforts to produce some prior understanding on basic principles, some frame of reference, so that negotiations would be held primarily to work out details, not to resolve fundamental issues. From October 5 on, Sadat had to rethink his strategy. Also, his relations with Syria were becoming increasingly strained.

By mid-October, then, the Israelis were in a relatively comfortable position. The pressure from Washington was off, and Dayan's achievement in New York had won the endorsement of the Israeli cabinet. The Israelis relaxed, but took no further initiatives. Meanwhile the Syrians gave voice to their doubts and skepticism, choosing to lecture Sadat on his duties as an Arab patriot, while doing little to convince Washington to take their concerns seriously. Sadat, by contrast, was restless, looking for ways out of the impasse. And Carter, who was increasingly frustrated, could think of nothing new to offer and was adamantly opposed to renegotiating the working paper to try to make it more acceptable to the Arabs.

In this setting something was bound to happen. And it did. In late October Sadat apparently decided he would go to Jerusalem to talk directly to the Israelis. This decision ushered in a new phase of the diplomacy, initially relegating the United States to the sidelines. Egypt and Israel began to move swiftly toward a bilateral agreement, as other Arabs stood by in impotent anger. For three months the United States, which had been pushing and prodding and taking most of the initiatives, was reduced to the role of little more than spectator. Then suddenly, in mid-January 1978, Sadat called a halt to his direct dealings with the Israelis and sought once again to bring the United States back to center stage, this time not as impresario for Geneva, but rather as broker of an Egyptian-Israeli agreement within a framework of general principles for a comprehensive agreement.

For the Carter administration this was a period of serious reassessment, the most intensive policy review since the initial discussions at the outset of the administration—a process that commonly takes place toward the end of a president's first year in office. The result was a significant shift in strategy, one that ultimately led to the Camp David negotiations and the Egyptian-Israeli peace treaty. But the change did not come immediately or easily.

Basic policy revision is a complex process, even in the face of major domestic and international pressures. Strong-minded men do not easily change their views, nor do they readily recognize that their policies have reached a dead end. But over time strategic adjustments can take place, as the period from October 1977 to February 1978 demonstrates. The Carter administration finally recognized some of the mistakes of the first year and adopted a more realistic, less ambitious set of guidelines for the Middle East in the second year.

CLINGING TO GENEVA

Some observers, mostly Arabs, have argued that everything was moving smoothly toward a convening of the Geneva conference when Sadat suddenly broke ranks and declared his intention to go to Jerusalem.[1] Others, mostly Israelis and Americans, believe that Geneva would have been impossibly rigid as a forum for real negotiations and that Sadat saved the peace process by circumventing Geneva.

Within the Carter administration the conclusion had been reached that Geneva, with all its likely imperfections, was a necessary step if more than an Egyptian-Israeli agreement was to be achieved. No one expected a multilateral conference to move easily to the much-touted comprehensive peace. Indeed, many believed that Geneva might break down shortly after it was convened and that a rocky period of negotiations might well lie ahead. But the goal was to get a process started, not to sit in Geneva, and everyone on the American side was convinced that little additional progress could be made until the parties to the conflict had committed themselves to negotiations. Once that had occurred, different channels could be used to move forward on substantive issues.

The hope was that if the Syrians and Palestinians showed up for at least the opening sessions, they would have little incentive to try to block progress on the Egyptian-Israeli front. If all worked well, Egypt and

1. Ismail Fahmy, *Negotiating for Peace in the Middle East*, pp. 215–32.

Israel would be the pacesetters, dragging the others along in their wake. In the end, this view was overoptimistic, and it seriously underestimated the depth of suspicion between Sadat and Asad, as well as the Syrian determination to retain control over the Palestinian issue.

After the meeting in New York with Dayan, Secretary Vance had worried about the Arab perception of U.S.-Israeli collusion. He was sensitive to the complaint that the United States had abandoned the October 1 U.S.-Soviet communiqué and had capitulated to Israeli pressures. He tried to argue against the idea that a U.S.-Israeli working paper was being presented to the Arabs on a take-it-or-leave-it basis. He genuinely felt there was no reason to apologize for the content of the communiqué, nor did he think the procedures outlined in the working paper were unfair, especially since they acknowledged for the first time the right of the Palestinians to be full participants in the conference. He was also heartened by the near agreement on how Palestinians would be selected for the conference.

On October 13 the draft of the working paper was finally sent to Egypt, Syria, and Jordan. Two days earlier, the Israeli cabinet had approved it. Not surprisingly, the Arab parties were reluctant to accept a document that was widely, if inaccurately, labeled the U.S.-Israeli Working Paper, and that Dayan had already publicly revealed to the Knesset. More haggling seemed inevitable.

Sadat wrote to Carter on October 19 and agreed to the original American draft of the working paper of late September, but not to the more recent version. He wanted some mention of the PLO as part of the unified Arab delegation and suggested a few other changes that seemed to reflect Egyptian Foreign Minister Fahmy's views.[2] Carter reacted negatively to this message. He did not want to go through another round of arguing over procedures. He felt that whatever differences remained should be sorted out at the conference itself. And he felt that Sadat was raising unnecessary quibbles.

Every Friday morning Carter would meet with his top foreign policy advisers—Vance, Brown, Mondale, Brzezinski, and usually Hamilton Jordan. On October 21, with Sadat's disappointing message in hand, the Friday breakfast group considered what to do. Carter decided to make a direct and very personal appeal to Sadat. He would send a brief

2. Ibid., pp. 243–44, gives the text of this important letter.

handwritten note to Sadat urging him to help break the impasse. During their meeting the previous April, Sadat had told the president to call on him whenever he needed help. Referring to that conversation, Carter said the moment had come. He pressed Sadat to endorse publicly the American proposals for Geneva.[3] The full text of the letter was as follows:

Dear President Sadat,

When we met privately in The White House, I was deeply impressed and grateful for your promise to me that, at a crucial moment, I could count on your support when obstacles arose in our common search for peace in the Middle East. We have reached such a moment, and I need your help.

Secretary Vance has provided clarifications to many of your questions regarding the procedures outlined in the United States working paper. There is adequate flexibility in the language to accommodate your concerns.

The time has now come to move forward, and your early public endorsement of our approach is extremely important — perhaps vital — in advancing all parties to Geneva.

This is a personal appeal for your support.

My very best wishes to you and your family.

Your friend,

Jimmy Carter[4]

To add some drama to the handwritten letter, Carter sealed it with wax and asked the Egyptian embassy to arrange to have it delivered by hand. (See pages 140–41 for a reproduction of the original letter.) Sadat later claimed that this letter started him thinking about his plan to go to Jerusalem. If so, it must have been because he shared Carter's frustration that the road to Geneva was being blocked by procedural wrangles and felt that the United States had no plan for overcoming the remaining obstacles. Carter's appeal may have indicated to Sadat that Carter could go no further, a conclusion that squared with the evidence of mounting domestic pressures that followed the October 1 communiqué. In his memoirs Sadat says as much. "What could the U.S.A. do? This was a subject that had to be dealt with, I thought, solely on the basis of the facts, and primarily the fact that President Carter's capacity for movement was governed by the current international situation. Furthermore, the

3. Jimmy Carter, *Keeping Faith*, p. 295; Anwar el-Sadat, *In Search of Identity*, pp. 301–04, refers to the importance of this letter, but gets the date wrong, placing it in late September instead of late October; and Fahmy, *Negotiating for Peace*, pp. 263–64, also refers to this letter, but mistakenly claims that it arrived about November 6.

4. I am grateful to President Carter for providing the text of this letter and giving me permission to reproduce it here.

October 21, 1977

Dear President Sadat,

When we met privately in
the White House, I was deeply
impressed and grateful for
your promise to me that, at
a crucial moment, I could
count on your support when
obstacles arose in our common
search for peace in the Middle
East. We have reached such
a moment, and I need your
help.

Secretary Vance has provided
clarifications to many of your
questions regarding the procedures
outlined in the United States
working paper. There is adequate
flexibility in the language to
accommodate your concerns.

WASHINGTON

The time has now come to move forward, and your early public endorsement of our approach is extremely important — perhaps vital — in advancing all parties to Geneva.

This is a personal appeal for your support.

My very best wishes to you and your family.

Your friend,

Jimmy Carter

extent of U.S. assistance in this connection was determined by the special relationship between the United States and Israel."[5]

In case there might be any misunderstanding of the president's letter, on October 22 U.S. Ambassador Hermann Eilts conveyed an oral message from Carter in response to Sadat's communication of October 19 seeking changes in the working paper. The United States would not agree to seek changes, Carter said. He reviewed the history of the document, arguing that it adequately protected the Arab position. While not explicitly including the PLO, it did not exclude them, and a procedure for selecting Palestinians who would be acceptable to all parties had been developed.[6]

A few days later Carter met in Washington with Saudi Foreign Minister Prince Saud bin Faisal. This was the last time Carter expressed his views directly to an Arab leader before Sadat's speech of November 9 in which the Egyptian president publicly announced his willingness to go to Jerusalem. As such, the meeting has particular importance for understanding the mood in the White House in late October.

Carter began by stating that Geneva was now necessary to break the stalemate. The parties should stop quarreling over details. Asad and Sadat were in deep disagreement. If the Arabs wanted to go to Geneva, they needed to sort out their own differences. No one would stop them from working closely together at Geneva, but the United States could not guarantee Arab unity. As for the working paper, Carter said the Arab parties should accept it the way it was and work out any remaining problems at Geneva.

Saud responded intelligently, spelling out the fears of the Syrians and the PLO. He explained why the Arabs were suspicious of the working paper and why they preferred the earlier version that had mentioned the PLO by name and had envisaged a role for the plenary session at Geneva.

Carter replied by saying that the PLO's role could not be explicitly mentioned in a document, but that Israeli Foreign Minister Dayan had indicated that PLO supporters in the West Bank and Gaza would be acceptable at Geneva. He criticized Syria for being too rigid and praised

5. Sadat, *In Search of Identity*, p. 304.

6. This same day, October 22, Sadat met with a Syrian envoy, Naji Jamil, who cast doubt on the ability and willingness of the United States to do anything to promote peace. See *Oktubar* (in Arabic), December 11, 1977, p. 6. See also *Al-Ahram*, November 27, 1977, as cited in Ibrahim Karawan, "Sadat on the Road to Jerusalem: Four Levels of Analysis," paper delivered to the Middle East Studies Association, Seattle, Washington, November 1981. According to other accounts, Jamil also lectured Sadat on his duty as an Arab nationalist, which greatly irritated the Egyptian president.

Dayan for having shown flexibility in their October 4 meeting. Carter said that nothing more could be done without Geneva. "The most difficult problem now is the lack of consensus among the Arabs."

Then Carter made one more offer to attract the Arab parties. If they would agree to accept the working paper and to go to Geneva on that basis, he would publicly state that the Palestinian question, the question of withdrawal, and the borders of peace must all be dealt with seriously if a comprehensive solution to the Arab-Israeli conflict were to be found. Saud said the idea was excellent, and the president promised to make such a statement.

On October 28, 1977, Carter sent an important message to Sadat; it was delivered to him the same day at the Cairo airport just as he was preparing to leave for a trip to Romania, Iran, and Saudi Arabia. In the letter Carter said that the effort to reach agreement on a working paper detailing procedures for the Geneva conference had gone far enough. " I do not frankly see any likelihood of reaching agreement on a paper acceptable to all parties nor do I believe that this is necessary." Carter suggested that any remaining problems could be worked out at Geneva.

Picking up on the promise he had made to Foreign Minister Saud, Carter said he understood the Arab concern that the Palestinian question would not be adequately addressed at Geneva. "In order to remove any doubts on this score, I am prepared, if the Arab side agrees to the course of action I am proposing in this letter, to make an unequivocal public statement that the Palestinian question, as well as the question of withdrawal and borders of peace, must be dealt with seriously at the conference with the aim of finding a comprehensive solution to all aspects of the Arab-Israeli conflict."

Carter concluded his letter by saying that the United States and the Soviet Union should now ask the U.N. Secretary General to invite all the parties to Geneva. The procedure used at the first session of the Geneva conference in December 1973 would be followed, which meant that neither superpower would be present in the negotiations at the subcommittee level.[7]

SADAT'S ROAD TO JERUSALEM

The pace of events now seemed to quicken. On October 31, 1977, the Egyptian ambassador, Ashraf Ghorbal, called the White House to say he

7. Most of the text of Carter's letter to Sadat of October 28, 1977, can be found in Fahmy, *Negotiating for Peace*, p. 246–49.

had a handwritten letter, complete with sealing wax, from Sadat to Carter. In it Sadat acknowledged Carter's recent appeal for help and promised a "bold step." Sadat's letter seems to have been sent before he had received Carter's message of October 28 and was meant to be a personal reply to the October 21 handwritten letter.

By the time this message from Sadat reached Washington, Sadat was already on his way to Bucharest. While in Romania, he apparently asked President Ceauşescu about Begin and was assured that Begin was a strong leader who would negotiate with Egypt in good faith. Sadat also reportedly raised with his foreign minister for the first time the possibility of his going to Jerusalem to address the Knesset. Fahmy and the other Egyptian advisers were reportedly shocked; Fahmy tried to dissuade the president by proposing as an alternative the idea of a multilateral conference, including all the permanent members of the U.N. Security Council, as well as the leaders of Israel, Egypt, Syria, Jordan, and the PLO, to be convened in East Jerusalem. He suggested that Egypt should simply issue invitations for such a superconference without any prior consultations, and if the conference took place, it would set the terms of reference for a subsequent convening of the Geneva talks. Sadat accepted the idea, but insisted on consulting with Carter first to make sure he would agree.[8]

On the evening of November 3, Sadat's message reached Washington. Only Carter, Vance, and Brzezinski were to see the message, according to Sadat. An answer was requested by November 5. Sadat referred to his October 31 handwritten note promising a "bold step." He spoke of the need to upgrade the level of the Geneva conference and to enlarge its membership. Sadat said he planned to outline his proposal in a speech to the Egyptian National Assembly on November 9. He then explained that he would propose a superconference in East Jerusalem. The text of an invitation was enclosed, along with four principles that should govern the conclusion of "peace treaties." In explaining the purpose of the conference, Fahmy had told Ambassador Eilts that it was intended to give momentum to the peace process and to take some of the domestic pressure off President Carter.

Carter and his top advisers reacted negatively to Sadat's proposal. The idea of inviting Soviet President Leonid I. Brezhnev and Chinese Premier Hua Guofeng, to say nothing of PLO Chairman Yasir Arafat, to East Jerusalem was a bit staggering. Brzezinski referred to the proposal as

8. Ibid., pp. 253–61.

"rather droll."[9] The Israelis would certainly have no part in it, and without their cooperation the idea was a dead letter.

Early on November 4 Carter met with Mondale, Vance, and Brzezinski to discuss the appropriate response to Sadat's message. One idea was for Carter to write to King Khalid of Saudi Arabia to ask that he use his influence with Syria to get President Asad to drop his objections to Geneva. After some careful redrafting by Carter, the letter was sent the next day.

On November 5 Carter sent a polite but negative letter to Sadat. He began by saying that after careful reflection he had concluded that Sadat's proposal might seriously complicate the search for Middle East peace. He urged Sadat to keep the focus on Geneva. In closing, he wrote: "Let me add that I am making intensive efforts to obtain agreement from all parties, and especially the Syrians, to recommend proposed procedures so that the Geneva conference can open soon."[10]

When Ambassador Eilts delivered this message to Sadat on November 5, Sadat was clearly disappointed. He nonetheless agreed not to call for the conference. He asked Eilts what the United States had to suggest as an alternative. Eilts had no answer.

Sadat then told Eilts that the Syrians were being difficult and that he was trying to get the Saudis to put pressure on them. Returning to a theme that had been much on his mind in recent weeks, Sadat said that he knew President Carter was under pro-Israeli pressure and that he would not add to Carter's troubles. He then urged that Carter ignore Syria, saying that Asad was simply "auctioneering." In conclusion, he repeated his belief that it was essential to have at least "agreed headlines" before Geneva convened.[11]

9. I am grateful to Zbigniew Brzezinski for allowing me to consult his diary notes for November 3–5, 1977, which provided much of the information here and in the following paragraph.

10. Fahmy, *Negotiating for Peace*, pp. 262–63, provides the text of most of the letter, except for the opening and closing lines cited here.

11. Carter, *Keeping Faith*, p. 296, says that on November 2 he called Sadat on the telephone to discuss the East Jerusalem conference proposal. This seems unlikely. Sadat on that day was in Saudi Arabia, and his proposal on the conference did not reach Washington in cable form until November 3 at the earliest. Moreover, Eilts's report of his meeting with Sadat on November 5 describes Sadat's disappointment on learning of Carter's negative opinion of the superconference. If Carter had already told him that three days earlier, it is hard to understand why he would have shown both surprise and disappointment. This suggests that Carter's phone conversation with Sadat must have come after November 5. Rosalynn Carter, *First Lady from Plains*, p. 240, repeats the story of the telephone conversation,

Carter's last public statement about the Middle East before Sadat's declaration of his intention to go to Jerusalem came on November 2, 1977, the sixtieth anniversary of the Balfour Declaration, which had called for a "national home" in Palestine for the Jewish people. After outlining again the basic principles that would have to be resolved in peace negotiations, Carter said the United States could not impose its will on the parties or do the negotiating for them. "For serious peace talks to begin, a reconvening of the Geneva conference has become essential."

Sadat did not share Carter's conviction that Geneva was the way to go, and when he spoke before the Egyptian National Assembly on November 9, with Arafat present in the audience, he stunned his listeners by saying that he was prepared to go anywhere for peace, even to talk to the Israelis in their Knesset in Jerusalem.[12] No one was quite sure whether Sadat meant what he said. Some thought his statement was just rhetoric, and the next day the Egyptian papers had deleted this portion of the speech from the printed text. Still, the White House took it seriously, especially after the exchange with Sadat over the idea of a conference in East Jerusalem. The Americans knew that Sadat was thinking in grandiose terms, but even they did not imagine that the trip would take place ten days later.[13]

It soon became clear that Sadat really did intend to go to Jerusalem and was anxious to receive an invitation from Begin. U.S. Ambassador Eilts in Cairo and U.S. Ambassador Samuel Lewis in Tel Aviv were instrumental in passing messages between the wary adversaries, and on

---

making it appear as if Carter played some role in shaping Sadat's decision to go to Jerusalem. From all the evidence available, Sadat made the decision to go to Jerusalem on his own, without informing Carter or anyone else in advance. Carter's letter of October 21 does, however, appear to have played a role in convincing Sadat to take some type of initiative.

12. Sadat's aversion to Geneva seemed to stem primarily from his view of the Syrians: "The Syrian Baath party will not go to Geneva, and if it did the picture would be like this: The Soviet Union has the Syrians in its pocket and Syria has the Palestinians in its pocket also. In Geneva, we would busy ourselves with all the things we have had enough of— semantic and legalistic arguments, the modalities, and the names of the topical, geographical and historical committees. All this, in addition to what we know about the nature of the Syrian Baath party. And the result would be that the Geneva Conference would greatly add to our level of disillusionment." *Oktubar* (in Arabic), December 25, 1977, p. 15.

13. Ambassador Eilts was informed a few hours before Sadat's speech that the Egyptian president might make some reference to the possibility of going to Jerusalem. Sadat had apparently raised the issue with his top foreign policy advisers but had not told them whether he was ready to make the proposal public or not.

November 15 Begin sent a letter to Sadat through the Americans inviting him to Jerusalem to address the Knesset.

Carter and his advisers admired the boldness of Sadat's decision and shared his belief that the visit would help break down some of the psychological barriers on both sides. They were less sure of what would happen after the visit. Sadat seemed to believe the Israelis would respond with enormous concessions, which was not exactly Begin's style, as the Americans tried to explain to Sadat before his departure. Meanwhile, the resignation of Egyptian Foreign Minister Fahmy was a reminder that Sadat's move would not be welcomed by all his countrymen, to say nothing of the other Arabs.

Despite some qualms about where Sadat's visit would lead, the Americans watched with fascination as Sadat arrived in Jerusalem after sundown on Saturday, November 19, 1977. It was a historic, unforgettable occasion. As Americans sat glued to their televisions, Sadat's plane landed at Ben-Gurion airport. Unknown to most onlookers, Israeli sharpshooters were positioned on the roof of the main terminal in case of a surprise attack from a planeload of terrorists.

But when the aircraft door opened, President Sadat emerged in a tan suit, with a look of great dignity on his face. As he set foot on Israeli soil, he began his campaign to win over a disbelieving public. Working his way down the receiving line, he made appropriate, often lighthearted comments as he met his former adversaries in person. When he reached former Prime Minister Golda Meir, with whom he had conducted famous long-distance feuds, he broke into a big smile and embraced her. It was a remarkable beginning to a visit that few had anticipated.

Sadat's speech the next day before the Knesset broke little new ground on substance; the fact of his standing there and delivering it was what counted. (See appendix C for the text of Sadat's speech.) Perspiring profusely and speaking in Arabic, Sadat stuck to the main lines of his known position, but raised hopes by calling for peace and an end to war. At American urging, he had also removed at the last moment a reference to the PLO, calling instead on Israel to respect Palestinians' rights. Begin's reply seemed somewhat stilted by comparison, though the Labor party leader, Shimon Peres, rose to the occasion with a generous statement of his own.

That Egypt and Israel were now capable of dealing openly with each other raised questions about what part the United States could or should play in the future. Carter had often complained about how much of his time was being consumed by Middle East issues, and he often seemed frustrated by the slow pace of diplomacy. But after his substantial investment in the Middle East issue, he was not entirely pleased with his new role of spectator. One could sense a tinge of jealousy within the administration that Sadat had thought of a dramatic move that cut across the American plans for Geneva. And no politician could ignore the enormous media exposure given to the event. Carter and his political advisers would no doubt have liked the president to have been somehow involved in such a major development.[14]

Apart from these concerns, there was the more important question of what would happen next. Within days of Sadat's visit, the American side began to take stock, listening to both the Israeli and Egyptian views of what had been achieved and what lay ahead.

WASHINGTON REASSESSES

Both Begin and Sadat sent Carter their accounts of the talks in Jerusalem on the same day, November 23. Begin noted that he and Sadat had agreed to go to Geneva as soon as feasible, but added that Sadat had said the conference should be well prepared. According to Ambassador Lewis, who had talked to Begin about the visit, both leaders saw Geneva as having only a ceremonial role.

Sadat, by contrast, said nothing to Carter about Geneva, though he did later tell Ambassador Eilts that his trip had opened the way to Geneva. Instead, he termed his trip to Jerusalem his greatest victory. He was elated by the response of the Israeli public and immediately felt a liking for Begin and Defense Minister Ezer Weizman. (Sadat never felt the same way about Dayan.) The next step in his plan was to arrange another meeting between Dayan and the Egyptian emissary Hassan Tuhamy in Morocco, and one between his defense minister, General Abd al-Ghani al-Gamasy, and Weizman, perhaps in Morocco. He reminded Carter that Dayan and Tuhamy had already met once and that Carter had been informed of this previously.

Sadat then gave credit to Carter for having encouraged him to take a bold initiative for peace. He added that the idea of a big conference in Jerusalem had been Fahmy's, and when Carter had rejected it, Sadat had reverted to his original idea of going alone to Jerusalem.

Turning to substance, Sadat informed Carter that Begin had given

14. Zbigniew Brzezinski, *Power and Principle*, p. 111.

him a copy of the Israeli peace plan of the previous September. Sadat agreed to security arrangements and no more war, but he would not endorse Israeli territorial expansion. Concerning the West Bank, Sadat raised the possibility of U.N. control over the area. He also hinted that Gaza might be handled differently: after the return of Sinai to Egypt he might be willing to cede the area of Yamit and Rafah to the Palestinians, making an enlarged Gaza the center of a Palestinian state closely tied to Egypt.

With these initial appraisals from Begin and Sadat in hand, Secretary Vance and his aides began the process of reassessing U.S. policy. In a memorandum to the president drafted on November 24, Secretary Vance noted that adjustments were now necessary in the American approach to Middle East peace. The most important points follow.

—The U.S. role as intermediary was now less central.

—An early reconvening of the Geneva conference was unlikely.

—Both Egypt and Israel believed that Syria and the Soviet Union could be ignored.

—Sadat wanted to show some movement on the Palestinian issue to protect himself from Arab criticism.

—Saudi support for Egypt was important, but Sadat did not want the United States to approach the Saudis on his behalf.

—The break between Sadat and Asad was serious. But the United States should try to prevent Syria from joining the rejectionists.

—Jordan was placed in a very awkward position by recent developments and was afraid of a separate Egyptian-Israeli agreement.

Vance went on to express his doubts about Sadat's most recent idea of a preparatory conference in Cairo. He was sure the other Arabs would not attend. He was more favorable, however, toward encouraging continued Egyptian-Israeli bilateral contacts. In closing, he added that Sadat had not thought through his strategy carefully and that he seemed too optimistic about Begin's willingness to make major concessions.

About the same time as Vance sent his memo to Carter, Brzezinski sent a handwritten memo of his own to the president called "Proposed Response Designed to Seize the Initiative to Turn the Begin-Sadat Plan to Our Purposes." The main point was to find a way of reasserting American leadership and to try to impose a wider peace process on top of the movement toward Egyptian-Israeli accommodation.

Carter met with his main advisers on November 28, the day after Sadat had publicly called for peace talks to be held in Cairo. After discussion, the president decided to ask Sadat to delay the Cairo conference so that the United States would have more time to consult with the Jordanians and Saudis and other Arabs and try to overcome their reticence. Carter also felt that an effort should be made to reach agreement with the Soviets on a date for Geneva in January and that the Soviets should be persuaded to deliver the Syrians. In the interim Vance would go to the Middle East to reaffirm U.S. support for a comprehensive peace settlement. Brzezinski argued that the president should praise Sadat and should not emphasize the Soviet role. Vance, by contrast, was more anxious to involve the Soviets and was somewhat reluctant to make another trip to the area.[15]

Carter was still unwilling to throw his weight fully behind a separate Egyptian-Israeli deal. He clung to the idea that a broader process was needed, and he feared that Begin was not showing enough flexibility in response to Sadat's dramatic gesture. On November 30 Carter opened a press conference with a carefully drafted statement on the Middle East. After praising both Sadat and Begin, he went on to say that the Cairo conference, scheduled for December 13, could be a constructive step. "The road toward peace has already led through Jerusalem, will now go to Cairo and ultimately, we believe, to a comprehensive consultation at Geneva."[16] With this statement, Carter hoped to overcome some of the criticism that had been expressed in the media about his alleged coolness toward Sadat's initiative and Begin's response.

Vance concluded that after Sadat's trip to Jerusalem it was clear that Egypt and Israel would move toward a bilateral agreement. The question remained of how, or whether, this move could be tied to some progress in working out an interim agreement on the West Bank and Gaza.[17] Henceforth, the American strategy would be to support talks between Egypt and Israel but to try to use the opening provided by Sadat to move forward on the Palestinian issue as well. The reasoning was fairly simple. Most of the Americans doubted that Sadat would be willing to conclude a peace treaty with Israel unless he could point to some progress on the Palestinian issue. This, after all, was what Sadat had said over and over. And the Americans felt that the Israelis could not be persuaded to make

15. Ibid., pp. 112–13.

16. "The President's News Conference of November 30, 1977," *Public Papers: Jimmy Carter, 1977,* vol. 2, p. 2054.

17. Cyrus Vance, *Hard Choices,* p. 195.

significant concessions to Egypt or on the Palestinian question without an offer of full peace from the largest and most powerful Arab country.

What changed as a result of Sadat's trip to Jerusalem was the American view of how to proceed with the negotiating process, not the preference to seek agreement on broad principles for a comprehensive settlement before getting down to the business of hammering out the texts of peace treaties. Egypt would now be the centerpiece for trying to develop an Arab position on the key issues of peace, security, borders, and Palestinian rights. Syria's hostility was anticipated, but largely discounted. More important would be the position adopted by King Hussein of Jordan and the Saudis. If they would tacitly agree to support Sadat's efforts, the opposition of the Syrians, the PLO, and the Soviets might be contained.

BEGIN'S PLAN FOR HOME RULE

Insofar as Sadat had a concept of how events should unfold after his talks with Begin in Jerusalem, he appeared to expect the Israelis to reciprocate with a grand gesture. In particular, he wanted Begin to commit Israel to the principle of full withdrawal on all fronts in return for peace and to agree that the Palestinians could exercise the right of self-determination if they were prepared to live in peace alongside Israel. Had Begin made such a statement, Sadat would have challenged Arab leaders to enter peace talks with Israel, at Geneva or elsewhere, and if they refused, he would have proceeded to negotiate a bilateral peace treaty with Israel.

Begin's next move thus assumed great importance, not only for Sadat and the viability of his strategy but also for Carter. On December 2 Carter met with Vance and Brzezinski to discuss the Middle East. Vance would go to the Middle East to seek moderate Arab support for the Cairo talks. He would try to arrange for Carter to meet with Sadat, King Hussein, and President Asad during the president's previously scheduled trip to Tehran and Riyadh in late December. (Carter noted on a memo that he would not see Begin unless the Israeli prime minister showed flexibility in Cairo on issues that went beyond the bilateral Egyptian-Israeli relationship.) Geneva would not be an immediate objective, though the Soviets would be urged to work on the Syrians and the PLO.

Carter wrote on a memo summarizing this meeting: "Also: discern desires/demands of Jordan and Syria prerequisite to going to Geneva and reaffirm our commitment to comprehensive settlement, not to exclusive bilateral agreement. Regain strong role versus USSR." Secretary Vance received a copy of these notes as a guideline for his upcoming trip to the area.

Sadat's strategy was gradually becoming apparent in Washington.[18] My own view, expressed in a memorandum to Brzezinski, was that Sadat was deliberately seeking to polarize the Arab world and to provoke a hostile Soviet response to his initiative. Sadat was escalating the conflict with Asad in public and had gratuitously attacked the Soviets before the Egyptian National Assembly after his return from Jerusalem. Disregarding Carter's advice, he had refused to discuss with Begin ways in which other Arabs might be brought into the peace process. When Ambassador Eilts asked him what might be done to encourage the Syrians, he said the United States should remind Asad that Cairo was the capital of the Arab world. When five Arab states decided to freeze relations with Egypt, Sadat responded by breaking diplomatic relations with them.

Sadat's motives, I surmised, were related to his hope for a positive Israeli and American response to his initiative. His willingness to break with Arab hard-liners should have added credibility to his position in both Washington and Jerusalem. Sadat also seemed to be appealing to Egyptian nationalism. "There is nothing quite like bearing the brunt of Soviet, Syrian, Iraqi, and Palestinian invective to bring out the Egyptian-first syndrome." Sadat appeared to be deliberately trying to keep a crisis atmosphere alive. "By striking out at Arab hard-liners, Sadat is paving the way for an Egyptian-Israeli separate agreement which may gain the support of Saudi Arabia. The Saudis will be most reluctant to weaken their support for Sadat if the alternative in the Arab world consists only of radical Arabs with strong Soviet backing."

Vance to the Middle East

Secretary Vance arrived in Cairo for talks with Sadat on December 10. Sadat appealed to Vance to urge the Israelis to make a public statement on full withdrawal and on the need to solve the Palestinian problem in all its aspects. This would undercut the argument of the Arab rejectionists. Sadat then went on to heap scorn on the Arab hard-liners, labeling them agents of the Soviet Union. Referring to Asad, he said the Syrian president wanted to join the peace process, but the Baath party always opposed him. Sadat claimed that the U.S.-Israeli Working Paper on Geneva had

18. The analysis in this and the following paragraph comes from a memorandum I wrote to Brzezinski dated December 12, 1977.

caused a big quarrel with the Syrians, and to break this impasse he had decided to go to Jerusalem. Otherwise Geneva would have dragged on for years in debates over procedures. Sadat was somewhat more generous in his comments about the Saudis and even more so about King Hussein, with whom he had just met.

The following day in Jerusalem Vance met with Begin. Despite a personal plea from President Carter, Begin was adamant in his refusal to meet Sadat's request for a statement on withdrawal. Begin, after all, was being asked to give up his overriding ambition to keep the West Bank as an integral part of Israel. Sadat's grand gesture of traveling to Jerusalem would not shake Begin's lifelong commitment to Eretz Israel, though it might well have convinced the Israeli prime minister to be forthcoming in Sinai.

Instead of meeting Sadat's request, Begin informed Vance that he intended to go to Washington toward the end of the week to present to Carter his ideas on "home rule" for the Palestinian Arabs of Judea, Samaria, and the Gaza District. This announcement was a bit of a surprise coming from someone who had taken pride in not coordinating positions with Washington in the past and who now could easily approach Sadat directly if he so chose.

In the course of Vance's meeting with Begin, it became clear that Israel had no intention of using the Cairo conference for serious negotiations with Egypt. Dayan had already informed Tuhamy in Marrakesh, Morocco, on December 2, 1977, at their second secret meeting, that Israel planned to put forward a plan for autonomy for the West Bank and Gaza. Dayan had also spelled out in some detail the Israeli position on withdrawal from Sinai, including the point that Israel wanted to retain the settlements around Yamit under its own control. Dayan had pressed Tuhamy on whether Egypt would make peace even if the other Arabs did not, but had not received a clear answer.[19]

Vance's next stop was Amman, Jordan, where he met with King Hussein. The king explained at length his view of the Sadat initiative and the risks and promises it entailed. He claimed that he was working hard to restrain the Syrians and keep them from attacking Sadat personally. His own recent talks with Sadat had been good, and he felt that their views on the need for some kind of transitional regime under international auspices for the West Bank and Gaza were similar. The king maintained

19. Moshe Dayan, *Breakthrough*, pp. 93–97.

that the key to Arab reaction to Sadat's initiative would be whether Sadat could deliver on the promises he had made. That would depend on the Israeli response. If Begin did not show flexibility, Sadat would be in deep trouble. Sadat would have to show some forward movement on the Palestinian question.

President Asad of Syria was more hostile to Sadat's moves than any of the other Arab leaders with whom Vance met. But even Asad's main complaint was that Israel would not respond with sufficient flexibility. As a result, Sadat would have broken the Arab front for nothing, leaving the Arabs without the option of pressuring Israel with the threat of military or economic actions.

Vance summarized the results of his trip in a lengthy cable to President Carter. The key to whether Sadat could win support for his initiative in Jordan and Saudi Arabia, Vance said, was tied to the Israeli response. Sadat felt his problems would be solved if Israel would agree in principle to withdraw to the 1967 lines with only minor modifications. He was less concerned with a plan for solving the Palestinian problem. For the moment he was content to live with generalities. Vance sensed that Begin's plan for the West Bank and Gaza would be very far from what Sadat wanted. Home rule, or autonomy, for these two areas would be offered as a permanent solution for the Palestinians, not as a transitional stage leading to the eventual withdrawal of the Israelis.

From these perceptions, Vance concluded that the U.S. role over the next several weeks should be to help Egypt and Israel work out the "peace for withdrawal" formula. Begin should be made to understand that his home rule idea might be a useful supplement to a statement on withdrawal, but it could not be a substitute for the statement. Autonomy might be desirable as a unilateral Israeli offer to move toward establishing a transitional regime, but Begin should not be given the impression that either Sadat or Hussein would ever accept autonomy as the basis for a final peace settlement. Begin should be told that the more he said on withdrawal, the less he would have to say on the Palestinian question. In conclusion, Vance noted that the Israelis had hinted that they could be more forthcoming if the United States was responsive to outstanding military requests. Vance argued that the premise could be reversed to say that unless Israel was forthcoming on the principle of withdrawal, the United States would find it hard to justify increased aid.[20]

20. Vance, *Hard Choices*, pp. 196–98, summarizes his trip to the Middle East.

Before Begin arrived in Washington, Carter and his advisers had agreed that they should not be seen as endorsing Begin's proposals. They were somewhat on their guard, since presumably Begin's purpose in bringing his proposals to Carter before discussing them with Sadat was to win just such an endorsement. In a curious way, Begin, the advocate of direct Arab-Israeli negotiations, was now dragging the Americans back into the process from the sidelines where Sadat's initiative had left them. But this time he obviously hoped to have Carter squarely in his corner.

Begin's Plan for the West Bank and Gaza

When Carter and Begin met on December 16, the president wasted no time in telling Begin that the world was awaiting his response to Sadat's initiative. Begin first reviewed his offer on Sinai, which was already known to the Americans. Israel would withdraw in stages to the old international border, phased to coincide with the establishment of normal diplomatic relations over a three- to five-year period. After Egyptian sovereignty had been restored to Sinai, Israeli settlers should still be able to live in Sinai with Israeli and U.N. forces present to protect them.

Responding primarily to Begin's willingness to withdraw to the international border, Carter said he thought Sadat would be pleased, though he added that there still might be details that he himself did not fully understand. (Later Begin was to claim that Carter had endorsed his Sinai proposal, including the point that settlers could remain after Israel's withdrawal.)

The new dimension of Israel's peace plan consisted of a twenty-one point document called "Home Rule, for Palestinian Arabs, Residents of Judea, Samaria and the Gaza District."[21] The document noted that this plan had not yet been approved by the government of Israel. There were two key points in the plan: the issue of sovereignty should be left open, and the Arabs in the West Bank and Gaza should elect an Administrative Council with limited powers. Israel would remain responsible for security. Some elements of reciprocity seemed to be built into the agreement. For

21. Begin had personally dictated the first version of this document to his close aide Yehiel Kadishai. He then asked Israel's Attorney General Aharon Barak to review the draft and to put it in proper legal form. Begin was afraid of leaks and showed the document to the inner cabinet only just before he left for Washington. The idea of autonomy was derived from Vladimir Ze'ev Jabotinsky's writings. According to Barak, the most difficult legal problem in this hastily improvised document was the "source of authority" for the self-governing body. Interview with Aharon Barak, February 1, 1985. See Oscar K. Rabinowicz, *Vladimir Jabotinsky's Conception of a Nation.*

example, Arabs in the occupied territories would be allowed to acquire land in Israel on the same basis that Israelis could acquire land in the territories. (This last point was subsequently modified to read that Arabs who became Israeli citizens could acquire land in Israel.)

Carter responded to Begin's presentation by saying that negotiations should be based on U.N. Resolution 242. Begin's plan said nothing about withdrawal. Nor did Begin say anything about the Palestinians outside the territories. Would they be allowed to return to the West Bank? And if the question of sovereignty were to be left open for now, how would it ultimately be resolved?

Begin responded with his well-known view that 242 did not require Israel to withdraw from the West Bank and Gaza. Under questioning from Brzezinski, however, he did say that Israeli sovereignty would not go beyond the 1967 lines. Who would have the right to expropriate land? asked Brzezinski. Begin said the elected Administrative Council would have that power, subject to the concept of public order. The Israeli military governor, however, would retain ultimate authority and in theory could revoke powers delegated to the Administrative Council.

Carter concluded this first round of discussions by saying that Begin's proposals might be viewed as a way of avoiding withdrawal and a fair solution to the Palestinian problem. This perception could hurt Sadat. In reply, Begin asked for public support for his proposals. Could Carter at least say they were a fair basis for negotiations?

When the American side caucused privately after Begin's departure, there was a general sense of disappointment with Begin's home rule proposal. Vance thought it was "far short" of what was needed.[22] Brzezinski was less critical, sensing the possibility of building on the proposal to develop the idea of a transitional arrangement that might be acceptable to all parties. He realized, however, that the home rule approach could resemble the South African–controlled black enclaves, or Bantustans, and even used the term "Basutoland" in front of Begin.

Carter then contacted Sadat to brief him on the proposals. On the basis of Carter's summary, Sadat said that the ideas seemed promising but that Israeli settlements could not remain in Sinai. As for home rule, Sadat liked the idea of leaving the question of sovereignty open, but said that Israel could not be responsible for security and that East Jerusalem should not be under Israeli control. Also, at the end of five years, the Palestinians should be able to exercise their right of self-determination.

22. Vance, *Hard Choices*, p. 199.

Meeting with Begin again on the morning of December 17, Carter told the Israeli prime minister that his proposals were "constructive" and that Sadat would probably react well to the Sinai proposal. Begin responded by reciting a long list of prominent Americans who reportedly favored his proposals. He quoted Senator Henry Jackson to the effect that the American people would support them. He even told the president he was sure the U.S. Senate would back them. This comment came very close to Israeli meddling in U.S. domestic politics and was not much appreciated by the White House. But since such behavior had long been part of the U.S.-Israeli relationship, no one objected.

Begin then said that Dayan, who had been left behind in Jerusalem, had suggested a few changes in the proposals. These made no essential difference, but added to the impression of flexibility and reasonableness that Begin seemed anxious to cultivate. Begin claimed that only security would remain in Israel's hands once the proposals went into effect.

Carter replied by urging Begin to use the phrase "withdrawal of Israeli forces to security outposts." "The determination of whether this appears as an empty proposal, or one full of meaning, will depend on how much autonomy or self-rule is being offered. This needs to be defined. If you have a military governor, and if the population is allowed self-rule just as long as it behaves, but the military governor can restore Israeli control whenever he wants, then this has no meaning." Carter went on to stress the importance of granting the Administrative Council authority over land and immigration, adding that the Arabs should also have a role in Jerusalem.

As the meeting came to a close, Carter observed that the proposals were serious and marked a step forward. Brzezinski added, however, that it might be best to present them to Sadat only in a general way, not as a written document with so much detail. Begin was clearly offended by this suggestion, saying that some of the ideas, such as the age of voting, were very good. Finally, responding to Begin's often expressed plea, Carter said the proposals could be a fair basis for negotiations, but he warned against dragging the negotiations on for too long.[23]

Begin apparently heard only the positive remarks about his ideas. Subsequently, he always claimed that Carter had said they were a "fair basis for negotiations" and then had changed his opinion. Carter, for his

23. Brzezinski, *Power and Principle*, pp. 115–20, gives the fullest version of the talks, including the text of a memorandum he sent to Carter assessing the good and bad aspects of Begin's proposals.

part, felt that Begin had claimed more than the president had implied and that the proposals shown to Sadat ten days later were significantly revised in ways that made them less attractive.[24]

The record makes clear that the Americans had reservations, especially Vance and Carter, but that they were unwilling to be seen in public as flatly opposing Begin's proposals. The stage was set for further misunderstandings, but first Begin had to try to win Sadat's agreement to his new ideas.

NEGOTIATIONS IN ISMAILIYA AND JERUSALEM

On Christmas day 1977 Menachem Begin arrived in Egypt for the first time. Accompanied by Dayan, Weizman, and Attorney General Aharon Barak, he met with Sadat and his advisers in Ismailiya, on the banks of the Suez Canal. In keeping with the pattern established by Sadat's trip to Jerusalem, no American representative was present. For the moment both sides preferred direct negotiations.

Just as the two leaders were settling down to talk, a phone call came through from President Carter, who was in Plains, Georgia. The connection was terrible, and the president was not even sure if his good wishes were heard on the other end of the line.

Carter was optimistic in his public statements at this time, and he insisted that the American role could now be limited to encouraging the parties from the sidelines. The United States, he repeatedly said, did not have strong views on what the parties should accept. Anything they could agree on would be all right with him. Apart from indicating a mild preference for a "Palestinian homeland or entity" affiliated in some way with Jordan, and for some type of transitional arrangements for the West Bank and Gaza, the president was careful not to imply that the United States had any proposals of its own to offer.[25]

24. Carter, *Keeping Faith*, p. 300, is partly correct in making this charge, but the proposals were not "attenuated substantially" as Carter maintained. Instead, some of the hints that Begin and Barak had made orally about the scope of authority for the Administrative Council were never acted on, and a few new points were added to the version shown to Sadat. For example, only Arabs who chose Israeli citizenship could buy land in Israel, according to the December 23 draft. In addition, Israel explicitly reserved a veto right over immigration into the territories. And Barak's view that the Administrative Council would have control over publicly owned land was never confirmed. Dayan, *Breakthrough*, pp. 359–61, gives the government-approved text of December 23, 1977, with the new title "Self-rule for Palestinian Arabs, Residents of Judaea, Samaria and the Gaza District, Which Will Be Instituted Upon the Establishment of Peace."

25. "Plains, Georgia: Informal Exchange with Reporters Prior to Visiting Allie Smith, December 25, 1977," *Public Papers: Carter, 1977*, vol. 2, pp. 2172–74; and "Conversation

Begin in Ismailiya

In Ismailiya, Begin and Sadat were unable to agree to anything of substance. Without difficulty Sadat accepted a proposal from Begin that two committees be formed, one to discuss political issues and the other, military matters. Begin also had the impression that Sadat's initial response to his proposals on Sinai and on "self-rule" for the Palestinians, as Begin now titled his plan, was positive. But it soon became obvious that the gap between the two sides was large. Begin tended to blame the gap on Sadat's hard-line advisers, especially his under secretary for foreign affairs, Usama al-Baz, and the Egyptian ambassador to the United Nations, Ismat Abd al-Magid. As yet the Israelis had no basis for judging Sadat's new foreign minister, Muhammad Ibrahim Kamil, a reticent and seemingly uncomfortable newcomer to the negotiations who was actually sworn into office during the Ismailiya talks.

From Ismailiya on, the Israelis repeatedly sought to deal with Sadat without the presence of his advisers; in due course the American side followed suit. Ismailiya convinced Begin that progress could be made only by isolating Sadat from the influences that surrounded him. Some Israelis at Ismailiya also claimed they could detect Sadat's clear preference for a bilateral agreement and his indifference to the Palestinian question. The Egyptian side, by contrast, seemed to feel that Ismailiya proved that direct talks with Begin were hopeless and that the Americans should be brought back into the picture.

Sadat's private comments to Ambassador Eilts after Ismailiya indicated that the Egyptian president was deeply disappointed that Begin had not responded magnanimously to his Jerusalem visit and his offer of peace. The only Israeli Sadat seemed to trust was Defense Minister Weizman, and it was significant that contact with Weizman was maintained even when other channels were closed.[26]

---

with the President, December 28, 1977," ibid., pp. 2188–91. Speaking from Poland on December 30, 1977, on the first leg of an overseas trip, Carter answered a question on the Middle East in a way that reflected his views at the time: "Any agreement which can be reached between Israel and her Arab neighbors would be acceptable to us. We are in a posture of expressing opinions, trying to promote intimate and direct negotiations and communications, expediting the process when it seems to be slow, and adding our good offices whenever requested. But we have no intention or desire to impose a settlement." "The President's News Conference of December 30, 1977," ibid., p. 2206.

26. Dayan, *Breakthrough*, pp. 102–05, gives his version of the talks at Ismailiya. Ezer Weizman, *The Battle for Peace*, pp. 122–35, provides a more detailed and graphic account of the talks, which he describes as a "blind alley." He notes that Dayan felt the Americans

The failure of the talks in Ismailiya dampened the hopes generated by Sadat's trip to Jerusalem. Not only was the substantive gap between Egypt and Israel very wide but also the atmosphere was beginning to cloud.

Carter's Aswan Declaration

On New Year's Day, as part of Carter's attempt to broaden the circle of Arab support for Sadat, the president met with King Hussein in Tehran. The mood was good, but Hussein remained noncommittal. Carter described his own views as favoring some minor modifications in the 1967 lines in the West Bank and a limited form of self-determination for the Palestinians that would preclude full independence.[27]

Meeting with the Saudi leadership on January 3 in Riyadh, Carter repeated these views and found the Saudis in a conciliatory mood, though they continued to insist that the Palestinians must have the right to an independent state. King Khalid told Carter that Sadat should not be allowed to fail in his initiative. Carter responded by saying he believed King Hussein would join the negotiations if Israel would agree to withdrawal and to Palestinian self-determination. Khalid agreed, and Carter replied that he would do his utmost to get Begin to accept these two principles of withdrawal and self-determination, as well as the idea of a transitional period. Khalid warned that the transition should not be too long.

Apparently pleased with the results of these talks, Carter promised King Khalid that when Congress reconvened he would proceed with the sale of F-15 interceptor aircraft to the kingdom. This had been a long-standing Saudi request, but it was not clear how urgent the Saudis felt it was to proceed. Possibly they were looking for reassurance after Sadat's unsettling moves. But the result was that Carter become involved in a major quarrel with the friends of Israel in Congress at precisely the time he was trying to make headway in the peace negotiations.

While King Khalid and President Carter were meeting, Secretary Vance and Foreign Minister Saud were trying to develop a formula that would come close to putting the United States on record as favoring self-determination for the Palestinians. The following day, during a brief

---

should be brought back into the discussions, whereas Weizman believed the military talks could proceed without them (p. 126). Additional detail on the talks can be found in Eitan Haber, Ze'ev Schiff, and Ehud Ya'ari, *The Year of the Dove*, pp. 114–37.

27. Carter, *Keeping Faith*, p. 300.

stopover in Aswan to see Sadat, Carter spelled out his well-known views on the need for real peace and on withdrawal in the context of security and normal relations. He then added: "Third, there must be a resolution of the Palestinian problem in all its aspects. The solution must recognize the legitimate rights of the Palestinian people and enable the Palestinians to participate in the determination of their own future."

The Aswan Declaration, as it came to be known, was not well received by the Israelis, and Arabs also were not quite sure what to make of it. Nonetheless, it acquired the status of acceptable compromise language in the course of Egyptian-Israeli talks and was eventually incorporated into the Camp David Accords.

New Israeli Settlements in Sinai

On the same day that Carter made his Aswan statement, the Israeli government began work on four new settlements in the Sinai Peninsula. This news infuriated Sadat and made Washington officials wonder what Begin thought he was doing.

Carter was particularly angry at Begin because of the promise that Dayan had made during his meeting with the president on September 19, 1977. According to the American record of the meeting, and the recollection of all the American participants, Dayan had said that Israel had plans to establish only six new settlements inside military camps over the next year. The cabinet had authorized those new settlements on October 10, 1977. A few days later, work had begun on an unauthorized settlement near Jerusalem, at a site called Maale Adumim, but Begin denied that this was a new settlement because it was close to a previous site. But four new settlements in Sinai, coming shortly after the Ismailiya meeting, could not be explained away so easily. [28]

Begin refused to budge, claiming that Dayan had promised there would be only six new settlements that year, meaning through the end of 1977, not for an entire year beginning September 19, 1977. [29] As much as anything else, this response helped convince Carter that Begin was not always a man of his word.

The long-standing difference over settlements was now to become a

28. According to Weizman, *Battle for Peace*, pp. 142–47, Ariel Sharon was the moving force behind the idea of building new settlements in Sinai as a form of pressure on Sadat.

29. Begin spelled this out in a letter to Carter informing him of the Israeli decision on January 8, 1978. Carter noted on the memorandum accompanying this letter: "It is obvious that they have violated a commitment. Sadat should raise hell. J."

constant irritation in U.S.-Israeli relations. Begin never openly accepted Carter's demand that no more settlements be set up during the negotiations, but in fact the four in Sinai were the last to be established in 1978. For the remainder of the year Begin observed a de facto freeze on settlement activity.[30]

Growing Strains between Sadat and Begin

Despite the rapid deterioration in the relations between Egypt and Israel after the Ismailiya talks and the Israeli decision to establish four new settlements in Sinai, both Sadat and Begin were committed to a continuation of the negotiating process. They had agreed that Weizman and his Egyptian counterpart, General Gamasy, should meet. In addition, a session of the "political committee" was scheduled for mid-January in Jerusalem. The meeting would take place at the level of foreign ministers, and, as Dayan preferred, the United States would be invited to participate.

In Washington, the upcoming Jerusalem talks, coupled with the palpable deterioration of the Sadat-Begin relationship, convinced Carter and his advisers to reconsider the comparatively passive stance they had adopted after Sadat's trip to Jerusalem. Vice President Mondale, in particular, thought Begin was vulnerable to pressure on two counts: his policy on settlements, which enjoyed little backing even among American friends of Israel; and his interpretation of U.N. Resolution 242, which excluded the West Bank from the provision calling for Israeli withdrawal. It was decided that on these two issues the United States would mount a public campaign in the hope of mobilizing domestic American support, as well as that of Israelis who opposed Begin. At the same time little more would be said about the Palestinians, and the PLO would be shunned. Mondale's reading of American domestic opinion was that the Palestinian issue could get the president into more trouble than settlements or 242.

The American side found it relatively easy to identify the general principles on which to base its public statements, but it still had no strategy. During January 1978 several points began to come into focus. First, left to themselves Sadat and Begin would get nowhere. Second, Sadat would insist on recovering all of Sinai, but would show flexibility

---

30. The one exception to this was the establishment of an "archeological site" at Shiloh on January 23, 1978, by Gush Emunim extremists. It was not officially recognized as a settlement at the time, but it did become one despite the Begin government's insistence that only authorized settlements would be recognized and protected.

on the details of a West Bank and Gaza arrangement for a transitional period. Third, Begin's ideas on self-rule would have to be substantially modified so that they would clearly apply only to an interim period during which substantial authority would devolve upon Palestinians pending a final settlement based on the principles of U.N. Resolution 242. Fourth, Sadat's tendency to act impulsively and without consulting Washington was a potential problem. Carter should try to build on his personal relationship with Sadat to ensure a better coordination of moves between Cairo and Washington.

As Carter's second year in office began, one could detect greater sensitivity to domestic politics but also a greater realism about the negotiating process between Egypt and Israel. The coincidence of these two developments made for a more viable strategy, though not one devoid of controversy over the next several months.

At this time some of Carter's advisers suggested moving toward a strategy of collusion with Sadat to help bring pressure to bear on Begin. Brzezinski and I were its prime supporters.[31] This strategy was politically dangerous, and both Carter and Vance were disinclined to use such manipulative techniques of diplomacy, but the idea began to be seriously considered as the more straightforward methods seemed to be leading nowhere.

Talks in Jerusalem

Before deciding on a strategy of close coordination with Sadat, the Americans first had to rejoin the negotiating process as part of the political committee talks held in Jerusalem on January 17, 1978. The talks did not get off to a promising start. Quarrels over the wording of the agenda nearly prevented the parties from meeting, and only after Secretary Vance had threatened not to participate unless a nonpolemical agenda was accepted did the parties finally get together.

Prime Minister Begin had concluded from his talks with Sadat in Ismailiya that it should be fairly easy to get Egyptian agreement to a

---

31. In a memorandum that I drafted for Brzezinski on January 12, 1978, I argued that the United States should not paper over the disagreements between Egypt and Israel. Instead, the current impasse should be allowed to develop into a stalemate. "In total confidence, we should develop a strategy for developing a mini-crisis, which will be resolved by an American proposal which Sadat will accept." It would be necessary, I wrote, to get Sadat's assurance in advance that he would accept the American compromise proposals so that pressure could then be mobilized against Begin on the issues of 242 and settlements, the issues on which he was most vulnerable.

declaration of principles that consisted almost entirely of the wording of
U.N. Resolution 242. His main goal in the political committee talks was
to press for such a declaration. If he was successful, the agreement might
provide the umbrella under which Sadat would be prepared to conclude
a bilateral peace treaty.

Unfortunately for Begin, the Egyptian delegation, led by Foreign
Minister Kamil, was not interested in reaching agreement on vague
principles. It wanted an outright Israeli promise of withdrawal to the
1967 lines and Palestinian self-determination as the quid pro quo for Arab
recognition and normal peaceful relations. This promise Begin would not
make, and anyone who understood how deeply he was committed to his
vision of Eretz Israel would never have been under the illusion that he
might. But the Americans and Egyptians were still not sure how rock
hard Begin's views on this issue really were.

In his first meeting with Vance, on January 16, 1978, before the official
talks began, Begin repeated the story of his near agreement with Sadat
at Ismailiya. Then he began to quote from the record of his December
talks with Carter, as if to imply that Carter had endorsed his proposals.
Referring to his insistence that Israeli settlements should remain in Sinai
and should be protected by Israeli forces, Begin said that a matter of
principle was involved and that the United States should respect Israeli
principles. The whole discussion was full of self-pity and wounded
feelings. Dayan tried to turn the discussion toward the impending
negotiations with the Egyptians, but Begin reverted to his disappointment
that the warm words of the previous December had somehow been
forgotten. He pleaded with Vance to repeat publicly that the Israeli
position was a fair basis for negotiation and that the settlements were not
illegal. Vance was unmoved.

In closing, Dayan added somewhat ominously that if Sadat would not
allow the Israeli settlements to remain in Sinai, the Israeli position would
have to be changed to include significant adjustments in the Egyptian-
Israeli border so that the settlements could remain as part of the sovereign
territory of Israel. Sadat's reaction to such an idea could easily be
imagined, coming as it did on the heels of renewed settlement activity.

The following day, January 17, the Egyptians and Israelis met, and
each side tabled draft declarations of principle. By the end of the day the
U.S. delegation was beginning to develop compromise language. Prime
Minister Begin hosted a large dinner that evening, in the course of which
he gave a toast that offended the Egyptians, especially Kamil, whom

Begin referred to as a young man, as if to imply that he was inexperienced and unaware of history. The atmosphere was tense, and no one expected the next day's talks to go smoothly.

During the afternoon of January 18, the Egyptian delegation came to see Vance to tell him that Sadat had ordered it to return immediately to Cairo.[32] The secretary consulted with President Carter, and Carter called Sadat. But the Egyptian president was adamant. He complained that Begin had not understood his initiative. Begin preferred land to peace. Sadat bitterly noted that the Israeli prime minister continued to insist on keeping settlements in Sinai. In response to a plea from Carter, Sadat said he would not break off the military committee talks with Weizman but that the political committee could not meet.

Sadat Invited to Camp David

As the American delegation headed home, some thought was already being given to next steps. Everyone believed Sadat had deliberately created a crisis, but no one was sure what he now had in mind.

On January 20 Carter and Brzezinski met to discuss the Middle East situation. For the first time they considered the possibility of inviting both Begin and Sadat to Camp David to try to break the impasse. Both men liked the idea. At a minimum it would mean that the leaders who were capable of making decisions would be directly involved.

The American side was increasingly aware that little could be accomplished at the level of foreign ministers alone. Sadat and Begin were crucial to the negotiating process—but with an important difference. On the Egyptian side, Sadat concerned himself with broad strategy, not with details. On the Israeli side, Begin not only controlled the overall strategy but also loved to immerse himself in detail. Defense Minister Weizman has well characterized the Egyptian and Israeli leaders:

Anyone observing the two men could not have overlooked the profound divergence in their attitudes. Both desired peace. But whereas Sadat wanted to take it by storm, capitalizing on the momentum from his visit to Jerusalem to reach his final objective, Begin preferred to creep forward inch by inch. He took the dream of peace and ground it down into the fine, dry powder of details, legal clauses, and quotes from international law.[33]

32. Muhammad Ibrahim Kamil, *The Lost Peace in the Camp David Accords* (in Arabic), pp. 96–122. Kamil gives an account of the talks in Jerusalem and Sadat's reasons for withdrawing the Egyptian delegation. Kamil was opposed to breaking off the talks and gives several reasons (p. 113).

33. Weizman, *Battle for Peace*, pp. 136–37.

Just as Carter and his advisers were beginning to regroup to set a new course, an important cable arrived from the highly respected American ambassador to Egypt, Hermann Eilts. Since no American knew Sadat better, Eilts's views on what was on Sadat's mind were read with particular interest. The cable was titled "Sadat and the USG: An Incipient Crisis of Confidence." First and foremost on the list of problems, said Eilts, was Sadat's growing doubt about the strength of the American commitment. The United States, Sadat believed, was not giving him enough support on the question of Israeli settlements in Sinai. He also reportedly feared that the United States was about to bend to pressure to sell more advanced aircraft to Israel.

With Eilts's analysis fresh in hand, Carter met with Vance, Brzezinski, Mondale, and others on January 23, 1978. Carter initially proposed inviting both Sadat and Begin to Camp David; Vance felt this was premature, and Brzezinski supported that view. Instead, they agreed that Sadat alone should be invited to meet with the president. Two purposes would thereby be served. Carter could draw on his personal relationship with Sadat to help restore mutual confidence, if indeed that was part of the problem. And Carter and Sadat could discuss a series of coordinated steps that would help to put pressure on Begin.[34]

CONCLUSION

For nearly three months after President Sadat announced his intention of going to Jerusalem, the United States was more observer than direct participant in Middle East diplomacy. Despite some doubts, and perhaps a twinge of jealousy at not being in the spotlight, the Americans would have been delighted if Sadat and Begin had been able to reach agreement. Carter, in particular, found the slow pace of negotiations, the quibbling over words, and the professions of bad faith to be extremely frustrating.

The Americans did not take long to conclude, however, that Sadat's initiative was not likely to succeed without some further involvement by the United States. Even Begin seemed to want Carter in the picture, if only as cheerleader for his proposals. And Sadat felt that the American role was essential, especially after his unproductive meeting with Begin in Ismailiya. Geneva was now out of the question, but direct negotiations

---

34. Brzezinski, *Power and Principle*, pp. 240–42, gives the most complete account of these deliberations and is the only one on the American side to refer openly to the secret strategy of collusion with Sadat.

also seemed unpromising. What Sadat now sought was an American proposal to break the deadlock.

Carter very much wanted to show a return on his investment of time and political capital in Middle East peacemaking. But over the previous year he had also learned much about the traps and dangers of playing the role of intermediary between two highly suspicious adversaries, one of whom had a strong constituency in the United States, and the other of whom was rapidly becoming a media star of consequence. Political considerations weighed more heavily in early 1978 than they had in 1977, a characteristic difference between the first and second year of a presidential term. Also, Carter had learned how controversial anything he might say on the Middle East could become. Public diplomacy was giving way to more conventional private exchanges. Vance was assuming a large share of the responsibility for the day-to-day conduct of diplomacy. The bureaucracy and the politicians were beginning to work together comparatively well.

Despite some caution in Washington as a result of the frustrations of the first year of Middle East peacemaking, Carter still attached great importance to making a breakthrough. Increasingly he seemed to feel that his personal involvement with Sadat and Begin, perhaps in a three-way summit, might be desirable. He had little real trust or confidence in Begin, but he respected the Israeli prime minister as a powerful and effective spokesman for his point of view. By contrast, Carter felt genuine affection for Sadat, though he was troubled by his moodiness and unpredictability.

Doubting that he could do much in the near future to change Begin's positions, especially on the question of withdrawal from the West Bank, Carter determined that the next step in his Middle East diplomacy should be to restore a close working relationship with Sadat. This decision opened a complex and confusing period of maneuvers that ultimately led to the Camp David summit in September 1978. But along the way there were many missteps and crossed signals, some of which had a significant effect on the eventual outcome. At the same time major progress was made in developing the idea of an interim regime for the West Bank and Gaza, an idea that was to become the centerpiece of the Camp David Accords and one of the chief innovations in the entire negotiations.

CHAPTER SEVEN

Inching toward Camp David

After one year of intensive involvement in Middle East diplomacy, President Carter found himself in late January 1978 with little to point to by way of concrete results. The search for comprehensive negotiations involving all parties had come to an end. Now even the prospects for salvaging something on the bilateral Egyptian-Israeli front seemed dim.

For most of the preceding three months, the Americans had been little more than spectators while Sadat and Begin occupied center stage, Sadat with his bold initiative and Begin with his detailed proposals. After the political committee talks collapsed in Jerusalem, Carter worried that the peace process would grind to a halt. Certainly there was little sign of confidence or mutual respect between the Egyptian and Israeli leaders. Their visions of peace, and especially their views on how to proceed with negotiations, were dramatically at odds.

During deliberations in late January among the American team, several points began to come into focus. Begin's rigidity was seen as a major obstacle to progress, especially his insistence on not accepting the principle of withdrawal as it applied to the West Bank. Nor could Begin's position on settlements possibly be accepted by Sadat or any other Arab leader. These substantive elements of the Israeli position would have to be changed if a negotiated agreement was ever to be reached. The question was how.

OUTLINE OF AN AMERICAN STRATEGY

The American strategy to bring about a change in Begin's position consisted of several elements. An effort would be made to introduce some revisions into Begin's plan for self-rule. The plan would be praised publicly for containing positive elements, but the Americans would stress that it was appropriate only for a transitional period. At the end of a five-year period the Palestinians should be able to participate, along with Jordan and Israel, in working out their political future in conformity with the "withdrawal for peace" equation of U.N. Resolution 242.

These changes, which Carter would try to obtain from Begin, should be enough to convince Sadat that he had adequate political cover to proceed in stages toward a full peace treaty with Israel. At this point few American officials believed Sadat would settle for a totally separate peace with Israel that offered nothing to the Palestinians. Speaking to both Americans and Israelis in private, Sadat insisted that he could not afford to make such an agreement. Some degree of cover was needed. No one was sure how much.

Carter and his advisers all felt that Sadat had shown considerable flexibility and imagination, and they were impressed by the way he had sought to win over American public opinion. Some were worried that his decision to break off the political talks in Jerusalem would cut into his popularity and would strengthen Begin's case that Sadat was not prepared for genuine negotiations. Thus the idea arose of trying to work out with Sadat a means for resuming the negotiating process that would put pressure on Begin, especially regarding the issues of 242 and settlements. To do so, Carter first had to regain Sadat's confidence and convince him to work from a common script in the coming months. If the United States was to play the role that Sadat wanted, it would have to be spared future surprises such as the abrupt cancellation of the Jerusalem talks.

One could sense in the American view as it developed in early 1978 some evidence of lessons learned from the previous year. The whole concept of Middle East peace had been scaled back to the idea of supporting a first step between Egypt and Israel, with a vaguely defined transitional period for the West Bank and Gaza. Syria was nowhere mentioned. The Palestinian issue was on the agenda, but talks with the PLO were not. Carter was still willing to engage his prestige in the negotiating process, but he was anxious for results and did not want Sadat to administer any of his famous shocks.

Domestic political realities, always lurking in the background, were much more on Carter's mind in 1978 than they had been in 1977. He had too many scars from skirmishes with the friends of Israel in his first year not to want to minimize frictions in his second year. This helped to account for the choice of issues on which to engage Begin. U.N. Resolution 242 and settlements were both comparatively safe, especially since many Israelis and American Jews were more in agreement with Carter's position on these points than with Begin's. Unfortunately for Carter, these were not bargaining positions for Begin and therefore even heavy pressure would not be enough to budge him. But the full appreciation of Begin's determination not to yield was still many months away.

Planning for Sadat

Carter had contemplated the possibility of a three-way summit with Begin and Sadat, but on January 23 the president decided to invite Sadat to come to Camp David for private talks.[1] Preparations for the visit began immediately, and Carter showed a strong interest in working out a general timetable for next moves that could be discussed with Sadat. He could hardly disguise his impatience as he noted on memorandums that things should be speeded up. Perhaps he already realized that the political calendar left him comparatively little time to deal with the Middle East.

High-level visits have a way of concentrating the mind and forcing the bureaucracy to disgorge concrete suggestions. At best, these can be moments of serious reflection and even creativity. Such were the stakes in the Middle East, and so unwilling was the American team to see the past year's investment produce nothing at all, that it spared no effort to provide the president with ideas of how to proceed in his talks with Sadat.

The State Department prepared a memorandum for Secretary Vance to send to the president which raised the basic question of what Sadat really wanted: was he serious about the West Bank, or did he simply need some kind of verbal agreement as cover for a bilateral deal with Israel? The president was urged to probe to get an answer from Sadat to this question. In the memo Vance made two recommendations: U.S. strategy should still aim for a good declaration of common principles that Sadat and Begin could endorse, and Carter should explore with Sadat a revised version of Begin's points as the basis for a transitional regime. Vance also cautioned that Sadat was not particularly interested in purchasing F-5 aircraft at present and that the president should hold off on such decisions for now.

Brzezinski and I were more interested than State in devising a strategy to get Sadat to help put pressure on Begin. The key point in our thinking was that the United States would eventually put forward a proposal, as Sadat wanted, and would pressure Begin on 242 and settlements. But Sadat first would have to agree to resume negotiations and would have to pave the way for the American proposal by introducing one of his own. The United States could not do all the negotiating of details with Begin while Sadat contented himself with making grand gestures.

1. Zbigniew Brzezinski, *Power and Principle*, pp. 240–42.

Sadat would be told of the political constraints on the president, including the importance he attached to getting early Senate ratification of the Panama Canal treaties. It would be hard for Carter to devote full time to the Middle East until the Panama debate had been concluded. In the meantime Sadat should put forward an Egyptian plan for the West Bank and Gaza. The plan should be built around the idea of a transitional period and should acknowledge Israel's security needs, but it should also include a few elements that would be unacceptable to the United States and Israel. These would give Carter the chance to engage in arguments with both Sadat and Begin. But Carter would have an understanding in advance with Sadat that at a mutually agreed moment an American compromise proposal would be put forward—and Sadat would accept it. Then the full burden of American influence could be turned on Begin, without Carter being vulnerable to the charge of applying one-sided pressure on Israel. This was a risky strategy, especially if it leaked to the press. But it had the great virtue that it would appeal to Sadat's theatrical instincts, and it might just work.[2]

The Nine Points

Brzezinski, more than most of Carter's Middle East advisers, was convinced that Begin's self-rule proposal could be reshaped into a viable transitional arrangement. Everyone on the American side agreed that the West Bank and Gaza had to be dealt with on a different time scale than Sinai, so some interim agreement seemed desirable. To the extent possible, drawing on Begin's own ideas would enhance the prospects for Israeli acceptance. From the Arab point of view, of course, the transitional period per se was unlikely to be of much interest, so some notion of what would follow had to be included. This perception led Brzezinski, in close consultation with State, to develop a nine-point proposal that would be discussed with the parties. It went through several drafts, but the version prepared on the eve of Sadat's visit and dated February 3, 1978, read as follows:

1. A self-rule arrangement would be established for a transitional five-year period.

2. Authority for this interim arrangement will derive from agreement among Israel, Jordan, and Egypt. The agreement will be negotiated among representatives of these states and of the Palestinians (from the West Bank and Gaza).

3. The agreement will provide for self-rule by an authority freely elected by

2. Ibid., pp. 242–43; and a memorandum from me to Brzezinski dated February 1, 1978. The memo included an illustrative calendar of steps that could be taken over the coming two months.

the inhabitants of the West Bank and Gaza. The agreement would define the responsibilities of that authority.

4. Neither Israel nor Jordan will assert their claims to sovereignty over the West Bank and Gaza during the five-year period.

5. Israeli forces would withdraw to limited and specified encampments.

6. During the five-year period, in order to implement UN Resolution 242 negotiations will be conducted and agreement will be reached among the West Bank–Gaza authority, Israel, Jordan, and Egypt on Israeli withdrawal from territories occupied in 1967, on secure and recognized final boundaries, including possible modifications in the 1967 lines, on the security arrangements which will accompany Israel's final withdrawal, and on the long-term relationship of the West Bank and Gaza to Israel and Jordan.

7. The agreement negotiated by the parties would come into effect by expressed consent of the governed to the substance of the agreement.

8. During the interim period the negotiating parties will constitute a continuing committee to reach agreements on:

a. Issues arising under the agreement regarding the conduct of the interim regime, not resolvable by the West Bank/Gaza authority.

b. The introduction of UN or Jordanian military presence on the West Bank and Gaza.

c. Provision for an economically practicable level of resettlement in the West Bank and Gaza of Palestinian refugees.

d. Reciprocal rights of residence in Israel and the territories for Palestinian Arabs and Israelis, and for land purchases with Israeli citizens and West Bank/Gaza residents entitled to buy land either in the West Bank/Gaza or in Israel.

9. A regional economic development plan would be launched, including Jordan, the West Bank/Gaza authority, Israel and Egypt.[3]

The nine-point plan was hardly a masterpiece of English prose, and it begged several important questions, but nonetheless it contained the essence of what the Americans thought was needed: a modification of Begin's proposal to make clear that it was only for a transitional period; a reaffirmation of the principles of U.N. Resolution 242 as the basis for a final agreement; a substantial change in the Israeli presence in the West Bank and Gaza during the transition; and a role for Jordan and the Palestinians in the negotiations.

SADAT AND CARTER AT CAMP DAVID

President Sadat arrived at Camp David on a cold Friday afternoon. He was accompanied by his wife, as was President Carter, and during the next two days the Sadats and Carters spent a great deal of time getting acquainted. This meeting forged a genuine friendship between the two men. It also marked an important step toward a joint U.S.-Egyptian

3. Cyrus Vance, *Hard Choices*, p. 204, summarizes a somewhat earlier version of the nine-point plan.

strategy designed to persuade Begin to change some of his deeply held positions on how to deal with the Palestinian question.

Sadat's Request for an American Proposal

On Saturday morning, February 4, 1978, Carter met alone with Sadat for a lengthy discussion of the negotiations. Sadat was discouraged and indicated that he was preparing to announce the suspension of all further contacts with the Israelis. His performance was convincing.[4]

Soon Carter and Sadat joined the American and Egyptian delegations, which had been waiting impatiently in a newly constructed conference room. Carter, as was often his habit, began by summarizing the discussion he had just had with Sadat. He gave a detailed account of the steps that had led Sadat to go to Jerusalem, and Sadat's bitter disappointment over Begin's response. Carter quoted Sadat as saying he had taken his initiative in part to overcome the influence of powerful lobby groups in the United States and to convince Americans that the Arabs were ready for peace with Israel.

According to Carter, Sadat's first disillusionment with Begin came in Ismailiya. Sadat had wanted a general declaration of principles, not detailed negotiations. Begin's proposals were not acceptable, especially his absurd idea of keeping settlements in Sinai after Israeli withdrawal. The Israeli actions in early January in creating new settlements in Sinai had angered Sadat. Now he was prepared to announce before the National Press Club on Monday, in Washington, D.C., that all contacts with Israel would be broken off. After reviewing some of the security arrangements in Sinai that Sadat had said he would accept, Carter noted that he would be discussing some political issues with Sadat after dinner. Then he turned the floor over to the Egyptian president.

Sadat began by adding a few details to the account of why he had decided to go to Jerusalem. He again said he had felt the weight of the Zionist lobby in the United States and had wanted to ease that burden on Carter by some bold action. When he received Carter's handwritten letter in late October, he began to think of how he might be able to break the impasse. He then declared that he was not worried at all about the reaction of the Arab rejectionists, but that Begin's stubborn attitude could hurt him badly and could discredit the whole peace process. Sadat added that his people did not believe Israel would be so stubborn unless it had full U.S. support.

4. Jimmy Carter, *Keeping Faith*, pp. 306–08, describes this meeting.

Carter intervened to put in a good word for Begin's autonomy plan as a possible basis, with suitable revisions, for an interim agreement on the West Bank and Gaza. Vance, Vice President Mondale, and Brzezinski all made the point that Sadat should not break off talks with the Israelis. If he did, American public opinion might begin to turn against him. Carter then said he needed Sadat's support if he was going to be able to force Begin to change his positions.

Turning to domestic politics again, Carter said he wanted to review some public opinion polls with Sadat. He also wanted to tell him about the status of the Panama and SALT negotiations. Time was becoming a problem. Next week the Senate would be voting on the Panama treaties, and Carter did not yet have the necessary votes. Several senators whose votes were needed on Panama were also strong supporters of Israel, and there could be complications if the Middle East talks broke down now.

During most of this discussion Sadat sat quietly, fingering his pipe and looking despondent. Finally he spoke, saying gravely that everything now depended on the American position. Israel would listen only to the United States. The time had come to state basic principles. No one should tread on other people's land or sovereignty. Israel had a right to feel secure, and Egypt accepted the fact that a special U.S.-Israeli relationship existed. Sadat then said he wondered if the time had not come for Carter to present a specific American position. He referred to the way in which Kissinger had put forward an American proposal to break the deadlock in the disengagement negotiations early in 1974.

After a brief pause President Carter said: "Let me reply. The answer is yes." But he quickly added that it would be a mistake for the United States to put forward a position immediately after the talks with Sadat. That would look like collusion. American Jews, public opinion, and Israelis would reject it. Carter should first talk to Begin, and then a U.S. proposal could be advanced. Egypt would probably be able to accept it, but Begin would have some difficulty.

Carter suggested that Vance and Brzezinski meet with the Egyptian delegation to work out a series of steps for the coming weeks. Brzezinski added that Egypt should come up with a plan of its own, which Israel would of course reject. Then the United States could come forward with proposals to break the deadlock.[5]

5. See Muhammad Ibrahim Kamil, *The Lost Peace in the Camp David Accords*, pp. 134–40, for an accurate summary of this discussion, including Sadat's question and Carter's reply.

Later that afternoon the American and Egyptian delegations met to work out a timetable. In the course of the meeting Vance and one of Sadat's advisers discussed the possibility of a three-way summit if agreement could be reached on a satisfactory declaration of principles.[6] The American version of the timetable, as conveyed to Carter and approved by Sadat, went as follows:[7]

1. Sadat's speech: door open to peace; 242; settlements.
2. Press statement—general—Atherton returning.
3. Departure statement—positive elements in Sadat's speech—Aswan language.
4. Dayan visit to Washington.
5. Begin invited to Washington.
6. Atherton returns to Middle East late February.
7. Begin visit to DC late February—early March.
8. Egypt outlines comprehensive settlement following talks with Jordan, mid-March.
9. Late March-early April U.S. comprehensive proposal.

A Joint Plan of Action

The Egyptian-American talks ended on February 4 with an appearance of wide agreement on substance and procedure. The Americans concluded that Sadat would not end the negotiations and that he would be prepared to put forward an Egyptian proposal on the West Bank and Gaza. This proposal would be rejected by Begin, and some parts would also be criticized by the United States. Meanwhile Carter, with support from Sadat, would keep hammering away at Begin on U.N. Resolution 242 and settlements, the two points on which he was believed to be most vulnerable. At an appropriate time, after it was clear that Egypt and Israel had reached a deadlock, the United States would put forward compromise proposals of its own, built around Begin's autonomy plan but clearly limiting autonomy to a transitional stage, which would be followed by an agreement based on the principles of 242, including withdrawal.

These moves might have led somewhere if both parties had been able to stick to the agreed strategy. But neither side was entirely convinced that

6. Vance also noted that Sadat had again raised the possibility of developing "sample treaties," an idea first broached the previous August and indicative of Sadat's desire to go quickly beyond general principles to concrete agreement.

7. Carter noted in the margin of the memorandum "Okay with Sadat." Kamil, *Lost Peace*, pp. 140–41, gives the text of six points that were agreed on as part of a joint scenario.

this was the best approach. The Egyptians were still reluctant to get into details about the West Bank and Gaza. Their idea was to stay with generalities and let the Americans put the pressure on Israel for concessions. The Americans, by contrast, were trying to get Egypt more involved in genuine negotiations over the Palestinian issue, and were hoping to maneuver Sadat into a position in which he would seem to be abandoning hard-line Arab demands under U.S. pressure. This stratagem was probably a bit too Machiavellian and could have placed Sadat in an awkward position if Israel had failed to make comparable concessions. And it was probably a foregone conclusion that Begin would not succumb to U.S. and Egyptian pressure.

As difficult as it would have been to carry out the understanding reached by Sadat and Carter in the best of circumstances, two elements intervened to further complicate the process. First, Sadat decided to request F-5 jet fighters from the Americans. He had previously given this demand low priority, but he now acted as if there were some urgency in getting a response. Since the United States also had requests for arms pending from Israel and Saudi Arabia, Sadat's insistence on an early answer led to the immediate consideration of all three cases. It is not clear why Sadat changed his position on this issue, for he had explicitly recognized on previous occasions that a debate over arms could sidetrack the diplomatic process.

The Temptation of a Bilateral Accord

Second, and more difficult to prove, Sadat and Carter may have reached some general understanding on the importance of moving quickly toward a bilateral Egyptian-Israeli agreement.[8] According to an Egyptian account, the agreement would be negotiated as soon as possible, but not signed until a declaration of general principles had been agreed on with Israel. Then, if the other Arab leaders failed to join negotiations based on these principles, Sadat would proceed to sign the bilateral accord.[9] Carter was

8. In an interview with me on May 22, 1985, President Carter could not recall any specific discussion along these lines with President Sadat. He also said that he was not sure when his own thinking began to shift from the idea of negotiations at Geneva toward the idea of bilateral Egyptian-Israeli talks.

9. Kamil, *Lost Peace*, p. 145. Kamil attaches considerable importance to an "agreement" between Sayyid Marei and Brzezinski, the text of which he gives on pp. 146–47. Its main points were that an early agreement should be reached on Sinai, with the actual signature of the accord being postponed until agreement had been reached on a strong declaration of principles. On p. 148, Kamil makes it clear that he did not like the thrust of the new

sufficiently drawn to the idea of pressing forward on the Egyptian-Israeli front to return from Camp David and ask Brzezinski to prepare a study of the consequences of a bilateral treaty.[10]

Increasingly, Carter and Sadat seemed to be thinking of an Egyptian-Israeli accord, one only loosely connected to an attempt to negotiate an agreement on the Palestinian question. Sadat focused his comments almost entirely on Sinai, where he insisted on full withdrawal by Israeli forces. He rarely talked in detail about the West Bank or Gaza, preferring to stress general principles such as the nonacquisition of territory by force and the right of the Palestinians to self-determination. He did not strongly support the American attempt to mobilize opinion behind a freeze on settlements and the applicability of U.N. Resolution 242 to all fronts. Carter was therefore left in the awkward position of appearing to be more pro-Arab than Sadat, a politically vulnerable position to say the least. Hence the effort was made to get Sadat to put forward a clear proposal on the West Bank and Gaza. When he proved reluctant to do so, Carter apparently began to conclude that Sadat's real interest was a bilateral Egyptian-Israeli deal. This appraisal was probably accurate, but it minimized Sadat's desire to preserve appearances. Sadat cared how he reached agreement with Israel. Face and prestige were involved.

It took many more months for the Americans to realize fully that Sadat's priorities were shifting; the Egyptians around Sadat continued strongly to reject the idea of a separate agreement. But the seed of the idea seems to have been planted at Camp David in February, and it came to fruition seven months later, again at Camp David, this time with Begin

---

agreement, which would involve Egypt in negotiating a bilateral agreement before working out a set of general principles that would apply to all fronts. On pp. 149–51, Kamil gives the Egyptian text of a very accurate account of what the two delegations agreed on. It corresponds with the American version described in this chapter, but provides more detail and gives the Egyptian understanding of what each point meant. This document, prepared by Ahmed Maher, includes four Egyptian "expectations": (1) that this approach will not delay serious efforts to reach agreement on a statement of principles; (2) that the United States will convince Israel to abandon its demand to retain the settlements and airfields in Sinai; (3) that the United States will work toward reaching a special agreement on Sinai very soon. This accord, based on respect for Egyptian sovereignty and the unity of its territory, will be signed at a later date in light of the progress made on other fronts. If, however, an Arab party rejects negotiations in spite of agreement on a statement of principles, Egypt will go ahead and sign anyway. And (4) that the U.S. will respond positively to an Egyptian request to purchase arms.

10. Brzezinski, *Power and Principle*, p. 244. "I suspect that this may have been stimulated by his private discussions with Sadat."

present to remove any last doubts about the possibility of linking progress on Sinai to the larger Palestinian question.

TO LINK OR NOT TO LINK

From the time Sadat left Washington until he returned to participate in the Camp David summit in September, most of the diplomatic maneuvering revolved around the question of linkage, as it came to be known. The question was essentially this: what kind of agreement, if any, on the Palestinian issue should accompany an Egyptian-Israeli treaty? Begin's position was clear. There should be no legal linkage. A treaty with Egypt should in no way depend on progress in solving the Palestinian question. Egypt and Israel might agree to some general principles, or to a variation of Begin's self-rule proposal, but these were separate matters from a treaty between the two states. There was logic in Begin's position, since in the end Sadat could not speak authoritatively for the Palestinians.

Sadat still hoped that any bilateral deal with Israel could be presented within a framework of general principles that would apply to the other fronts of the conflict. In his view Egypt should establish a model on which peace could be reached between Israel and each of its Arab neighbors. The key ingredients would be Israeli withdrawal to the 1967 lines and Arab recognition of Israel and acceptance of security arrangements. Once these principles were established in the context of Egyptian-Israeli talks, it would be up to other Arab leaders to join the negotiations to get the best deal possible within the framework of the principles. Egypt would not wait for them to do so and would proceed to conclude a peace treaty once the general principles were agreed on. The principle of withdrawal on all fronts was even more important for Sadat than Palestinian self-determination, because without the first the second would remain a moot point.

Sadat seems to have gone a bit further in his talks with Carter in February to suggest that a bilateral agreement could be negotiated even before agreement on general principles had been reached, though it would not be signed until after such agreement. His foreign minister, Muhammad Ibrahim Kamil, opposed that approach, fearing that pressure would eventually be brought to bear on Egypt to sign the bilateral agreement regardless of whether Israel had accepted the more general principles of withdrawal on all fronts and Palestinian self-determination.

Carter, who had originally favored a comprehensive set of negotiations with all parties involved, still hoped in early 1978 that something more than an Egyptian-Israeli agreement could be achieved. He was prepared to try to persuade Begin to show flexibility on the West Bank and Gaza. He realized that Sadat's political position at home and in the Arab world would be enhanced if the Egyptian president could demonstrate that he had got more for his trip to Jerusalem than concessions in Sinai. But Carter was also beginning to feel that almost any agreement was better than none at all, and that whatever Egypt and Israel could agree on would be fine with him. As time went by he seemed to think the primary strategic objective for the United States was to conclude a peace treaty between Egypt and Israel, not to resolve the Palestinian question. Begin and his foreign minister, Moshe Dayan, certainly shared this view, and now it seemed that Sadat did as well. By holding firm, the Israelis were wearing down both the Egyptians and the Americans.

Despite the slow shift of focus toward Egyptian-Israeli bilateral negotiations, much of the debate over the ensuing months concerned the West Bank and Gaza—as well as arms sales to Egypt, Israel, and Saudi Arabia. In a discussion with Secretary of Defense Harold Brown on February 6, Sadat had confirmed his interest in early purchase of 120 F-5s. A week later, on February 13, 1978, Secretary Vance recommended to the president that he agree to sell 50 F-5s to Egypt, 60 F-15s to Saudi Arabia, and 75 F-16s and 15 F-15s to Israel. These sales would be presented to Congress as a package so that all the cases or none would be approved. In that way Congress could not proceed with only the Israelis' requests and turn down the Arabs'. Carter approved Vance's recommendation the same day, a decision that had considerable bearing on the diplomacy of the next two months.

PRESSURE ON ISRAEL

The day Sadat left Washington, February 8, 1978, the White House issued a statement on the Middle East, emphasizing that "Resolution 242 is applicable to all fronts of the conflict" and that "Israeli settlements in occupied territory are contrary to international law and an obstacle to peace, and that further settlement activity would be inconsistent with the effort to reach a peace settlement." The White House also repeated in full the Aswan statement on the legitimate rights of the Palestinians.[11]

11. "Visit of President Sadat of Egypt: White House Statement on the Final Meeting, February 8, 1978," *Public Papers: Carter, 1978*, vol. 1, pp. 291–92. Moshe Dayan, *Breakthrough*, pp. 115–19, describes his negative reaction to this statement and to what he saw as the administration's deliberate attempt to create an anti-Israeli mood.

Dayan in Washington

On February 16 both Secretary of State Vance and President Carter met separately with Israeli Foreign Minister Dayan. Vance began the discussions by spelling out in detail Sadat's need for a declaration of principles. With such a declaration, Vance argued, King Hussein might join the negotiations. If a declaration was agreed on between Egypt and Israel, and if Jordan refused to join the talks, Sadat would have a problem. Vance said he did not know what the Egyptian leader would then do. He was sure, however, that Sadat did not require Syria's participation before proceeding toward a bilateral agreement.

Dayan replied by saying that Israel wanted peace with Egypt, but would not be able to reach it through face-to-face talks. The United States would have to be involved and would have to contribute ideas of its own. Dayan then turned to the issue of 242, stating bluntly that Israel would not accept withdrawal on all fronts. Evacuating the West Bank was not part of the Israeli plan. Other parties could make such proposals in negotiations, but Israel would not do so. Israel, he said, wanted a peace agreement with Jordan without withdrawal. Israel intended to keep its military positions, its settlements, and its right to settle. He acknowledged that this might not be consistent with 242 or with the position of the previous Israeli government, but it was the Begin government's position.

In his meeting with Dayan later the same day, Carter stated forcefully that Sadat could not move further without Hussein. Israel would have to agree to the language of 242 as it applied to all fronts. Dayan restated Israel's position, and then asked, as he was to do over and over, if Sadat would be content with words alone or if King Hussein actually had to join the negotiations. Shifting his earlier assessment, Carter said Sadat might be satisfied with just a framework for a comprehensive settlement.

During his talks in Washington Dayan showed the Americans a curious document that supposedly represented what Carter had told a group of American Jewish leaders a few days earlier. In it Carter allegedly said that Israel might be able to keep one airfield in Sinai; that Israel could retain a military presence in the West Bank beyond five years; and that the West Bank Palestinians would be allowed to participate in a referendum after the five-year transitional period and would have the choice of affiliation with Jordan or Israel, or continuation of the status quo, but not the choice of an independent state. Carter reportedly had told the

Jewish leaders that even the Saudis did not favor an independent Palestinian state. Some of these points did indeed accurately reflect Carter's thinking, but some, such as the possibility that Israel could retain an airfield in Sinai, were clearly misunderstandings. The net effect was to cause some confusion in the negotiating process and to make Carter and Vance wary of what they said before Jewish audiences in the future.[12]

Clarifications from Sadat

After the talks with Dayan, Carter sent a cable to Sadat requesting his answer to Dayan's questions. If a strong declaration of principles could be agreed on, and if King Hussein still refused to join the talks, how far would Sadat be prepared to go? And in those same circumstances, how would Egypt react if Syria refused to negotiate?

Two days later Sadat's reply was in hand. If there was a strong declaration and King Hussein stayed out, Sadat would go forward and sign a peace treaty with Israel. It would help if Hussein agreed to participate in the negotiations, but the important thing was the declaration of principles. Syria's attitude was no problem. Sadat insisted, however, that the declaration must call for withdrawal from the West Bank, Gaza, and Golan by name, or at a minimum from the West Bank and Gaza. Sadat might be prepared to accept a first-stage withdrawal in Sinai with only a declaration of principle, but the second stage of agreement with Israel should be postponed until the West Bank–Gaza issue was settled. Jordan and the Palestinians should have responsibility for the West Bank, and Egypt would deal with Gaza. Sadat also noted that he had urged a prominent Israeli politician to allow one of the moderate PLO leaders to represent the Palestinians in any talks.

The next step on the American side was to send Assistant Secretary Alfred L. Atherton, Jr., back to the Middle East to try to make headway on a declaration of principles. While Atherton was in Cairo on March 1, Sadat gave him a letter to deliver to Begin containing extremely critical language. Sadat claimed that Begin was wasting time by quibbling over words, whereas Sadat felt the whole problem could be solved in a few days if only Israel would agree to the principles of withdrawal, Palestinian rights, and mutual security. Expanding on this last point, Sadat said he recognized that Israel would have security concerns in the West Bank even after the five-year transitional period. Begin's reply a few days later

---

12. See Dayan, *Breakthrough*, pp. 119–20, for an account of his meeting with Carter.

was argumentative and included the point that Israel did not need Egypt's recognition, because recognition of Israel's right to exist came only from God.

In brief, the Egyptian-Israeli relationship was deteriorating, and the groundwork was gradually being laid for an American intervention to break the impasse. But first Sadat had to put forward a proposal of his own, and Carter had to get both the Panama treaties and the arms package through the Senate. Meanwhile the United States tried to keep pressure on Begin.

An Egyptian Proposal

In accordance with the time schedule discussed between Sadat and Carter in early February, the Egyptians prepared a document called "Basic Guidelines for the Solution of the Palestinian Question." Sadat gave a copy to Atherton on March 7, but asked that it not be shown yet to the Israelis. The paper consisted of four sections and was limited to a general restatement of the Egyptian position. It called for full Israeli withdrawal, including withdrawal from Jerusalem and from the settlements; it supported the principle of self-determination for the Palestinians 'and the right of refugees to choose between returning to their homes or receiving compensation; it called for a short transitional period for the West Bank and Gaza under U.N. supervision, ending with a plebiscite in which the Palestinians would decide on their political future; and in a final section it briefly mentioned security arrangements and guarantees. In passing, the paper noted that Egypt believed that a Palestinian state should have a link to Jordan.

The American reaction to the Egyptian document was one of disappointment. Carter and Vance had hoped to see the Egyptians develop the idea of a transitional regime in more convincing detail. The gap between the Israeli position and the Egyptian was so large that an American compromise could not possibly bridge it. As a result, the Americans urged Sadat to come up with another proposal, this time spelling out more completely Egypt's views on the transitional period.

Strains with Israel

While waiting for a new Egyptian proposal, Carter kept up the pressure on the Israelis. On March 9 he again insisted in a press conference that U.N. Resolution 242 must apply to the West Bank, Gaza, and the Golan. The same day, Mark Siegal, an aide to presidential assistant Hamilton

Jordan who had maintained close ties with the Jewish community, had resigned in protest over the proposed sale of advanced aircraft to Saudi Arabia. Carter did not appear to be disturbed and kept up his criticism of Begin's unwillingness to give the Palestinians a voice in determining their own future.[13]

Israel's flamboyant defense minister, Ezer Weizman, arrived in Washington at this time. He found the atmosphere chilly, but was surprised to hear from the president that Begin's plan for self-rule, with certain modifications, could serve as the basis for a transitional arrangement. But before Weizman could enjoy this apparent softening of Carter's views, the president added that the Palestinians might be given the right at the end of five years to hold a plebiscite on their future. While ruling out an independent Palestinian state, Carter was trying to keep open the option of linking the West Bank to Jordan. To try to sweeten the idea for the Israelis, however, Carter spoke of the possibility that Israeli forces would remain even after the five-year transition. Weizman was not convinced, but he might well have been confused.[14]

As the United States continued to try to maneuver the Egyptians and Israelis toward some common ground, it became aware that extremists among both the Arabs and Israelis might seek to disrupt the negotiating process. That was precisely what happened on March 11, 1978, when PLO guerrillas attacked an Israeli bus along the coastal road, leaving more than thirty Israelis dead. Within days the Begin government reacted, launching Operation Litani, a full-scale invasion of southern Lebanon designed to drive the PLO out of the area near the border.

Carter was appalled by the PLO attack, but he refused to accept the legitimacy of the Israeli response. It was disproportionate to the threat; it entailed the use of American weapons for purposes other than self-defense; and it ran the risk of compromising the chances of progress in the negotiations with Egypt. If the United States were to appear to condone the Israeli invasion, there would be little chance of convincing Jordan and moderate Palestinians to join the peace talks. Carter therefore supported a U.N. Resolution calling for Israeli withdrawal and the creation of a U.N. force, dubbed UNIFIL, to patrol south Lebanon. Over the next several months Lebanon was a continuing irritant in U.S.-Israeli relations, but the peace process was not brought to an end.

13. "The President's News Conference of March 9, 1978," *Public Papers: Carter, 1978*, vol. 1, pp. 491–94.
14. Ezer Weizman, *Battle for Peace*, pp. 260–62.

BEGIN'S SIX NOES

In his first two meetings with Prime Minister Begin, Carter had been relatively mild, listening with patience to the Israeli leader's explanations. He had hoped to win his trust and confidence, apparently believing that Begin's intransigence might melt under a healthy dose of southern hospitality. But after their first meeting, in July 1977, the word had got back to the White House that Begin considered Carter weak. Their second encounter, in December 1977, had done little to firm up Carter's reputation, but by March 21, 1978, when Begin arrived in Washington, Carter was in a fighting mood. Part of his attitude was no doubt a deliberate ploy to put more pressure on Begin, but much of it was genuine irritation with Begin's rigidity.

In their first session Begin blamed the breakdown of negotiations on Sadat's insistence that Israel agree to the principles of full withdrawal and Palestinian statehood as preconditions for further talks. Carter took strong exception to this assertion, noting that Sadat would accept some border modifications in the West Bank (though only minor ones), and that he favored a Palestinian entity tied to Jordan, not a fully independent state.

After a lengthy review of how the impasse had come about, Carter returned to the attack, pressing Begin hard on the question of the applicability of the withdrawal provision of U.N. Resolution 242 to the West Bank. Carter said the issue was not that Sadat insisted on full withdrawal, but rather that Begin refused to consider any withdrawal at all. Even if Israel was allowed to keep some security forces in the West Bank and Gaza during a transition, and perhaps beyond, Israel would not withdraw politically from these areas. Carter reminded Begin that Sadat would proceed with negotiations for a peace treaty once a declaration of principles was reached even if King Hussein refused to join the talks.

Dayan and Attorney General Barak tried to put a positive face on the Israeli position, arguing that nothing in the self-rule proposal was contrary to 242. The Begin government simply had a different interpretation of the resolution. For example, in its view the offer to abolish the military government could be seen as a form of withdrawal. If this was accepted, there would be no dispute over 242 and the West Bank. Carter correctly noted that Begin had changed the policy toward the West Bank from that of the preceding Israeli government. For this reason a clarification on 242 was needed. Begin acknowledged that there had indeed been a change.

The discussion then turned to what might happen after five years of self-rule in the West Bank and Gaza. Would the Palestinians have the right to join with Jordan? Begin said a plebiscite could not be accepted. Carter responded by saying that this attitude on the part of Israel would make it impossible to reach any agreement with Egypt. Vance added that the Palestinians had to be given some choice at the end of the transition. Carter chimed in, saying the self-rule plan would give Israel a permanent veto. He, for one, would never want to participate in such a scheme if Israel could always veto the results.

As this first session came to an end, Carter said the main obstacle to peace between Egypt and Israel was Begin's determination to keep political control over the West Bank and Gaza, not just for now, but for the foreseeable future, with or without a peace agreement. Carter urged Begin not to close the door to peace. Israel should accept the idea of eventually relinquishing political control over the West Bank in return for adequate security guarantees. This would be the best basis for an agreement. Adding a few words of praise for Sadat, Carter ended by saying he was very discouraged.

In subsequent talks with Vance, the Israelis kept pushing the idea that withdrawal could be interpreted in many ways. At one point Vance pressed again for precision on what might happen at the end of five years. Could Israel be more explicit about the process by which a final agreement would be worked out? Dayan said he would raise the question with the prime minister.

On March 22 Carter and Begin met again. The president had spent the previous evening with Begin, but there had been no give. Carter was blunt in his criticism of the Israelis. He said he had become reconciled to the idea that peace would come first between Egypt and Israel, and not in the comprehensive framework that he had first envisaged. But now he doubted that even this more limited outcome could be achieved.

Carter then reviewed his position. He did not insist, nor did most of the Arabs, on complete Israeli withdrawal or on a fully independent Palestinian state. Begin was using these as excuses for his own unwillingness to withdraw. The United States could support the self-rule proposal, with modifications, as the basis for a transitional regime for the West Bank and Gaza, but there must be some means for reassessing the situation after five years. Authority for the transitional period should be derived from agreement among the parties, not from the Israeli military government. Claims of sovereignty would be left in abeyance. The West

Bank and Gaza should be demilitarized, except for some Israeli military encampments into which Israeli forces would be withdrawn. During the interim period Israel would have an effective veto over a number of security-related issues, but there should be no new settlements or any expansion of existing settlements.

Turning to the Israeli position, Carter said that even if Israel was not required to withdraw completely from the West Bank, and even if there was no Palestinian state, Begin would still not show flexibility. He would not stop settlement activity; he would not give up the settlements in Sinai; he would not allow the Sinai settlements to remain under U.N. or Egyptian protection; he would not agree to withdraw politically from the West Bank even if Israel could retain military outposts; he would not recognize that 242 applied to all fronts; and he would not give the Palestinians the right to choose, at the end of the interim period, whether they wanted to be affiliated with Jordan or Israel, or to continue the self-rule arrangements.

Begin agreed that Carter had accurately described his views, but claimed that the six points had all been put in the negative. There was a way they could be stated in the positive. As the talks came to an end, the mood on the Israeli side was somber.[15]

Carter was quick to brief congressional leaders on Begin's negative attitudes, and before long the press was filled with reports of the Israeli position, often labeled the "six noes." Even Kissinger told one of Carter's advisers that the Israeli position was hopeless. For once, Carter reached the American public with his interpretation of events before Begin had done so. All Carter's actions were in conformity with the deal worked out with Sadat the previous month at Camp David. The stage was now set for receiving an Egyptian proposal, carrying on a sharp debate with both sides for some time, and then intervening to break the deadlock with a carefully drafted American compromise. But over the next few months this strategy began to crumble, and once again domestic political realities were part of the cause.

15. Several accounts of these meetings exist: Carter, *Keeping Faith*, pp. 311–12; Vance, *Hard Choices*, p. 207; Brzezinski, *Power and Principle*, pp. 246–47; and Dayan, *Breakthrough*, pp. 120–29. The "six noes" are summarized accurately by Don Oberdorfer, "Carter Summary of Begin Stand Is Bleak," *Washington Post*, March 26, 1978. In his book (p. 129) Dayan correctly notes that the session was difficult, but adds that it showed that the American side would not insist on full withdrawal and would accept elements of the self-rule proposal as the basis for an interim agreement. In interviews with other Israeli participants in this meeting I was told that it was seen as the low point for Israel in the entire negotiating process.

A PARTIAL RETREAT

As President Carter became more and more involved in discussing the details of a possible settlement on the West Bank and Gaza, he also became vulnerable to the charge that he was trying to impose his views on the Israelis and was colluding with Sadat. Carter was particularly open to the criticism that he was more concerned with the Palestinian question than Sadat was, a point the White House political advisers were sensitive to. From the outset, Carter had recognized that Egypt had to be involved in genuine negotiations with Israel for the United States to assert its influence. Carter did not want to give the impression that the United States was negotiating with Israel on Sadat's behalf. Fresh from his recent skirmishes with Begin, Carter now needed Sadat to rejoin the game.

Carter's deep involvement in the detail of the talks was not only politically controversial. It also ran the risk of getting the presidential stamp of approval on formulations that, at times, were improvised and troublesome. For example, in his talks with Senate leaders at the time of the Begin visit, Carter had said that, during the interim period, matters involving security would require unanimous agreement among Israel, Egypt, Jordan, and the Palestinian elected authority for the West Bank and Gaza. The wording of this suggestion was meant, of course, to give Israel a veto over security questions, but it also would have given a veto to everyone else. It was a careless formulation, but it was the kind of statement that would put a man like Begin on his guard. After all, his attention to words was legendary, and he tended to be wary if others were using them imprecisely.

Similarly, Carter and Vance were pressing for some sort of plebiscite for the Palestinians at the end of five years. But to allay Israel's stated fears, the option of a Palestinian state was to be explicitly precluded. This omission was not enough to reassure Begin, who opposed the idea of returning the West Bank to Jordan as much as he opposed an independent Palestinian state. Nor could any Arab leader readily exclude in advance the one goal that most Palestinians supported. As a result, the United States found itself carving out some rather shaky middle ground, less by design than through the impromptu comments of its top leaders. Some tighter discipline over the evolution of the American position would be needed as the negotiations moved forward.[16] One step in this direction

16. These points were contained in a memorandum from me to Brzezinski dated April

was Carter's decision to name Atherton as ambassador-at-large for Middle East peace negotiations and to appoint Harold H. Saunders as assistant secretary of state for Near East and South Asian affairs.

With the Panama treaties scheduled for a Senate vote in mid-April, the moment was also approaching for the administration to send the Middle East arms package, including the controversial F-15s for the Saudis, to Capitol Hill.[17] A prominent Democratic party leader with close ties to the Jewish community had approached the White House with an offer. He urged the administration to delay sending the arms package to Congress for one or two months and to throw its weight solidly behind an Egyptian-Israeli bilateral agreement. In return, the administration could count on substantial Jewish and congressional support for pressing Begin to change his position on 242 and eventually for the sale of the F-15s to Saudi Arabia. A debate over the arms package at this time would cause an irreparable breach between the friends of Israel and the administration. Carter ignored this offer and decided to proceed with the sales. The package was sent to Congress on April 28.

Meanwhile contacts between Egypt and Israel had been resumed. In late March Weizman and Barak had met with Sadat and Defense Minister Gamasy. They had tried to find out if the Egyptians would sign a separate treaty. Weizman had the impression that Sadat wanted only a fig leaf, and that this could be provided by real autonomy for the Palestinians.

11, 1978. The memo suggested that the idea of a plebiscite should be replaced by that of a referendum that would be held after the five-year period to ratify the terms of the final peace treaty dealing with the status of the West Bank. The memo concluded with the following observation: "The weakness of this approach is that it provides no assurance that the parties will negotiate in good faith to conclude a peace treaty that could be submitted for ratification at the end of five years. But this will be a potential problem in any scenario involving the West Bank–Gaza once Egypt has concluded its own agreement with Israel. Sadat realizes this and has therefore thought of the possibility of tying the first stage of implementation of his own bilateral agreement to the conclusion of the negotiations on the Palestinian question. Whether this is the best means or not, we do need to think of how momentum can be maintained in negotiations once a Sinai agreement has been reached. Once Egypt has settled with Israel, much of the pressure on Israel for further movement will be removed, which is precisely why Jordan and Syria are so afraid of a separate deal."

17. In an interview with me on May 22, 1985, President Carter said he normally paid little attention to his political advisers when they urged him to postpone one controversial move in order to enhance the chances of positive action on another issue. But in the spring of 1978 he was working simultaneously on Panama, the Middle East, normalization of relations with China, and SALT II. He recognized that to win the Senate vote on the Panama treaties, which he saw as vital to U.S. interests, he would have to have support from pro-Israeli, pro-Taiwan, and anti-SALT senators. Therefore, until the Panama vote was concluded, he had to hold back on issues that might irritate some of these senators.

But Weizman worried that Begin had reduced the autonomy plan to a caricature of genuine self-rule.[18]

The next move came in talks between Vance and Dayan on April 26 and 27. Barak reviewed at length the recent meetings in Egypt, saying that Sadat still insisted on a declaration that would include Israeli withdrawal and Palestinian self-determination. If this point could be achieved, Sadat had indicated considerable flexibility on other issues. Gamasy, he said, had even suggested that Egypt and Israel should negotiate and initial two secret agreements, one on Sinai and one on the West Bank. Then a declaration should be issued by both parties, spelling out common principles for peace and inviting other parties to join. If Jordan chose to stay out, the two secret agreements could be signed and implemented.

Dayan placed emphasis on reaching an understanding on what would in fact happen in the West Bank and Gaza during the interim period. If Egypt and Israel could agree on that, a declaration of principles should not be so difficult. But not all the details could be worked out at present. Dayan then tried out an idea that few other Israelis seemed to share: unilateral implementation of the self-rule proposal. In his view, if Egypt and the United States were in general agreement, Israel could simply proceed to carry out the key provisions of autonomy on its own. The military government could be abolished; military redeployments could take place; elections could be called. The details of what would happen after five years could be left vague.

During the second day of talks Vance returned to the question of the final status of the West Bank and Gaza, arguing that not everything could be left vague as Dayan preferred. Dayan again raised the possibility of secret agreements with Egypt, arguing that Sadat could not be expected to do everything in public. Dayan urged the United States to make proposals of its own, but balked when Vance asked him if Israel could provide answers to the questions raised during the recent Begin visit on whether and how the final status of the West Bank would be resolved after the interim period. With a distinct lack of enthusiasm, Dayan agreed to seek answers to Vance's questions from his government.[19]

18. Weizman, *Battle for Peace*, pp. 292–301. Weizman recounts that Sadat retreated from some concessions after consulting with Palestinians from Gaza and failing to convince them of his views. The Egyptian foreign minister was furious that Sadat had agreed to receive Weizman while the Arab foreign ministers were meeting in Cairo and Kamil was trying to patch things up with them. Kamil, *Lost Peace*, pp. 225–32.

19. Dayan, *Breakthrough*, pp. 129–33.

On balance, little was achieved in the talks with Dayan, but once again the American side felt that Dayan's pragmatism, coupled with Barak's creativity, held out the best hope on the Israeli side for genuine progress. If only Begin could be as reasonable, some headway might be made. In any case, some of the sharp edges that had marked the Carter-Begin meeting had been removed. On the eve of a big battle with Congress over the aircraft package, that was some consolation. It also reflected a gradual drift from the confrontational strategy agreed on with Sadat at Camp David.[20]

PROPOSALS, PLANES, AND PLEAS

During much of May and June 1978, the Middle East group around Carter worked simultaneously to encourage the Egyptians to put forward a proposal of their own on the West Bank and Gaza, to convince Congress not to veto the sale of sophisticated aircraft to Saudi Arabia, and to get Israeli answers to questions about how the future of the occupied areas would be decided after five years of autonomy. In the end the administration got some or all of what it asked for on each score, but the result did little to move the peace process forward. The Egyptian proposals were generally disappointing; the plane sale used up much scarce political capital; Sadat was becoming apprehensive that a U.S. proposal might be counterproductive;[21] and the Israeli answers, when they finally arrived, were useless.

A New Proposal from Sadat

On May 1 a revised version of the Egyptian proposal was given to the Americans, called "Guidelines for the Solution of the Palestinian Question."[22] It included somewhat more detail on the transitional period than

---

20. On May 1, 1978, Carter met briefly in New York with Begin. To improve the atmosphere of relations with Israel, and to enhance the chances of passage of the aircraft package, Carter went out of his way to identify with some of Begin's views: "My belief is that a permanent settlement will not include an independent Palestinian nation on the West Bank. My belief is that a permanent settlement will not call for complete withdrawal of Israel from occupied territories. My belief is that a permanent settlement will be based substantially upon the home-rule proposal that Prime Minister Begin has put forward." Bernard Gwertzman, "Begin Arrives in U.S. and Will See Carter about Mideast Issues," *New York Times*, May 1, 1978.

21. See Kamil, *Lost Peace*, p. 263–64, for the text of a letter from Sadat to Carter warning that a U.S. proposal along the lines of the nine points would "complicate matters for us and have negative repercussions in the Arab world."

22. Ibid., pp. 623–26.

the March 7 draft. Full authority would be vested in the U.N. secretary general, and Jordan and Egypt would have advisory roles in the West Bank and Gaza, respectively. No mention was made of Israel having any role at all during the transition.

On the same day the Egyptian proposal arrived, Carter met briefly with Begin as part of ceremonies to mark the thirtieth anniversary of Israel's independence. The talks were cordial, with Begin expressing his pleasure at finding again the good atmosphere of his visit the previous July. On substantive matters, Carter told him that an Egyptian proposal could be expected imminently. Begin seemed pleased. Carter stressed the importance of getting the Israeli answers to the questions about how the final status of the territories would be determined. Begin promised an answer within a short time.

The Arms Package

For the next two weeks much of the administration's time was taken up with the debate over the arms package. Carter and all his top aides spent time lobbying the Senate for votes. On May 12, 1978, the president sent a strong letter to every member of the Senate and House leadership stressing the importance of the sales.[23] Three days later the Senate voted by a comfortable margin not to veto the sales. The Israelis had fought hard against the sale of planes to Saudi Arabia and had lost. But Carter did not feel emboldened by this victory. If anything, he seemed to conclude that he could not afford many more such confrontations with Israel and its friends in Congress.[24]

Reassessment

Two days after the Senate vote, on May 17, 1978, I sent a memorandum to Brzezinski raising concern about the lack of direction in Carter's strategy. My purpose was to try to call attention to problems that were already visible on the horizon:

With the successful conclusion of the debate over the arms sales, we must now

23. "Middle East Arms Sales: Letter to Members of Congress, May 12, 1978," *Public Papers: Carter, 1978*, vol. 1, pp. 896–97.

24. Carter, *Keeping Faith*, pp. 313, noted that shortly after his cordial meeting with Begin on May 1, 1978, he "still had serious political problems among American Jews, and a few days later we had to postpone two major Democratic fund-raising banquets in New York and Los Angeles because so many members had canceled their reservations to attend." Many political advisers were urging Carter to become less involved in the Middle East. Ibid., pp. 315–16.

turn again to the diplomacy of the Arab-Israeli peace negotiations. I am concerned that we are approaching a critical moment without having given adequate thought to our basic strategy. In particular, I detect at least *four potentially serious flaws in our present approach*:

—*Timing.* We have assumed that time would work to soften the Israeli unwillingness to accept that the principle of withdrawal applies on all fronts. Despite the internal Israeli debate, we have no reason whatsoever to expect a softening of Begin's position on the West Bank/Gaza. Sadat may be willing to stick with the negotiations for lack of a better alternative, but he is beginning to hedge his bets and has few cards left to play. Time is now working against us and against moderation and added flexibility.

—*Cooperation with Sadat.* In February, we tried to develop a joint approach with Sadat. With the passage of several months, it is unclear how much of a common strategy remains. Sadat takes initiatives without informing us in advance; he holds back on what he is saying to Weizman; he lets his officials turn out worthless legalistic documents in the guise of serious negotiating proposals; and yet he seems to be disappointed with our reluctance to become a full partner. We do not have a satisfactory political understanding with Sadat as we enter a crucial phase of the negotiations. The reason, in my view, is that he has little idea of how to proceed and counts on us to bail him out. His impatience with details is becoming a real problem, as is his reluctance to engage in sustained negotiations.

—*Jordan.* We have assumed that Jordan would be able to play a constructive role in helping to solve the West Bank/Palestinian part of the problem. But Hussein is deeply suspicious of the "self-rule" proposal. In addition, Sadat's success in getting Egyptian sovereignty over Sinai recognized by Israel stands as a measuring stick against which his own efforts will be judged. He cannot expect to do as well and does not want to take the blame for selling out the Palestinians. With the PLO out of the picture, the local West Bank/Gaza Palestinians demoralized, and Hussein pessimistic, only Sadat remains to negotiate with Israel over the West Bank and Gaza. This will require him to hold out firmly for virtually full withdrawal, since otherwise he also will be accused of sacrificing Arab rights and he will have little to show for his initiative of last November. Even if he could strike a deal with Dayan, could he deliver on his part of the bargain?

—*Declaration and Nine Points.* We have relied upon formal paper exercises as the means by which to move forward. Both Israel and Egypt have apparently lost interest in this. All Sadat really wants is a public Israeli affirmation of a willingness to withdraw once Israel has achieved peace, security and recognition through negotiations. He will not get this, and vague 242 language will not be an adequate substitute. The other essential requirement is broad agreement on an interim arrangement for the West Bank/Gaza, but on this there has been virtually no productive dialogue and our own approach needs some rethinking (e.g., the limited-choice referendum is not acceptable to anyone). Dayan may have been on the right track in suggesting that we get away from these legalistic exercises, but he fails to address Sadat's political need for an Israeli response to his initiative that goes beyond the offer to return Sinai.

Options

We are approaching a difficult period. If we could get a clear, albeit conditional, Israeli commitment to eventual withdrawal from the West Bank/Gaza, that would open the way for Egypt and Jordan to work out with Israel the details of a five-year interim arrangement and for Sadat to conclude his negotiations on Sinai. This should remain our primary objective. *If we cannot get such a clear Israeli commitment on withdrawal, the only realistic alternatives will be continued stalemate or a bilateral Egyptian-Israeli agreement on Sinai. At some point we may have to ask ourselves whether a bilateral deal is better than none at all.*

The central question, if we still prefer a broad-based peace effort, is whether we can persuade Begin to change his position on the West Bank. We have already gone about as far as possible with reasoned argument and with adjustments in our own positions.

— We have come out strongly against an independent Palestinian state and have relegated the PLO to obscurity. We no longer even speak of a Palestinian homeland.

— We have publicly stated that 242 does allow for border changes, and have dropped our emphasis on only "minor modifications" in deference to Begin's sensibilities.

— We have spoken of an Israeli military presence in the West Bank/Gaza for an interim period and beyond, which the Israelis have viewed as endorsement of a permanent military presence, to the acute embarrassment of the Egyptians, Jordanians, and Saudis.

—We have left the strong impression that Israel will remain in control of a unified city of Jerusalem; will have a veto over the return of refugees; and will be able to keep existing settlements in the West Bank.

— We have suggested to Israel a bilateral mutual security treaty and have foresworn the use of military and economic aid as a form of pressure.

— We have made it clear that Israeli withdrawal from the West Bank/Gaza would be conditional upon the achievement of full peace, security, and recognition.

What have we gotten in return from Begin? A vigorous defense of his "self-rule" proposal; a repetition of the litany that everything is negotiable and that there are no preconditions; and a vague promise to give us some idea of what would happen after a five-year interim period on the West Bank. This is pretty thin, especially in light of the rather extensive efforts we have made to deal seriously with Israel's security concerns. If Begin really has any intention of reaching an agreement on the West Bank/Gaza, he would ask us to pin down with Sadat and Hussein some of the points we have explored with him. But instead he has acted as if his proposals are fully adequate until Egypt comes forward with a counterproposal of its own. Dayan and Barak, to their credit, recognize what a sterile approach this is, but they cannot break out of it without our help.

There will be a temptation after the arms package to try to make amends with the Israelis. This will no doubt take the form of assurances about our commitment to Israel's security. But we should not feel guilty about the positions we have taken to date. We have been very forthcoming, and it has gotten us very little. Begin will act the aggrieved party, and he will convince many of his own people.

But the truth is that Begin has not moved an inch in his thinking on the West Bank/Gaza, in contrast to his rather forthcoming proposals on Sinai. For nearly five months negotiations have remained stalemated, primarily because of Begin's unwillingness to accept the principle of "withdrawal for peace" when it comes to the West Bank. He must assume that either Sadat will cave in and agree to a bilateral deal, or that we will give up in despair. He may be right on either or both counts.[25]

As the tone of this memorandum makes clear, my sense of frustration was mounting. The next round of diplomacy did little to ease the strain. When the American ambassador to Israel, Samuel Lewis, met with Dayan on May 6, Dayan had said that Israel could provide positive answers to the questions about the final status of the West Bank and Gaza if Sadat could clarify his position on four points. (1) Will Egypt negotiate and conclude an agreement on the West Bank and Gaza if Jordan refuses to join the negotiations? (2) Will Egypt drop its insistence on total withdrawal and accept "minor modifications" in the 1967 lines? (3) Will Egypt accept a continuing Israeli defense force presence in the West Bank and Gaza in limited areas at strategic points? (4) Will Egypt accept the Aswan language on the Palestinians rather than insist on self-determination and an independent state?

These questions were dutifully conveyed to Sadat, who said that he would answer them once Israel had clarified its position on withdrawal from the West Bank and Gaza. Lewis returned to see Dayan on May 19 to urge that the Israelis be forthcoming. Negotiations by questionnaire were getting nowhere.

A Secret Planning Group

Meanwhile Vance had urged the Egyptians to revise their May 1, 1978, proposal for fear that its tone and content would strengthen the hard-liners in Israel. On May 17 the Egyptians sent a long memorandum to Washington defending their proposal, arguing that they too had a public opinion to worry about.

Finally, the American side decided that a new look was needed. In complete secrecy, a planning group was formed under Secretary Vance. Its membership consisted of the vice president; Brzezinski and his deputy David Aaron; Under Secretary David Newsom, Atherton, and Saunders from State; and myself from the National Security Council staff. Hamilton Jordan and press secretary Jody Powell were also occasional participants

---

25. Memorandum from me to Brzezinski dated May 17, 1978.

to ensure that domestic political realities were taken into account. For the next several weeks this group met regularly, reporting to the president and trying to find a way out of the apparent impasse.

The first meeting of the group took place on June 1, 1978. Vance posed the question of when the United States should put forward a proposal of its own. Mondale outlined in some detail the concerns of the American Jewish community. The arms sales to Saudi Arabia had apparently created a strong reaction. Mondale and Aaron were reluctant to press forward with a proposal in these circumstances. Instead, they argued for getting Egypt back to the negotiating table and refocusing attention on the "withdrawal for peace" formula under U.N. Resolution 242. Vance said the Egyptians would be told that their proposal was unacceptable and would have to be revised. It was agreed that a draft of an American proposal should be developed, based on the nine-point plan of the previous February. Finally, it was noted that Mondale would be going to the Middle East in late June and that his trip could serve a useful purpose in sounding out both the Israelis and Egyptians.

For the next several weeks the main thrust of the U.S. effort was to encourage the Egyptians to put forward their revised proposal and to agree to a resumption of negotiations. On June 11 Ambassador Eilts met with Sadat and his advisers to suggest some changes in the Egyptian draft of May 1.[26] The most important changes were that there should be negotiations to work out the details of the transitional regime and that Israel could retain a security presence during the transition. Sadat's reaction to the American suggestions was generally positive, though he said the United States should force him to accept the point about an Israeli security presence. When the United States made such a proposal, he would initially complain about it for the sake of Arab public opinion, but Carter could be sure he would accept it in the end. More interesting was Sadat's caution about an American proposal. Before any such step, Sadat warned, the United States and Egypt should work out the minute details of such a plan. In the meantime Sadat suggested that Carter should propose the resumption of talks at the level of foreign ministers. This would help President Carter with his own public opinion.

A few days later, on June 18, the long-awaited Israeli answers finally arrived in Washington. In essence, Israel agreed that "the nature of future relations between the parties will be considered and agreed upon at the suggestion of any of the parties" after five years of autonomy. Agreement

26. See Kamil, *Lost Peace*, p. 291. Sadat also told Kamil at this time that Carter had requested a meeting of Vance, Dayan, and Kamil. Sadat had agreed. Ibid., p. 292.

would be reached through negotiations. No mention was made of 242 or of any role for Jordan or Egypt in deciding the future of the West Bank and Gaza. And the Israeli cabinet made clear that the whole five-year autonomy scheme would not even go into force until peace treaties had already been signed with Egypt and Jordan. The Americans tried to shrug off their disappointment, and Dayan could hardly conceal his distaste for the exercise in questionnaire diplomacy.

By the time the Middle East group met on June 21, 1978, it had plenty of paper to look at but little enthusiasm for the exercise. Many American drafts had been developed; the revised Egyptian proposal had been received on June 15; and Dayan had explained in some detail the meaning of the Israeli answers. Even though there was little new to work with, Vance decided he should meet with Kamil and Dayan in London in mid-July.[27]

Mondale to the Middle East

Vice President Mondale's trip to Israel and Egypt was the next step in the process of regaining some momentum in the peace talks. A carefully designed speech was prepared for Mondale to deliver in Jerusalem spelling out the American position in general terms. It explicitly reaffirmed that the principles of U.N. Resolution 242, including withdrawal, must be applied to all fronts. In a crucial passage in the speech, which he delivered at the Knesset on July 2, 1978, the vice president stated: "In the Sinai, Israel has proposed a peace treaty in which there would be negotiated withdrawal and security would be achieved while relinquishing claims to territory. This approach can be applied in the West Bank and Gaza."[28]

In talks with Dayan, Mondale encountered deep anger and skepticism. Dayan bluntly said Sadat would never agree to a separate peace. He would always have to ask for major concessions for the Palestinians, which Israel could not grant. The Israeli foreign minister told Mondale that it was futile to seek a declaration of principles or greater clarity from Begin on 242. The only way to proceed, he said, was through private understandings with Sadat. In a separate meeting Mondale encountered

27. See ibid., pp. 627–28, for the text of the Egyptian proposal; see also Dayan, *Breakthrough*, pp. 136–37. Brzezinski, *Power and Principle*, p. 249, discusses the mid-June shift to a different strategy: delaying the introduction of an American proposal until after another meeting at the foreign minister level. He notes that Mondale in particular was beginning to talk of the need for a more politically attuned "top-level negotiator."

28. Texts of the speeches by Mondale and Begin are contained in Meron Medzini, ed., *Israel's Foreign Relations*, vol. 5, pp. 445–55; quotation is from p. 453.

a blast from Israel's burly agricultural minister, Ariel Sharon, who accused the United States of sowing the seeds for war by overpressuring Israel and overpromising the Arabs.

The following day Mondale met with Sadat in Alexandria. By now the Americans were used to surprises from Sadat; it came as no great shock when the Egyptian president said he no longer insisted on self-determination for the Palestinians. Sticking to that position could hinder the prospects of reaching an agreement with Israel. Instead, Sadat proposed that Gaza should be returned to Egypt and the West Bank to Jordan. After five years under their administration, the Palestinians could take part in solving the problem. If the Israelis were not prepared to accept this plan, the United States should come up with some other proposal. Sadat went on to make rude remarks about King Hussein, the Saudis, and Syrian President Asad.

On the more constructive side, Sadat did agree to a charade of sorts by formally giving the United States the text of the Egyptian proposal dated June 15, now redated July 3. He also spelled out in some detail the ideas he had for reassuring the Israelis about their security. Finally, he agreed to send his foreign minister to meet with Vance and Dayan in London.

When Mondale returned to Washington, he made a full report to the president and included his recommendation that the time had come for a "political negotiator." This idea was not immediately accepted by Carter, but it came to the surface a year later after the signing of the Egyptian-Israeli treaty.

Looking for Alternatives

At a meeting of the Middle East group on July 6, U.S. strategy was again debated. Brzezinski defined the alternatives by asking whether the time had come for a confrontation with Israel or whether the United States should walk away from the negotiations. Mondale argued the case for pulling back and rebuilding confidence with the Jewish community. Hamilton Jordan interjected that Carter felt he had already paid a high price with the Jewish community and could rebuild his ties only by achieving a peace settlement. Jordan also thought Carter could not break his word to Sadat. If a confrontation with Israel were inevitable, it should be staged so that only part of the Jewish community would side with Begin. U.S. proposals would have to be reasonable.

During this session Vance showed considerable interest in convening a U.N. conference to provide a forum in which the United States could put forward its ideas. The project aroused little enthusiasm from the others. The key issue for discussion was whether to proceed with a U.S. proposal—and what to do if Israel rejected it—or to adopt a less ambitious strategy. Political considerations were very much on everyone's mind, and the fall congressional elections were discussed. Interestingly, the president's top political advisers, especially Hamilton Jordan, seemed to feel that Carter should press forward. Only positive results, Jordan argued, could help Carter politically. Mondale's recommendation to pull back was put aside for the moment, but it reflected a serious alternative and would be resurrected once the Egyptian-Israeli treaty had been secured—and once the election year was more nearly in view.

While the Carter administration was trying to sort out its next moves, Sadat was also returning to the game. By now Sadat seemed to have concluded that Begin was impossible to deal with and that he, Sadat, would do the Israeli people a great favor by helping to bring about his political demise. He clearly hoped that Weizman might be Begin's successor. In a meeting on July 13 with Weizman in Vienna, Sadat pleaded for a unilateral gesture in the form of the return to Egypt of Al-Arish and Mt. Sinai. To sweeten the picture, he spoke of a future in which Egypt would sell oil from Sinai to Israel and would provide water from the Nile to help irrigate the Negev.[29]

Sadat also began to cultivate the Labor opposition, and he arranged for a separate meeting while in Vienna with Shimon Peres. In a talk with Ambassador Eilts after that meeting, he praised Peres and said that the time had come for an American proposal designed to put pressure on Begin. Sadat also tried out his new idea about Nile water on the ambassador. If the Israelis would agree to get out of the West Bank, he said, he would be ready to give them water to irrigate the Negev. Although the Americans paid little attention to this exotic notion at the time, Sadat kept it in the back of his mind; he seemed to believe he could use it as a trump card of sorts to gain Israeli acceptance of withdrawal from the West Bank in the end.

MARKING TIME AT LEEDS CASTLE

Secretary Vance left for London to meet with Dayan and Kamil without great hope of success. Part of the point of the conference, in any event,

29. Weizman, *Battle for Peace*, pp. 313–24.

was to show that progress could not be made without a more forceful involvement by the United States.

For reasons of security, the meetings were not held in London, as originally scheduled, but rather at Leeds Castle, which provided a dramatic setting for the talks, including a moat for protection and attractive medieval surroundings. Whether the setting was responsible or not, the talks turned out to be surprisingly productive for the American partici-pants. No agreements were reached, but many ideas were generated, both by the Egyptians and the Israelis, that ultimately helped narrow the differences between the two sides. The talks also proved to all parties that little more could be done by foreign ministers alone and that the top political leaders in all three countries would have to confront some tough decisions before real progress could be made.

Vance met separately with each of the foreign ministers at Leeds; there were also several three-way sessions with full delegations present. In his first meeting Dayan suggested to Vance that the discussion of Israeli withdrawal should be superseded by a discussion of abolishing the Israeli military government in the West Bank and Gaza. A number of concrete and visible steps could be agreed upon if this formulation was accepted for the period of autonomy.

In a "nonpaper" that Dayan handed to U.S. Ambassador Lewis on July 18, Dayan summarized the Israeli position in three points. First, any proposal for a peace treaty based on Israeli withdrawal to the 1967 lines in the West Bank would be rejected even if there were to be minor border changes and security arrangements. Second, if the Arabs made a proposal for concrete territorial compromise, Israel would consider such a proposal. Third, if the Israeli plan for self-rule was accepted, Israel would be prepared after five years to discuss the question of sovereignty and, according to Dayan, an agreement would be possible. These statements represented a slight improvement over the previous Israeli position, but not enough to make the Egyptians happy.

In a meeting of the full delegations of the three countries on July 18, the Egyptians, primarily through their able under secretary of state for foreign affairs, Usama al-Baz, made a strong case for meeting Israeli security concerns. Egypt would agree to a transitional Israeli military presence on the West Bank and Gaza. But Egypt would not agree to any Israeli territorial gains. Foreign Minister Kamil asked bluntly if Israel wanted security or territory; the Israelis could have the first but not the second.

At one point Dayan asked if the Egyptians objected to Israel's Sinai proposal. If so, Israel would withdraw it and start again. Kamil bluntly said the talks should focus on the Palestinian question. The discussion then turned to both the Egyptian and Israeli proposals for the West Bank and Gaza. Dayan again asked whether Egypt would conclude an agreement on the West Bank and Gaza even if Jordan and the Palestinians did not join the negotiations. Al-Baz said an effort should be made to broaden the talks, but if that proved impossible, Egypt would probably proceed on its own to negotiate with Israel if an acceptable framework could be agreed on.

As the talks continued, the Egyptians put forward the idea of negotiating in stages on the West Bank and Gaza. First, Egypt and Israel would work out the general principles. Then Jordan would join the talks to establish the transitional regime. Finally, once the Palestinians had elected their own representatives, they would join the talks to work out the final status of the territories and to clarify the functioning of the transitional regime.[30]

The following day, July 19, Dayan met with Vance. He was pessimistic. Israel could not meet the Egyptian demand for a clear statement on withdrawal. But, Dayan said, Sadat had raised another possibility with Weizman during their talks in Vienna. Sadat had asked for a unilateral Israeli withdrawal to a line running from Al-Arish to Ras Muhammad at the tip of the Sinai Peninsula. Dayan said this could not be done as a unilateral Israeli gesture, but it could be a result of negotiations.

Vance in turn raised with Dayan an issue that the foreign minister had informally discussed over dinner with me the night before. For the Israelis, Dayan had said, the principle of being able to buy land in the West Bank was terribly important. But this could be thought of as an individual right. For example, state-owned lands in the West Bank and Gaza could be placed under the Administrative Council, and neither Israelis nor Palestinians would be able to buy those lands. Only individual land transactions between Palestinians and Israelis would be legal. This seemed like a promising idea, said Vance, and if agreement could be reached on land and on security, a major step forward would be made.

Vance then picked up on Dayan's idea about "ending the occupation" as opposed to talking about withdrawal. Vance felt this could be a useful formulation if the Israelis were really prepared to change the existing

30. See Kamil, *Lost Peace*, p. 355.

arrangements in the territories. Vance pressed on, asking if Israel would cede its claim to sovereignty if it received assurances on security and land purchases by individuals. Here Dayan drew the line, saying Begin would never agree. The most Israel could accept, he maintained, would be an end to the occupation, withdrawal of the occupying forces, and a discussion of sovereignty after five years.

Vance left the Leeds Castle conference with a few new ideas to consider, but with still no reason to be optimistic about the chances of bridging the gap between the two sides. On his return to Washington he met with the president and his advisers. Brzezinski had urged the president to decide how far he was prepared to go. If the United States made a proposal, it could not afford to back down in the face of Israeli rejection.

CARTER DECIDES ON A SUMMIT MEETING

At a breakfast meeting on July 20, Carter told his advisers that he was considering a summit meeting with Begin and Sadat. Instead of working against Begin, he wanted to work through him. He later told Brzezinski that for political reasons he wanted the summit to have a dramatic impact.[31]

While Carter was considering his idea of a summit, he received a lengthy message from Sadat on July 26, saying that an important and crucial crossroads had been reached. The Egyptian president expressed disappointment in the results of the Leeds talks and told Carter that further meetings with the Israelis could not be justified.[32] Sadat also decided to break the last remaining direct link to Israel by closing down the Israeli military mission in Egypt.

Meanwhile Assistant Secretary Harold Saunders began to develop a new proposal on the West Bank and Gaza. It contained ideas from the Leeds Castle talks, the nine-point proposal, and Begin's original self-rule plan. The idea of negotiations in three stages was incorporated. At the same time the American side was acutely aware of a promise made by President Ford in a letter to the Israelis dated September 1, 1975, at the time of the Sinai II agreement, which said that no American proposal would be put forward without first consulting on it with the Israelis. Perhaps realizing how slim the chances for peace really were, Saunders

31. Brzezinski, *Power and Principle*, pp. 250–51.

32. Kamil, *Lost Peace*, p. 374. Sadat was particularly angry at Begin's rejection of the idea of a unilateral Israeli pullback from Al-Arish and Mt. Sinai. For the full text of Sadat's letter to Carter, see ibid., pp. 375–79.

had also asked his staff to prepare a paper on the consequences of failure in the current negotiations.

On July 30 a flash cable from Ambassador Eilts reached Washington. Sadat had just met with Atherton and Eilts and had confirmed that further meetings with the Israelis were impossible. Sadat was visibly agitated, charging that Begin had been consistently negative. The Israeli prime minister had rejected Sadat's idea of a withdrawal to the Al-Arish line and had done so in a way that angered Sadat, particularly since Begin's message included a lecture on how Sadat could not expect to get something for nothing.³³ Sadat now felt that the United States should insist on principles only, no details: the nonacquisition of territory by war, the illegality of settlements, and the nonnegotiability of territory and sovereignty. He pointedly observed that the Saudis were urging him to call off the negotiations entirely. Sadat maintained that this was his final word, and Eilts reported that he had rarely seen Sadat so agitated.³⁴

With all these currents in play, Carter met again with his top advisers on July 30 and told them he had decided to hold a summit at Camp David with Begin and Sadat. Vance would go to the Middle East to issue the invitations. No one outside of a very small group would be told. There should be no leaks before Vance met with Begin and Sadat. And there were none.³⁵

CONCLUSION

How did President Carter move from a confrontational approach toward Prime Minister Begin early in 1978 to a belief that he could work with him to attain a peace agreement between Egypt and Israel? Does the answer lie in the character of the man, in the circumstances of the Middle East, or in domestic American politics?

No doubt Carter felt somewhat uneasy with the strategy of collusion discussed with Sadat in February 1978. It was a bit too manipulative.

---

33. See Weizman, *Battle for Peace*, p. 330, for a partial text of Begin's message.

34. See Kamil, *Lost Peace*, pp. 406–21, for details of Sadat's meeting with Eilts and Atherton.

35. Brzezinski, *Power and Principle*, pp. 251–52; and Carter, *Keeping Faith*, pp. 315–16. Carter emphasizes that he was worried that Sadat might do something rash. The Egyptian president had hinted that if no progress was made by the time of the third anniversary of the Sinai II agreement in September 1978, he would consider resigning, or perhaps reverting to a posture of belligerency. In an interview with me on May 22, 1985, President Carter said he had not been worried that Egypt and Israel might go to war, but had been concerned about the possibility of the negotiating process breaking down completely.

Vance disliked it from the beginning. And it would have been enormously difficult to carry through to a successful conclusion. And yet, if Carter wanted to salvage the broader peace effort, something like that strategy for putting pressure on Begin was needed. One thing was certain: Begin would never relinquish Israel's claim to the West Bank without a fight. Gentle persuasion would not do. The trick was to find a sustainable means of applying pressure and to work from an American proposal that would appeal to many Israelis, and to many American Jews, even if Begin rejected it. Sadat was more than willing to do his part even if it included some theatrical jousting with Carter in order to make it easier for the president to be tough with Begin.

Whatever qualms Carter may have harbored about the strategy he had worked out with Sadat, he nonetheless continued to reassure the Egyptians that the agreement reached at Camp David in February was still binding.[36] And he might have stuck with that strategy a bit longer had it not been for Sadat's own inconsistency and the pressure of American domestic politics.

Sadat was a difficult partner to work with in a strategy of collusion. He spoke of the need to pressure Begin to agree to withdraw from the West Bank and Gaza, but at the same time he seemed to have left Carter with the impression that he really wanted only a fig leaf behind which to conclude a bilateral Egyptian-Israeli peace. He talked of the need to bring King Hussein into the negotiations, but in private and in public he was abusive toward Hussein and other Arabs, spurning American advice that he should quiet his rhetorical attacks on those whose cooperation was being sought.

Sadat was also inclined to come up with new ideas that he would throw out carelessly. Instead of working with Carter toward the minutely detailed plan he professed to want, he constantly surprised the Americans with his views. Sometimes he said he was ready for the Americans to put forward a proposal; then he would say there was no rush. He suggested that the foreign ministers should meet, but even before they had done so he had told Weizman that their talks would fail and that an alternative approach should be considered. His meetings with Weizman and Peres seemed like attempts to interfere in domestic Israeli affairs and could be expected to produce a sharp reaction from Begin.

Had Sadat made his moves as part of a deliberate strategy, they might

36. For example, Carter told this to Sadat's friend and adviser, Sayyid Marei, on June 22, 1978.

have led somewhere. But instead, some of Sadat's comments in the meetings with the Israelis must have conveyed to Begin a sense of Sadat's mounting frustration, perhaps even desperation. And Begin was a good enough bargainer to know that this frustration could be turned to his advantage. Also, Carter was finding it increasingly difficult to coordinate with Sadat.

Even if Carter had had the stomach for a showdown with Begin, and even if Sadat had been a steadier ally, it would have been hard to pursue the strategy set at Camp David in February. The crucial missing ingredient in the original calculation was the domestic political climate. Carter was not a particularly popular leader at this time. His decision to sell F-15s to Saudi Arabia brought him into sharp conflict with the Jewish community. He won the battle, but seemed to conclude that it was a costly victory. Mondale certainly became more cautious after the fight over the arms package, whereas previously he had advocated a tough policy toward Begin on 242 and settlements.

As Carter felt his political fortunes slipping, he probably began to see a success in the Middle East as a way to recover his tarnished reputation. All his other victories—the Panama treaties, the arms package—had cost him political support. A peace agreement in the Middle East, by contrast, would be a big plus, even though the process of achieving it might often be painful and time consuming. But the American electorate would not care much about the details of the agreement. Any agreement that Sadat and Begin could accept would be fine.

The temptation arose to aim for the attainable, not necessarily the preferred, a calculation typical of presidents in the second year of their term. As a result, Carter decided to work through Begin, not against him. Whatever Begin could be brought to accept without a confrontation would define the outer limits of the agreement. Sadat, Carter had reason to believe, would go along with this in the end, even though he might still hope to see the Americans impose a broader agreement that dealt also with the Palestinian question. At this point Carter probably understood better than the rest of us that Sadat was prepared to yield on the West Bank and that Begin was not.

 As Carter contemplated the upcoming summit meeting, he must have realized that he had to succeed. The one thing he could be fairly sure of was that both Sadat and Begin wanted to reach an agreement on Sinai. Carter was determined to be the midwife of that agreement, with or without a link to the broader settlement of the West Bank and Gaza. It was here that domestic politics entered in. A success—almost any success—was needed. And Sadat and Begin could be counted on to ensure the necessary drama for the event. Carter's decision to call a summit certainly entailed risks, but it also held out the prospects for substantial gains, both domestic and international.

CHAPTER EIGHT

The First Ten Days

President Carter's decision to invite Sadat and Begin to Camp David was the result of both his frustrations and his hopes. In the course of the previous year, Carter had become intensely irritated with the slow pace of the Middle East peace negotiations to which he had devoted so much of his time. From the high expectations generated by Sadat's trip to Jerusalem in November 1977, little remained by the summer of 1978. Instead, Sadat and Begin continued to be deeply distrustful of each other, and diplomatic exchanges seemed to be sterile. At the same time Carter realized that his continued involvement in the Middle East morass was costing him precious political capital at home, something he could ill afford.

Offsetting these sources of frustration was Carter's belief that Middle East peace, or at least an Egyptian-Israeli settlement, was both obtainable and necessary. From his reading of the issues that divided the two countries, the gap did not seem too large. Part of the problem, Carter felt, was a lack of political courage, especially among the advisers to Begin and Sadat. Negotiations at the foreign minister level would be unable to break the impasse. Only Begin and Sadat could do that, and Carter felt he could help to persuade each leader to make concessions.

Carter's optimism about the outcome of a summit was not based entirely on his confidence in his own persuasive powers. The president knew that Begin would be tough and that there was a limit beyond which Sadat could not be pushed. But he genuinely believed that part of the problem between the Egyptian and Israeli leaders came from a distrust and lack of confidence that could be overcome by helping each to understand the other better. Camp David, in his view, would provide an ideal setting for Begin and Sadat to discover their common interest in, and commitment to, peace in the Middle East. His role would be that of impresario more than mediator.

Carter's initial concept of Camp David was a far cry from the strategy he had discussed with Sadat the previous February. Gone was any hint of orchestrating the summit to produce a deadlock that could be blamed on Begin. Instead, Carter genuinely wanted an agreement.

Sadat and Begin immediately accepted President Carter's invitation to Camp David when Secretary Vance met with them in early August. The Israelis may have sensed a trap, but they gave no hint of their possible suspicion that Carter and Sadat might have already reached some kind of agreement behind their backs. Some of the Egyptians seemed apprehensive that a summit meeting would lead to demands for concessions, but Sadat appeared to be genuinely pleased, noting with approval the U.S. promise to be a "full partner" in the negotiations. He also reminded Vance that he expected the long-promised American proposal to be finally unveiled.

PREPARATIONS FOR THE SUMMIT

The American team spent much of August in lengthy, and typically paper-heavy, preparations for the summit. The State Department and the National Security Council worked both together and separately on strategy memos and briefing papers. Personality profiles were developed of Sadat, Begin, and other members of the Israeli and Egyptian teams. The Department of Defense devised ways of dealing with Israeli security concerns in Sinai and the West Bank. The president's domestic advisers offered suggestions on the kinds of inducements that might be attractive to Israel. All this activity generated the expectation within official Washington that a moment of truth was approaching. If anyone had any bright ideas on how to make the summit a success, this was the time to get them on paper and to the president.

Although Carter welcomed the massive flow of paper, and as always read diligently, he already had in mind a concept for Camp David. It was not identical to that of most of his foreign policy advisers. For Vance and Brzezinski, the crucial test would be whether Carter could persuade Begin to make some concessions on the Palestinian question. Such concessions, they believed, were not only important for the future of the peace process but were also the sine qua non of Sadat's agreeing to peace with Israel.

Carter, by contrast, no doubt drawing on his judgment about Sadat's real bottom line, was more intent on reaching an Egyptian-Israeli accord, with or without much of a link to the Palestinian issue. The linkage issue was to bedevil the talks at Camp David and the subsequent negotiation of the peace treaty. In the end Carter proved to be correct in his belief that Sadat, despite his strong initial position, would not continue to insist on much for the Palestinians, at least not at the expense of recovering Egyptian territory. But that was not the way it looked to most observers, including Israelis, on the eve of the Camp David meetings.

Sadat himself almost certainly expected much more out of Camp David than he got. To begin with, he apparently believed that he had an agreement of sorts with President Carter that would force the Israelis to make significant concessions. Thus his approach to the negotiations was to coordinate his plan with Carter, to put virtually all his cards face up on the table before the president, and to help Carter manage the inevitable confrontation with Begin. As he repeatedly told the Americans, U.S.-Egyptian agreement was more important to him than an Egyptian-Israeli agreement.[1]

Begin came to the negotiations with one trump card that neither Carter nor Sadat possessed. He could afford to walk out of the talks at any time and return home in a strong political position, blaming the failure on the extreme position of the Egyptians or the clumsiness of the Americans. Domestically, his militant supporters could be counted on to back him regardless of the outcome. For Carter and Sadat, by contrast, the failure of the talks would be seen as a personal political setback and would take a lot of explaining. Begin's only real fear, it would seem, was that Carter might blame him for the failure, go public with that judgment, and try to mobilize American public opinion against him. But Carter had repeatedly pledged never to threaten to cut economic or military aid to Israel as a form of pressure, and he had vowed not to impose an American peace plan. So Begin could anticipate that little more than a verbal disagreement would result if the Camp David talks failed. At most, a modest agreement on common principles might be achieved, coupled with a commitment to resume negotiations.

The key players at Camp David each came to the summit with quite different purposes. Each brought a distinctive personal style, a world view, a coterie of advisers, and a strategy. Carter was obviously in a pivotal position, because each of the other parties was anxious for him to side with it. Much of what happened at Camp David would be shaped by Carter himself; thus his preparations for the negotiations, and his early adjustments in the American strategy, took on particular significance.

---

1. The Egyptians expected the summit to break down after a few days. For the full text of the Egyptian foreign ministry's strategy memorandum for Sadat dated August 28, 1978, see Muhammad Ibrahim Kamil, *The Lost Peace in the Camp David Accords*, pp. 453–62.

THE PRESIDENT'S BRIEFING BOOK

Shortly after his trip to the Middle East to invite Begin and Sadat to Camp David, Secretary Vance began to prepare for the summit. On August 11, together with Ambassador-at-Large Atherton, Assistant Secretary Saunders, and myself, Vance left Washington for the calmer atmosphere of rural Virginia. For several days we stayed at Averell Harriman's estate near Middleburg working on the president's briefing book.

Preparations in Middleburg

At this point in the preparations, none of us thought a full agreement could be worked out during the summit. Instead, we hoped that a few key principles could be agreed on so that a framework for future negotiations could be developed. No one expected the Sinai to be the focus of the discussions, since the problems there were comparatively well defined and seemed susceptible to resolution through normal diplomatic exchanges. In fact, the Israeli and Egyptian defense ministers had already made considerable progress in direct talks without U.S. mediation. The impasse involved the Palestinian question, and to find a way around that problem was the reason, we thought, for the summit.

Vance and the Middle East team expected the major difficulty at Camp David to stem from Begin's unwillingness to go much beyond the narrow confines of the autonomy proposal that he had first presented to Carter and Sadat in December 1977. From everything the Americans had heard from the Egyptians, Sadat would not move further toward a bilateral agreement with Israel unless Begin adopted a more forthcoming position toward the Palestinians. No one knew exactly what Sadat would settle for, but he seemed most insistent that Begin should affirm that he had no designs on Arab territory seized in the 1967 war. Almost anything else could be discussed calmly with Sadat—security arrangements, transitional periods, limits on the expression of self-determination for the Palestinians, the need for normal diplomatic relations—but Sadat was adamant when it came to territory and sovereignty. Israel could have peace and security, he said, but not at the expense of Arab land.

Anyone with the slightest knowledge of Begin's true position could appreciate the problem faced by the Americans. Sadat said Israel could have everything except land, and Begin was just as firm in saying he would never be the prime minister of Israel who would agree to relinquish the West Bank, to say nothing of East Jerusalem. These were fundamental parts of Begin's ideology, of his political raison d'être. His great concession had been to drop, as an active issue, Israel's claim to the East Bank, that is to Jordan, and to leave in abeyance the question of sovereignty in the West Bank. It was hard to see that he could be persuaded to go much further.

Vance had repeatedly pressed Begin for signs of flexibility on these issues. The most encouragement he ever got was a remark from Begin that he would never agree to withdraw from any of the West Bank, but that he would not be prime minister of Israel forever. Perhaps his successor would have a different view. This firm position was one of the reasons we had come to favor the idea of a five-year transitional period before the issue of sovereignty in the West Bank and Gaza would have to be solved. By then, we expected, Begin would no longer be in charge.

The firmness of Begin's stance on the West Bank led us to the idea of trying to get Begin to agree at Camp David to a transitional period based largely on his concept of autonomy, followed by negotiations that would resolve the final status of the West Bank and Gaza by the end of five years according to all the principles of U.N. Resolution 242. This arrangement was as close as we thought Begin would get to an agreement on eventual withdrawal, but it might at least help keep the "territory for peace" option open for his successor and give Jordan and the Palestinians some incentive to cooperate during the transitional period.

Because of the inevitable clash between Sadat and Begin over territory, the success or failure of Camp David would come down to how that issue would be handled. Theoretically, agreement could come if either Begin or Sadat changed his stated position; or if the withdrawal issue was broken down so that each leader could claim victory on at least one front, Sadat in Sinai and Begin on the West Bank; or if the issue was fuzzed over with imprecise language, as in U.N. Resolution 242, and the search for a workable formula put off until later, perhaps until after Begin had left the political scene.

Vance and the rest of us at Middleburg were fairly sure that Sadat would be able to get all the Sinai back in an agreement with Begin. He would, of course, have to accept certain limits on deployments of his own forces in Sinai, and he would have to offer Israel the main elements of peace, in particular the exchange of ambassadors, which seemed to count for a great deal in Begin's legalistic view of the world. We did not expect the question of Israeli settlements in Sinai to be insurmountable; we in fact underestimated how tenaciously Begin would fight to keep them.

If Sinai seemed unlikely to become the primary stumbling block at Camp David, it was clear to Vance that the West Bank and Gaza, and more generally the Palestinian question, would be complicated. To begin with, Sadat had no mandate to negotiate on behalf of the Palestinians, and previous experience suggested that the Egyptians were reluctant to go much beyond the enunciation of broad principles when it came to those issues.

For Sadat, the most likely strategy would be to use the bait of major Egyptian political and security concessions to extract from Begin a commitment to withdrawal from occupied territories. If Sadat could get the Israelis clearly on record as accepting the territory for peace formula for all fronts—Egypt, Syria, and Jordan—he would be ready to go ahead with a bilateral agreement of his own with Israel, leaving other Arab leaders to work out the best deal they could in their own negotiations with Israel. He had little interest per se in these details, a point he made repeatedly. But he did want credit in Egypt and the Arab world for establishing the principles on which a fair peace could be negotiated. In his view the Egyptian-Israeli peace treaty should be a model that other Arab leaders could copy if they were willing to take the risk of negotiating with Israel.

Sadat was sensitive to the charge that he was prepared to sell out the Arab cause, to abandon the Palestinians. In private, his remarks about other Arab leaders were often caustic, but he still saw himself as an Arab leader. He did not want to be accused of taking Egypt out of the conflict with Israel while the Israelis clung to the West Bank, Gaza, and especially East Jerusalem, an issue of special concern to his devout Muslim population. He also correctly sensed that Begin, Foreign Minister Moshe Dayan, and in particular Defense Minister Ezer Weizman were eager for an agreement with Egypt, and to reach that goal, they would be prepared to show some flexibility on the Palestinian issue. Sadat thus became the prime proponent of linkage, that is, of making some elements of a bilateral Egyptian-Israeli agreement conditional upon movement on the Palestinian question. On this point he expected American support; only when he found it wanting did he begin to back away from his insistence on a close link between the Egyptian-Israeli agreement and the Palestinian question. Sadat, like Carter, was eventually worn down by Begin's adamant refusal to dilute Israel's claim to the West Bank.

Vance was generally disposed to agree with Sadat that some link had to be maintained between an Egyptian-Israeli agreement and the Palestinian question. If Egypt concluded a separate agreement, Israel would have few incentives to move ahead with negotiations on other fronts. The diplomatic trick would be to keep the weight of Egypt in the scales of future Arab-Israeli peace talks as both an incentive for Israel and a moderating influence on other Arabs, while at the same time not making Egyptian-Israeli relations hostage to possible intransigence on the part of other Arab leaders.

In brief, without any linkage Sadat might refuse to negotiate. And even if he and Begin reached a bilateral agreement, it could result in Egypt's isolation in the Arab world and would certainly bring the peace process on other fronts to a halt for a long time. But complete linkage between the Egyptian-Israeli negotiating track and movement on other fronts would return the situation to where it was in the fall of 1977, when disagreements among the Arab parties had brought the situation to an impasse.

Somewhere between these two extremes might be a point at which Egypt and Israel would begin to move toward full agreement, but in stages that could be related to progress in negotiations on other fronts. Sadat seemed to be confident that other Arab leaders would have no choice but to follow in his footsteps once he had made it clear that Egypt was firmly committed to a diplomatic settlement. But he also wanted them to know that whatever he agreed to with Israel would be a precedent for their own negotiations with the Jewish state, if and when they followed his lead. Such had been the pattern in 1974, when Egypt and Israel reached the first disengagement agreement, to be followed within months by the Syrian-Israeli disengagement agreement. This time, however, Sadat thought it would be King Hussein and the West Bank Palestinians who would be next in line. And he counted on the Americans to deliver Saudi support for Egypt's negotiations with Israel.

A Strategy for the Summit

With these thoughts in mind, Vance, Saunders, Atherton, and I worked at Middleburg to sketch out a plan for the Camp David talks. We prepared a paper called "The Pivotal Issue: The Sinai/West Bank Relationship." Saunders had also begun work on an American proposal for dealing with the status of both the West Bank and Gaza and the Sinai. It was meant to be a framework for negotiations and incorporated many of the ideas that the Egyptians and Israelis had put forward, as well as some points that had emerged from the discussions at Leeds Castle in July. The key idea was to refashion Begin's autonomy plan into a proposal for an interim regime for the West Bank and Gaza that would offer the Palestinians a serious measure of self-government. The proposal would include a clear commitment to a second phase of negotiations toward the end of the transitional period to resolve the questions of borders, sovereignty, and Palestinian rights in accordance with U.N. Resolution 242—territory for peace—and Carter's promise at Aswan that Palestinians should have the right to participate in determining their own future. Everyone agreed that at some point an American proposal would be needed.

Besides developing a basic strategy memorandum and a draft American proposal, we also tried to sketch a scenario for negotiations during the first few days of the summit. These included talking points for the president to use with Begin and Sadat in his private sessions and suggestions for trilateral meetings as well. At this stage of the preparations, success was being measured in modest terms. Little more was expected than a joint statement from the three leaders that could serve as a guideline for renewed negotiations.

I prepared an early analysis of the negotiating situation for Brzezinski on August 17. It reflected some of the ideas developed at Middleburg. It read in part:

Begin wants an endorsement for his proposals, and he will concentrate on procedure, not substance. By contrast, Sadat will want us to endorse the 1967 borders with only minor modifications. Both of these politicians are masters at manipulation, and they will be trying with all of their persuasive powers to draw the president closer to their positions in order to bring pressure to bear on one another.

While we will want to provide opportunities for Begin and Sadat to talk directly, we should have no illusion that Begin-Sadat-Carter meetings will be very productive at the outset. The most important talks that the president will have will be his bilateral private talks with each of them. . . .

With Sadat, the president will have to find a way to persuade him that agreement on general principles alone serves little purpose. If principles are to have some meaning, Israel must know what she will get for agreeing to these principles. Will there be assured movement on the Sinai negotiations? Will Jordan join the talks? Or will Egypt assume responsibility for negotiating a five year regime for the West Bank and Gaza? Sadat should understand that his ability to answer these questions concretely will have a significant influence on whether Israel can be persuaded to agree to general principles.

Sadat also will have to understand that Israel cannot be brought to the position of accepting the 1967 borders with minor modifications as a basis for an eventual settlement. . . . The most that we can expect from Begin is the acceptance of the principle of withdrawal on all fronts, and an agreement that at the end of the five year period negotiations would resolve the question of sovereignty and would establish the precise location of secure and recognized borders in conformity with the principles of resolution 242. We cannot even be sure that Begin will go this far, but this would seem to be the outer limits of his flexibility. We can assure Sadat that our own view remains that Israel can be persuaded to withdraw to something approximating the 1967 lines provided that concrete security arrangements have been established and Israel has had the chance to test those arrangements and to experience normal relations and open borders for a five year transitional period. . . .

With Begin, the president will have to try to persuade him that Israel's present position on the West Bank and Gaza is a serious obstacle to the resumption of negotiations. If Israel can be assured that the consequences of accepting the general principle of withdrawal on all fronts will be progress in the negotiations on Sinai, Israel should then be prepared to publicly accept that the principle of withdrawal does indeed apply on all fronts, and that the question of sovereignty and the precise location of final borders will be resolved by the end of the five year period through negotiations based on the principles of 242.

Somehow the president will have to convey to Begin that if he is unwilling to go this far with us in accepting the applicability of the basic principles of 242, there is little chance that the negotiations can move forward and there is a serious risk that the United States and Israel will be moving on different paths in the coming months as a result of Israel's abandonment of its commitments under 242. This will be a hard message to deliver to Begin, and it will be virtually impossible to get him to focus concretely on the choices he must make unless he can be assured that by modifying his position he will have a significant chance of advancing the negotiations on Sinai.[2]

While the American team was working to develop a strategy for the summit negotiations, it was also trying to figure out what Sadat and Begin would be seeking from the talks. According to a reliable report, Sadat was hoping for two agreements from Camp David. One would be a general declaration of principles based on Resolution 242 and the Aswan formula on the Palestinians. This agreement would be made public. The second document would be a precisely written secret agreement on the framework for the Middle East peace settlement. These two documents would be signed by Sadat and Begin and witnessed by Carter. More detailed negotiations could then take place to resolve remaining problems. Sadat would be very flexible, except on territory and sovereignty. He would not go beyond considering some minor border adjustments in the West Bank. In the secret agreement Sadat would be prepared to give Israel some assurances about who the future Palestinian leaders of the

2. Memorandum from me to Brzezinski called "Strategy for Camp David," August 17, 1978.

West Bank would be. In conclusion, Sadat told the informant that he had lost all confidence in Begin and was counting heavily on Carter for support in the coming talks.

Further insight into Sadat's strategy came from a long talk between Sadat and the U.S. ambassador to Egypt, Hermann Eilts. On August 26, 1978, Sadat emphasized that his objective at Camp David was not a declaration of principles, but rather a framework for a comprehensive settlement. According to Sadat, Carter should be ready for a "confrontation" between Sadat and Begin. But Carter could count on Sadat not to let him down. He would talk strategy with Carter during their first meeting, but he wanted the president to know that everything was negotiable except land and sovereignty. He would be flexible on the West Bank, but he would make no concessions on Sinai or the settlements there. He would not speak for Syria, but anything that Egypt got should be applicable to the Golan Heights as well. By contrast, he would be prepared to talk about the West Bank and Gaza.

Sadat went on to tell Eilts that the position of Saudi Arabia was terribly important to him. He had received a message from the Saudis that they would support him as long as he held firm on land and sovereignty. Sadat emphasized that he could not agree to a separate peace. That would open the area to the Soviets and would undermine Egyptian leadership in the Arab world. Sadat then went on to denounce Begin in forceful terms, saying it would be far better to deal with Shimon Peres, Weizman, or even Golda Meir.

The most intriguing of Sadat's comments to Eilts was his closing remark, that he would be giving Carter a written paper on the Egyptian position and strategy. The United States might not have to put forward a proposal of its own at this stage. In fact, said Sadat, he was thinking of "saving President Carter for a major coup." He would not elaborate on what he had in mind, but did refer to a "Dullesian exercise in brinkmanship." In short, though Carter may have drifted away from the collusive strategy of the previous February, clearly Sadat had not.

On the last day of August Secretary Vance forwarded to the president the formal briefing book for the summit. In his covering memorandum the secretary noted that the purpose of the summit was to break the negotiating impasse by reaching decisions at the level of heads of government so that talks could then resume at the foreign minister level. A detailed agreement could not be expected. Instead, the broad aim of the talks would be to establish a basis for negotiations on the West Bank and Gaza that would allow Jordan to join the process. An agreement on basic principles would allow talks on Sinai to go forward after the summit.

"The pivotal issue in the talks will be Israel's need to know whether they can get an agreement on the Sinai and what price they must pay for it in concessions on the West Bank," the memo read. Vance noted that the American position on this point would be crucial, and that at a minimum Carter should seek a freeze on settlements and the applicability of the principles of U.N. Resolution 242 to the West Bank and Gaza, including the clause on the inadmissibility of the acquisition of territory by war.

In an attachment to the basic memo, the following cautionary note was included: "Sadat resorts to generalities as a defense against decisions which are difficult for him to make, and it will frequently be necessary for you to summarize what you have heard him say. Whereas Begin has a tendency toward literalism and an obsession with detail, Sadat is often imprecise with words and has little patience for precision and for real negotiating. In this situation, the danger of genuine misunderstanding, followed by feelings of betrayal and recrimination, is very great."

Another part of the briefing book was called "The Issues of Withdrawal, Security, Borders, Sovereignty, and the Palestinians." Here the idea of treating the concept of withdrawal as a continuum was developed. "In brief, our objective will be to get both parties to agree that the principle of withdrawal, as embodied in Resolution 242, does apply on all fronts, but that its application must be adapted to specific circumstances and is not incompatible with an Israeli security presence over a prolonged period." In summation, the following objectives were defined for the negotiations:

—The principle of *withdrawal on all fronts*, in conditions of peace and security, should be established.

—*Withdrawal is a multidimensional concept*. Some elements of the Israeli presence on the West Bank and Gaza can be withdrawn at an early date; other elements can be removed later; and some may remain for a prolonged period.

—*Security and withdrawal are intimately related*. A long-term Israeli security presence in the West Bank and Gaza is a legitimate objective of negotiations.

—*Sovereignty and borders are issues that cannot be resolved at this stage*, and will require the participation of the Jordanians and the Palestinians. A preceding *interim* period in which the entire West Bank and Gaza are placed under a new administration, and in which new security arrangements can be tested, is a necessary prior condition for a rational discussion of final borders and sovereignty.

—The Aswan language on the Palestinians is a minimal acceptable compromise between the Egyptian demands for self-determination and the Israeli position of self-rule.

—Israel should be asked to agree to an indefinite moratorium on settlement activity.[3]

It is noteworthy that the briefing book paid little attention to the problems of Sinai. We felt that the details of an Egyptian-Israeli agreement would not be particularly difficult to work out. The obstacle to agreement seemed to be political, namely Sadat's insistence that he would not sign a separate peace and that he needed at least some progress on the West Bank and Palestinian issues before he could go any further in discussing Sinai. Thus almost all the American effort was aimed at breaking the impasse on that front.[4]

Convening of the National Security Council

Before reading through the various papers prepared for the summit, Carter convened a meeting of the National Security Council on September 1, 1978. Present was the full Middle East team that would be at Camp David, including Ambassador Eilts and the American ambassador to Israel, Samuel Lewis.

Stansfield Turner, the director of Central Intelligence, opened the meeting with an assessment of the consequences of failure at Camp David. His judgment was that many in the Arab world would welcome Sadat back into the fold with open arms. Brzezinski was more pessimistic about the impact of failure on Sadat's position. Some discussion also took place concerning Lebanon, where once again it seemed as if a new round of violence might break out at any moment. If it did, Turner noted, the responsibility would lie primarily with the right-wing Christian forces. Carter commented that he had been afraid one month earlier, about the time he decided to invite Begin and Sadat to the summit, that the situation in the Middle East might explode.

Secretary of Defense Brown then reviewed Israel's security concerns as they might be affected by a peace agreement. He spelled out a variety of ways to deal with Israeli security in the West Bank, and then went on to discuss the possibility of a U.S.-Israeli defense treaty as part of an overall settlement. Brown argued that such a treaty might have political

---

3. Memorandum and attachments from Vance to Carter, August 31, 1978.

4. Zbigniew Brzezinski, *Power and Principle*, pp. 253–54, quotes from his own briefing memorandum to the president dated August 31, 1978. He also placed more emphasis on the West Bank issue than on Sinai.

value in the negotiations, but that it held little attraction for the United States on strictly military grounds. Carter agreed.

President Carter finally took the floor to spell out his idea of how the summit should unfold. He would first meet privately with Sadat and Begin, then with both together. He would try to reassure them of the good intentions of the United States. All proposals would be shown to both leaders, and no U.S. ideas would be formally presented without prior consultations. Sadat and Begin would be urged to deal directly with each other, though the United States would make available its good offices. Carter said he would try to convince them of the benefits of peace and the risks of failure in the talks.

The president went on to say that he did not intend to rush things. He would not pressure either Begin or Sadat. By the end of one week at most, he thought, all the issues should have been covered. Then he added that Vice President Mondale was the American the Israelis trusted most. By contrast, the Israelis viewed Carter and Brzezinski as somewhat suspect. Vance was seen as objective.

From his comments it was clear that one of Carter's goals was to win the trust of both leaders. If he could accomplish that, and if Begin and Sadat could overcome their mutual suspicions, Carter seemed to believe a positive result could be achieved from the summit. This goal was, of course, a far cry from the "brinkmanship" strategy that Sadat seemed to be counting on. For Carter, the psychology of the meeting seemed to be more important than the issues or the strategy.[5]

On the weekend before Camp David, Carter left Washington, taking with him the bulky briefing books. He apparently read them carefully and made copious notes, but he was not satisfied. They were too modest, primarily because they did not aim for a "written agreement for peace between Egypt and Israel."[6] This idea, which seems to have crystallized in Carter's mind during his talks with Sadat at Camp David the previous February, derived from a fundamentally different judgment from that of Vance and the rest of us on what Sadat needed as political cover. Most of the State Department specialists, as well as Brzezinski and I, felt that a strong link between an Egyptian-Israeli agreement and a formula for the West Bank and Gaza was not only desirable but necessary. Carter disagreed. He was not opposed to some degree of linkage, but he did not think it that important, and in any event it should not obstruct the search

---

5. Jimmy Carter, *Keeping Faith*, p. 322.
6. Ibid., p. 321.

for a bilateral agreement. The American team was thus not entirely united on its strategy as it approached Camp David. And in the end it was Carter, not Vance, who had the last word.

AT THE SUMMIT

The thirteen days at Camp David were in some ways like a microcosm of the preceding year and one-half. The same issues were debated, often with little change in the script. Hopes rose, then fell, and then sober realism began to take hold. But everything happened so much more quickly, and the normal domestic political constraints that operated on all the parties were somewhat minimized by their remaining secluded from the public and conducting the talks in almost total secrecy.

Each party came prepared with positions and strategies; each came with ambitions and illusions as well. There were to be fierce arguments, moments of real despair, considerable good humor, and a constant process of revision and reassessment as the negotiations unfolded. No one could have told on September 5 what would eventually come out of the talks on September 17. By the end, the process came to resemble an endurance contest in which the party that could least afford failure was brought under the greatest pressure to make concessions. This turned out to be Sadat. Instead of cornering Begin with his strategy of brinkmanship, in which Carter was to be assigned the crucial role as co-conspirator, Sadat found himself the target of relentless pressures for concessions.

Begin's steamroller tactics, coupled with his willingness to leave Camp David without any agreement if necessary, proved to be more successful than Sadat's flamboyant concept of confrontation. For unlike Begin, Sadat was not prepared to leave Camp David empty-handed. At a minimum, he needed a clear agreement with Carter. But Carter now wanted an agreement between Begin and Sadat, not the appearance of American-Egyptian collusion against Israel.

Carter's Preparations

Carter prepared himself carefully for his first meetings with Sadat and Begin on September 5. In the margins of the briefing book Vance had sent him he made numerous notations. On one memo he wrote cryptically: "To Begin and Sadat—analysis of consequences of failure. —More ambitious goals. —Communications with Hussein. —Inform Soviets at all?" On one of the attachments that listed points for inclusion in a joint statement, Carter noted in the margin: "Should conclude agreement on

Sinai." On another paper that referred to Jordan's role in negotiations, Carter wrote: "Jordan's timidity could block progress."

Finally Carter sat down and wrote in his own hand two pages of notes to refer to during his initial meetings. Most of the points were familiar ones that had been repeatedly discussed, such as the importance of 242 as the basis of negotiations on all fronts. The points seemed to be a checklist, a reminder to the conscientious mediator, not the outline of an American plan. But the notes do reveal a confidence that anything Carter, Sadat, and Begin could agree upon could be made to work. Success in the talks, Carter believed, would bring in Saudi Arabia and Jordan, though how this might be done was left unstated. Carter seemed confident of success as he listed areas of agreement between Egypt and Israel.[7] At the end of one page he carefully penned the sentence: "First Egyptian-Jewish peace since time of ~~Joseph~~ Jeremiah." The Bible was never too far from Carter's thoughts.

Day One, September 5, 1978

President Sadat and Prime Minister Begin arrived at Camp David accompanied by their delegations on the afternoon of September 5, 1978.[8] Sadat met briefly with Carter and indicated that he had a plan he wished to discuss the following day. He would be flexible on everything except land and sovereignty, he said. He would be putting forward a proposal of his own, so that Carter would not have to do so.[9] These comments were consistent with what Sadat had told Eilts, but Sadat gave no further hint of what his strategy was. He was tired and soon withdrew to his cabin.

Begin arrived after Sadat and met that evening with Carter for more than two hours. He made it clear that he feared that Carter and Sadat would confront him with a common position. He carried with him a copy of a letter from President Gerald Ford signed in conjunction with the Sinai II agreement on September 1, 1975, stating that the United States would consult with Israel before putting forward any peace proposals. Begin stressed that his priority was to reach agreement with the United States—much the same point that Sadat had earlier made. He went on to note that he would insist on keeping Israeli settlements in Sinai.

7. See ibid., pp. 325, 327, for examples of these lists.
8. Ibid., p. 326, provides the full list of delegation members.
9. Ibid., pp. 328–29.

Carter was discouraged after these first encounters.[10] Instead of dwelling on areas of agreement, he now listed the likely problems that would be most difficult to resolve in the negotiations. It proved to be quite accurate.

—Reference to the inadmissibility of the acquisition of territory by war, language used in 242 but rejected by Begin.

—How to provide the Palestinians with a voice in determining their own future.

—Egypt's demand that there be no new Israeli settlements.

—The applicability of 242 to the West Bank and Gaza.

—Israeli relinquishment of settlements and airfields in Sinai.

—Participation by Jordan in the negotiations.

—The source of authority for the interim administration of the West Bank and Gaza.

—Security arrangements in Sinai.

—The Arab demand for full Israeli withdrawal from the West Bank and Gaza.

—How to resolve the question of sovereignty on the West Bank and Gaza after a five-year transitional period.

Carter wondered if some of these issues might be resolved by offering Israel a mutual defense treaty. He was not enthusiastic about the prospect, but he realized it might give him some leverage with Begin.

While Carter was meeting alone with Sadat and Begin, the Egyptian and Israeli delegations were generally keeping their distance from one another. At dinner, they sat at separate tables, with members of the American delegation sprinkled among them. On the Israeli side, only Defense Minister Ezer Weizman broke away from his colleagues to sit with the Egyptians and to banter with them in somewhat broken Arabic. Foreign Minister Dayan, a much less outgoing person, made no effort to talk to the Egyptians, but seemed envious of Weizman's easy familiarity with them.

Day Two, September 6, 1978

On Wednesday Sadat met with Carter in the morning and unveiled his plan. He had with him a written Egyptian proposal called "Framework for the Comprehensive Peace Settlement of the Middle East Problem." The eleven-page document consisted of a preamble and nine articles.[11] It

10. See ibid., pp. 332–37, for a detailed account of his meeting with Begin.

11. See appendix D. The full Arabic text can be found in Kamil, *Lost Peace*, pp. 629–34. According to Kamil, Sadat had decided to develop a detailed "framework for peace" instead of a more general "declaration of principles" as a way of producing a sharp confrontation with Begin. Sadat told his colleagues that he expected Carter to side with him and that Begin would be toppled. Ibid., pp. 468–69.

was a tough document, insisting on full Israeli withdrawal; dismantlement of settlements; banning of nuclear weapons; transfer of authority in the West Bank and Gaza to Jordan and Egypt, respectively, for a transitional period of five years, at the end of which the Palestinians would exercise their right of self-determination; return or compensation for Palestinian refugees; and compensation by Israel for war damage and for the oil pumped from Sinai. In return, Egypt would agree to sign a peace treaty, would accept various security measures, would recognize Israel, and would support free access to religious shrines in Jerusalem.

Carter realized that Begin would violently reject almost all of the Egyptian document. But Sadat quickly reassured the president that this proposal did not represent his final position. Presumably it was intended primarily to provoke the confrontation that Sadat had often spoken of. This result, after all, was what Carter and Sadat had both envisaged at Camp David in February, and now Sadat had come with a plan guaranteed to raise the temperature of the negotiations.[12]

Sadat then played an important card. He would give Carter in advance a series of concessions to be used at appropriate moments in the negotiations.[13] He handed the president three typewritten pages, the first of which was marked for the president's eyes only. According to this document, Carter could propose several modifications in the Egyptian document and Sadat would agree. For example, he would accept safeguards and qualifications on the return of Palestinian refugees. He would also be more forthcoming on normalization of ties with Israel, including diplomatic and consular relations, free movement of peoples across the borders, and trade relations. These last points were important to Carter, and presumably to Israel, and Carter was pleased to know he would be able to take the sharp edges off the Egyptian proposal at some point by adding these elements.

On the second page of the document Sadat made a few additional points, the most important being a willingness to agree that Jerusalem should not be a divided city. Finally, on the last page Sadat indicated that he would agree that representatives of the Palestinians should come

12. If the negotiations had broken down, Egypt was prepared to publish this proposal immediately. Representatives were waiting with drafts in Washington, London, and Paris and were ready to launch a media campaign denouncing Israel. Sadat had told the Egyptian delegation that he would "turn the tables" on Begin. Interview with Nabil al-Arabi and Ahmed Maher, Cairo, January 24, 1985.

13. Carter, *Keeping Faith*, pp. 340–41.

exclusively from the inhabitants of the West Bank and Gaza. Even with these concessions in hand, Carter knew the gap between Sadat and Begin was enormous. But Sadat had shown a willingness to compromise, and that was what gave Carter hope.[14]

The first meeting between Sadat and Begin took place Wednesday afternoon. Carter had forewarned the Israeli prime minister that Sadat would be putting forward a tough proposal. After some preliminary discussion, Sadat read the proposal aloud. Begin listened without making any comments. Carter joked that it would save a lot of time if Begin would just sign. An atmosphere of surprisingly good humor prevailed, but it was not to last long. As soon as Begin was alone with Carter, he strongly denounced the Egyptian proposal. Later that evening the president met with the American delegation to discuss the day's event. He was in a reflective, thoughtful mood.

Day Three, September 7, 1978

Thursday, September 7, proved to be a crucial day. Carter, Sadat, and Begin met together twice. The atmosphere was electric, with Begin making a detailed, point-by-point rebuttal of the Egyptian proposal. Sadat angrily replied that Begin wanted land more than he wanted peace.[15]

While the trilateral meeting was going on, Vance met with the Israelis and Egyptians to explore ideas on the West Bank and Gaza issues. In the course of his discussions with Weizman and Dayan, the Israelis mentioned that there were still two outstanding problems in Sinai: settlements and airfields. Weizman also noted that though there had been a great deal of talk about the Sinai, there was no written agreement. Dayan asked if the Sinai agreement could be put in writing. He and Weizman also hinted that the settlements in Sinai would not be an obstacle, and that some type of moratorium on settlements in the West Bank should be possible.

---

14. Among Sadat's advisers, only one was aware of Sadat's intention to reveal these fallback positions to Carter. This adviser urged the Egyptian president to wait until later in the talks, but Sadat felt he could win Carter's confidence by showing a willingness to be flexible at the outset. Although Sadat probably read Carter correctly, the result was that Carter was inclined to disregard the Egyptian proposal and to believe that Sadat could be persuaded to make concessions whenever a stalemate was reached. In an interview with me on May 22, 1985, President Carter said Sadat had immediately made it clear that he was not wedded to the formal Egyptian proposal. He did insist, however, on two points: any agreement should deal with the West Bank and Gaza, and no Israelis could remain anywhere in Sinai after withdrawal.

15. Carter, *Keeping Faith*, pp. 346–60, provides a detailed account of these talks.

Later that day Dayan specifically urged the United States to put forward a proposal of its own, arguing that Egypt and Israel could go no further on their own.

Vance's meetings helped to offset the negative results of the Sadat-Begin encounter. At least some of the Israeli advisers were indicating areas of flexibility. As the negotiations proceeded, Carter and Vance came to rely on Dayan, Weizman, and Attorney General Barak to persuade Begin to drop his most rigid demands, while on the Egyptian side they dealt directly with Sadat, fearing that all his advisers would be more adamant.

Summing up the day's events late on September 7, I made the following notes for myself:

One can begin to draw some tentative conclusions from the talks so far. First, Begin and Sadat are not speaking the same language and they do not get along personally at all. This is causing concern in the Israeli delegation. [A member of the Israeli delegation] approached me in the evening and pleaded with me to find some way to get the message through to the president to keep Begin and Sadat apart. He said that Begin was beginning to harden his position and was already thinking of how the summit could end in failure without his being blamed for it. [He] said that the time had clearly come for the Americans to put forward ideas of their own since the Egyptian proposal was unacceptable as a basis for serious negotiations. He also urged that we pay more attention to Dayan and less to Weizman. Weizman is good at a general level, but Dayan will be the one who helps find the formulations to solve problems when the drafting begins.

By contrast with the Israelis, the Egyptians seem more anxious to identify their positions with those of the United States than to reach any kind of agreement with Israel. They have deliberately incorporated language used by American presidents in the past in their own proposal. At this stage, it would seem that their preferred outcome from Camp David would be agreement between the United States and Egypt, with Israel isolated and under strong American pressure to change positions. The expectation is still that the talks may end this coming Sunday.

Late in the evening on Thursday, Carter met again with Sadat and raised the possibility that the United States would develop a proposal. On the West Bank and Gaza problems, the proposal would be couched in general terms and would deal primarily with the transitional period, but on Sinai, said the president, "it can be much more specific, because you and Israel, the principal parties, can now negotiate directly with one another."[16]

16. Ibid., p. 362. The following day, September 8, Vance met with Kamil to preview

Henceforth the American side would take the lead in drafting a document. Begin and Sadat did not meet again for negotiations until the Camp David Accords were ready for signature. Carter's hope that he could encourage Sadat and Begin to trust each other and to work out their differences had fallen flat. Now Carter would have to inject himself more forcefully into the discussions, and he already knew what he wanted as a minimum—an outline of a full Egyptian-Israeli peace agreement.

Day Four, September 8, 1978

On Friday Carter held an important meeting with Begin. He was alarmed at the Israeli prime minister's negative mood, his dwelling on the Egyptian proposal. Carter essentially told Begin that the Egyptian proposal was not Sadat's final position and that he already had a number of compromises in hand.[17] What the effect of this revelation was on Begin can only be surmised, but from then on Begin adopted an unyielding position on settlements in Sinai. Perhaps he concluded that if Sadat could use the tactic of adopting a deliberately hard position at the outset, then he might do the same. But, unlike Sadat, he had no intention of telling Carter what his fallback position really was.

While Begin was seeking to convince Carter that he would never recommend abandoning the settlements in Sinai, the other members of the Israeli team were gradually modifying their stand on some West Bank–Gaza issues. None of these changes amounted to much because the Israelis continued to maintain that they would retain their claim to sovereignty in these areas. But they did agree that at the end of the five-year transitional period a decision on sovereignty would be reached only by agreement among the parties, including the elected representatives of the Palestinians. While this plan seemed to ensure deadlock if the issue of sovereignty ever arose, at least it would preclude outright Israeli annexation.

It soon became clear to the American side—though not as early as the first Friday—that the Israeli strategy was to hold off making any concessions on the things most important to Sadat, such as settlements in Sinai, until he had agreed to drop most of his unacceptable demands on the West Bank and Gaza. Meanwhile the Israelis would make minute, incremental, largely symbolic adjustments in their position on the West

---

the American compromise proposal. Much of what Vance said made the Egyptians optimistic. See Kamil, *Lost Peace*, pp. 522–23, for a summary.

17. Carter, *Keeping Faith*, p. 365.

Bank and Gaza, hoping the Americans would seek to match each of their mini-concessions with a major one from Sadat. The goal of all this maneuvering was, of course, a separate Egyptian-Israeli agreement, only thinly disguised as part of a broader framework. Begin, Dayan, and Weizman had all openly acknowledged that such an agreement was their aim, and increasingly Carter was leaning in that direction as well.

Late Friday evening Harold Saunders began to work on the first version of an American proposal. Eventually there would be twenty-three such drafts, and in many respects the first draft was drastically modified. But it did contain ideas that survived, especially the notion of several stages of negotiations for the West Bank and Gaza, with broader participation on the Arab side at each stage. Surprisingly little attention was paid to the issues of Sinai, though the important principles of withdrawal to the international border and a freeze on settlements during negotiations were included.[18]

Day Five, September 9, 1978

During the day on Saturday no formal meetings took place among the delegations. Instead, the American team worked on revisions in the draft proposal. Carter met with the drafting team in the afternoon. He had prepared a list called "Necessary Elements of Agreement" that included some thirty items.[19] About half made it into the final version of the Camp David Accords in recognizable form.

18. The first draft of the American proposal contained the following provisions, among others: during the interim period in the West Bank and Gaza, the Israeli military government would be abolished; Egypt and Jordan would provide liaison officers to cooperate with U.N. forces in helping to provide security during the interim period; the final status of the West Bank and Gaza would be resolved through negotiations based on all the principles of U.N. Resolution 242, including the mutual obligations of peace, security arrangements for all parties, the withdrawal of Israeli forces, a just settlement of the refugee problem, and the establishment of secure and recognized borders; and "the boundaries and security arrangements must satisfy the aspirations of the Palestinians and meet Israel's security needs. They may incorporate agreed modifications in the temporary armistice lines which existed between 1949 and 1967." Point 6 of the draft said that during these negotiations no new Israeli settlements would be established and that there would be no expansion of existing settlements. In a later revision of this draft during the day of September 9, Carter deleted a provision that would have linked the implementation of the Egyptian-Israeli peace treaty to the establishment of the self-governing authority on the West Bank and Gaza. He suggested that the third draft, point 2-C, should be revised to read that the secure and recognized boundaries might "incorporate agreed *minor* modifications" in the armistice lines (emphasis added).

19. See Carter, *Keeping Faith*, p. 371, for a summary of this list.

Late Saturday evening, I wrote the following:

Although there were no formal meetings today between Egyptians and Israelis, Weizman did meet with Sadat twice during the day. Weizman apparently asked Sadat the following questions: Can Egypt and Israel reach an agreement at Camp David that deals just with the two of them? Sadat said no. Weizman asked if Sadat would agree to an Israeli military presence in the West Bank and Gaza after five years. Sadat said no. (He has told Carter that he agrees to the concept in general, but will not openly agree to it as long as Prime Minister Begin is prime minister.) Weizman asked if the Yamit/Rafah area could be joined to the Gaza district? Sadat said no. Weizman asked if Sadat would agree to open borders and diplomatic relations and Sadat said that he would recognize Israel, but that he was not prepared for full diplomatic relations and open borders. (Again, Sadat has told us that he agrees in principle to these steps, but not while Begin is prime minister.) Weizman also asked if Israel could keep Etzion airfield near Eilat. Sadat said no. But he talked of helping Israel build a new airport within Israel proper and delaying withdrawal from Etzion for a period of two years.[20]

Weizman was discouraged by this conversation because he saw Sadat backing away from some of the points that had been agreed upon in their previous conversations. To some extent, Sadat is reflecting his genuine irritation with Begin's positions, but also seems to be trying to convince the Israelis that only an American compromise proposal can be the basis for further negotiations. He is giving them no encouragement in the direct contacts that he will be forthcoming.

The American delegation spent most of the day working on a draft proposal. The first version, prepared by Saunders, was discussed in the morning with the Secretary and the full delegation. By two o'clock in the afternoon, a revised draft had been sent to the president to get his preliminary reactions. At four o'clock, the president met with the full American delegation to discuss the draft and to make suggestions of his own.

The most important of the suggestions was the addition of the word "minor" to the language on agreed modifications in the 1967 lines on the West Bank and Gaza. The president said that he wanted to do this in order to have something to bargain with in his talks with Begin. He does not expect that language to remain in the final draft, but he has told both leaders that this represents the American position and he is prepared to include it in an initial draft. He thinks that Sadat will understand the need to remove it later, but that he can get something from Begin in return for its removal. . . .

The president talked about the need to try to conclude an agreement on the Sinai while at Camp David. There should be three years for implementation of such an agreement. Everything should be accomplished while at Camp David except the problem of settlements. There would be limited armament zones in Sinai. We would not make any reference to sovereignty in the West Bank and Gaza in the general framework document. He was beginning to think of how to

20. See Ezer Weizman, *The Battle for Peace*, pp. 360–62, for his version of his meeting with Sadat.

solve the airfields problem in Sinai as well. The president was very frank in saying that we should try to get an Egyptian-Israeli agreement started and concluded. If there are any delays in negotiation of the West Bank/Gaza agreement, that is somebody else's problem. He said that he hoped both agreements could move in parallel, but it was clear that the Egyptian-Israeli one took priority, and if nothing happened in the West Bank for ten years he would not really care very much. He began to refer to the possibility of side-letters dealing with a number of issues. For example, on sovereignty Israel might restate its position, while Sadat and the United States would say that they saw sovereignty as residing with the inhabitants in the area. On Sinai, Sadat would make a commitment not to send his main forces beyond the [Mitla and Giddi] passes. On the airfields, the Israelis might be able to use them for three years, and then they should be abandoned.[21]

During the evening, further drafting took place and near midnight a final draft was prepared for the president's consideration with notations made in the margins to reflect likely Israeli and Egyptian reactions to the proposal. The president wants to see this early tomorrow morning before he meets with the Israelis for the first discussion of this proposal.

Day Six, September 10, 1978

During the day on Sunday Carter received the latest version of the American proposal, with marginal notes indicating the likely Israeli and Egyptian reactions to various provisions. (See appendix E for the full text of the draft.) For instance, the language on the "inadmissibility of the acquisition of territory by war" was judged "very difficult for Begin," as would be the applicability of the principles of 242 to all fronts. Begin would most likely object as well to language calling for a solution of the Palestinian problem "in all its aspects." He was also expected to reject the provision that spelled out the need to base a final agreement on the West Bank on the principles of 242, including withdrawal of Israeli forces. The reference to "minor modifications" in the 1967 borders was also seen as a red flag for Begin, as was the point on including Egyptian and Jordanian officers, along with U.N. forces, in the West Bank and Gaza during the transition. Sadat was seen as more likely to find the draft acceptable, though he would have a hard time agreeing to the provision for keeping some Israeli forces in the West Bank and Gaza beyond the five-year transition.

Carter reviewed the new draft with Secretary Vance. Further changes

---

21. During the afternoon meeting with the American delegation, Carter also noted that Sadat wanted a statement of principles, but he termed this partly "subterfuge." Carter expressed the view that Sadat did not really care about such a declaration.

were suggested, and another version was ready by early Sunday afternoon after the president returned from an outing to Gettysburg. The president then reviewed this draft with Mondale, Vance, and Brzezinski and made further changes. The most important was the removal of the reference to "minor modifications" in the 1967 lines. Mondale argued strongly for deletion, and Carter accepted his advice.[22]

The Israelis were presented with the American proposal late in the afternoon. Begin was aggressive in his criticism. After an hour of heated discussion, the talks were suspended, to be resumed at 9:30 p.m. That meeting went on for five and one-half hours and resulted in little substantive progress.[23]

During these sessions, however, Carter did tell the Israelis of his priorities. The question of eventual sovereignty in the West Bank and Gaza would not be solved at Camp David. The question of settlements was not included in the U.S. draft at this point, but it would have to be dealt with before the talks were over. (Carter had feared that if it was included in the early drafts, it would be the only topic of discussion.) Finally, a specific agreement on Israeli withdrawal from Sinai should be concluded at Camp David.[24] Carter went on to play one of the cards that Sadat had handed him earlier, telling the Israelis that he would try to ensure that only representatives of "the permanent residents of the West Bank and Gaza will participate in the negotiations—not all Palestinians."[25]

Day Seven, September 11, 1978

By 3:00 a.m. on Monday, when the session ended, the Israelis promised they would give the Americans their written suggestions by midmorning so that these could be taken into account before a new draft was shown to the Egyptians. This set the pattern for the remainder of the negotiations, with each side being given the chance to make suggested changes in the U.S. draft, which the Americans might or might not incorporate into the next version that would be shown to the other party.[26]

22. When the Egyptians finally saw the American proposal the next day, they were angry that the reference to "minor modifications" had been removed, and they knew that Mondale had been responsible for the removal.

23. Carter, *Keeping Faith*, pp. 371–79, describes these meetings in detail.

24. Ibid., p. 373.

25. Ibid., p. 377.

26. I noted in my diary on Sunday, September 10, 1978: "The Egyptians were extremely nervous during the day on Sunday as they saw intensive consultations going on between the United States and Israel. They fear a joint U.S.-Israeli document, which will then be

Between eight and ten o'clock on Monday morning, September 11, the Egyptian delegation, which was housed some twenty yards away, witnessed a remarkable spectacle. Someone from the Israeli delegation would come running or cycling up to Holly Lodge, where Carter, Mondale, Vance, Brzezinski, and the rest of the U.S. delegation were sitting around a table. The Israeli would hand over a few pages of a document and then disappear. A few minutes later one of the Americans would dash out of Holly, hop on a bicycle, and ride off.

Inside the lodge the American side was reviewing the written Israeli reactions and deciding what, if anything, to incorporate in a new draft to be shown to President Sadat later in the morning. Once changes had been decided on, someone would rush off to get a page retyped.

Finally a new draft was ready, and the president turned it over to Sadat before noon. Sadat's initial reaction was generally positive, though he wanted stronger language on an Egyptian and Jordanian military presence in the West Bank and Gaza during the transitional period.[27] Sadat asked for some time to consult with his colleagues before giving Carter his final comments.

While awaiting the Egyptian reactions, Carter and Vance began to explore with the Israelis the possibility of parallel talks on the Sinai. Over lunch with Dayan, Vance asked how the Sinai negotiations could be made more precise. Dayan was interested, but recognized that Sadat needed agreement on a general framework in order to go forward with a deal on Sinai. Until this time the negotiators had been considering only one "framework document," but now they began to discuss the idea of two separate but related documents.

Later in the afternoon Carter met with Weizman and Avraham Tamir, director of the Israeli Army Planning Branch, to review the Sinai issue. Afterward he had another session with the Israelis, this time with Dayan and Barak. Dayan urged the president to come up with a proposal on Sinai, and Carter agreed to do so.

---

presented to them for approval or disapproval. This is not the spirit in which the U.S. side is consulting with the Israelis, but the Egyptians fear collusion nonetheless. The Israelis also today developed a proposal of their own entitled 'Response to the Egyptian Framework Document Submitted on 6 September 1978 at Camp David.' They initially intended to present it to the Egyptians, but at our urging did not do so, and there was no further discussion of this particular document. It was primarily a restatement of the known Israeli positions."

27. Carter, *Keeping Faith*, pp. 379–80. The full English text of the American proposal, as presented to the Egyptians on September 10, 1978, is found in Kamil, *Lost Peace*, pp. 635–44.

While Carter was beginning to turn his attention to the Sinai, Vance was meeting with the Egyptian delegation to hear their preliminary reactions to the U.S. draft. The news was not encouraging. Foreign Minister Kamil, who had frequently warned the Americans that Sadat did not pay much attention to details and that this fact could hurt him politically in Egypt as well as in the Arab world, argued strongly that the draft was unacceptable. Kamil protested, for example, the deletion of language from an earlier draft that had referred to the 1949 armistice lines as the basis for future borders with only minor modifications. Vance told him that Sadat had already agreed to the new and vaguer formulation. Kamil then argued that the Palestinian question was not being adequately addressed, and he complained that the American document said nothing about settlements. Vance reassured him that settlements would be mentioned in the final draft and that the United States favored their removal from Sinai and a freeze on them in the West Bank and Gaza.

Day Eight, September 12, 1978

On Tuesday the Egyptians gave full vent to their dissatisfactions with the draft American proposal. On the same day Carter himself penned the first version of a Sinai accord on a legal-sized yellow pad.

When the president met with Sadat in the morning, he found the Egyptian leader somewhat discouraged. He seemed preoccupied with the likely Arab reaction to the Camp David documents and mentioned Saudi Arabia in particular. Sadat was also having trouble with his advisers, who were strongly opposed to much of the U.S. draft.[28] Nonetheless, he told Carter that he would agree to the American proposals in the end, but that he might have to go through the motions of fighting on some issues.

During the afternoon the Egyptians, with the under secretary for foreign affairs, Usama al-Baz, taking the lead, presented their official response to the American proposal. Al-Baz argued that the document concentrated too much on the process of negotiations and not enough on substance. Also, the concessions being asked from the two sides were not equivalent. Concerning the West Bank and Gaza, Egypt could accept the idea of a transitional period, but the current draft left open the possibility of perpetual Israeli control. There was no clear Israeli commitment to

---

28. On September 13, Kamil sent a long memo to Sadat arguing that the talks had reached a dead end. Kamil did not, however, want Camp David to finish in a way that would damage U.S.-Egyptian relations. See the full text of his memo in Kamil, *Lost Peace*, pp. 548–52.

eventual withdrawal; even the military government was not to be abolished in this draft. The draft made no mention of Arab Jerusalem as part of the West Bank. In conclusion, al-Baz stated that Egypt would agree to diplomatic recognition of Israel, but that did not necessarily entail the exchange of ambassadors.

The Egyptians were not the only ones who were gloomy. During an informal talk between Dayan and Vance, the Israeli foreign minister said that probably no agreement could be reached on the Sinai because of disagreement over the settlements. Dayan argued that some effort should be made to reach limited agreements, leaving the intractable issues until later. Vance rejected this advice, and Dayan shrugged, saying he had tried his best and he could now see no positive outcome from the talks at Camp David. History would show, he said, that his conversation with Vance had been the last chance to salvage something, and it had not worked.

Meanwhile Carter was busy drafting the first version of an agreement on Sinai. It concentrated on phases of withdrawal, security arrangements, and some technical issues. Originally he called his handwritten draft "Outline of a Settlement in Sinai"; he then changed "Outline of" to "Framework for." The key sentence in the four-page draft read: "The exercise of full Egyptian sovereignty will be restored in the Sinai, up to the internationally recognized border between Egypt and mandated Palestine." After some minor changes, including the setting of a three-month goal for negotiation of a peace treaty—a point recommended by Saunders—the draft was typed and delivered by Carter to Sadat. (A facsimile of the draft is presented in appendix F.) The Egyptian president read the document and said it was largely acceptable. From this point on, Carter handled the Sinai proposal very much on his own.

Day Nine, September 13, 1978

Wednesday was almost entirely consumed by a lengthy meeting involving Carter and Vance on the American side, joined by only al-Baz and Barak. Carter's idea was to deal with the principal draftsmen on the Egyptian and Israeli sides to clean up some of the language in the general framework document. Carter was becoming concerned that Begin would create two new problems for every one that was solved. By engaging the lawyers to work on the smaller issues, Carter hoped to avoid that situation. As disputes over language in the text were resolved, the larger political problems that could be resolved only by Carter, Begin, and Sadat stood out all the more clearly.

The Israelis' refusal to include the language from 242 on the inadmissibility of the acquisition of territory by war was finessed by referring generally to 242 in all its parts in the preamble and then appending the entire text of the resolution to the framework document. But the question of settlements could not be so easily dealt with, nor could the problem of how to resolve the final status of the West Bank and Gaza. These were now the main stumbling blocks, and no one was sure that any way around them could be found.

At a late-night session on Wednesday, Vance, Begin, and Dayan discussed the Sinai proposal in detail, but found no openings. Both Begin and Dayan were adamant in refusing to agree to the removal of Israeli settlers from Sinai. Dayan's unhelpful suggestion was to include language in the draft saying that these issues could be addressed in later negotiations and that until then the status quo would prevail. This was one point on which the Americans were sure that Sadat would not yield.

During the talks at Camp David, Carter had developed a special fondness for Barak, the Israeli attorney general who constantly seemed to be looking for ways to solve problems, whereas some others seemed to specialize in creating them. Barak also seemed able to soften some of Begin's harshest positions. By contrast, Carter found al-Baz and the other Egyptian advisers more difficult to deal with than Sadat; whenever he encountered problems at their level, he would appeal over their heads to Sadat. Carter had intended to do so late on Wednesday, but was told that Sadat had retired for the evening. At four o'clock the next morning, Carter became alarmed that something might be wrong with Sadat, either illness or perhaps worse. He called Brzezinski and the Secret Service. When the sun rose, Sadat was out for his usual morning walk, and Carter breathed a sigh of relief.

Day Ten, September 14, 1978

On Thursday the negotiations seemed to reach an impasse. No agreement could be found for the settlements in Sinai. Several other problems remained. During the day some changes were made in the U.S. draft to make it more attractive to the Egyptians.

Carter appeared to have concluded that a full agreement was now beyond reach, but that at a minimum he must try to preserve his close working relationship with Sadat. If necessary, the talks could end with a statement that Carter and Sadat had reached agreement on all issues, and that only Begin's refusal to withdraw settlements from Sinai and accept the applicability of all the principles of U.N. Resolution 242 to the West Bank and Gaza stood in the way of an accord.

Because the Americans had long hoped that Dayan and Sadat might be able to work out some of the remaining problems, they enjoyed a brief moment of optimism when they learned that Sadat had finally agreed to receive the Israeli foreign minister. But when Dayan reported to Carter on his talks, he predicted that there would be no agreement.[29] For the first time Carter seemed to be convinced that the Camp David talks were headed toward failure.

In a paper that reflected the grim mood of that Thursday night, I outlined how the talks might end:

1. Priority to Egypt and Israel signing a joint statement, even if content of document is vague on key issues and postpones decisions on hard issues until later.

Plus — produces apparent progress and momentum; possible resumption of negotiations; short-term political gains here.

Minus — could embarrass Sadat; Hussein will refuse to join; each side may interpret statement differently, leading to charges of bad faith. Risk of our appearing to oversell results of Camp David.

2. Hold firm on key issues, even if Begin is reluctant; get Sadat to agree and sign. Key issues include:

— settlements (freeze in West Bank; eventual withdrawal in Sinai).

— West Bank–Gaza issues resolved in negotiations by end of transitional period.

— Inadmissibility language, if Sadat insists (simply quote preamble).

— Egyptian commitment to diplomatic, economic relations in return for above points.

Plus — Sadat has a chance of drawing support from other Arabs, including Jordan and Saudi Arabia; some prospects for internal debate in Israel, leading eventually to more flexibility; will be seen as partial success, without excessively raising expectations in US.

Minus — US and Israel will be in confrontation over settlements issue; possible charges of US-Egyptian collusion; Begin may succeed in short-term in rallying support.

CONCLUSION

After ten days of intense discussions and negotiations at Camp David, almost everyone believed the talks had reached an impasse. Carter's

---

29. Moshe Dayan, *Breakthrough*, pp. 171–72.

original hope that Begin and Sadat would come to trust each other now seemed terribly naive. They were literally not on speaking terms. Nor had there been any breakthroughs on the crucial issues, although many less important problems had been resolved.

Even Carter's belief that the tranquil atmosphere of Camp David would make it easier to reach an agreement was not holding up. Despite the lovely surroundings, claustrophobia was setting in. Almost everyone wanted to get away, if only for a few hours. The outside world was beginning to seem remote and exotic. Jokes were being made about "prison" and the "concentration camp" atmosphere. Psychologically and politically, time seemed to be running out.

Faced with the real prospect of failure, Carter was obliged to reconsider his initial strategy. Should he settle for a vague joint statement that papered over the differences? Should he keep pressing hard for a breakthrough on the key issues even if this effort led to a collapse in the talks? If the negotiations were to end in failure, should he remain neutral or seek to side with one party against the other?

Carter was now facing a classic political problem. If he held out for a strong agreement on both Sinai and the West Bank and Gaza, he risked not getting anything at all. The alternative would be to aim lower and to raise the chance of salvaging at least something. This is the point at which every politician must recall to himself the maxim that "politics is the art of the possible." And every negotiator must decide whether to consolidate his gains while still short of some objectives, or to suspend talks as a bargaining tactic in the hope of improving prospects for the next round.

Two fundamental and related issues now had to be addressed. One was the question of Israeli settlements in Sinai, which had become a surprisingly large stumbling block. The other was the way in which the future of the West Bank and Gaza would be eventually resolved. All the U.S. drafts to date had made explicit mention of finding a solution based on the principles of 242, including withdrawal. This point had not been much discussed, but Begin's rejection of it was predictable.

Carter had two choices. The first was to hold firm on both issues, winning a few more concessions from Sadat on security and normal relations with Israel, and then preparing a final draft that Sadat would accept and Begin would reject. The president could then bring the talks to an end and report to Congress and the American public on what had and had not been achieved in the talks. In doing so, he would be pointing the finger at Begin as the primary obstacle in the negotiations, hoping that he could win American support for his proposal and could even generate a hot debate within Israel. This was the confrontational strategy that Sadat favored, and as of Thursday, September 14, Carter had still not ruled it out if all else failed.

The alternative was to get Sadat what he most wanted, the removal of Israeli settlements and airfields from Sinai, but at the price of watering down the already rather vague draft on the West Bank and Gaza. No one could be sure that this approach would work. But it was reasonable to assume, from the comments made earlier by Dayan and Weizman, that Begin might consider giving up the settlements in Sinai, provided he could protect what most mattered to him, namely Israel's claim to future sovereignty over all the West Bank and Gaza. The obvious trade, if this assessment was correct, was to drop reference to withdrawal from the West Bank and Gaza in exchange for Israeli willingness to leave the Sinai completely.

Carter rarely spoke of political considerations when he confronted tough choices. But he must have been aware that the first alternative of confronting Begin would be politically unpalatable and might result in a complete failure. It was risky for him personally, and for the chances of any form of peace agreement. The second approach of trying for a compromise agreement would at least keep the peace negotiations on track for a while longer and would certainly be popular domestically.

The first ten days of Camp David set the stage for the choice that Carter now had to face. During the next three days he wrestled with Sadat and Begin and with himself to find a way to get from impasse to agreement. In the process he flirted with the more confrontational strategy, the possibility of going to the brink with Begin, but in the end that approach must have seemed too costly. Still, he fought hard to get what he believed to be the best obtainable agreement. The result was the Camp David Accords.

CHAPTER NINE

Success

Bringing the Camp David negotiations to an end proved to be almost as complicated as launching them. The pressures of time were beginning to weigh on all three leaders by late in the second week. The political costs of leaving the summit empty-handed must have been apparent not only to Carter and Sadat but also to Begin. If agreement was now to be reached, someone was going to have to make major concessions.

As of Friday, September 15, the gap between Egypt and Israel was still large. Sadat continued to demand that Israel withdraw from the settlements and airfields in Sinai, and Begin still refused. Sadat also insisted on some language that would commit Israel to eventual withdrawal from the West Bank and Gaza and to some form of Palestinian self-determination. Here Begin showed no give. Sadat was also refusing to cede on one point of importance to the Israelis, the exchange of ambassadors. This, he said, was a matter of Egyptian sovereignty and did not automatically follow from the establishment of diplomatic relations.

In the three days of talks that remained, each leader tried to pressure the others by threatening to walk out of the negotiations or to bring them to an end on unsatisfactory terms. Carter pleaded with both Sadat and Begin for concessions, and they explained at length the constraints they felt in going any further. The Americans tried to put pressure on Begin from within his own delegation, whereas they sought to give Sadat arguments to use to convince his advisers.

As the final phase of negotiations began, each leader had to decide what trade-offs were worth making. It was a critical moment: no one wanted to budge too readily from previously "nonnegotiable" positions, but everyone knew some movement was needed. Under the pressure of time, it was also the moment when mistakes could easily be made and when the whole effort could collapse.

For Carter, this was the most trying period of the negotiations. Sadat and Begin now made major efforts to win him to their side and to use him to pressure the other party for concessions. It was the time when a mediator was most needed, since neither party wanted to deal directly with the other. American proposals to package comparable concessions would be much easier to handle than direct demands from the opposing party. This situation gave Carter great power, but also placed enormous responsibility on his shoulders. For if the talks were now to break down, he would certainly be blamed.

END GAME: DAY ELEVEN, SEPTEMBER 15, 1978

Carter awoke on Friday morning with the conviction that the negotiations were reaching their crucial phase. In his own hand he wrote a letter to both Sadat and Begin that Vice President Mondale delivered. It read:

To Pres. Sadat and P.M. Begin:

We are approaching the final stage of our negotiations. With your approval, I propose that today we receive your most constructive recommendations, that tomorrow (Saturday) be devoted to drafting efforts, and that we conclude the meeting at Camp David at some time during the following day. We will, at that time, issue a common statement to the press, drafted together. Additionally, we should agree not to make any further public statements prior to noon on Monday. Please let me know if you object to any of these proposals.

J.C.

Sadat's Threat to Leave

The Egyptian president did object. He had apparently been deeply disturbed by his meeting on Thursday with the Israeli foreign minister. For some reason, he did not much care for Dayan, preferring to deal with Defense Minister Weizman. Dayan had been blunt in his remarks, arguing that Israel had the right to keep settlers in Sinai and suggesting that the issue of settlements be left unresolved for the moment, with the parties aiming instead for another partial agreement. Sadat had rejected this idea, and Dayan had replied that in that case Israel would stay where it was and would keep on pumping oil from Sinai.[1]

Whatever the reason for Sadat's black mood on Friday morning, he seemed to have reached the conclusion that further progress was impossible. He called Vance and informed him that he was preparing to leave that day. The Egyptian delegation was packing its bags.

---

1. Sadat's foreign minister was later to write: "In my opinion, Dayan's discussion with Sadat, which lasted less than an hour, was the straw that broke the camel's back and a turning point toward Sadat's involvement in a series of concessions, arriving at the point of total surrender and, in the end, his signing something beyond Israel's most optimistic dream." Muhammad Ibrahim Kamil, *The Lost Peace in the Camp David Accords*, p. 524.

Because Sadat had once before broken off talks, in January 1978, his threat could not be taken lightly. But he was also something of an actor, and one could not be sure how much he was staging his departure for dramatic effect on Carter. In either event, Carter took the threat seriously and went to Sadat's cabin for a private talk.

According to Brzezinski, Carter was very rough with Sadat. Carter reportedly warned of these results if Sadat left:

It will mean first of all an end to the relationship between the United States and Egypt. There is no way we can ever explain this to our people. It would mean an end to this peacekeeping effort, into which I have put so much investment. It would probably mean the end of my Presidency because this whole effort will be discredited. And last but not least, it will mean the end of something that is very precious to me: my friendship with you. Why are you doing it?[2]

Sadat appeared to be shaken by the force of Carter's argument. He explained that he had concluded that the Israelis did not want peace. He had obviously been angered by what Dayan had said the previous day. He also feared that were he to reach agreement only with the United States, which had originally been his goal, that would become the baseline for further concessions if negotiations resumed at a later date. It would be better to have no agreement at all. Carter assured him that Egypt would not be held to its concessions if Begin proved to be recalcitrant, and with this assurance Sadat agreed to stay.[3]

Sadat later informed his colleagues that Carter had said that he needed an agreement at Camp David to ensure his reelection. Once that hurdle was passed, he could turn his full attention again to Middle East peace negotiations.[4]

---

2. Zbigniew Brzezinski, *Power and Principle*, p. 272, quoting from what Carter told him several days after the incident. Carter's somewhat milder version can be found in Jimmy Carter, *Keeping Faith*, pp. 392–93.

3. According to Carter, the entire conversation lasted less than fifteen minutes. The two men remained standing, and Carter made it clear that he was deadly serious. They discussed the political impact of a collapse of the talks. Some Egyptians have argued that Carter, in a bid to convince Sadat to stay, promised Egypt a massive aid program equal to Israel's. Carter has strongly denied that any such promise was ever made. Interview with President Jimmy Carter, Plains, Georgia, May 22, 1985.

4. Kamil, *Lost Peace*, p. 574 and especially p. 595, where he quotes Sadat as saying to him: "President Carter told me that success at Camp David in reaching agreement on a framework for a comprehensive peace will easily guarantee his success in the upcoming election." Ezer Weizman, *The Battle for Peace*, p. 372, also refers to Carter's telling Sadat how an impasse in the talks would endanger his political prospects. Weizman does not say how he got this information. Sadat also told Kamil after his meeting with Carter that he

Sadat's threat to bring the talks to an end led the Americans to try to find solutions to the remaining issues in Sinai and to make additions to the West Bank–Gaza section of the framework that might make it more appealing to an Arab audience. Somehow Begin would have to be persuaded to relinquish the airfields and settlements in Sinai.

If possible, Carter hoped to add some words on the rights of the Palestinians, including their right to choose their own form of government and to vote for or against the results of the negotiations on the final status of the West Bank and Gaza. With these concessions from Israel, it was hoped, Sadat might be able to argue that he had protected the essence of the Palestinian demand for self-determination, provided, of course, that during the interim period of autonomy the Israelis would be constrained from building more settlements and expropriating more land.

The Speech That Never Was

If Begin proved to be intransigent, Carter seemed determined that he and Sadat would nonetheless leave Camp David in agreement. On Friday Carter asked that a draft speech be prepared that would be used if the talks failed. In it he would spell out the progress that had been made. He would explain the gap that had existed on the eve of Camp David. He would then announce that Sadat was prepared to make major concessions, which he would enumerate, such as full recognition of Israel, detailed security provisions, and an interim period of autonomy for the West Bank.

The climax of the draft speech that I prepared for Carter was a paragraph saying that only two issues now prevented agreement. One was Begin's unwillingness to give up the settlements in Sinai. The other was his refusal to acknowledge that the withdrawal provision of U.N. Resolution 242 would govern the final negotiations on the status of the West Bank and Gaza. On both points Carter was prepared to say that he sided with Sadat. He would ask the American public for understanding as the diplomatic process continued, and he would appeal to the Israeli public to urge its leaders not to miss the chance for peace. Doing so would of course mean a confrontation of some kind with Israel and could prove to be politically painful for the president.

Carter reviewed my draft of the "failure speech." He made a few

---

would sign anything without even reading it. In Kamil's words, he was a "changed man." Interview with Muhammad Ibrahim Kamil, January 24, 1985.

marginal notes and then gave his conditional approval. But it was clear that this speech was to be used only as a last resort. The president still had in mind finding solutions to the remaining problems, or at least creative ways of papering over the differences. Had he given the speech, he would have been launched on the course that had been discussed with Sadat the previous February. At that time such a course had seemed possible, perhaps even inevitable, but now it appeared to hold little promise and even less attraction for Carter.

Solving Sinai

Among the Israeli delegation, Weizman was most keen on reaching an agreement with Egypt. On Friday morning he began to explore with members of the American team the possibility of getting U.S. help to build new airfields in the Israeli Negev to compensate for giving up the three modern bases in Sinai. Secretary of Defense Brown favored the idea, as did Secretary Vance. During the day Carter gave his approval, even though the project would cost the American taxpayer $3 billion in concessional loans, and Carter was wary of having to "buy" peace between Egypt and Israel.

With the airfields off the agenda of remaining obstacles, Carter returned to his pet project of working out the details of the Sinai agreement. On two handwritten pages he listed how he thought various problems should be resolved. On the width of one zone in Sinai he was inclined to side with Egypt. On another point he urged that the Egyptian-Israeli difference be split, and so on through eight points. He concluded by observing that he would like the negotiations on these details to be concluded as quickly as possible after Camp David, preferably within a few days. Sensing the risk of losing control once his guests departed, Carter added: "Let's do as much as possible now."

The only remaining obstacle to a Sinai agreement seemed to be the settlements. Unbeknownst to the Americans, members of the Israeli team had arranged to have the hawkish minister of agriculture, Ariel Sharon, telephone Begin to say he would agree to give up the settlements if that was the price for peace with Egypt. Within the Israeli delegation, Weizman reinforced that message.[5] Begin held back a bit longer, however, presumably eager to know what he might get in exchange for this long-held concession.

5. Weizman, *Battle for Peace*, pp. 370–71.

During the day on Friday Vance and Brzezinski had been looking for ways of softening up the Israelis. For the first time they raised with Dayan the possibility of a U.S.-Israeli security treaty as part of an overall settlement. Dayan must have seen this proposal as something of a trap, as offering American protection if only Israel would make further territorial concessions. He therefore showed little interest, and the issue was quickly dropped.

At the same time the Americans tried to persuade Sadat to let the United States take over one of the Israeli airbases as a training facility. The airbase would provide a U.S. buffer of sorts between the two parties and was something Dayan had sought. Sadat flatly refused. The Americans did not press the issue further, because they had little interest in the base per se and Weizman had already signaled an alternative way of solving the problem.

By the end of the day the American team produced another draft of a framework document. Next to most paragraphs the notation "ok" was added. There was, however, one glaring exception, paragraph 1-C, which attempted to spell out how the final status of the West Bank and Gaza would be resolved by the end of the five-year transitional period. Amazingly enough, this crucial paragraph had barely been discussed. It would now become the focus of serious debate, and once again the negotiations would seem to reach an impasse.

WAFFLING ON THE WEST BANK: DAY TWELVE, SEPTEMBER 16, 1978

If Friday was the day of a near breakthrough on Sinai, Saturday was spent primarily on the West Bank and Gaza. Up to now, the main concession made by the Israelis on the issues of concern to the Palestinians had been to agree that the final status of the occupied territories could be decided by the end of the five-year transitional period. But they had not specified how such a decision would be made, nor on what basis. Certainly Israel had not dropped its claim to ultimate sovereignty over those areas.

Egypt was curiously absent from this discussion. Sadat had insisted that reference be made to the "nonacquisition of territory by war," which in his mind should mean that Israel would have to give up the West Bank and Gaza eventually. He had also mentioned the possibility of returning the West Bank to Jordanian administration and Gaza to Egyptian control during the interim period. And when that had been rejected by Begin, he had suggested that Jordanian and Egyptian officers might join U.N.

forces to provide security during the interim period. This, too, Begin had rejected.

With the decision to append the full text of U.N. Resolution 242 to the framework agreement, Sadat was as close to getting a reference to the "nonacquisition of territory by war" as he was to come, and from that point on he showed little concern with details of how the West Bank and Gaza would be dealt with. So the American side, still believing something tangible had to be achieved for the Palestinians if there was to be any hope of winning Jordanian, Saudi, and even Egyptian support, was left with the daunting task of trying to whittle away at Begin's lifelong position on Judea and Samaria, as he always called the West Bank. Adding to the sensitivity was Sadat's desire for some explicit mention of an Arab role in Jerusalem, which he considered part of the West Bank, a point totally rejected by Begin.

The United States and Israel Search for a Formula

Dayan and Barak met with Vance and other members of the American team at 11:30 on Saturday morning. This encounter proved to be crucial to the eventual resolution of the West Bank and Gaza issues. Up to this point the U.S. drafts had envisaged three stages of negotiations for these territories. In stage one, Egypt and Israel would agree on certain basic principles, such as the interim period, elections to a self-governing council, and the withdrawal of the Israeli military government. This agreement would be part of the Camp David framework.

The second stage of negotiations over the West Bank and Gaza would be broadened to include Jordan if King Hussein could be persuaded to join. If not, Egypt would continue negotiations anyway. This phase would deal with setting up the interim regime, electing the self-governing body, and working out security arrangements for the transition.

No later than three years into the interim period a third phase of talks would begin, this time including the elected representatives of the Palestinians in the West Bank and Gaza. These four-party discussions would address the final status of these areas, and agreement, based on the principles of 242, should be reached by the end of the fifth year. This phase proved to be the most controversial.

Dayan and Israeli Attorney General Barak opened the meeting by explaining in detail that Begin would never accept the idea that the final status of the West Bank and Gaza should be determined on the basis of the principles of 242. To do so would imply that Israel was prepared for withdrawal, as in Sinai, but this was not the case. The Israeli plan called only for autonomy, and that had nothing to do with 242.

Dayan suggested that 242 be referred to only with regard to future Jordanian-Israeli peace negotiations. Since in Begin's view King Hussein had no valid claim to the West Bank, and certainly none to Gaza, the issue of withdrawal should not arise. For those areas, Begin would agree to only one of two possible outcomes: perpetual autonomy or the imposition of Israeli sovereignty at the end of the five-year transitional period. This position was the same one the Americans had heard before. In fact, they had insisted on including reference to 242 as the basis for resolving the final status of the West Bank and Gaza in order to try to force a change in Begin's position.

At about noon Carter called Dayan away from the discussions. Barak continued to argue for a separation between Jordanian-Israeli negotiations on peace and the four-party talks on the final status of the West Bank and Gaza. Vance insisted that the two could not be so easily dissociated and that 242 had to be made to apply to both negotiating tracks.

Barak, who had a creative legal mind, expressed his view that there was not enough time to find a satisfactory resolution to this problem. This was the point at which the talks should have begun, he said. It would take at least another two weeks to find the appropriate language. As far as he was concerned, the effort should be made. But if there were only twenty-four hours left to negotiate, a formula would have to be found to fuzz over the issue rather than resolve it.

Barak had little support for his desire to continue the Camp David talks until the crucial West Bank and Gaza issues could be fully resolved. So his alternative of finding ambiguous language was implicitly accepted.

The central idea, worked out between Barak and Vance, was to have two synchronized sets of negotiations, one involving Jordan and Israel and one involving Israel and the elected representatives of the Palestinians in the West Bank and Gaza, joined by Egypt and Jordan. The draft would say that the principles of 242 applied to "the negotiations," without spelling out what that meant in reality. Egypt and the United States could claim that it meant that 242 did apply to the West Bank and Gaza, but Israel would maintain that it applied only to the peace treaty negotiations between Jordan and Israel, where the question of the future of the West Bank and Gaza would not be raised.

Few outside observers would have been able to follow the logic of this arcane discussion, but if they had, they would have seen that a basis for future arguments was being laid. The American side recessed for lunch to try to come up with acceptable wording. With some qualms I put pen to paper to draft a new paragraph 1-C that said, in reference to the final status of the West Bank and Gaza and the Israeli-Jordanian peace treaty, that the results of these negotiations should be in accordance with all the principles of U.N. Resolution 242, including withdrawal of Israeli armed forces, termination of all claims of belligerency, respect for the sovereignty and territorial integrity of all states in the area and their right to live in peace within secure and recognized boundaries, and a just settlement of the refugee problem. The ambiguity was deliberate, and probably essential. The draft also included a statement that these negotiations should recognize the legitimate rights of the Palestinian people.

During the afternoon the revised language of paragraph 1-C was forwarded to Carter and approved by him. He then tried to convince Sadat that the new wording was acceptable, which he did after some difficulty. Finally the task of persuading Begin had to be confronted. The decisive moment had finally been reached by late Saturday.

Saturday Night Fever

Early in the evening Begin, Dayan, and Barak arrived for their fateful meeting with Carter and Vance. It was there, in tense and difficult negotiations, that the final trade-offs were made that resulted in the Camp David Accords. It was also there that the seeds of future misunderstandings were sown.

Carter's main objective was to convince Begin to give up the settlements in Sinai. The Israelis presented their opening position: if all other elements of a peace treaty were successfully negotiated, Begin would then ask the Knesset to vote on whether the settlements should be removed. Carter said this proposal was not good enough. A firm Israeli commitment was needed now. Finally Begin agreed that the Knesset could vote within two weeks on the proposition: "If agreement is reached on all other Sinai issues, will the settlers be withdrawn?" (When Hamilton Jordan learned of this stratagem, he quipped that Begin had decided to "finesse it at the Knesset.") Begin even agreed to lift party discipline in the vote, though he did not promise that he would recommend acceptance. Still, the outcome did not seem to be in doubt, and Carter thought he could persuade Sadat to accept this formulation.

The discussion continued until well into Sunday morning. Carter felt that he had considerable leeway to deal with the remaining West Bank and Gaza issues.[6] Many points that could not be otherwise resolved were to be handled by an exchange of letters in which each party would restate its own position. For example, on Jerusalem it was decided that nothing would be included in the text of the agreement, but that each party would restate its well-known views. Likewise, Begin would write a note explaining how he interpreted the words "Palestinians" and "West Bank and Gaza," a device both for protecting his ideological position and for making clear that he did not mean that autonomy in the West Bank should apply to any part of Jerusalem, which for him was separate from Judea and Samaria. Begin also asked that the term "Administrative Council" be added in parentheses after the words "self-governing authority." (Begin later argued that inclusion of the words Administrative Council meant that the self-governing authority could not have legislative powers.) Carter attached little importance to these linguistic changes at the time.

More controversial was the language in the draft agreement that called for respect for the "legitimate rights of the Palestinian people," a phrase that Begin had previously rejected as synonymous with a Palestinian state. Now he accepted the words without much argument, later explaining to his colleagues that they had little meaning in any event.[7]

In return for his concession on "Palestinian rights," Begin was handsomely rewarded. On the difficult paragraph 1-C, which dealt with the final status of the West Bank and Gaza, Begin asked for several important changes. First, the text said that "the results of the negotiations" should be based on all the principles of U.N. Resolution 242, and the principles, including withdrawal, were then enumerated. Begin argued that the wording should be changed to read that "the negotiations" should be based on 242, not "the results of the negotiations." By this he meant that any party could raise the points mentioned in 242 during the negotiations, but that the final agreement need not reflect those principles. Begin also asked Carter to delete the listing of the principles of 242. The word "withdrawal" would therefore not be in the text dealing with the final status negotiations. Carter agreed to make these deletions, which watered down even further the vague wording of the agreement.

6. Carter, *Keeping Faith*, pp. 396–97. "I had a lot of latitude in dealing with the West Bank–Gaza questions. Fortunately, Sadat was not particularly interested in the detailed language of the Framework for Peace, and with the exception of the settlements, Begin was not very interested in the details of the Sinai agreement."

7. Weizman, *Battle for Peace*, p. 373.

One major issue remained. The question of the settlements in Sinai had been resolved, but those in the West Bank and Gaza had yet to be tackled. Carter had originally wanted a freeze on all settlement activity during the negotiations to establish the institutions of self-government in the West Bank and Gaza. Early drafts of the American proposal had specified that such a freeze would apply to land, buildings, and numbers of settlers. Dayan had argued that this plan was unrealistic, especially the attempt to place a clear limit on numbers of settlers. Carter was willing to soften the language somewhat, but he still wanted the Israelis to agree to the following language: "After the signing of the Framework Agreement and during the negotiations, no new Israeli settlements will be established in the area, unless otherwise agreed. The issue of further Israeli settlements will be decided and agreed by the negotiating parties."

Begin and Dayan argued vigorously that they could not accept that proposal. It would mean a freeze on all Israeli settlement activity for at least five years. Carter continued to insist. Finally, toward 1:30 Sunday morning the talks came to an end. Carter and Vance thought Begin had agreed to sign a letter confirming their understanding of the need for a freeze on settlements during the negotiations over the West Bank and Gaza. With the issue apparently resolved, the Americans finally concluded that an agreement could be reached the next day.

THE SETTLEMENTS FLAP

Nothing caused more ill will between the Israelis and Americans who were at Camp David than the issue of what they had supposedly agreed on concerning Israeli settlements in the West Bank and Gaza. Five people—Carter, Vance, Begin, Dayan, and Barak—were direct participants in the meeting at which the settlements were discussed, and each has given his own version. A clear picture does not emerge from these accounts, but by drawing on them and on some additional evidence, one can piece together what probably happened.

Carter's account is straightforward and detailed:

Late in the evening, Saturday, September 16, 1978, Prime Minister Begin, Foreign Minister Dayan, Attorney General Barak, Secretary Vance, and I were concluding discussions on the final wording of the section on the West Bank and Gaza. Section 6 referred to the Israeli settlements and as drafted the American proposal stated: 6. After the signing of the framework and during the negotiations, no new Israeli settlements will be established and there will be no expansion of physical facilities in existing settlements unless otherwise agreed by the parties.

Prime Minister Begin objected to this language, and began to make several alternative proposals. They included: A. A fixed time (three months) during which no new settlements would be constructed; B. prohibition against civilian settlements only; C. right to build a limited number of new settlements; etc. All of these proposals were rejected by me.

Finally, we agreed on the exact language concerning the settlements, and that the paragraph would be removed from the West Bank-Gaza section and included in a letter from Begin to me. I told him it could not be a secret letter and the Prime Minister replied that the text should be made public.

The agreed text was: "After the signing of the framework and during the negotiations, no new Israeli settlements will be established in this area. The issue of future Israeli settlements will be decided and agreed among the negotiating parties."

It is clear and obvious that the negotiations applied to the West Bank and Gaza.[8]

Vance, who was attuned to all the nuances of the discussion, has essentially confirmed Carter's account. In his mind the discussion of a freeze on settlements was linked to the negotiations on autonomy for the West Bank and Gaza. According to Vance, Begin did say he would give Carter a letter stating that Israel would establish no new settlements until the autonomy negotiations were completed. In his memoirs Vance argued that it is hard to understand how Begin could have "misinterpreted" what the president was asking, and he also expressed the view that Begin changed his position when he became aware of the adverse reaction of Israeli public opinion.[9]

The position of Begin was that he never agreed to more than a three-month moratorium on settlements. In the letter that he eventually wrote to Carter, he stated that Israel would build no more settlements in the West Bank and Gaza during the three months envisaged for the negotiations of an Egyptian-Israeli peace treaty. When first challenged by Carter on this interpretation, Begin seemed somewhat unsure of what he had agreed to on Saturday night and turned to his colleagues to confirm his interpretation.[10]

In his memoirs Dayan maintained that all Begin promised to Carter in their late night meeting was to think over the president's suggestion

8. The quotation comes from a handwritten note of President Carter's, probably drafted on September 18, 1978, a copy of which was sent to Prime Minister Begin. Carter, *Keeping Faith*, p. 397, only briefly mentions this episode.

9. Cyrus Vance, *Hard Choices*, pp. 225, 228–29.

10. See "An Interview with Begin," *Time*, October 2, 1978, p. 21, where the prime minister said: "There are some divergences of opinion about what was actually agreed upon on this issue. But as my two colleagues [Dayan and Barak] who were with me during the conversation with President Carter are now in Israel, I just have to consult them."

and to give him an answer the next day.[11] But on September 19, 1978, Dayan gave a somewhat different account of what had happened. On his arrival at Ben-Gurion airport in Tel Aviv, Dayan was asked what had been agreed upon concerning settlements in the West Bank and Gaza. He replied: "For this coming period, which is the period of the negotiations, which has not been defined—the duration of the negotiations on the Israeli-Egyptian issue has been determined to be 3 months, but the duration of the negotiations on the Palestinian issue has not been determined at all, but let us assume that it will indeed take 2 or 3 months—for the period of those negotiations, after we clarified things in Israel, it transpired that in effect the question of establishing additional settlements within the next 2 or 3 months or even maybe beyond that is not relevant now, at the moment, even if there had been no agreement and the question had not been raised at all." Dayan went on to say that after the establishment of the autonomy regime, "an agreement on this issue will have to be reached," referring to the possibility of new Israeli settlements during the transitional period.[12]

Dayan's contemporaneous account, then, confirms Carter's version that the freeze was linked to the autonomy negotiations, not to the peace treaty talks with Egypt. But Dayan did imply that there was no real difference, since the autonomy talks might be completed within three months in any case.

The only other eyewitness was Barak, who was taking notes during the meeting but has claimed not to be able to recall independently of his notes what was said. His notes confirm that Carter asked for Begin's agreement on a settlement freeze during the autonomy talks, to which Begin responded that he would think about it and would give Carter his answer the following day.

The only additional piece of evidence comes from my own notes of what Vance told the American negotiating team immediately after the meeting with Begin on Saturday night had broken up. Vance began by saying that there had been lots of haggling. I then wrote: "Begin letter to us—public—no new settl during neg except as agr—Freeze for period of neg—(*he keys to three months—could be extended*). Won't put in agreement."[13]

11. Moshe Dayan, *Breakthrough*, pp. 184–86.

12. Foreign Broadcast Information Service, *Daily Report: Middle East and Africa*, September 20, 1978, p. N7, quoting Israel Defense Force's Radio on September 19, 1978.

13. This passage was taken verbatim from my notes called "Pres with Begin Sept 16 evening." Translated it meant: "Begin will write a letter to Carter that will be made public. There will be no new settlements during the negotiations except by agreement. This means

Exactly what took place in the meeting between Carter and Begin on Saturday night will never be known. But apparently Carter was correct when he said that the entire discussion of the freeze of settlements in the West Bank and Gaza was tied to the negotiations on autonomy, not to the Egyptian-Israeli bilateral talks for which a three-month deadline had been set. The language on a settlements freeze being discussed was taken directly from the part of the draft framework document dealing with the West Bank and Gaza. The Saturday night talks gave Begin no basis for his subsequent decision to link the freeze to the Egyptian-Israeli peace treaty negotiations. At the same time it is clear from most accounts that Begin did say something about a freeze for only three months though he apparently implied that it could be extended.

It seems most likely that on Saturday night Begin did not give Carter a firm agreement to a freeze on settlements for the duration of the autonomy negotiations. But he may have wanted to leave the president with the impression that such an agreement had almost been reached. When he reportedly told Carter that he would give him a letter the following day, he may well have hoped that the president would interpret that as tantamount to acceptance of Carter's proposed language. This is only speculation. But clearly when Vance briefed us after the meeting, he knew that there was still some ambiguity in Begin's position. Presumably it would be clarified once the letter actually arrived.

No doubt Carter and Vance felt they had Begin's essential agreement on all points. On the crucial issue of the settlements in Sinai, they had a clear commitment from Begin. By early Sunday morning everyone was exhausted. Vance was still worried about how the wording of paragraph 1-C could be finally resolved. It had been substantially altered since Sadat had given his approval. Much remained to be done on Sunday.

With so many issues in mind, Carter and Vance were apparently willing to wait until the next day to pin Begin down on West Bank settlements. They had stated their point of view forcefully and thought Begin had acquiesced. Begin, who was always careful with words, had come close to agreeing, but had left himself room for maneuver. In any event, until he had given his commitment in writing, it would not be possible to know exactly what he had accepted. Sunday would prove to the Americans that they still did not have Begin's agreement. But by

there will be a freeze on settlements. (*Begin sees the freeze lasting only three months, but it could be extended.*) This understanding will be put in a separate letter, not in the framework agreement itself."

then they were so close to concluding the negotiations that they chose to overlook this "misunderstanding." It was a costly mistake.

THE FINALE: DAY THIRTEEN, SEPTEMBER 17, 1978

Summing up the results of the talks on Saturday, I wrote the following:

In the course of the day, it was decided to leave some issues vague and unsettled, knowing that there would be a moment of truth further down the road when some of the vagueness would have to be removed. In these negotiations, there comes a time when one opts for clarity at the risk of reaching no agreement at all, or settling for vagueness, which means postponing problems until a later date. On the West Bank and Gaza, we have chosen to postpone until later what cannot be solved today.

Sadat clearly wants an agreement with the United States, and not particularly one with Begin. But we have made it clear to him that we prefer an agreement between the two parties themselves. The Egyptian delegation fears that Sadat has given too much away and that he will be vulnerable in the Arab world.

Sadat's lack of interest in detail and in language is very frustrating to his colleagues. Sadat has bargained hard on Sinai and has achieved everything that he wants there, assuming that the Israelis do agree to pull out the settlements.

Begin held firm on his basic West Bank/Gaza position and managed to get Sadat to back down on a number of key issues there, and in return only gave a few symbolic positions away, such as reference to the legitimate rights of the Palestinians.

The Egyptians feel that the only big concession that they have gotten out of Begin is the removal of settlements from Sinai and a freeze on settlements on the West Bank and Gaza. Otherwise they have little with which they can sell the agreement to the rest of the Arab world. The Egyptians fear that this will be seen as a formula for a separate Egyptian-Israeli peace agreement and nothing more. It is difficult to see how Hussein can join the talks.

Despite the apparent breakthroughs on Saturday night, agreement was still not certain. On Sunday morning Carter met with Sadat and informed him of the most recent developments, including Begin's apparent willingness to accept a freeze on settlement activity in the West Bank and Gaza during the negotiations to establish self-government there.[14] Sadat was pleased, but there were still questions concerning Jerusalem that needed to be solved. Carter had reached the conclusion that no mention of Jerusalem should appear in the framework document, and that instead

14. According to Eilts, "Sadat, who was told of Begin's alleged agreement, signed the Camp David accords that Sunday night believing U.S. assurances that a protracted settlements freeze, even if not inscribed into the accords, constituted part of the Camp David package and would be confirmed by letter the following day." Hermann Frederick Eilts, "Improve the Framework," p. 8.

each party would simply restate in separate letters its well-known position. This was acceptable to Sadat.

With Sadat's agreement on nearly all points in hand, Carter and Vance now had to work quickly to produce a final version of both the general framework for peace and the agreement on Sinai. In addition, letters had to be drafted for world leaders explaining what had been accomplished, and plans had to be made for announcing publicly the Camp David Accords. After all, there had been a virtual press and diplomatic blackout during the negotiations. No one on the outside knew if the lengthy talks at Camp David were on the verge of success or failure.

At about noon on Sunday another crisis erupted when the United States conveyed to the Israelis the text of the letter stating the U.S. position on Jerusalem. Quoting from statements by two former U.N. ambassadors, Arthur Goldberg and Charles Yost, the American letter confirmed that in the official U.S. view East Jerusalem should be considered occupied territory, subject to the provisions of the Geneva Convention of 1949, and its final status should be resolved in future negotiations. There was nothing new in these formulations, but nonetheless Begin found them totally unacceptable.

In response to the American draft letter on Jerusalem, Begin threatened to walk out of the negotiations. He seemed to be deadly serious. Dayan, who had been brooding all morning and had been predicting that the talks would fail, was fully behind Begin on this point. Even Barak feared that an impasse had been reached. Finally it was agreed that the United States would restate its position by referring to the Goldberg and Yost statements, but would not quote from them. In substantive terms this changed nothing, but somehow Begin was able to accept the less precise formulation.

In midafternoon, as the last details were falling into place, Barak brought Carter the drafts of two letters from Begin, one on the settlements in Sinai and the other on the settlements in the West Bank and Gaza. Carter argued that neither letter conformed to what had been agreed and spent some time redrafting the language on how the Knesset would vote to remove settlements from Sinai.

A red flag should have gone up for Carter when he read the Begin letter on settlements in the West Bank and Gaza. In black and white Begin had spelled out that a freeze on settlements would take place for only the three-month period set for the Egyptian-Israeli negotiations. Carter told Barak this was unacceptable, and read to him from his notes of the previous evening where he had written down the formulation he thought Begin had accepted.[15]

At this time Carter knew that he did not have a clear-cut agreement with Begin on the question of settlements in the West Bank and Gaza. It was an act of faith, to say the least, to think that Begin would change his mind and sign the text of the letter Carter had requested. Careful, prudent negotiators would have insisted on seeing the final draft instead of relying on hope. But it was late in the afternoon, much work remained to be done, and Sadat was not insisting on greater clarity on this point. As a result, the Americans made their most serious technical mistake.[16] They failed to get Begin's signature on the letter concerning settlements, agreeing instead that it could reach them the next day. By then, of course, the Camp David Accords would be signed. Instead of pinning Begin down on this admittedly crucial issue, Carter turned his attention to ensuring that Sadat was ready to conclude the agreement. Then he could think about how to announce it to the world.[17]

Late in the afternoon Carter met with Sadat and al-Baz to go over the final document. The atmosphere was tense. Sadat was far from enthusiastic about the results. Al-Baz realized that by now an agreement was inevitable, but he was still unhappy with the result.

As Sadat took leave of President Carter, he was quiet, almost grim. There was no sense of victory or elation. After seeing Sadat to the door, Carter turned to his aides and said he thought an agreement was now in hand, but he had been afraid to ask Sadat directly.[18]

At about 5:30 p.m. Vance finally told the president that the last details of the text had been worked out. The mood among the Americans was

15. Carter, *Keeping Faith*, p. 400, says Barak confirmed that the President's language was accurate, but in a memo that Carter drafted shortly after the meeting he merely noted that Barak "did not disagree with the agreed text."

16. Looking back on Camp David more than six years later, Carter wrote that his most serious omission had been in "not clarifying in writing Begin's promise concerning the settlement freeze during the subsequent peace talks." He also notes that neither he nor Sadat kept King Hussein adequately informed during the talks and this "undoubtedly contributed to his refusal to join the subsequent autonomy talks." Jimmy Carter, *The Blood of Abraham*, p. 169.

17. Dayan was later to write: "The truth was that if the US President wanted clear and specific commitments from us, he should have demanded and tried to get them before the signing of the Camp David accords. Since he was then satisfied with the limited commitment Begin was prepared to give, he could not now blame us but only himself." Dayan, *Breakthrough*, p. 229.

18. See Vance, *Hard Choices*, p. 226; and interview with Harold Saunders, May 27, 1985.

surprisingly subdued. Shortly after six o'clock Carter asked media adviser Gerald Rafshoon and press secretary Jody Powell how long it would take to organize a signing ceremony at the White House. Rafshoon said he needed four hours. Carter looked at his watch. It read 6:08 p.m. The president replied: "You have my approval eight minutes ago. Let's have the ceremony at ten o'clock." Rafshoon and Powell pleaded for a bit more time, and the signing was finally set for 10:30 p.m.

Just as the American team was about to leave the president's cabin, the weather, which had been good throughout the previous thirteen days, took a sudden turn for the worse. Thunder and lightning began, accompanied by heavy rain. It seemed an ominous start for the Camp David Accords.

But a few hours later at the White House a much more hopeful atmosphere was created as Sadat, Begin, and Carter made gracious comments about one another, pledged themselves to keep working for peace, and then smiled and clasped hands in a picture that was seen around the world.

THE SCORECARD

Two agreements were signed on September 17, 1978, by Sadat and Begin, and witnessed by Carter. The first stated general principles and set forth an outline for dealing with the West Bank and Gaza. The second, loosely tied to the principles stated in the first, was a detailed formula for reaching an Egyptian-Israeli peace treaty. (See appendix G for the full text.) The Camp David Accords were essentially one more step, but an extremely significant one, in the continuing process of negotiations.

The texts of the two agreements were precise on some issues, vague on others. They were certainly subject to different interpretations. And they left many issues to be dealt with in the future. Still, each party felt it had achieved something by signing the agreements, while no doubt realizing that many difficult times lay ahead. In any case, the framework for subsequent negotiations was now set. The next stage, difficult as it proved, was primarily one of detail, filling in the blanks, along with occasional attempts to revise the basic formula.

Egyptian Gains and Losses

Egypt's most tangible gain from Camp David was an Israeli commitment to full withdrawal from Sinai, including from the oil fields, settlements, and airbases. To get this commitment, Sadat had offered a period of three years to complete the withdrawal, concrete security arrangements that would be monitored by the United States and the United Nations, and a promise to "normalize relations" with Israel once the first phase of withdrawal had been reached. In Egyptian terms, the agreement was a good one, meeting virtually all Sadat's demands.

On issues of concern to other Arabs, especially the Palestinians and Jordanians, Sadat had much less to point to. The document containing general principles referred to "the legitimate rights of the Palestinian people" and the right of the Palestinians to choose their own form of government, but all the details dealt with procedures and arrangements for the transitional period, not for the final status of the occupied territories. Even a cursory reading of the text would show that Israel had made no commitment to eventual withdrawal from the West Bank and Gaza; nothing was said about Jerusalem; and settlements in the West Bank and Gaza were nowhere mentioned, though the Americans were telling everyone that Begin had in fact agreed to a freeze for the duration of the negotiations on autonomy.[19]

Had Egypt not aspired for nearly thirty years to lead the Arab world, these shortcomings would not have mattered so much. But Sadat, and certainly his chief aides, had not given up on Egypt's Arab vocation; they were thus keenly disappointed by the results of Camp David. Their pride was hurt, even though Egypt's vital national interests had been well defended.

Sadat did not come away from Camp David with any specific commitments of American aid, either military or economic. But from his discussions with Carter he could conclude that American support of Egypt in both spheres would depend on achieving a peace treaty with Israel. Carter had also apparently implied that a success at Camp David would strengthen his hand in dealing with Israel in subsequent negotiations.

Israel's Gains and Losses

Begin was no doubt the most able negotiator at Camp David. He understood best how to play the cards in his hand, he was meticulous in

19. In letters that Carter sent to world leaders the night of September 17, 1978, he included this sentence: "There will be no new Israeli settlements in the West Bank and Gaza during the negotiations to establish self-government in this area." Brzezinski made the same point in his briefing to the press that evening.

turning words to his advantage, and he credibly used the threat to break off the talks to extract concessions at crucial moments. He kept his eye on specific issues, sometimes giving in on a symbolically important but intangible point to obtain something more concrete. He knew how to play the game of brinkmanship, holding back on his final concessions until everyone else had put his cards face up on the table.

Admittedly, Begin had to concede the entire Sinai to Sadat, thus giving up something tangible and very valuable. But in return, Begin had won not only peace with Egypt, which by its nature might not prove durable, but also a comparatively free hand for Israel in dealing with the West Bank and Gaza. For Begin, Sinai had been sacrificed, but Eretz Israeli had been won.

Because of his skill and fierce determination, Begin protected himself against considerable U.S. and Egyptian pressure on the key issues of the future of the West Bank and Gaza and on any form of linkage between the Egyptian-Israeli agreement and the Palestinian question. While promising "full autonomy" to the West Bank and Gaza, Begin refused to spell out what that might mean in practice. He did not agree to abolish the military government, only to "withdraw" it. (It later emerged from discussions that he meant that the military government would be physically moved from the West Bank during the interim period, but it would continue to exist and would have ultimate control over the "self-governing authority" that the Palestinians were to elect.)

Central to Begin's sense of success was the fact that he had not been forced to accept language on the "inadmissibility of the acquisition of territory by war," the applicability of the principles of 242 U.N. Resolution "to all fronts of the conflict," and the need for eventual Israeli withdrawal from the West Bank and Gaza. Nor had any dilution of Israel's claim to sovereignty over all of Jerusalem been insinuated into the agreement. Finally, Begin had gone no further than to promise a three-month freeze on settlements in the West Bank and Gaza.

By the time he arrived at Camp David, Begin had already ceded the point of recognizing Egypt's international boundary that dated from the days of the Palestine Mandate. But until the very end he had held firm on not removing Israeli settlements, and even when he left Camp David, he had not gone beyond promising that the Knesset would vote on whether to abandon the settlements in Sinai if all other issues could be resolved in negotiations with Egypt.

Some of his critics in Israel were violently opposed to Begin's willingness to return all the Sinai to Egypt. The question of settlements was indeed a sensitive one, especially for the sizable town of Yamit on the northern Sinai coast. But Begin was in a good position to defend himself, particularly with the backing of Ariel Sharon, one of the main architects of Israel's settlements plans.

Finally, Begin could point to the early normalization of relations with Egypt, something to which he attached great importance. Within nine months of signing a peace treaty with Egypt, and even with Israeli troops and settlers still in Sinai, diplomatic relations would be established and ambassadors might even be exchanged. This arrangement went well beyond what most Israelis had thought possible, and Begin was proud of his achievement.

The American Role

Carter's role in helping to broker the agreements was central. Left to themselves, Sadat and Begin would probably not have overcome their suspicions and would have broken off the talks over any number of issues. For both leaders it was easier to accept suggestions from Carter than from each other. Direct negotiations may sound fine in theory, but they had little part in achieving the Camp David Accords.

Carter's positions on substance influenced the outcome. He wanted an Egyptian-Israeli agreement on Sinai, and he was prepared to press Begin hard on withdrawal and on settlements to get it. He was less concerned with the details of a West Bank–Gaza agreement and did not think that any explicit linkage with the Palestinian question was desirable or necessary.

Vance was more concerned with the Palestinian part of the framework than Carter. He favored some degree of linkage. He had hoped to persuade Begin to accept the applicability of the withdrawal provision of 242 in deciding the final status of the West Bank and Gaza. In his own account of Camp David, most of the attention is paid to those issues, not to Sinai.

But in the end, on the American side it was Carter who made the final judgments on what to accept and what not to accept, and it was Carter who used his influence with Sadat to get him to stay and to sign an agreement that both men knew was imperfect. No one other than Carter could have gone to Begin on the last day and insisted on a signed letter confirming the discussion of the previous evening, in which Carter believed Begin had promised a prolonged freeze on settlements in the West Bank and Gaza. But Carter did not do so.

Carter was thus very much the architect of the Camp David Accords. He had played the role of draftsman, strategist, therapist, friend, adversary, and mediator. He deserved much of the credit for the success, and he bore the blame for some of the shortcomings. He had acted both as a statesman, in pressing for the historic agreement, and as a politician, in settling for the attainable and thinking at times of short-term gains rather than long-term consequences.

In many ways the thirteen days at Camp David showed Carter at his best. He was sincere in his desire for peace in the Middle East, and he was prepared to work long hours to reach that goal. His optimism and belief in the good qualities of both Sadat and Begin were reflections of a deep faith that kept him going against long odds. His mastery of detail was often impressive. And he was stubborn. He did not want to fail. These were precisely the qualities that he had brought to his electoral campaign in 1976 and that the American people had apparently admired. As in 1976, he surprised many of his critics by showing what hard work, determination, and faith could produce.

But Carter, well into the second year of his presidency, had also become more aware of what could be attained from Begin and what the costs of a confrontation with Israel might be in domestic political terms. These realizations had convinced him to pull back from his original ambitious plan for a comprehensive peace and had made him particularly cautious in dealing with the Palestinian question.

Camp David was not the end of the road, either in the search for Middle East peace or in Jimmy Carter's political career. Over the next several months there would be many more tests. Once again the negotiations would grind to a halt, and once more Carter would have to throw himself into the breach to salvage what he could. And once again, faced with the choice of pressuring Begin or Sadat for concessions, he turned to Sadat. At Camp David, after all, he had taken the measure of the two men and had concluded that Begin could not be made to budge. Sadat, whom he genuinely liked and admired, would. That perception, as much as any other, influenced the final outcome.

CHAPTER TEN

Interpretations

The two agreements reached at Camp David marked an important watershed in the peace negotiations, but a long road remained to be traveled before peace would actually be achieved. Along the way there would be pauses, detours, some backtracking, and many dead ends. Egypt and Israel would finally reach their goal of a formal peace treaty, but the broader objective of finding a peaceful resolution to the Palestinian question remained elusive. And this failure could ultimately jeopardize the hard-won peace between Israel and the largest Arab country.

So Camp David represented a possibility of peace, but did not guarantee its achievement. Much remained to be done, many of the blanks would have to be filled in, and many of the ambiguities would have to be resolved one way or another. In short, the negotiating would continue.

The phase of detailed drafting was now to begin, a seemingly technical task, but in fact a complex process during which major political battles were still fought and attempts to revise the basic framework of negotiations were still made. Although the technicians were sitting at the table drafting documents, the political leaders were still deeply involved.

Begin, Sadat, and Carter each devised strategies for this phase of negotiations, but the special circumstances of the summit could not be recreated. Isolating the leaders from the press and their own public opinion had no doubt been a prime ingredient in reaching the two framework agreements. Now, however, each leader would have to return to the real world in which domestic constituencies would have their say.

As each of the Camp David participants felt compelled to justify what he had done at the summit, the gap separating them began to widen again. By the time of the self-imposed target of three months for negotiating the peace treaty between Egypt and Israel, the talks had come to a halt.

POST-SUMMIT STRATEGIES

Carter left Camp David with a feeling of real satisfaction. The reaction in Congress, the press, and the public at large to the news of agreement between Begin and Sadat was overwhelmingly positive. Carter received much of the credit, and his political fortunes appeared to improve significantly as a result.

To sustain this political boost, however, Carter needed to make sure that the Camp David frameworks did not remain dead letters. Time was of the essence in reaching a formal peace treaty. Among other considerations, midterm congressional elections were scheduled for early November, and it would probably help Democratic candidates, and therefore Carter, if a peace treaty could be signed by then.

While Carter was no doubt pleased with the domestic American reaction, he was worried by the early signs of disenchantment in the Arab world. He had implied to Sadat that he would make a major effort to win support from Jordan and Saudi Arabia, and in his more careless moments he had said that anything he and Sadat agreed to would have to be accepted by King Hussein and the Saudis. But Hussein was wary of the accords reached at Camp David and refused to meet with Sadat on the Egyptian president's return trip to Cairo.

Carter's sense of urgency in pressing the negotiations forward was tied in part to his belief that Arab opposition to the agreements would grow if the momentum seemed to be waning. An Arab summit was scheduled to be held in Baghdad in late October, where Jordan and Saudi Arabia would undoubtedly come under strong pressure to denounce the accords.

Carter's clear priority after Camp David was to conclude the treaty negotiations as quickly as possible, literally within days. As usual, the president tended to see the remaining issues as technical and therefore susceptible to rapid resolution. The deeper political problems faced by both Begin and Sadat were harder for him to fathom. Carter found it difficult to accept the fact that neither shared his own sense of urgency.

Not only did Begin not share Carter's feeling that time was of the essence, but he also wanted to slow down the pace of negotiations for fear that too much pressure would otherwise be put on Israel. Whenever Carter showed himself too eager for quick results, Begin seemed to dig in his heels to resist demands for Israeli concessions. He was particularly recalcitrant about the settlements in the West Bank and Gaza. As hard as Carter might press to resolve this issue, Begin simply said no to the idea of a prolonged freeze on new settlements. And that was that.

Begin, who often seemed to have the clearest strategic overview of the negotiations, was also determined to keep the focus on peace with Egypt, not on the Palestinian question. Since an early achievement of peace with

Egypt would mean an early commencement of talks on the Palestinian question, Begin was probably not eager to sign the treaty within the envisaged three-month period.

If Begin was attentive to the rhythms of American politics, and surely he was, he must have realized that it would be increasingly difficult for Carter to play a strong role in the negotiations as 1979 unfolded. At some point the preelection atmosphere would take hold, and Carter would have to turn to shoring up his political position. He would not then want to engage in confrontations with Israel. Begin was well aware that Carter tended to side with Sadat on the Palestinian question and that the negotiations over the West Bank and Gaza would be extremely difficult. It would be far better, then, not to begin talks on autonomy until sometime well into 1979, when Carter would have other preoccupations.

For Begin, time was far less important than maintaining the integrity of his position. For him that meant there could be no formal link between the Egyptian-Israeli peace treaty and the negotiations to establish a Palestinian self-governing authority. He had fought hard at Camp David to resist linkage and had essentially succeeded, but the battle was likely to go on.

Begin also faced domestic problems, especially within his own Herut party within the Likud bloc. He returned to Israel to find some strong criticism for his having agreed to abandon the settlements in Sinai. He had of course done so to secure an agreement with Egypt, and in the process had protected Israel's claim to the West Bank and Gaza, which was of primary importance to him. But there was still opposition, including attacks on the Camp David Accords from those who saw in "full autonomy" for the Palestinians the embryo of a future Palestinian state. Begin went to great lengths to deny this, and in doing so he gave such a narrow interpretation to autonomy that both the Egyptians and Americans felt he was retreating rapidly from what he had promised at Camp David.

Unlike Begin, Sadat did not seem to be worried about his domestic public opinion, but he was concerned about Arab reaction. He knew he could not be criticized for recovering Egyptian territory, but he would inevitably be accused of having sold out the Palestinians. Anyone with the patience to read through the Camp David Accords might have found a few passages that looked promising for the Palestinians, but the magic words "withdrawal from occupied territory" and "self-determination" were not there, and nothing in the agreement precluded indefinite Israeli control of the West Bank and Gaza. Even the envisaged freeze on settlements in the West Bank and Gaza seemed to vanish within days after Camp David.

Sadat had the most difficult political task of the three leaders in trying to build broad support for the Camp David Accords. He had just received the resignation of another foreign minister, Muhammad Ibrahim Kamil. (Ismail Fahmy had quit after Sadat went to Jerusalem.) Some of the Egyptian foreign ministry officials had boycotted the signing ceremony at the White House, including the chief draftsman, Usama al-Baz. Egyptian intellectuals, journalists, leftists, and Islamic groups would all be critical. Elsewhere in the Arab world Sadat would be abused for making a separate peace with Israel.

None of this mattered too much in the short term; Sadat's political position seemed secure, and he was able to govern without much regard for the ups and downs of public opinion in Egypt or the Arab world. But Sadat was a proud man, and he was determined to show that he had not sold out at Camp David.

Sadat was not particularly thin-skinned. He had been sharply criticized before, especially after the Sinai II agreement in September 1975. He was not, however, reconciled to letting Begin have peace with Egypt without any concessions to the Palestinians. He continued to think that a U.S.-Israeli confrontation was needed before a final agreement could be reached. He had failed to establish the principle of linkage at Camp David, but now he would try to repair that mistake.

In many ways Sadat was in a weaker position than Begin. If the talks now broke down, Israel would stay put in Sinai. Sadat would have nothing to show for his "historic initiative." And his hope for American economic, military, and technological assistance would fade if the peace negotiations collapsed because of his actions. Carter had already warned him of that at Camp David. Sadat worried less about time than Carter, but he too must have seen that Carter's role would have to change as the election year of 1980 approached. But Sadat also knew that any show by him of impatience or eagerness to conclude the negotiations would be used by Begin to try to extract further concessions.

When viewed from the perspectives of Carter, Sadat, and Begin, the post-summit phase of negotiations was bound to be difficult. The unique circumstances of the thirteen days at Camp David had facilitated reaching agreement, but now most of the pressures were working in the opposite direction. It was not a propitious atmosphere in which to resume the talks.

PREPARING FOR THE NEXT ROUND

According to the Camp David agreements, negotiations would not begin on the peace treaty until the Israeli Knesset had voted in favor of removing the settlements in Sinai as part of the final withdrawal to the international border. The vote was to take place within two weeks.

Controversy over Settlements

Carter was not content to sit and wait for the results of the Israeli vote. There was one item of unfinished business. On Monday, September 18, 1978, Begin had sent Carter the promised letter on the settlements in the West Bank and Gaza. The text was identical to the one Carter had rejected the previous day. Referring to his notes of the Saturday night conversation, Carter wrote down what he thought had been agreed to and had Assistant Secretary of State Saunders deliver his version to the Israelis, along with the original of Begin's letter, which Carter refused to accept.

For several days American and Israeli officials tried to find language that might resolve the difference. An Israeli embassy official pointed to Foreign Minister Dayan's public remarks of September 19 and seemed to think a formulation such as the following might be acceptable: "There will be no new settlements authorized by the Government of Israel in the West Bank and Gaza during the period of negotiations to establish the self-governing authority. The question of future settlements will be discussed with the objective of reaching agreement among the negotiating parties." Carter would have easily accepted this formulation, but Begin would not hear of it. And Sadat did not help matters when he said to the press on September 19 that he understood there would be a freeze for three months and that Israel had also agreed not to expand settlements during this period.[1]

Carter continued to look for ways to pressure Begin into agreeing to

1. Middle East News Agency (Cairo), September 20, 1984. Israelis frequently quote Sadat's remark to prove that Begin was correct in his interpretation of what was agreed on. But Sadat was not present when the issue was discussed between Carter and Begin. When Sadat spoke on September 19, he had already been told that Begin had agreed only to a three-month freeze. Sadat is also wrong in saying that Israel had agreed not to expand settlements. That language had been dropped at Israeli insistence. According to Sadat's aides, the Egyptian president chose to play down the issue of settlements in the West Bank in order not to put pressure on Carter. He assumed that Carter would find a solution in due course.

a freeze on settlements for the duration of the negotiations on self-government for the Palestinians. At one point Carter decided that until he had received the letter he sought on settlements, he would not send a letter to Begin promising to help build two airfields in the Negev. On September 22 he signed a letter to Begin spelling out once more what he thought had been agreed on, pointedly noting that he had so informed Sadat on September 17. But the letter was never sent. A few days later, however, he dispatched an oral message to Begin, repeating his view on what had been agreed on and warning that "the settlements could become a serious obstacle to peace. Construction of new settlements during the negotiations could have a most serious consequence for the successful fulfillment of the agreement."

When Begin met with the American ambassador, Samuel Lewis, on September 27, 1978, he provided the text of Israeli Attorney General Barak's notes from the meeting on the night of September 16. According to Begin, the notes proved that he had not agreed to the freeze that Carter had requested. He had agreed only to consider it. He went on to say he would never agree to give Arabs a veto over where Israelis could settle. In his view, Jews had as much right to settle in Hebron as in Tel Aviv. That was precisely the crux of the disagreement.

Neither Carter nor Begin would budge, but soon Carter turned to other matters. To the many bystanders who were waiting to see the outcome of this dispute, round one seemed to go to Begin—not an encouraging sign for Sadat or King Hussein.

Vance to the Middle East

While Carter was trying to untangle the controversy over settlements, Secretary Vance was traveling in the Middle East. His goal was to try to win Jordanian and Saudi support for the Camp David Accords. What he found instead was deep skepticism, coated only with a formal politeness that some Americans interpreted as an expression of hope that the next round of negotiations would succeed.[2]

Carter and Vance both felt that some of Begin's public interpretations of the Camp David Accords were making it difficult for King Hussein

2. On September 19, 1978, the Saudi News Agency released an official Saudi cabinet statement critical of the Camp David Accords because they did not call for full Israeli withdrawal and did not provide for Palestinian self-determination. Nonetheless, the cabinet statement went on to say that it did not dispute Egypt's right to recover Sinai. See Foreign Broadcast Information Service, _Daily Report: Middle East and Africa_, September 20, 1978, p. C3.

and the Saudis not to reject them.[3] The Americans were also frustrated by Sadat's seeming unwillingness to communicate with either the Jordanians or the Saudis.[4] Through some unknown trick of arithmetic, Sadat came up with the notion that Egypt, supported by Sudan, represented 90 percent of the Arab world and that therefore he did not need to worry about the views of the "dwarfs and pygmies," as he was fond of calling other Arab leaders.

Despite all these problems, Carter remained somewhat optimistic that Jordan would join the negotiations.[5] Vance was more skeptical, especially after his visit to Amman and Riyadh. King Hussein had raised many questions, and Vance knew it would be difficult to overcome his doubts. In an attempt to do so, however, Vance did agree to give the king written answers to questions he might have about the accords.

Questions from the Arabs

Meanwhile through intelligence channels the PLO was making queries to Washington about the meaning of the agreements. Arafat was also skeptical, but he showed a serious interest in finding out if there might be more to Camp David than met the eye. Although the Americans had no reason for optimism, they could see that an Arab consensus had not yet formed. If the Arabs took Begin's interpretations, or Sadat's contemptuous expressions, as the final words on the matter, the case would be closed. But the Americans hoped they might succeed in giving a more open-ended interpretation to the framework dealing with the Palestinians and thus prevent a strongly negative Arab reaction. They therefore decided to use the questions from King Hussein as the means for offering a liberal American interpretation of Camp David.

Not everyone in the administration was pleased with the idea of responding in writing to King Hussein. Vice President Mondale, for example, thought it was undignified for the United States to submit to

---

3. See Jimmy Carter, *Keeping Faith*, p. 405, in which he notes that Begin seemed to want to keep both the peace with Egypt and the West Bank; and Cyrus Vance, *Hard Choices*, p. 229. Begin had made some particularly hard-line public comments on the day after signing the Camp David Accords. Carter was so angry that he took Begin aside during their joint appearance before the U.S. Congress and told him, in Sadat's presence, that his remarks could cause serious problems. Interview with President Jimmy Carter, Plains, Georgia, May 22, 1985.

4. Sadat had the impression from Carter that the United States would deliver Saudi support for Camp David. See Hermann Frederick Eilts, "Improve the Framework," p. 9.

5. Zbigniew Brzezinski, *Power and Principle*, p. 274.

this sort of interrogation. But Vance had given the king his word, and Carter decided to provide written answers. As soon as the fourteen questions arrived on September 29, the bureaucracy began to churn out answers. Most of them consisted of repeating well-known American positions, but in some cases they involved interpretations of Camp David. For example, the United States went on record as favoring the inclusion of the Palestinians in East Jerusalem in the election for the self-governing authority. And in an early draft the Americans had taken the position that sovereignty in the West Bank and Gaza resided with the people who lived there. When Mondale saw the draft, he strongly opposed such a formulation, and it was removed from the final version signed by Carter.[6] (See appendix H for the full text of the questions and answers.)

Carter's Talks with Begin and Sadat

While the Americans were working to convince other Arabs to be open-minded about Camp David, the Israeli Knesset met on September 27, 1978, to vote on the Camp David Accords, including the provision for withdrawing settlements from Sinai. After lengthy arguments, the vote was 84 in favor and 19 opposed, with 17 abstentions.

Carter phoned Begin the next day to congratulate him on the outcome of the Knesset debate. He also mentioned his hope that the "difference of opinion" between them over settlements in the West Bank and Gaza would soon be resolved. Begin said he had already sent the president a letter on the topic. Carter repeated that he was determined to solve this problem and that he and Begin should try to minimize their differences. He added that he would like to see a Sinai agreement within days. Begin said it should be possible if everyone agreed to use the standard form of a peace treaty and just fill in the blanks with appropriate details. (Begin had a fixation with the concept of peace treaties and often seemed to imply that the treaty per se was a guarantee of peace. Some of his Israeli colleagues felt this legalistic attitude made him willing to pay too high a price for the formality of peace with Egypt and prevented him from concentrating enough on the content of peace.)

Carter then called Sadat, and the two agreed that negotiations on the peace treaty could begin in mid-October. With these conversations, Carter

6. Vance, *Hard Choices*, pp. 230–31, summarizes the answers to Hussein's questions, but mistakenly includes the point that sovereignty resides with the people in the West Bank and Gaza. *Al-Dustour* (Amman), October 20, 1978, and *Al-Ahram* (Cairo), October 28, 1978, carried partial texts and summaries.

seems to have given up the idea of trying to force Begin to change his position on West Bank and Gaza settlements. By continuing to dwell on that topic, Carter would risk the Sinai agreement he so badly wanted. He would also be reminding the other Arabs of one of the flaws in the Camp David framework. Instead, he apparently decided to end the public debate over the issue. For three months, in any case, there would be no more Israeli settlements, and during that period Carter hoped that a solution might be found. So that same day, September 28, he authorized Secretary of Defense Brown to sign a letter to Israeli Defense Minister Ezer Weizman promising American support in building two airfields in the Negev.

Vance at the United Nations

On September 29, 1978, Secretary Vance spoke before the U.N. General Assembly. He had urged Carter to allow him to say something on the Palestinian question that might change the negative atmosphere that was growing in the Arab world. Carter agreed, and Vance included the following phrase in his text: "As the President said, our historic position on settlements in occupied territory has remained constant. As he further said, no peace agreement will be either just or secure if it does not resolve the problem of the Palestinians in the broadest sense. We believe that the Palestinian people must be assured that they and their descendants can live with dignity and freedom and have the opportunity for economic fulfillment and for political expression. The Camp David accords state that the negotiated solution must recognize the legitimate rights of the Palestinian people."[7]

Lebanon on the Brink

While Vance was speaking, Lebanon was threatening to erupt again. Carter had made an offhand reference on September 28 to the need for an international conference on Lebanon. As often happens, a presidential statement forces the bureaucracy to come up with ideas of what to do. No one in the administration much liked the idea of a big conference, but there was some sentiment for calling a meeting of the U.N. Security Council to try to get the fighting in Lebanon stopped. On October 5 a message was sent to Syrian President Asad saying that the United States

7. Vance speech in "United Nations: 33d General Assembly Convenes, Statement at the Opening Session of the U.N. General Assembly on September 29, 1978," *Department of State Bulletin*, vol. 78 (November 1978), pp. 45–51; quotation referred to is on p. 49.

favored an immediate cease-fire. Vance was worried that Asad would think the violence directed at Syrian forces in Lebanon was an American-instigated punishment for his refusal to support Camp David.

As a further step in quieting the situation in Lebanon, the hot-line to Moscow was used to request Soviet help for immediate action in the Security Council. On October 6 the United Nations called for a cease-fire in Lebanon.

At about this time, Richard Parker, a veteran State Department Arabist, was due to leave his post as ambassador to Beirut. Summing up his long experience, he warned that the Maronites were bringing great trouble on themselves by refusing to show respect for the Muslim majority in Lebanon. "They have insisted on affirmative action carried to its ultimate extreme, i.e., preservation of a dominant position for themselves." After criticizing the Israelis for undermining the authority of the Lebanese government by supporting various Lebanese militias, he warned, pro-phetically, "Those who think the Lebanese infection can be isolated do not understand the nature of social diseases."

But for the moment the warnings on Lebanon did little more than briefly divert American attention from the arena of Egyptian-Israeli relations. Carter had noted on a State Department memorandum that reviewed the options on Lebanon open to the United States: "There don't seem to be any really good ideas. Saudis and UN best hope."

THE BLAIR HOUSE TALKS

To prepare for the next phase of negotiations, the American team had drawn up a draft of an Egyptian-Israeli peace treaty. Vance wanted to use the same procedure that had proved successful at Camp David. Each side would be asked to comment on the American draft, but changes in the text would be made only by the American side after consulting with the others. The device of a "single negotiating text" was one of the methodological devices the Americans had found useful, and both the Egyptians and Israelis had come to accept it.

Carter reviewed the draft treaty on October 9. His only comment was that Israel should withdraw fully from Sinai in two, not three, years. The draft treaty was a fairly simple document. It formally ended the state of war and established a relationship of peace. Israel would withdraw to the international border according to details to be worked out by the parties. On completion of an interim phase of withdrawal, diplomatic relations would be established. The border between the two countries was defined as the former international boundary between Egypt and mandated Palestine. Article 3 of the treaty called for normal peaceful relations, the details of which were to be spelled out in an annex. Article 4 called for security arrangements in Sinai and along the border. Article 5 dealt with freedom of navigation. And article 6 spelled out the relation between this treaty and other international obligations of the parties.

From the beginning the Americans realized that several issues would be contentious. For Israel, there was the question of the timing of withdrawal. Israel's fear was that Egypt might get most or all of its territory back before entering into any form of peaceful relations with Israel. For the Israeli public, all the concessions would then seem to be coming from the Israeli side. Israel therefore insisted that Egypt should establish diplomatic relations before final withdrawal and that some aspects of normal relations should begin at an early date. For Egypt, this timing posed a problem. Sadat wanted to withhold the exchange of ambassadors until Israel had at least carried out the provisions of the Camp David Accords that called for elections for the Palestinians in the West Bank and Gaza to establish their own self-governing authority. This was the famous issue of linkage, which here boiled down to when Egypt would send its ambassador to Israel. Since that was a matter of great importance to Begin, it acquired significance for Sadat as well. A test of will quickly developed over the issue.

A second issue of likely contention was the so-called priority of obligations. Israel wanted the treaty to contain a clear statement that it superseded other Egyptian commitments, such as Egypt's many mutual defense pacts with Arab countries. Sadat found it intolerable to say in public that commitments to Israel counted for more than commitments to Arab states. For example, if Israel carried out aggression against an Arab state allied to Egypt, Sadat did not feel it would be a violation of the treaty if he went to the aid of that state. In reality, of course, whatever was written on paper would not guarantee what would happen in some future conflict, but these were issues of high symbolic importance for each party, and each was trying to make its position clear to the United States in the event of future disputes. Much more was to be heard about the "priority of obligations," though at the outset I thought it was largely a legalistic quibble that would be resolved with some artfully ambiguous formulation. Vance, the experienced international lawyer, realized from the outset that this issue would be a sticking point.

Perhaps most difficult was the question of how the two parties would express their continuing determination to work for a solution to the Palestinian question after they had signed the treaty. Begin wanted only a vague commitment to negotiate, whereas Sadat insisted on deadlines and specific commitments that would make clear that Egypt had not concluded a "separate peace." Here again was the linkage issue in its pure form.

Besides these difficult conceptual problems, there were also some complicated details. Israel wanted to retain access to Sinai oil, and wanted some form of guarantee from the United States if Egypt later refused to supply the oil. Some of the specific issues involving security arrangements in Sinai might also prove difficult, even though the military men on both sides had a good record of finding concrete compromise solutions.

This phase of the negotiations differed from Camp David not only in content but also in format and personnel. On the American side, Carter was less involved. He felt that he had spent too much time on the Middle East and that he now had to turn his attention to other issues. Normalization of relations with China and the conclusion of SALT II with the Soviet Union were high on his foreign policy agenda. Vance was designated as the principal negotiator on the American side, though he too had other responsibilities. He hoped to delegate much of the day-to-day work to Ambassador Atherton.

On specific issues the State Department was able to field an impressive array of talent, including help from the legal office headed by Herbert J. Hansell. The military designated General Richard Lawrence to work with his Egyptian and Israeli counterparts on the security annex to the treaty. Consequently, the Americans were well prepared to deal with specific problems, provided they were not too controversial, but they were not as well positioned to tackle politically sensitive topics like linkage or the priority of obligations.

The Egyptian team was also somewhat different. In the past Carter had relied heavily on his ability to deal directly with Sadat over the heads of the Egyptian delegation. Now that the time had come to put words to paper in a peace treaty, the Egyptian lawyers would have their chance again to push Sadat toward harder positions. Kamil had resigned, and then without much explanation Sadat had also replaced Minister of Defense Abd al-Ghany Gamasy. The new minister of foreign affairs and head of the Egyptian delegation was Kamal Hassan Ali, who was assisted in the negotiations by Boutros Ghali and Usama al-Baz, both veterans of Camp David. Sadat also soon named a new prime minister, Mustafa Khalil, who had played no previous part in the negotiations.

The Israeli participants were more familiar, most of them having been at Camp David. Dayan and Weizman led the negotiating team to Washington, accompanied by Barak and Meir Rosenne, a legal adviser to the prime minister. Begin refused to delegate much authority to the team, however, and the Israeli cabinet as a whole wanted to be kept abreast of most of the details of the talks. As a result, the comparative moderation of the negotiating team meant little.

Even at a distance of several thousand miles, Begin kept an iron grip on the Israeli position in the negotiations. But sitting in Jerusalem, he was even more aware than he had been at Camp David of the state of Israeli public opinion, and at least one important current of opinion, that within Begin's own party, was worried that the whole peace effort was a fraud. For some Israelis, Sadat wanted only to get his territory back; he would then resume his posture of hostility toward Israel and would seek rapprochement with the Arab world. All that Israel would get for giving back Sinai would be a piece of paper that would prove worthless when the next Middle East crisis erupted. Even if the worst did not take place, there was no way to make sure that Egypt would proceed with full normalization of relations once Israel was out of Sinai.

The delegations arrived in Washington in the second week of October, and the first sessions were scheduled for October 12. Carter met with both the Israelis and Egyptians before the formal resumption of the talks in order to urge both sides to move toward agreement quickly. In his talks with the Egyptians on October 11, Carter said the negotiations in Washington should be used to deal with the problems of Sinai and the West Bank and Gaza. He urged the Egyptians not to give up on the Jordanians and Palestinians. At the same time, he said, the issues involving the West Bank and Gaza should not be allowed to impede progress toward an Egyptian-Israeli peace treaty.

In the meeting with Carter, Boutros Ghali took the floor for the Egyptians to make the case for linkage, or the "correlation" between the two agreements, as he was fond of calling it. After Egypt and Israel reached agreement, he asked, what pressure would there be on Israel to do anything about the West Bank and Gaza? If Egypt received some advantages in Sinai, the Palestinians must also have something. Otherwise Egypt would be isolated in the Arab world. That could jeopardize some $2 billion that Egypt was receiving from Saudi Arabia. Al-Baz interjected the thought that the opposition to Camp David had already peaked in the Arab world and that within a few months King Hussein would be ready to join the talks. Carter concluded by repeating that he was committed to finding a solution to the West Bank and Gaza, but that he did not want to risk the treaty between Egypt and Israel because of problems with Jordan or the Palestinians.

Vance met with both delegations on October 12. The talks took place at Blair House, across from the White House. Normally used by visiting heads of state, Blair House provided an elegant, if too formal, setting for the negotiations. As time went on, many meetings also took place at the Madison Hotel, the State Department, and the White House, but Blair House was the official site for the peace negotiations.

OPENING BIDS

Vance's bilateral discussions on October 12 revealed much about the priorities on both sides. Dayan was worried that Carter might travel to the Middle East soon and meet with PLO figures. Weizman raised the problem of paying for the withdrawal of the Israeli armed forces from Sinai. The cost could be as high as $2 billion. Dayan returned to political issues, arguing that as soon as the treaty was signed the Israeli public must see something positive. An Israeli ship must immediately be allowed to pass through the Suez Canal. Diplomatic relations must also be established right away.

The Egyptians, by contrast, used their meeting with Vance to press the case for Israeli "confidence-building measures," as they came to be called, on the West Bank and Gaza. For example, Israel should agree that public lands would come under the authority of the self-governing council. Palestinians in East Jerusalem should be allowed to vote, and the elections should be held under third-party supervision. Unilateral steps by Israel, they argued, could help improve the climate in the occupied territories. Israel should help Egypt to retain its leadership in the Arab world by showing that Sadat had been able to win concessions for the Palestinians, not just for Egypt alone. The next day the Egyptians formally presented Vance with an aide-mémoire listing several major steps the Israelis should take in the occupied territories.[8]

For several days after these initial meetings the talks dragged on without any breakthroughs. The technicians were able to make some headway on the annexes, but the problems at the political level remained. Carter

8. See "Egyptian Aide-Memoire on Confidence Building Measures in the Occupied Palestinian Territories," October 13, 1978, in *The Egyptian Position in the Negotiations Concerning the Establishment of Transitional Arrangements for the West Bank and Gaza*, pp. 21–23.

began to show signs of impatience. He was thinking of flying to the Middle East in late October, and even hoped, unrealistically, to be able to preside over the signing of the Egyptian-Israeli peace treaty at that time. An Arab summit was being talked about in early November, and Carter wanted to pin down the treaty before it convened. He also had his eye on the congressional elections.[9]

Carter Joins the Talks

To speed up the talks, Carter decided to meet both delegations on October 17. Dayan complained about three issues: the language on priority of obligations in the treaty; linkage between the treaty talks and the West Bank–Gaza issues; and Egypt's reluctance to speed up normalization. Then, in a shrewd gesture seemingly calculated to win Carter's support, Dayan announced that Israel was prepared to accelerate withdrawal to the interim line in Sinai. (The Camp David Accords called on Israel to pull back its forces from about two-thirds of Sinai, within nine months of signing a peace treaty.) The town of Al-Arish, which had great symbolic value to Sadat, could be returned within two months instead of the nine envisaged in the framework agreement. Carter was pleased and saw the offer as a welcome sign of Israeli flexibility. In return, Carter agreed to talk to the Egyptians about moving quickly on normalization; he undertook to resolve a technical problem involving the location of the interim line; and he agreed to consider helping to finance the withdrawal of the Israeli military from Sinai, but not the cost of removing the settlers.

A few hours later Carter met with the Egyptian delegation. Kamal Hassan Ali informed the president that agreement had been reached on the delineation of limited-force zones in Sinai. Boutros Ghali then argued the case for some correlation between the treaty negotiations and the Palestinian question. In particular, he put forward the idea of establishing diplomatic relations in stages that would somehow be related to progress on the West Bank and Gaza. First would come the formal recognition of Israel, then a chargé d'affaires would be sent to Tel Aviv, and only later would ambassadors be exchanged. Carter was unhappy with this proposal and reminded the Egyptians that Sadat had orally agreed at Camp David that ambassadors would be exchanged at the time of the interim withdrawal. He then gave the Egyptians copies of his answers to King

9. Brzezinski, *Power and Principle*, p. 276, says that Carter had hoped to have the treaty signed by election day.

Hussein's questions and said they should help deal with the problem of linkage.

Carter also informed the Egyptians that the Israelis were prepared to accelerate withdrawal to Al-Arish. Now, he said, the Egyptians seemed to be backsliding on the timing of sending their ambassador to Tel Aviv. He argued that Egypt should reciprocate Israel's constructive attitude on withdrawal by agreeing to an early exchange of ambassadors. Carter ended the talks by asking the Egyptians to tell President Sadat of his desire to visit the Middle East, before November 1 if possible.

Carter was now back in the middle of the negotiations. On October 20 Carter held a sometimes acrimonious meeting with the Israeli delegation. The Israelis began the meeting by telling Carter that they had just been to Yale University to consult with several American experts on international law, including Eugene Rostow, and that the American lawyers supported the Israeli position on the question of priority of obligations in the treaty. This statement led to a lengthy and legalistic discussion, which prompted Carter to ask if Israel really wanted peace with Egypt. Carter charged that Israel was ignoring the fact that the Egyptian-Israeli framework was part of a broader commitment to work for a settlement on the West Bank and Gaza as well.

Barak asked if Carter thought the treaty should be made contingent on whether an agreement could be reached on the West Bank. Carter said that was not his intention. After all, the West Bank formula might fail because of the actions or inactions of third parties, in particular the Jordanians or Palestinians. But, Carter asked, what if Israel was the party responsible for the failure of the West Bank framework? Did Israel think that in those circumstances the treaty would be unaffected? Barak answered that the treaty must be legally independent of whatever happened on the West Bank and Gaza, even though some degree of political linkage might exist.

Carter then told the Israelis that he was sure he could get Sadat to agree to an exchange of ambassadors within one month of the interim withdrawal. Dayan asked if the United States could write a letter guaranteeing that the treaty would be carried out.

Answers to King Hussein

On the same day that Carter was having his difficult talk with the Israelis, Assistant Secretary of State Saunders was in Jerusalem meeting with Prime Minister Begin. He had previously been to Amman to deliver

Carter's answers to Hussein. He had also stopped in Riyadh and was planning to meet with West Bank Palestinians.

First Saunders reported to Begin on Hussein's attitude, which was not entirely negative. The king had told Saunders that he was not ready to make a decision on entering negotiations until after the Baghdad summit in early November, but that he would encourage Palestinians in the West Bank to cooperate with the Camp David process. The Saudis had said they would adopt a neutral attitude.

Begin complained that the Americans seemed to have great understanding for the political problems of Arab leaders, but none for his own. He had been bitterly attacked by some of his oldest friends in the Irgun. The Americans should appreciate the concessions he had already made for peace. Then he told Saunders to convey to Carter his "deep sadness." There had been no prior consultation with Israel over the answers to King Hussein. Begin proceeded to launch into a point-by-point criticism of the answers, emphasizing what he considered to be all the deviations from Camp David that they contained. He argued at length that the deletion of the word "also" in reference to Palestinian rights constituted a grave threat to Israel, since without that word Israel's rights were not protected. Begin also criticized the United States for repeating its postion on Jerusalem, for mentioning "political institutions" when discussing the "self-governing authority," and for supporting the vote for Arab residents of East Jerusalem. Although Carter's signature was on the answers to Hussein, Begin and his colleagues preferred to speak of the "Saunders document," and for several weeks Saunders was the target of a harsh campaign in the Israeli press.

Near Agreements

Despite these contretemps with the Israelis in Washington and in Jerusalem, agreement ad referendum was reached on the text of the treaty. Each delegation had to refer back to its own capital for final approval, but the basic elements of the treaty were seemingly all in place. The Egyptians, however, had proposed during the talks that a parallel letter be signed by Sadat and Begin dealing with the West Bank and Gaza. The letter should coincide with the treaty and would commit the two parties to conclude the negotiations on the West Bank and Gaza by a fixed date, with elections to be held within three months of signing the treaty.

Egypt also mentioned in the negotiations its special responsibility for Gaza, a reminder of Sadat's interest in the "Gaza first" option whereby self-government would first be established in Gaza and only later in the West Bank, after King Hussein joined the negotiations. Al-Baz referred to this as a ploy to scare King Hussein and the Palestinians, in essence telling them that if they did not get into the negotiations soon they would be left out. He argued strongly that Israel should take a number of unilateral steps in Gaza before the withdrawal to the interim line in Sinai was completed.

Carter wrote to Sadat on October 22, spelling out the terms of the treaty as negotiated in Washington. He asked that Sadat accept the text in its current form, and that in addition he agree to a letter committing Egypt to send an ambassador to Israel within one month of the interim withdrawal. Carter repeated that he had asked the Israelis to withdraw more rapidly to the interim line than was called for at Camp David. Carter concluded the letter by saying he would like to visit the Middle East for the treaty signing, which he hoped could be at a very early date. A similar letter was sent to Begin. Carter noted that he did not yet have Sadat's approval to send an ambassador to Israel within one month of the interim withdrawal, but he hoped that Sadat would have a positive attitude.

Sadat's reply came on October 24. He was willing to accommodate Carter on several points, including the exchange of ambassadors, provided some changes could be made in the text of the treaty. Egypt could not agree to permanent force limits in Sinai. Up to twenty-five years would be acceptable. (Carter noted "Not a problem.") Second, article 6 of the treaty, the priority of obligations issue, made it seem as if Egypt's commitments to Israel were greater than those to the Arab League.[10] The language of the treaty should not downgrade Egypt's obligations under previous agreements. (Carter noted "A problem.") Third, the treaty must clearly say that Egypt has sovereignty over Sinai. (Carter wrote "Okay.")

A letter from Begin arrived the same day. In it the Israeli prime minister complained at length about the answers provided to King Hussein. The full transcript of Begin's talk with Saunders was appended to the letter. Then Begin reviewed the dispute over settlements in the West Bank and Gaza, noting that he had told the president there were plans to add several hundred families to the settlements in Judea and Samaria even during the three-month moratorium.

---

10. According to Ambassador Eilts, Sadat was irritated with the way his negotiating team in Washington had handled the language of article 6 of the treaty. This was one of the reasons he brought Mustafa Khalil more directly into the negotiations from that point on. Interview with Eilts on November 30, 1984.

Meanwhile Dayan and Weizman were in Israel seeking to win cabinet approval for the draft treaty. They ran into considerable criticism, but nonetheless Begin pressed for cabinet support of the existing draft and won a sizable majority on October 26. For reasons of his own, and perhaps as a reward to some of the hard-line cabinet members, Begin accompanied the announcement of the cabinet's decision on the treaty with a decision to "thicken" settlements in the West Bank.

Carter was furious. He perfunctorily congratulated Begin on the cabinet vote, and then commented on the decision to thicken settlements: "At a time when we are trying to organize the negotiations dealing with the West Bank and Gaza, no step by the Israeli government could be more damaging." In his own handwriting Carter added, "I have to tell you with gravest concern and regret that taking this step at this time will have the most serious consequences for our relationship."

In light of these developments, it was somewhat ironic that the Nobel peace prize was awarded the next day to both Begin and Sadat. Some of Carter's aides were bitter that the president was not included, but for the moment the more important problem was that peace itself seemed to be slipping away. Reports had even reached Washington that Sadat was about to withdraw his delegation and break off the talks. Carter contacted him and convinced him not to take any rash action, but the mood at the White House was gloomy. At a minimum, Carter would not be able to make his hoped-for trip to the Middle East before the end of the month.

Talks resumed in Washington, with the Israelis showing increasing interest in pinning down the United States on what commitments it was prepared to make as part of the treaty. For example, Dayan was still pressing for a letter on how the United States would guarantee the implementation of the treaty. He also wanted to revise and update all previous U.S.-Israeli memorandums of understanding. Weizman added that Israel's final withdrawal from Sinai should be made contingent on the completion of the new airfields in the Negev. (Carter skeptically added a question mark next to this point when it was called to his attention in a memo.)

During the last days of October the American team became increasingly aware that the Israelis were insisting on a very narrow definition of self-government for the Palestinians in the West Bank and Gaza. Dayan, in an unusually frank session with Vance on October 30, conveyed the most recent Israeli cabinet decisions on the treaty, and then went on to talk about the West Bank problem. Israel, he said, was prepared to talk to Egypt only about the "modalities" for holding elections. It would be a mistake to get into the question of the "powers and responsibilities" of the elected self-governing authority. To do so would open a Pandora's box. The Egyptians would inevitably argue that state lands should be under the control of the self-governing authority; Israel would reject that. Far better to limit the talks to holding elections, and then Israel could work out with the Palestinians the powers of the body to which they had been elected.

Dayan also used this meeting to reject the notion that Egypt had any special status in Gaza. Sadat seemed to think that by getting something started in Gaza, he could put pressure on Hussein to join the talks, but Dayan warned that this appoach would probably backfire. The Palestinians would see it as a further attempt to fragment the Palestinian community. Those living in Gaza would come under intense pressure not to participate in elections.

The next day Dayan made many of these same points before the Egyptian delegation. Dayan presented a strong case to limit the discussions between Egypt and Israel to the question of how to organize the elections in the West Bank and Gaza. Otherwise the talks would drag on indefinitely. Al-Baz, speaking for the Egyptians, disagreed. The Palestinians had to know, he argued, what they were voting for. Unless the powers and responsibilities were defined in advance, the elections would be seen as a fraud. It would not be easier to grapple with this problem later. Dayan, who knew his prime minister well, said he would refer this issue to Begin if the Egyptians insisted. But he could tell them now that if Israel did consent to discuss powers and responsibilities, the negotiators would spend years trying to reach agreement.

In a side conversation with me, Dayan elaborated on his ideas about the self-governing authority. First, he said, the Israeli military government would not be abolished. It would keep its authority, and it might not even be physically withdrawn from the West Bank for many years after the election of the self-governing authority. Israel, he said, also was planning about eighteen to twenty more settlements in the Jordan Valley over the next five years and would need to keep at least 20 percent of all public lands for itself. Summing up my impressions of the conversation, I wrote: "My prediction is that the Egyptian-Israeli treaty negotiations will be concluded within ten days, depending on how Begin reacts. On the basis of my understanding of the Israeli position, I doubt if we will ever get very far with the West Bank–Gaza negotiations."[11]

11. Memorandum from me to Brzezinski, October 31, 1978.

When Carter read the accounts of these meetings, he was outraged. He saw them as further evidence of Israeli backsliding from the commitments made at Camp David. Mondale, Vance, Brzezinski, and Hamilton Jordan were called to the White House on November 1 for a strategy session. They decided to slow down the pace of the negotiations, to review Israel's commitments under the Camp David Accords, and to develop a series of steps to bring pressure on Begin to live up to those commitments. Responses to Israeli requests for arms could be delayed, and several other steps could be taken.

The next day Vance flew to New York for a brief meeting with Begin, who happened to be in town on his way to Canada. Dayan had made it clear that Begin and the cabinet had ultimate authority and that he could do little more to resolve the disputes on remaining issues. Begin found most of the treaty text acceptable, but had problems with the side letter dealing with the West Bank and Gaza. Dayan and Weizman had indicated that it should be possible to mention a target date for the holding of elections, but they did not want that date to coincide precisely with the interim withdrawal in Sinai. That would give the appearance of too much linkage. Begin, however, now said that Israel was adamantly opposed to the idea of any target date for elections. He argued that if for some reason beyond the control of Egypt and Israel the elections could not be held, that would call into question everything else, including the peace treaty. By contrast, Begin, always the legalist, found no problem in agreeing to the Egyptian request that powers and responsibilities of the self-governing authority be defined in advance of elections. On both these crucial issues, Begin ignored Dayan's advice. This was the first concrete evidence that Dayan's authority in this phase of the negotiations was much less than it had been in the preceding year.

Then Begin turned to bilateral issues. Israel would need $3.37 billion from the United States to help finance the withdrawal from Sinai, including removal of the settlers. This aid should take the form of a loan at low interest rates. The cabinet would never approve the treaty, he said, unless the question of aid was solved first. Vance was noncommittal, refusing to give up one of the few elements of leverage that the United States possessed.

As tensions rose in the U.S.-Israeli relationship, largely over the perception that Begin was diluting his already modest commitments concerning the Palestinians, pressure was mounting on Egypt to adopt a tougher position in support of Palestinian rights. The Arabs had held a summit meeting in Baghdad, and on November 5 they announced their conclusions. They criticized the Camp David Accords, and they decided that the headquarters of the Arab League was to be moved from Cairo if Egypt and Israel reached a peace treaty. The conference participants sent a small delegation to Cairo to meet with Sadat to dissuade him from continuing with the peace negotiations, but the Egyptian president refused to meet it. Instead, he publicly referred to the summit participants as "cowards and dwarfs." He would not pay any attention, he said, to "the hissing of snakes."

Still, within days the Egyptian position seemed to harden.[12] Sadat sent a message to Carter on November 8 saying there must be unequivocal agreement on what was to take place on the West Bank and Gaza. Otherwise he would be accused of making a separate deal with the Israelis and abandoning the Palestinians. Sadat was not prepared to open himself to such accusations from the other Arabs.

The time had come for the Americans to pause and assess the situation. A memorandum was prepared for Carter reviewing what Begin had been saying since Camp David about the West Bank and Gaza. On at least eight points, Begin seemed to have deviated from what Carter felt was the agreed interpretation of the Camp David Accords. He noted on the memo: "To Cy and Zbig—Any aid-loan program *if* agreed *must* be predicated on Israeli compliance with Camp David agreements. J.C."

Carter met with his senior aides to review the negotiations on November 8. He was in a bad mood. Brzezinski was arguing for a tough line with Begin. He urged Carter to consider reducing aid to Israel by a certain amount for each new settlement that Begin authorized. "We do not intend to subsidize illegal settlements and we will so inform Congress." No decisions on aid should be made until Begin accepted a target date for elections.

Carter decided that Vance should not go to the Middle East again as had been proposed. It was pointless for him to spend full time on a nonproductive effort. Carter had concluded that Israel wanted a separate treaty with Egypt, while keeping the West Bank and Gaza permanently. The creation of new settlements, he thought, was deliberately done to prevent Jordan and the Palestinians from joining the negotiations.[13] Carter

12. According to Kamal Hassan Ali, after the Baghdad summit Sadat was very sensitive to the priority of obligations issue. This slowed up the negotiations on the Egyptian side. Interview in Cairo, February 4, 1985.

13. Carter, *Keeping Faith*, p. 409; Brzezinski, *Power and Principle*, pp. 276–77; and Vance, *Hard Choices*, p. 238.

and Vance now felt they must try to pin down the agenda for the West Bank and Gaza, even if that meant delaying the signing of an Egyptian-Israeli treaty. As usual, their sympathies were more with Sadat than with Begin.

The next day the Egyptian delegation, which had just been in Cairo for new instructions, met with Vance. Boutros Ghali said that linkage was now the main problem. A target date for elections must be mentioned in the letter concerning the West Bank and Gaza. Israel must commit itself to several unilateral steps to build confidence among the Palestinians. Some reference must be made to Egypt's special responsibility for Gaza. Also, problems still remained with the language in article 6 of the treaty concerning priority of obligations. Kamal Hassan Ali added that there was also a problem relating to Israel's demand for oil from Sinai.

Vance was firm in saying that the text of the treaty should not be changed. The same point had been made to the Israelis. A few issues remained to be resolved in the annexes, including the timing of the exchange of ambassadors, and the text of the side letter on the West Bank and Gaza still had to be agreed upon.

Over the next few days the American side worked to complete the text of the treaty and all its annexes, as well as a letter on the West Bank and Gaza. Carter reviewed the entire package, and it was ready to present to the Israelis and Egyptians on November 11. In a late session at the State Department that same evening, Vance and Dayan tried to resolve some remaining issues in anticipation of a meeting between Vance and Begin in New York the next day. Dayan informed Vance that the Israeli cabinet was adamant in not agreeing to accelerate withdrawal to the interim line. He personally was inclined to accept a target date for elections in the West Bank and Gaza, but the date should not correspond to the interim withdrawal. As for the text of the treaty, Dayan seemed to be satisfied.[14]

MOUNTING PRESSURES

Vance's meeting with Begin the next day did not go well. Vance carried a letter from Carter to the prime minister saying that the conclusion of the peace treaty was now in doubt. Vance would soon have to turn to

14. The text of the November 11, 1978, draft of the treaty was leaked to the press by the Egyptians and Israelis. It is available in Meron Medzini, ed., *Israel's Foreign Relations*, vol. 5, pp. 577–81.

other duties. Carter strongly urged Begin to accept the documents that the secretary brought to him.

Begin was not in a conciliatory frame of mind. He refused to accept the idea of a target date, adding that Dayan had had no authority to imply otherwise. He repeated his refusal to consider accelerated withdrawal. And as if he should be rewarded for his intransigence, he demanded that the aid for the withdrawal from Sinai take the form of a grant, not a loan. He had made a mistake, he said, when he earlier requested a loan, and promised that every penny of it would be repaid.

Sadat Loses Patience

Meanwhile Carter telephoned Sadat in Cairo to urge him to accept the same package. Sadat was more agitated than usual. He argued at great length that the Baghdad rejectionists should not get the upper hand. He must show that he had got something for the Palestinians, at least in Gaza, before Israel completed the interim withdrawal. He would even be willing to have the withdrawal delayed by a few months if that would make it possible to hold the elections for Palestinian self-government so they would coincide with the return of most of Sinai. Somewhat awkwardly, Sadat said he would not agree to the first phase of withdrawal without at least the beginning of self-government in Gaza. Carter made it clear that he did not favor treating Gaza differently from the West Bank. Elections should be held in both areas by the end of 1979, he said.

Sadat repeated that the first phase of withdrawal should coincide with the day the Palestinians started their self-government in the West Bank and Gaza, or at least in Gaza. He accused Begin of trying to delay everything until the start of the American elections. Carter responded by urging Sadat to stop attacking Hussein and the Saudis. Sadat replied that he was punishing them for what they had done at the Baghdad summit. Give me Gaza, he pleaded. Carter was skeptical, but he agreed to try to come up with a new formulation.

Carter then called Begin in New York, pointing out that the prospects of agreement were now quite remote. Begin responded by saying that Israel had broken no promise in refusing to accelerate the withdrawal. Weizman should never have agreed to such an idea. In any case, Egypt had no right to use the Israeli decision as a pretext to refuse to send an ambassador to Israel, as Boutros Ghali had implied. Carter reassured him that Sadat would stand by his agreement to send an ambassador within one month of the interim withdrawal.

The next day Ambassador Eilts met with Sadat and found him in an angry mood. Sadat said that he and Carter were no longer speaking the same language. Egypt would not agree to peace with Israel without having reached an agreement at the same time on the West Bank and Gaza. Even if the interim withdrawal had to be delayed until November 1979, he said, that could be done if by then the Palestinians had their self-government, at least in Gaza. Sadat also said he could not accept article 6 of the draft treaty, since that made it seem as if his obligations to Israel took precedence over his obligations to his Arab allies. The only solution, he said, was for a confrontation between Carter and Begin to take place. He was planning to send his vice president, Husni Mubarak, to see Carter the next day to discuss such a strategy.

Meanwhile a Saudi emissary arrived in Washington to meet with U.S. officials. He explained the position that the Saudis had taken in Baghdad, arguing that it would give the Saudis more influence with the radicals in the future. If only Egypt did not make a separate peace, and if there was some form of linkage, then Saudi Arabia could help defend the Camp David Accords in front of the other Arabs. But there had to be some mention of ultimate Israeli withdrawal from Arab occupied territories and some mention of Jerusalem.

Mubarak met with Carter at the White House on November 16. Only two points remained to be solved, he said: the West Bank and Gaza letter, and article 6 of the treaty concerning the priority of obligations. He made a clear case for trying to reach agreement on self-government in Gaza first. Egypt would have more influence over the Palestinians there, he said. Also, the problems were easier in Gaza. The question of Jerusalem's status would not arise, for example. If Hussein could see a model agreement in Gaza, he would then want to join the negotiations.

Carter again urged the Egyptians to stop attacking the Saudis and Jordanians. He argued against separating Gaza from the West Bank, and said that the treaty text should be considered closed, including article 6, which by now had become a real issue with Sadat. Mubarak said he planned to talk some of this over directly with Weizman while he was in Washington.

Several days later, on November 21, Begin telephoned Carter to say that the Israeli cabinet had voted to accept the text of the treaty and its annexes. Carter was pleased, but asked about the letter on the West Bank and Gaza. Begin replied that the cabinet had rejected the idea of setting a target date at the end of 1979 for elections in the West Bank and Gaza.

And he added that there were also other problems. First, Israel wanted to resolve the question of a grant from the United States to help cover the costs of withdrawal from Sinai. Second, Israel needed assurances on oil, especially in light of the turmoil in Iran, the country from which Israel normally received its oil.

Carter tried to explain Sadat's position on the need for the interim withdrawal to coincide with the onset of self-government. Then Carter suggested that Israel might agree to delay the interim withdrawal until elections were held in the West Bank and Gaza, without setting a date for either event. Begin was surprised by this suggestion and said he would have to think about it.

Carter spoke by phone with Sadat the next day to inform him of the Israeli position. Sadat was still angry at Begin. Although he said little to Carter at the time, he was also annoyed at Carter's suggestion that the interim withdrawal might be delayed until elections were held for Palestinian self-government. Without some deadline, that could mean no withdrawal would take place at all. Sadat had suggested that there might be a brief delay in withdrawal to make it coincide with elections, but he was not ready to accept the possiblity of no withdrawal at all.

Sadat remained in a foul mood for the next week. On November 28 he met with Senate Majority Leader Robert Byrd of West Virginia. Ambassador Eilts, who attended the meeting, reported that in more than 250 meetings with Sadat he had never seen the Egyptian president so emotional or upset. Two days later Eilts was handed a letter from Sadat to Carter strongly criticizing Begin for wanting only a separate peace. The talks had reached a crossroads. An Egyptian presence in Gaza was now essential. Article 6 of the treaty on priority of obligations was impossible to accept, and article 4 needed to be revised so that it did not imply permanent limits on Egyptian forces in Sinai. When Israel reneged on accelerated withdrawal, Sadat said, this upset the equation on an early exchange of ambassadors. He could no longer agree to send an ambassador to Israel one month after the interim withdrawal. Sadat also provided the Americans with the text of a sixteen-page letter he was sending to Begin.

Eilts tried to account for Sadat's temper. Egypt, he said, was feeling isolated in the Arab world. Sadat totally distrusted Begin and resented the narrow Israeli interpretation of the Camp David Accords. The debate over settlements had angered Sadat as well. The United States did not show much understanding of his problems with the other Arabs. And, Eilts concluded, Sadat was annoyed that the United States seemed to consider him the line of least resistance whenever the Israelis took a hard stand.

Sadat's lengthy and argumentative letters to Carter and Begin—probably written by Usama al-Baz—did little to advance the peace negotiations. Begin's reply was predictably self-righteous and combative.

Carter Reassesses

More constructive was Sadat's decision to send his prime minister, Mustafa Khalil, to Washington to consult with Carter. Khalil made a good impression on the Americans as a man of reason and as an able spokesman for the Egyptian side. In a meeting with Carter on December 1, Khalil pressed hard on the importance of simultaneity of Israeli withdrawal to the interim line and the establishment of the self-governing authority. He also wanted to revise article 6 of the treaty. Carter objected to the idea of revising the treaty, but did suggest that interpretive notes could be appended to it.

Several days later, on December 4, Carter met with his Middle East team to review the details of the proposals Khalil had brought with him. Carter and Vance were both eager to know what Sadat's bottom line was. Would he insist on a fixed date for elections in the West Bank and Gaza? Carter favored a less precise formulation of a target date. On article 6, Carter thought Sadat might settle for some cosmetic change of words. But Carter was convinced that Sadat would insist on some explicit relationship between the implementation of the Sinai agreement and the establishment of self-government in the West Bank and Gaza. Brzezinski noted that the Camp David Accords were ambiguous on this issue of linkage, but Carter responded that Sadat was correct that some degree of linkage was implied by the agreements.[15]

Vance made it clear that he did not want to make another trip to the Middle East. He suggested that Ambassador Atherton might go. Carter said there was no point in having anyone other than Vance or Mondale talk to Begin and Sadat. In a somber mood Carter said that if the negotiations failed, he wanted it to be clear that Sadat was not to blame. He wanted to be on Sadat's side. The Israelis would have nowhere else to go in any event.

Hamilton Jordan added the thought that at this point only success in

15. Ezer Weizman, *The Battle for Peace*, p. 375, essentially agreed with Carter and Sadat when he wrote that it was naive to believe there was no link at all between the two agreements. After all, they were signed together.

the negotiations could help Carter politically. Once the treaty was signed, Carter would be in a stronger position to deal with the West Bank and Gaza issues. Carter seemed to be willing to take some political risks. He told Vance to press Israel hard, even if that ended up costing him the election and Jewish support.[16]

VANCE TO THE MIDDLE EAST

Vance set off for Cairo on December 9, 1978, with two clear objectives and one new proposal. First, he wanted to complete negotiations on the text of the treaty. Second, he wanted to make sure that the letter on the West Bank and Gaza would mention a target date of the end of 1979 for the establishment of self-government, or at least for the conclusion of the negotiations before the holding of elections.

Vance's new idea was one that originated with Carter in response to his belief that Sadat would be adamant on some form of linkage. The Camp David Accords had specified that diplomatic relations would be established after the interim withdrawal in Sinai, but there was no mention in writing about when ambassadors should be exchanged. Carter had earlier convinced Sadat that the exchange should be made right away, but after the Israelis dropped the idea of an accelerated withdrawal, the Egyptian position had become less certain.

Carter now felt it would be justified for Sadat to say that he would establish diplomatic relations after the interim withdrawal, but that the actual exchange of ambassadors would not take place until the self-governing authority in the West Bank and Gaza had actually been established. Sadat was likely to see considerable merit in this form of linkage, and Begin would inevitably react with horror.

Vance with Sadat

Vance met privately with Sadat on December 10 and reviewed the new position on the timing of the exchange of ambassadors. As predicted, Sadat was pleased. In return, he indicated some flexibility in accepting a target date instead of a fixed date for setting up the self-governing authority. He also agreed that article 6 could remain essentially unchanged, provided an interpretive note could be added making clear that this treaty did not prevail over other treaties to which Egypt was a party. In the side letter Sadat also wanted to mention the possibility that the self-

16. Brzezinski, *Power and Principle*, pp. 277–78.

governing authority might start first in Gaza, and he also inserted a provision for Egyptian liaison officers to be stationed in Gaza because of Egypt's former administrative role there.

Sadat readily informed Vance that a basis for agreement now existed, but that he expected Begin to react negatively. Cheerfully, he said Vance should be ready for a big confrontation that might last for several months.

Over the next forty-eight hours the Americans hammered out a new package of documents. The treaty text was essentially unchanged, along with the annexes. Several interpretive notes were drafted. The side letter on the West Bank and Gaza was redone to reflect several of Sadat's demands. The United States agreed to draft a legal opinion of its own on the meaning of article 6, to the effect that nothing would prevent Egypt from honoring its commitments under other treaties in the event of armed attack against one of its allies. Most important, Sadat was now asked to write a letter to Carter committing himself to the exchange of ambassadors after the establishment of the Palestinian self-governing authority, at least in Gaza.

Vance and Sadat met again on December 12 to go over the entire package. At 7:45 p.m. Sadat said he was willing to accept everything in it, despite some remaining complaints by Khalil and al-Baz. But he stressed to Vance that this was as far as he could go. He pleaded with Vance not to come back to him to ask for more concessions. In his words, there was no further room for compromise. He wanted the United States at his side in this final round. Vance said he would do his best.

As he set off for Israel Vance was aware that the three-month deadline for completing the negotiations was approaching. If at all possible, he wanted to have a package agreed on by December 17. He knew that there would be some tough bargaining in Israel, but he had Carter's clear instructions to press the Israelis hard.

Begin's Negative Reaction

Vance began his meeting with Begin and his colleagues by reviewing the recent evolution of the Egyptian position. He explained that he had convinced Sadat to drop demands for changing the treaty and for a fixed date for establishing self-government. There would, however, have to be some interpretive notes to articles 4 and 6. Vance also mentioned the idea of a target date and the possibility of reaching agreement first on Gaza. Then he explained Sadat's new position on not exchanging ambassadors until after the self-governing authority was established.

Begin, always suspicious of U.S.-Egyptian collusion, looked tense during this presentation. When Vance was done, Begin did little to hide his anger. He accused Sadat of deviating from Camp David, especially on his promise to exchange ambassadors after the interim withdrawal. He rejected the idea that Egypt should have any special role in Gaza, and he maintained that Israel would never accept a target date for setting up the self-governing authority. Nor did he like the idea of interpretive notes. These seemed to dilute the strength of the peace treaty and might open loopholes for Egypt not to live up to its obligations.

Begin then went on at length to review all the concessions he had made and all the risks Israel was required to take. The United States, he said, was unfairly siding with Egypt, when it should instead be supporting Israel. He resented the fact that the United States had not consulted Israel on the new elements of the package. He felt he was being told that he had to accept the package simply because Sadat said so. The Americans were joining the Egyptians in making demands on Israel. These were not negotiations. Vance somewhat defensively said he had simply expressed his view that the Egyptian position was reasonable. Begin said that was just what he feared.

Vance spent another day trying to explain some of the changes. He managed to defuse the Israeli concern over the minor issue of an interpretive note to article 4 of the treaty. Dayan even indicated some interest in the idea of proceeding with autonomy in Gaza first. He also privately told Vance that there might be a way for Israel to accept the delay in the exchange of ambassadors, but that this point should not be spelled out in a letter. Any delay in exchanging ambassadors should be left vague until after the treaty was signed, and then Sadat could say whatever he wanted. On this suggestion, however, Dayan was clearly not speaking for Begin.

In a meeting with the entire Israeli cabinet, Vance heard a long litany of complaints. At one point Ezer Weizman tried to introduce a positive note by suggesting that Dayan should accompany Vance to Cairo to talk directly to Sadat. Begin contemptuously rejected the idea by saying the cabinet would discuss Weizman's suggestion the following day. (Vance was planning to leave for Cairo within a few hours.)

Then Ariel Sharon, the minister of agriculture, unleashed a bitter denunciation of American policy. He said Sadat was clearly not interested in peace and was only offering Israel a piece of paper. Sadat would never agree to a separate peace. Israel could not afford to leave anything vague if it was to withdraw from Sinai. As Jews, he said, Israelis did not owe anything to anybody. Nor, he seemed to be saying, could they trust anybody, least of all the Americans.

Vance was obliged to leave the Middle East somewhat ahead of schedule. The decision had been made to announce the normalization of relations with China, and Carter wanted him to be in Washington for the occasion. Vance had time to make only a quick stop in Cairo before he left.

There he informed Sadat of Begin's angry reaction. Sadat smiled and expressed his pleasure. Vance said he had told Begin in private that the United States supported the Egyptian position.

While flying back to Washington, Vance received word that the Israeli cabinet had met and had issued the following statement: "The Government of Israel rejects the attitude and the interpretation of the U.S. government with regard to the Egyptian proposals." For once, Vance was genuinely angry. His inclination was to let the negotiations remain temporarily in limbo. An impasse had been reached, and nothing more could be done for the moment.

CONCLUSION

The Camp David Accords were no doubt an important watershed in the negotiating process between Egypt and Israel. But the struggle between the two countries did not end with the signing of the two framework documents on September 17, 1978. Instead, a new test of wills began, and once again the United States found itself in the middle.

In this phase of the negotiations, time acquired great importance. Carter was the most impatient, for his political calendar required quick movement. He also had a large backlog of other issues. His political advisers were urging him to conclude the Egyptian-Israeli treaty as soon as possible.

Begin was the best able to deal with the pressures of time. He was in no hurry to reach agreement. For him it was far more important for the ultimate document to reflect his view that the Egyptian-Israeli treaty would stand on its own, in no way dependent on what might happen in the West Bank and Gaza. He was also determined to pin down the United States on several bilateral issues, including financial assistance, before signing the treaty.

Sadat was in a bind. He wanted to conclude the talks, but as time went on he was increasingly worried that Begin would insist on an entirely separate peace, which would result in a split between Egypt and other Arab countries. Sadat had handled the linkage issue carelessly at Camp David, but now he seemed determined to reestablish a degree of interdependence between the two frameworks.

Sadat was still convinced that a confrontation between Carter and Begin was necessary. He was prepared to accommodate Carter on any number of details in order to keep the American president on his side for the eventual showdown with Begin. As of mid-December 1978 he had reason to believe that his strategy was finally paying off. The Americans, for the first time, had reached an agreement with him that they had endorsed in front of the Israelis. Sadat viewed the resulting strain in U.S.-Israeli relations as a good sign.

But if Sadat had been a more attentive reader of the indications of comparative strength in the U.S.-Israeli struggle, he might have been less sanguine. After all, Carter had already lost a major round immediately after Camp David, when Begin managed to resist pressure for a freeze on settlements in the West Bank and Gaza during the negotiations on autonomy. Adding insult to injury, Begin had even gone so far as to announce in late October that settlements would be thickened immediately. So much for the idea of restraint or of confidence-building measures to encourage Palestinians and Jordanians to join the negotiations.

Carter seemed to feel by early December that Sadat could not be pressed much further. Carter was irritated by Begin's positions and his attitudes. As on many other occasions, he began to look for some way to pressure the Israelis. The best he could do was to withhold some bilateral commitments and to support Egypt on not sending an ambassador to Israel until self-government was set up, at least for the Palestinians in Gaza.

Carter was prepared to tilt in Sadat's favor on these points, but he had still not figured out how to bring Begin along. Thus the impasse that had been reached by mid-December had little strategic purpose. It marked a pause. Each side would wait to see who would flinch first.

In the end, events outside the immediate scope of the Egyptian-Israeli negotiations broke the stalemate. The shah of Iran fell from power in early 1979, and then everyone flinched, Carter most of all. For political and strategic reasons he concluded that he could not let the chance of peace between Egypt and Israel slip away while Iran was caught up in revolution. Even at some risk to his own reputation, he was prepared once again to make a major gamble to reach an agreement. And if Begin could not be moved, then Sadat would have to be.

CHAPTER ELEVEN

The Treaty

As 1978 came to an end, the prospects for peace anywhere in the Middle East looked dim. Not only were the Egyptian-Israeli talks at an impasse, but also Iran was in turmoil. The shah's regime was on the verge of collapse, and no one in Washington seemed to know what to do about it.[1]

For the next several months American thinking about the Camp David negotiations was colored by what was happening in Iran. The strategic balance of power in the region was changing, and the positions of the negotiating parties were hardening. Israel seemed to be reacting by becoming even more insistent that the peace treaty with Egypt be independent of any commitments involving the Palestinians. Furthermore, access to Egyptian oil assumed special importance as Iranian production, hitherto Israel's main source of supply, dried up. And the spectacle of a pro-American regime in a Muslim country being swept aside by religious extremists did little to increase Israeli confidence in the long-term value of Sadat's promises.

In Egypt there was also a retreat from the idea of a peace treaty. The Iranian revolution had reverberations everywhere in the Muslim world. Leaders were finding it risky to be portrayed as pro-Israeli or pro-American, since the popular mood seemed to be flowing in the opposite direction. In addition, with Iran in turmoil the Egyptians saw a role for themselves in helping to stabilize the oil-rich Arab regimes around the Gulf. But this would be difficult if the Arabs were to break with Egypt over the impending peace treaty with Israel.

As usual, the United States was pulled in several directions. The Iranian revolution made it increasingly important to conclude the peace negotiations between Begin and Sadat successfully. A peace treaty was not only desirable for strategic reasons; Carter also needed a political success to offset the enormous failure in Iran. At the same time Carter sympathized with the Egyptian argument that Egypt should not be

---

1. See Gary Sick, *All Fall Down*, pp. 130–40.

isolated from the rest of the region because of peace with Israel. If possible, Carter still wanted Sadat to be able to defend what he was doing with Israel before the moderate Arab regimes. Egypt's potential role as a stabilizing force in the Arab world seemed essential now that Iran had become a new source of unrest in the region.

In brief, the American role in this last phase of the peace negotiations was heavily influenced both by Iran and by the domestic political clock. Iran provided a strategic rationale for pressing for a quick conclusion of the Camp David process; the political calendar told Carter that he would soon have to turn his attention to other matters, namely reelection. Either he needed a quick and dramatic success, or he would have to back away from further involvement in the negotiations and hope that the electorate would not accuse him of losing the chance for peace between Israel and the largest Arab country.

TALKS RESUME

When Secretary Vance left the Middle East on December 15, 1978, the talks seemed deadlocked, and Vance was frustrated. He authorized his staff to prepare a "white paper" explaining what had happened in the talks since Camp David. The obvious purpose was to answer the Israeli charge that Washington was being unfair. A draft was in fact produced on December 17 that tended to place the blame for the recent crisis on Begin. Some thought was given to making the document public, but in the end more cautious counsel was taken.

Indeed, soon the United States was once again helping the two parties to resume contact. Vance suggested that Egyptian Prime Minister Khalil and Israeli Foreign Minister Dayan should meet with him in Brussels on December 23. Both accepted, and for two days the parties reviewed both the specific stumbling blocks in the negotiations and the broader strategic concerns raised by events in Iran.

During the Brussels talks Khalil insisted that Egypt should not be isolated from the other Arabs. This would not be in Israel's interest or that of the United States. With Iran in revolution, Egypt had to be ready to help the small countries in the Gulf, as well as Saudi Arabia, North Yemen, and Sudan. Therefore, the treaty with Israel should not appear to be a separate peace. Egypt must be seen as working for a just settlement of the Palestinian question. And above all, Egypt's obligations under the treaty must not appear to supersede Egypt's promises to its Arab neighbors.

(This last issue was the source of the debate over article 6, the priority of obligations.)

Dayan listened carefully, but argued that he must have assurances that if Syria, for example, attacked Israel, Egypt would not claim that the treaty allowed it to join Syria in "self-defense." Dayan, of course, knew that the words on paper could not guarantee how Egypt would behave in hypothetical circumstances. But he did want to make sure, primarily because of the important role of the United States, that Washington would not accept the argument that Egypt could go to Syria's help in a future war and still be true to its treaty commitments to Israel. (Dayan, after all, remembered the promises that Egypt and the United States had made to Israel in 1957, when Israel pulled its forces out of Sinai. In 1967 not only did President Nasser violate the understandings, but the Americans even seemed unsure of what commitments they had made.)

Dayan and Khalil appeared to get along well, but the talks made no real headway. Dayan had little authority, and it was clear that many in his own cabinet were suspicious of him. The hints that he had made to Vance two weeks earlier of areas of Israeli flexibility had all vanished. Begin was in charge, and he was not in a conciliatory frame of mind.

Rethinking the Issues

After returning to Washington, Vance spent the weekend at Camp David with Carter to discuss the foreign policy agenda for 1979. The president felt that things were falling apart in the Middle East. Dealing with that region had also become his heaviest political burden. And it was incredibly time-consuming. But the stakes were too high to let the negotiations drop. Carter decided to "continue to move aggressively on it and not postpone the difficult discussions, even though they were costly to us in domestic politics."[2]

In early January the Americans began to think of separating the unresolved issues into those that seemed technical, which would be handled at the subministerial level, and those that were more political, which would be addressed later by the president and Vance.

Included in the technical category were interpretive notes to articles 4 and 6 of the treaty and American legal interpretations of the priority of obligations issue. The political questions involved linkage—specifically, setting a target date for establishing self-government in the West Bank

2. Jimmy Carter, *Keeping Faith*, p. 412.

and Gaza and the timing of the exchange of ambassadors—and the more concrete questions of guaranteeing Israel's supply of oil, U.S. bilateral aid commitments, and clarification of the U.S. role if the treaty was violated.

At this point in the negotiations Sadat was rarely in evidence. Instead, Prime Minister Khalil began to play the principal role. Sadat seemed to have given him wide authority, and Khalil was much more attentive to detail than Sadat. The linkage issue was critical in his thinking.

Meanwhile, on the Israeli side Dayan seemed to be losing authority. He made it clear that Begin and the rest of the cabinet would have to decide all the difficult matters. When Samuel Lewis, the American ambassador to Israel, met with Begin on January 10, 1979, to discuss ways of resuming the talks, he found Begin to be totally unyielding on substance, with the insignificant exception of article 4 of the treaty. (The article called for nothing more than a review of security arrangements at the request of either party, and amendment by mutual consent.)

By mid-January the Americans were thinking of several ways of reviving the talks. Khalil and Dayan could be invited to Washington; another summit could be arranged; a new U.S. proposal could be put forward. Most felt it would be best to resolve the minor issues before engaging the president and Vance once again. They therefore decided to send Ambassador Atherton and the State Department's legal adviser, Herbert Hansell, to the Middle East to work on articles 4 and 6 and any necessary legal interpretations. March was frequently mentioned as the time by which an agreement should be reached on the entire treaty.

While Vance was thinking of ways to regain momentum in the peace talks, Brzezinski was taking the lead in reassessing the security situation for the whole Middle East, and especially for the Persian Gulf region. During this period several papers were written that looked at the possibility of strengthening the American military presence in the area.

The Policy Review Committee met on January 23, 1979, just as the Iranian revolution was about to sweep away the shah's regime. Much of the discussion focused on what Saudi Arabia might be able to do. Most participants were impressed by the limits on the Saudis' ability to act. No one thought of Saudi Arabia as a substitute for Iran.

One concrete result of the meeting was the decision to send Secretary of Defense Brown to the area to review the security situation. David C. Jones, the chairman of the Joint Chiefs of Staff, noted that the United States needed to clarify its security commitments in the area, and he spoke of the desirability of a "Carter Doctrine" for the Gulf. (One year later, in January 1980, such a doctrine was in fact announced.)

On the same day that the Carter Doctrine was being discussed for the first time, Brzezinski sent a memorandum to the president spelling out his concerns on the Arab-Israeli issue. "Events may make it difficult for us to pursue such a strategy, but I am firmly convinced for the good of the Democratic Party we must avoid a situation where we continue agitating the most neuralgic problem with the American Jewish community (the West Bank, the Palestinians, the PLO) without a breakthrough to a solution. I do not believe that in the approaching election year we will be able to convince the Israelis that we have significant leverage over them, particularly on those issues. . . . We have little time left."[3]

Toward the end of January the Atherton-Hansell shuttle was able to report back on the results of talks in Cairo and Jerusalem. In brief, there was no significant give from either party. The Americans did, however, begin to consider dropping the legal interpretations the United States had offered to both Israel and Egypt on the meaning of priority of obligations in article 6.

On February 6 Carter wrote to Begin and Sadat asking them to agree to a meeting in Washington involving Dayan, Khalil, and Vance. The talks would begin on February 21 and be held at Camp David. Vance had recommended this course of action in a memorandum to the president on February 1. There he suggested that Carter should ultimately persuade Sadat to drop the linkage of the exchange of ambassadors to the establishment of the self-governing authority in return for stronger commitments from Begin to do something on the Palestinian question. He also proposed some slight revisions of articles 4 and 6 and the text of a new letter on the West Bank and Gaza.

CAMP DAVID II

In preparation for the talks at Camp David, the Middle East team undertook one of its periodic assessments. I tried to pull together the events in Iran and Carter's domestic political standing to assess the current negotiating situation. My memorandum to Brzezinski began by stating that the Dayan-Khalil talks would not succeed.[4] At some point Carter would have to deal directly with Begin and Sadat. Many in the Middle

---

3. Memorandum from Brzezinski to Carter, January 23, 1979.
4. Memorandum from me to Brzezinski, February 17, 1979.

East now believed that the United States had lost its way. The only conceivable success on the horizon for Carter in foreign policy was an Egyptian-Israeli peace treaty. Both Egypt and Israel knew that the United States needed a success after Iran, and Israel had concluded that Carter would not fight hard for the West Bank.

"This means that we are going to have to exert a major effort for little more than a thinly disguised separate Egyptian-Israeli treaty. This is an unpalatable reality, and it will produce a sharp polarization within the Arab world. The Soviets will have opportunities to enhance their influence. Saudi Arabia's choices will be the key to whether this strategy works."

My memo went on to argue that the president should be tough with Begin on settlements, telling him that U.S. aid would be reduced by a fixed amount for each new settlement established in the West Bank and Gaza. I concluded, however, that Carter could not afford to fail. That would discredit Sadat's entire strategy. Egypt would then proceed to become the Bangladesh of the Middle East, the Saudis would retreat, and the United States and Israel would be faced with an increasingly radical, Soviet-oriented Arab world (and possibly a Soviet-oriented Iran). "And the Saudi role will be crucial, unreliable, and unpredictable."

On February 19, 1979, shortly after Secretary of Defense Brown returned from his Middle East foray, Carter assembled his Middle East team, along with Brown, Ambassador Eilts, and Ambassador Lewis. Brown gave his assessment, which boiled down to two points: everyone he had talked to was nervous about Iran, and Begin and Sadat were prepared to keep working for a peace treaty.

Carter realized he would probably have to meet again with the Egyptian and Israeli leaders. As he cast around for new ideas he argued that Sadat should not try to speak for the West Bank. The president even speculated in front of his Middle East advisers that Sadat really "did not give a damn about the West Bank." He was more concerned with Gaza. If he would drop his interest in the West Bank, he could have his separate treaty with Israel, get something in Gaza, and embarrass Hussein.

Carter stated clearly that he did not want a public confrontation with Israel. This was a time for progress on the overall negotiation, with details to be resolved later. Carter acknowledged that he had to take some of the blame for urging Sadat to link the exchange of ambassadors to the establishment of self-government, but Sadat would now have to drop that demand for linkage. Carter also said two mistakes had been made at Camp David. Too much emphasis had been placed on the timing of the exchange of ambassadors, and Sadat should not have agreed to negotiate in place of King Hussein if Jordan refused to join the talks.

The Saudi role was raised by Eilts, who said Sadat still wanted Saudi support, but would be ready to go ahead even without it. Somewhat cavalierly, Carter said the Saudis would have nowhere else to go after the treaty was signed. "They have to work with the United States and Egypt."

The following day I wrote a memorandum to Brzezinski in reaction to Carter's remarks, called "The Gaza Option and Saudi Views." I argued that it was a mistake to believe that the main difficulty for Sadat was that he found himself on the West Bank hook. No problem would be solved by dealing with Gaza first. That would simply highlight the separateness of any Egyptian-Israeli agreement. If there was a time for dealing with Gaza, it should be later, after the signing of the treaty. "Sadat is simply wrong to assume that the Gaza option will enhance his credibility in the Arab world and put pressure on Hussein." As for Saudi Arabia, it was not useful to say the kingdom had nowhere else to go. That ignored important nuances, and it was dangerous to take Saudi Arabia for granted. "For two years we have been operating on the assumption that a totally separate Egyptian-Israeli peace ran the risk of damaging the Egyptian-Saudi relationship and could push the Saudis back toward their parochial, ostrich-like posture. Nothing has happened to change the basic validity of that assumption, including the events in Iran."[5]

The second round of talks at Camp David began on February 21. Vance, Dayan, and Khalil were the principal participants, and each was accompanied by several aides. Khalil continued to insist that Egypt could not afford to be isolated, especially with the turmoil in Iran. Any treaty must be defensible before reasonable Arab opinion. On specifics, Khalil showed some interest in holding elections only in Gaza, and he implied that the exchange of ambassadors need not necessarily be tied to West Bank and Gaza developments.

Dayan had little room for negotiating, and he repeatedly said Vance would have to deal directly with Begin on the outstanding issues. He did, however, imply that Israel might be able to make some unilateral gestures toward the Palestinians, a point the Egyptians had pressed hard.

Talks at this level seemed to hold little promise of further progress. Khalil had authority to negotiate, but Dayan did not. So Carter invited

5. Memorandum from me to Brzezinski, "The Gaza Option and Saudi Views," February 20, 1979.

Begin to join the talks. On February 27 the Israeli cabinet rejected Dayan's recommendation that the prime minister attend, saying Begin would not participate in a summit with Khalil. Only Sadat would do. Carter was irritated, but decided to ask Begin to come to Washington just to meet with him. Things now seemed to be working toward a climax.

CARTER AND BEGIN IN WASHINGTON

In preparation for his meeting with Begin, on February 28, 1979, Carter called together his top advisers—Mondale, Vance, Brzezinski, and Hamilton Jordan. Brzezinski bluntly stated that Israel seemed to want a separate peace and wanted Carter not to be reelected. Jordan agreed. Mondale drew the conclusion that Carter should therefore not confront Begin and should stand back and let things take their natural course.[6]

Begin arrived in Washington without Dayan or Defense Minister Weizman in his delegation. These comparatively moderate voices seemed to have lost Begin's confidence. Carter and Vance noted their absence with regret.

The first session between Carter and Begin took place on Friday, March 2, 1979. Begin opened with a strong argument that the United States should help Israel because only Israel stood in the path of a Soviet takeover of the whole Middle East. He maintained that Israel could help prevent a communist takeover in Saudi Arabia, and even went so far as to offer the United States an airbase in Sinai that he had already promised to return to Egypt. None of these remarks had much effect on Carter.

Next Begin turned to the outstanding issues in the negotiations. He said the talks were in a deep crisis. The American interpretations to article 6 on the priority of obligations were tantamount to making peace between Egypt and Israel contingent on the achievement of a compre-

---

6. See Zbigniew Brzezinski, *Power and Principle*, p. 279. Brzezinski thought that Iran made it impossible for Carter to stand aside. "To let the Camp David Accords slip away would be to turn a triumph into disaster, with unforeseeable consequences for the Middle East as a whole." Carter by this time had also concluded that all that could be attained was a separate peace, followed by prolonged negotiations on the West Bank and Gaza. Carter, *Keeping Faith*, p. 413. In a memorandum to Carter written on February 28, 1979, Brzezinski had said that Begin believed he could afford a failure and Carter could not. "He believes that election year realities will increasingly weaken our hand in the negotiations." It was also clear that the United States would have to be very forthcoming on aid to get Israel to budge on the remaining issues of the treaty. Bilateral issues were now as important as Egyptian-Israeli differences.

hensive peace in the region. Such linkage would allow Egypt to use any pretext to tear up the treaty. Begin added that he was sure that some future Egyptian leader would recommend doing so. No interpretive notes would be acceptable. The text of the treaty must stand unchanged, whether Sadat liked it or not.

Begin then raised his objections to the side letter dealing with the West Bank and Gaza. It contained deviations from Camp David. There was no reason to separate Gaza from the West Bank, as Sadat now wanted to do, though if Egypt was prepared to drop all interest in the West Bank, Israel might consider discussing Gaza alone with Egypt. But Gaza would not then be a precedent for what might later be done on the West Bank.

Begin also introduced his own deviation from Camp David by claiming that Israel was under no obligation to discuss the West Bank unless Jordan joined the negotiation. Carter reminded him that Sadat had signed a letter, which was part of the Camp David Accords, saying that Egypt would assume the Jordanian role if Hussein did not step forward. Begin replied that the letters did not have the same value as the text of the agreement, a point that Carter quickly rejected.

Next on the list of Begin's objections was the idea of setting a target date for elections to the self-governing authority. If for some reason the date was not met, Israel might be accused of violating the treaty with Egypt, and Egypt might then break some of its commitments. Israel could not accept such linkage between the treaty and the future of the West Bank and Gaza.

Finally, Begin turned to the question of oil. Since signing the Camp David Accords, he said, Israel had lost access to Iranian oil. More than ever, Israel needed a firm guarantee from both Egypt and the United States that its oil supply would be met. If Egypt refused, Israel would not evacuate the oil fields in Sinai.

Carter was very discouraged by this meeting. There seemed to be no openings. Still, Vance was prepared to continue the talks over lunch at the State Department.

Brzezinski had made the argument to Begin that Sadat could not be pressed to renounce his commitments to Arab countries as the price of peace with Israel. That was going too far. Vance picked up on this point at lunch and told Begin that Sadat needed to be able to say the Egyptian-Israeli treaty "did not prevail over" other treaties. Begin said he did not object to that language, provided it was clear that if Egypt's treaty with Israel conflicted with its other treaty obligations, the treaty with Israel would be honored. In brief, Begin signaled a willingness to allow interpretive notes on article 6, so long as the priority of obligations went to the Egyptian-Israeli treaty. This essentially meant that Begin would say that the treaty was not meant to prevail over others, but that in practice it must do so. As Vance later wrote: "Of such are diplomatic compromises made; six months of negotiations to reach agreement with Begin on two contradictory statements in the same interpretation."[7]

Vance and his team took some time on Saturday to develop new language on article 6 and on the target date for elections in the West Bank and Gaza. The most significant alteration was tying the target date to the conclusion of the negotiations between Egypt and Israel rather than to the actual holding of elections. Meanwhile Carter had another session with his top advisers, in which he raised the possiblity of going to the Middle East to bring the negotiations to a dramatic conclusion. Hamilton Jordan in particular favored it. As Carter was later to say, "My proposal was an act of desperation."[8] Later in the evening Carter had another unproductive private meeting with Begin.

A final session between the two leaders was scheduled for Sunday morning, March 4. They met against a backdrop provided by a message from Sadat, who said he was planning to come to Washington to denounce Begin for his intransigence. Carter had already begun to think the best way to proceed was for him to go to the Middle East, and he hardly welcomed the telegenic Sadat stealing the show in Washington with ringing denunciations of Israel. So an effort was made to resolve some of the issues and therefore to justify a trip by the president to the region.

Somewhat surprisingly, Begin was in a rather conciliatory mood on Sunday morning. Vance reviewed the new formulations on article 6, and after a brief discussion among the Israeli delegation in Hebrew, Begin made a minor suggestion for a change in wording and agreed to seek cabinet approval, provided the United States formally withdrew its previous legal opinion on article 6. Similarly, Begin said the new American proposal on setting a target date for concluding the negotiations on autonomy was serious and would be considered by the cabinet. After all, he commented, Egypt and Israel could assume responsibility for the

---

7. Cyrus Vance, *Hard Choices*, p. 244. The language quoted by Vance is the text as it was finally agreed on, but at this stage the Americans had proposed, and Begin had accepted, language saying that the note to the effect that the Egyptian-Israeli treaty did not prevail over other treaties "did not derogate from" the provisions of article 6, paragraph 5, wording to which the Egyptians later took exception.

8. Carter, *Keeping Faith*, p. 416.

timing of the negotiations, but the actual holding of elections for the Palestinian government could be blocked by "third parties." That was why he had opposed a target date for elections, but could accept one for concluding the negotiations. This was a lawyer's point, but it gave Begin a pretext for changing his position without appearing to back down on a matter of principle.

The problem of oil supplies remained, along with the timing of the exchange of ambassadors, but Carter implied that he would deal directly with Sadat on both issues to find a satisfactory solution. To his surprise Carter found that the United States and Israel were now in agreement on most issues. The reason, it seemed, was not so much that Begin had been won over by Carter's argument, but rather that the new American formulations went just far enough to overcome his suspicions. Begin must have also realized that the moment had come to clinch the bilateral deal with Sadat.

As soon as the meeting was over, Carter sent a message to Sadat informing him that some progress had been made in the talks and that he did not want Sadat to say anything further in public, and especially not to commit himself to coming to Washington. In fact, said the president, he was considering a trip to the Middle East himself in the next few days.

The following day, March 5, 1979, the Israeli cabinet approved all the new American proposals. Carter now felt that success was at hand. A trip by him to the Middle East would produce a peace treaty and a much needed political boost.

Carter immediately decided to send Brzezinski to Cairo to see Sadat. He wanted Brzezinski to have a broad strategic review with the Egyptian president, to inform him of the new proposals and ask for his support of them, and to tell Sadat "very privately that the President's domestic political situation was becoming more difficult and that Begin might even wish to see the President defeated."[9]

Brzezinski met with Sadat on March 6 and delivered the president's messages. Sadat made it clear that the new formulations would pose no problem for him. He was, however, reluctant to go back to the idea of sending an ambassador to Israel after the interim withdrawal.

Sadat then told Brzezinski of his most important "secret weapon" —

---

9. Brzezinski, *Power and Principle*, p. 282. Carter, in an interview on May 22, 1985, did not recall having sent any such message to Sadat. Brzezinski, in an interview on June 3, 1985, recalled in some detail his conversation with Carter. Because Brzezinski was carrying a "political" message to Sadat from Carter, Vance did not object to his going to Cairo.

a proposal that Carter would be allowed to convey to Begin for building a pipeline from the Sinai oil fields directly to Israel. Sadat denounced the Israelis as idiots for ignoring his proposal on Gaza, but nonetheless said he would do everything possible to make Carter's visit a big success. The treaty should be signed while Carter was in the Middle East. If all went well, Sadat would even invite Begin to Cairo for the signing. Carter was very pleased by this prospect.

Sadat then turned his anger on the Saudis, describing them as a scarecrow and a U.S. protectorate to which the Americans attached too much importance. The Saudis, he said, were indecisive and incapable of action. Sadat treated King Hussein in similar fashion, asserting that the United States should dismiss him altogether. Somewhat surprisingly, he urged the Americans to improve their relations with Iraq.

CARTER TO THE MIDDLE EAST

By the time Carter arrived in Cairo on March 7, 1979, he had every reason to believe that his trip would be crowned with success. Sadat had essentially said Carter would have carte blanche to negotiate the final text of the treaty with Israel.[10]

Success in Egypt

Carter spent much of his time in Egypt celebrating the close ties between Egypt and the United States. Sadat put on an impressive show, including a train ride to Alexandria, which exposed the American president to larger and friendlier crowds than he was used to seeing at home.

Just before leaving for Israel, Carter and Secretary Vance met with Sadat and his top advisers at the Maamoura rest house near Alexandria. Carter pledged to get the best possible agreement for Egypt while in Israel and spoke as if he had Sadat's proxy in hand. Once the treaty was a reality, the United States and Egypt could plan for a "massive" government-to-government relationship in the military and economic fields. Carter also expressed the hope that the American private sector would invest in Egypt after the peace treaty was signed. In addition,

---

10. Carter had called Sadat on March 5 to tell him of Brzezinski's visit, and Sadat had promised him that the president's trip would be a great success. Carter felt he had a guarantee from Sadat that the negotiations would not fail because of any U.S.-Egyptian differences. As Carter later wrote, "Once more, I wanted Begin to have his way with particular phrases and depended on Sadat to be flexible on language and to take the long view concerning the effect of the agreement." Carter, *Keeping Faith*, p. 417.

Carter promised to use his maximum influence to get Jordan and Saudi Arabia to back the fait accompli of the treaty.[11]

While Carter and Sadat were congratulating each other on the achievement of peace, the Egyptian foreign ministry officials were showing anxiety. They still wanted Carter to persuade the Israelis to make some unilateral gestures to the Palestinians, and they hoped that Israel would agree to some form of special status for Egypt in Gaza. They also wanted a few minor changes in the treaty, including the replacement of a word in the notes to article 6 that they did not like. Carter and Vance promised to do their best.

Problems in Israel

Carter arrived in Israel after sundown on Saturday, March 10, 1979. He immediately drove to Jerusalem for a private dinner with Begin. To Carter's surprise, Begin made it clear that there was no chance of concluding the negotiations and signing the peace treaty while Carter was in the Middle East. The president was angry and suspected Begin of wanting him to fail. Begin was standing on procedure, arguing that the Knesset must have a chance to debate the agreement before it could be signed. Carter reminded Begin that this had not been necessary at Camp David, but Begin would not be rushed.

After all, for Begin a peace treaty with Egypt was an extraordinarily important achievement. He would not be stampeded into signing just because Carter had decided to put his prestige on the line by traveling to the Middle East. And even if Begin might agree to the text of the treaty, the Knesset did have to have its say, much as the Senate would in the United States.

Carter had little sympathy for Begin in the best of times. It was a bad start for what proved to be a difficult few days. The upbeat mood of Cairo had suddenly been replaced in Jerusalem by mutual suspicions and recriminations. And in that atmosphere, once again it seemed as if the chance for peace might be lost.

On Sunday, March 11, Carter and Begin met with their full delegations. Carter began by sketching his preferred scenario. Negotiations on the treaty text should be concluded within the next day or so; Sadat would

---

11. While in Cairo, Carter had a strained meeting with his ambassador to Saudi Arabia, John C. West. He told West in no uncertain terms that he was disappointed with the Saudis and instructed him to be blunt in telling Crown Prince Fahd that he expected Saudi support in the future.

fly to Jerusalem to sign; then Begin, Sadat, and Carter would all travel
to Cairo together for a second signing ceremony.

Begin immediately poured cold water on the president's idea. The
cabinet, he explained, would have to debate the matter fully, and then
the Knesset would have to vote before any signature could be put on so
solemn a document as a peace treaty. All this would take at least two
weeks. Then Begin asked to hear the new Egyptian proposals.

Sadat and his advisers had not liked the wording of the proposed notes
to article 6. The notes had been included to meet Sadat's desire to portray
the Egyptian-Israeli treaty as part of the comprehensive peace mentioned
in the Camp David Accords. To this end, the notes had said that article
6 of the treaty did not contravene the framework for peace agreed on at
Camp David and that the treaty was not to be seen as prevailing over
any other treaties to which the parties were bound. But to meet Israeli
concerns, the notes went on to say these provisions did "not derogate
from" the language of article 6, which in essence said that the provisions
of the Egyptian-Israeli treaty would be respected without regard to actions
of other parties even if a conflict arose with other obligations.

The Egyptians were bothered by the word "derogate." Carter therefore
suggested that Israel accept the substitution of the following phrase: "The
foregoing [the notes to article 6] is not to be construed as inconsistent
with the provisions of article 6." From the Americans' standpoint, there
was no substantive difference. The point was that the notes to article 6
should not be seen as changing the meaning of the treaty.

Carter also said Egypt was insisting on having liaison officers in Gaza
to help prepare for self-government there. Vance then passed around the
new texts of the notes to article 6 and the letter on the West Bank and
Gaza.

Begin frostily replied that the United States and Israel had already
agreed on the language of the notes when he was recently in Washington.
Sadat had the right to object, but Begin would not budge. He rejected
the new language and expected Carter to stand by the text that had been
worked out in Washington. The two phrases "does not derogate from"
and "is not inconsistent with" were worlds apart, he said. Article 6 was
the heart of the treaty. Without it the treaty would be a sham document.
Israel would not knowingly sign a sham document. At one point he said
that if the words "is not inconsistent with" were used instead of "does
not derogate from," it would mean that Egypt would start a war while
it had a peace treaty with Israel.

Carter denied that Egypt was looking for a pretext to attack Israel. Begin then pulled out a sheaf of newspaper articles and began to read extracts from the Egyptian press that he saw as threatening to Israel. Carter asked him what the point of such a display was. Begin referred to the terrible atmosphere in which the peace talks were being conducted and asked that the American ambassador in Cairo raise with Sadat the question of anti-Israeli articles in the Egyptian press.

Carter then asked if Begin had any counterproposals to make. Begin said no. He would stand by what had been agreed on in Washington. Begin went on to make a lengthy critique of the new note to article 6, paragraph 2. He had agreed in Washington to say in a note to the article that it should not be construed as contravening the framework for peace in the Middle East agreed to at Camp David. Sadat had wanted to add that Camp David had called for a "comprehensive peace," as it in fact did. Begin argued that by adding these two words, "comprehensive peace," Sadat was seeking a pretext to violate the treaty with Israel by making it contingent on other Arab states also making peace with Israel. Syria, he said, would then be able to render the treaty null and void by refusing to negotiate.

Toward noon, Begin turned his impressive critical powers to the new letter concerning the West Bank and Gaza. He strongly objected to the possibility of implementing autonomy in Gaza first. Nor would he accept Egyptian liaison officers there. Then, for what must have been the tenth time, he objected to the term West Bank, giving a lesson to the president on the geographic and historical inappropriateness of the term and the importance of using the words Judea and Samaria. Only if Sadat were to renounce entirely his interest in those two areas, said Begin, would he agree to discuss Gaza alone with Egypt.

Other members of the cabinet joined the discussions, and for a while it seemed as if no headway would ever be made. Ariel Sharon intervened with his standard lecture on "Jordan is Palestine" and called the Hashemites the only foreigners in Jordan. He promised Carter that within twenty years one million Jews would be living in the West Bank and Gaza. No line would ever separate Israel from these areas.

After a break for lunch, the talks resumed at 3:00 p.m. Carter tried to regain Begin's confidence by promising an American guarantee of Israel's oil supply. He also said he was sure that he could persuade Sadat to exchange ambassadors after the interim withdrawal if Israel would expedite the withdrawal, as originally agreed the previous November. He also said the United States would sign a memorandum of understanding with Israel on steps to be taken if Egypt violated the treaty.

Turning to bilateral U.S.-Israeli relations, Carter maintained that the two countries were equal partners. He added that what the United States did for Israel was more than balanced by what Israel did for the United States, a point that Begin had long been pressing on American audiences and that Carter really did not believe. Israel, he said, was a tremendous strategic asset to the United States, especially if it was at peace with Egypt, the other major regional friend of the United States. With these sweeteners, Carter urged the Israelis to try to find words to resolve the dispute over article 6.

For at least an hour that afternoon, the two delegations sat in different rooms, each poring over a dictionary and a thesaurus to find words that would be acceptable. There was something unreal about Carter, Vance, Brzezinski, Brown, Ambassador Lewis, Atherton, Harold Saunders, and me all struggling to find synonyms for *derogate* or *inconsistent*. The mood was generally gloomy; most of the Americans interpreted Begin's antics as little more than filibustering. In their view Begin had decided this was not the time for an agreement. They suspected that his real purpose was to hurt Carter politically by depriving him of a much needed foreign policy victory.

Late in the afternoon the two delegations reconvened. Begin announced proudly that his group had found a solution. An addition should be made to the appended note stating that it "does not affect" article 6 of the treaty. The Americans were stunned. The whole point of the note was that it added to the text of the treaty, but was not meant to contradict it. Vance pointed out that the Israeli proposal was totally unacceptable. Begin replied that no one could say that Israel had not made an honest effort to solve the problem.

With his frustration now clearly showing, Vance suggested that the note should say that its qualifications did not "contravene" the provisions of the treaty. Begin replied that this was a serious proposal, worthy of consideration. After some delay, the Israelis sent back word that they could not accept Vance's suggestion but that they would agree to say: "The foregoing [the note] is not to be construed as contravening the provisions of Article 6."[12]

The Americans, who had little notion of what all the verbal gymnastics

12. Begin's version of this session is found in his presentation to the Knesset on March 20, 1979, reproduced in Meron Medzini, ed., *Israel's Foreign Relations*, vol. 5, pp. 673–74.

were about, and who saw no important difference in the various formulations, gladly agreed. Begin, once again, had shown himself a master at controlling the agenda. For most of one day the negotiations had concentrated on one word in a note to one article of the treaty, and in the end Begin's version was accepted.

During this late afternoon session Begin told Carter that the Israeli cabinet would meet that evening to make its formal decisions on the matters under discussion. Then Vance could go to Cairo, and Carter could return home. In about two weeks, if all was proceeding smoothly, the Israelis might be ready to sign the treaty.

Carter responded by saying that Vance would not go to Cairo. The Egyptian position was already known to the Americans. They could conclude the negotiations right now. Begin replied that he was very tired and that the meeting should now be adjourned. Once again, the Americans felt Begin was deliberately trying to keep Carter from enjoying the fruits of his high-stakes trip to the Middle East.

Just before the meeting broke up, Carter again pleaded with Begin to try to reach agreement in the next day or so. Begin replied that the sky would not fall if agreement was not reached.

The next morning Carter and Begin and their advisers met again at 10:20. The cabinet had been in session all night, breaking up at 5:30 a.m. The Israelis looked exhausted.

Carter began by making a strong case for the strategic benefits to Israel of peace with Egypt. He argued that the U.S.-Israeli relationship would grow even stronger and the United States could be even more forthcoming on aid if the peace treaty was concluded. Egypt and Israel could work together to prevent the kind of radicalism seen in Iran from spreading to the rest of the region. If the opportunity for peace was now lost, it would be hard to recover.

The Israeli cabinet had essentially confirmed the new wording of the notes to article 6, and Carter was satisfied. But the cabinet had adamantly refused to consider giving Egypt any special status in Gaza. Carter argued that its refusal would be hard for Egypt to accept. He pleaded with Begin to reconsider, but Begin refused.

Vance reminded the Israelis that Egypt was also unwilling to agree to sell a fixed amount of oil to Israel. The most Sadat would promise was to sell oil to Israel on a nondiscriminatory basis. Sharon interjected a strong statement to the effect that Israel did not want to depend on the United States for its oil. Nor would Israel allow any Egyptian liaison officers in Gaza. Nor should the United States have anything to do with the negotiations over the West Bank and Gaza. And just for good measure, Sharon reminded Carter that Israel planned to build more settlements in Gaza, in the West Bank, and in Golan.

The meeting broke up at 11:20 a.m. Begin and Carter left to prepare for their addresses to the Knesset. That event turned out to be somewhat less than edifying. In his remarks Carter rather undiplomatically implied that the Israeli public wanted peace more than its leaders did. During Begin's speech opposition members interrupted so frequently that it was hard to follow what was being said. Begin's old ally Geulah Cohen was ordered off the floor of the Knesset when she refused to observe parliamentary decorum. Begin seemed to enjoy the battle, but the Americans were less happy. Still, Begin had shown that he was not the most extreme hard-liner among the Israelis.

Carter went from the Knesset to a lunch with the members of the Foreign Affairs and Security Committee. During the lunch Carter revealed that he essentially had carte blanche from Sadat to conclude an agreement. Begin doubtless suspected this anyway, but now he must have become certain that Carter could be persuaded to cede on his insistence that Egypt be given a special role in Gaza.

Vance was scheduled to have one more session with the Israeli delegation on Monday afternoon, March 12. Carter hoped that the remaining problems on Gaza, on oil, and on the timing of withdrawal from Sinai and the exchange of ambassadors could all be settled.

Impasse

Begin opened the meeting by saying that the cabinet had been in session for two hours and had decided to reconfirm its position on all issues. There would be no further changes from the Israeli side. Israel needed, he said, a clear-cut Egyptian promise to sell 2.5 million tons of oil to Israel each year. Begin did say he would agree to consider an Egyptian proposal to start the autonomy talks in Gaza, but this issue could not be included in the side letter. Nor could any mention be made of Egyptian liaison officers. Even on article 6 Begin insisted that the words "comprehensive peace" be removed from one of the notes, arguing that otherwise the treaty would appear to depend on the action of other Arab parties in making peace with Israel.

Begin did suggest that some expedited withdrawal to the interim line might be possible, but only if Sadat agreed to send an ambassador to

Israel shortly thereafter. From this point on, the discussion quickly deteriorated. Begin accused the Americans of always showing an understanding of Sadat's concerns but never of his. Sharon harshly interjected that the Egyptians would never be allowed into Gaza in any form. They would only try to stir up the local population. Even the usually moderate Dayan and Deputy Prime Minister Yigal Yadin seemed to think that Carter should not support the Egyptian claim to a special role in Gaza.

Vance tried to salvage the situation by urging that both the Gaza and oil issues be dropped from the agreement. Neither had been included in the Camp David Accords, and both could be dealt with later. Begin said oil was a matter of life and death and could not be left out of the agreement. Nor would Israel agree now to put in writing its willingness to accelerate withdrawal to the interim line.

To the surprise of the Americans, Begin then said that the talks were over and a joint communiqué should be issued announcing that some progress had been made, but that some questions still needed to be resolved. A text to this effect, obviously prepared well in advance, was passed over to Vance for his agreement.

Carter was immediately informed of the outcome of the talks. He decided there was no point for him to stay in Israel any longer. Begin clearly did not want an agreement at this time. The president ordered his plane to be prepared to return directly to Washington. But the hour was late, and to get all the presidential party and its luggage assembled in time would be difficult. Reluctantly Carter agreed to spend the night in Jerusalem, but he was a bitterly disappointed man.

FINALE

When the Americans reconvened at the King David Hotel, the mood was gloomy. No one saw much point in trying to come up with new formulations on the outstanding issues. Most of the Americans drifted off to have dinner together. No working sessions were planned.

Toward 9:00 p.m. one of Dayan's associates called Vance to suggest that the secretary should invite Dayan over for an informal talk. Dayan, it turned out, had been caucusing with members of the cabinet who were unhappy with the way the negotiations seemed to be ending. Dayan had got Begin's permission to see Vance. Weizman was apparently threatening to resign if the peace treaty was jeopardized by Begin's obstinacy.

Dayan made several suggestions and confirmed that most of the cabinet would accept the U.S. proposals on guaranteeing Israel's supply of oil and for accelerated Israeli withdrawal to an interim line in Sinai. In return for those concessions, Dayan suggested that the side letter should omit reference to Gaza as a special case and to a role for Egyptian liaison officers there. He urged Carter to meet again with Begin the next morning to put these proposals forward as new American suggestions. Meanwhile Dayan would try to prepare the way with Begin. Vance agreed to try, and for several hours the American team worked on a new set of proposals.

While Vance and Dayan were working to prevent a collapse of the talks, Jody Powell was briefing the press on the situation as it stood at 9:00 p.m. He painted a bleak picture, and this was the basis for the pessimistic accounts that most Americans read in their papers on Tuesday, March 13.[13]

By the time the American press accounts were being digested, the situation had already changed. Carter met with Begin alone on Tuesday morning; they were then joined by Dayan and Vance. Begin, as usual, held back from making a complete commitment to the new proposals. If Egypt accepted them, and if Sadat agreed to an early exchange of ambassadors, Begin would recommend the new proposals to the Knesset. Carter knew that was tantamount to having Begin's agreement. Pressing his luck a bit, he asked Begin if Israel would agree to undertake some unilateral gestures to improve the atmosphere for the Palestinians in the West Bank and Gaza. This issue was of great importance to the Egyptians. Begin said he would sympathetically consider this request. Carter finally knew he had an agreement in hand.

Carter then flew directly to Cairo, where he met with Sadat at the airport. Sadat's aides still had some objections, but Sadat was in no mood to quibble.[14] He had promised the president a success, and he was prepared to say that agreement had now been reached on all issues. At 5:00 p.m. Carter said that full agreement had been reached, and he placed a call to Begin from the airport to tell him so. Begin agreed to go to the cabinet the next day for final approval, but the outcome was no longer in doubt.

Carter and Sadat then walked out on the tarmac to tell the awaiting press corps that a peace agreement had been concluded. After so many

---

13. Jody Powell, *The Other Side of the Story*, pp. 93–97.

14. When Khalil asked Carter to try to change the text of the agreement in several places, the president replied: "For the last 18 months, I, the president of the most powerful nation on earth, have acted the postman. I am not a proud man—I have done the best I could—but I cannot go back to try to change the language."

ups and downs, and after the previous evening's pessimistic briefing, many of the journalists were amazed—and somewhat irritated that their previous day's stories would look bad.

On the plane back to Washington Carter's political aides were ecstatic. At long last Carter could point to a major foreign policy achievement that would be genuinely welcomed by most Americans. The foreign policy advisers were a bit less jubilant, thinking as always of the many problems that lay ahead. Most of all, they were exhausted and grateful that the talks were over, at least for the moment. When we arrived at Andrews Air Force Base later that evening, a large crowd was waiting to congratulate Carter, Vance, and the rest of us. It had been quite a day, starting in Jerusalem and ending in Washington.

SIGNING THE PEACE TREATY

As we returned with President Carter from the Middle East in mid-March 1979, we all realized that major historical forces were being unleashed in the region we had visited so briefly and knew so imperfectly. The impact of the Iranian revolution could already be felt. And peace between Egypt and Israel, now almost a reality, was also bound to set off shock waves. How it would all balance out in the coming years was beyond anyone's understanding.

Carter, Vance, and the rest of us on the Middle East team were profoundly satisfied that our lengthy diplomatic efforts had finally paid off. To be sure, the result was quite different from what we had envisaged in early 1977. Many adjustments had been made in strategy as initial preconceptions clashed with stubborn realities. Ambitious objectives had been scaled back, in part in response to adverse domestic American reactions. What had seemed possible and desirable early in Carter's term had become less and less plausible as the president's popular support ebbed and his attention to political considerations grew.

The comprehensive Middle East peace that Carter had originally hoped for was still far off, but the largest of the building blocks in that design, the Egyptian-Israeli peace, was nearly a reality. Carter was ambivalent about whether the peace treaty would by itself bring stability to the Middle East, or whether it would set in motion an inevitable process that would widen the circle of peace around Israel. He certainly did not believe it could make matters worse than they already were.

Little time was spent pondering these questions once we returned to Washington. Arrangements had to be made for the formal signing ceremony, an event of considerable political importance for Carter. And an attempt needed to be made to minimize adverse Jordanian and Saudi reactions.

To contain the negative actions of key Arab states, Carter decided to send a high-level delegation to Saudi Arabia and Jordan to discuss the new strategic realities with Crown Prince Fahd and King Hussein. Brzezinski was chosen to head this team; he was accompanied by David Jones, the chairman of the Joint Chiefs of Staff, and Warren Christopher, the deputy secretary of state.

In Saudi Arabia Brzezinski felt he made some headway. The Saudis affirmed that they were prepared to continue funding the F-5 aircraft program for Egypt.[15]

Brzezinski arrived late for his meeting with King Hussein and left abruptly for Cairo. Not surprisingly, the king was not forthcoming. Although an effort of sorts had been made, Carter basically seemed to share Sadat's view that the reaction of the other Arabs did not much matter. They would simply have to accept the new facts. This was a serious misjudgment. Little could have been done, in my view, to win the overt support of King Hussein for Camp David and the peace treaty, but we might have been able to gain his tacit endorsement for our endeavors. But we never made the necessary effort, nor did Sadat.

Before the signing, a few remaining issues had to be resolved. Ezer Weizman visited Washington to work out the new phases of withdrawal and to appeal successfully for additional military assistance.[16]

Bilateral U.S.-Israeli questions remained to be answered. In particular, how would the United States guarantee Israel's supply of oil if Egyptian oil was not available to meet Israel's requirements? And what would the United States promise to do if Egypt violated the treaty? What provision should be made for the contingency that U.N. peacekeeping forces would not be available for the Sinai after Israeli withdrawal? On all these points the United States had to find solutions. In some instances, the final wording was not worked out until the actual day the peace treaty was signed.

15. Brzezinski, *Power and Principle*, p. 286, somewhat overstates the case when he writes that he obtained a secret Saudi pledge not to adopt any damaging sanctions against Egypt. In fact, the Saudis were prepared to continue the F-5 program until Sadat issued a ringing denunciation of the Saudi leadership by name. At that point they withdrew the offer of funding and severed all government-to-government aid programs.

16. Ezer Weizman, *The Battle for Peace*, p. 381; and Leon H. Charney, *Special Counsel*, pp. 147–54.

But the problems of the draftsmen and mapmakers would not stand in the way of the signing ceremony on March 26, 1979. Carter was joined by Begin and Sadat on the north lawn of the White House. A large audience was invited to attend. Many political debts were paid that day. Egyptians and Israelis mingled freely and expressed hopes that peace might be at hand. Across the street in Lafayette Park some Palestinians and their supporters held a small demonstration against the treaty, a reminder that the next phase of negotiations would encounter opposition. But the day was one of optimism and good feeling, and it was crowned that evening by a magnificent banquet on the south lawn of the White House.

The formal Egyptian-Israeli agreement consisted of a thick file of documents that few people would ever read in their entirety. (See appendix I for the key documents.) Besides the text of the treaty, there were three annexes dealing with security arrangements, maps, and normal relations between the parties. Seven interpretive notes were attached to the basic documents. Sadat and Begin also signed a letter to Carter concerning negotiations on the West Bank and Gaza issues. Carter added in his own handwriting an explanatory note to the letter saying, "I have been informed that the expression 'West Bank' is understood by the Government of Israel to mean 'Judea and Samaria.'"

Sadat signed another letter to Carter promising that a resident ambassador would be sent to Israel within one month of the interim withdrawal. Carter conveyed this information to Begin in a letter, and Begin acknowledged its receipt. Carter also wrote to both Sadat and Begin to spell out what the United States would do to help monitor the security arrangements in Sinai and how the United States would use its best efforts to organize a multinational peacekeeping force if U.N. troops were unavailable.

On the day of the signing of the peace treaty, Vance and Dayan also put their signatures to a memorandum of agreement. Most of the commitments made in this document were hedged with qualifications, but it put the weight of the United States behind Israel in the event that Egypt violated the treaty. Promises made as part of previous memorandums of understanding were reaffirmed. An agreement on oil supply was signed at the same time.[17]

As for military aid to Israel, Secretary Brown wrote to Ezer Weizman committing the United States to $3 billion to help construct new airfields

17. See Moshe Dayan, *Breakthrough*, pp. 356–58, for the texts of these two memorandums.

in the Negev. Of that amount, $800 million would be in the form of grants. The United States also informed Israel that it was prepared to act positively on a number of weapons systems that had been requested earlier. (During the negotiations Carter had deliberately held off on making major decisions on arms so that he would have some remaining leverage over both Israel and Egypt.)

Brown wrote a similar letter to the Egyptian minister of defense, promising $1.5 billion in aid over the next three years. A list of military equipment that Egypt would be allowed to purchase was appended to this letter.

Inevitably, a few loose ends were handled by memorandums for the record written by the legal adviser or other participants in the negotiations. None of the memos changed the basic outline of what had been agreed upon. They largely involved putting the United States on record with an interpretation of some ambiguous point in the treaty or in the annexes, or recording some informal understanding that had been reached after the text of the treaty had been completed.

At the last minute Carter was also required to write a secret letter to Begin affirming what Begin and Sadat had orally agreed upon on March 26 concerning oil supplies. Carter also wrote to Egyptian Prime Minister Khalil to inform him of the results of his discussions with Begin about unilateral gestures toward Palestinians in the West Bank and Gaza.

Khalil, who had not known of the U.S.-Israeli memorandum of agreement until the last moment, wrote two letters to Vance spelling out sixteen reasons why Egypt rejected it. The day after the peace treaty was signed, Khalil also wrote to Carter protesting that Carter had not done enough to commit Begin to take positive actions in the West Bank and Gaza. But these were faint notes that attracted little attention, and Carter had long ago learned that Sadat would not make an issue out of such matters.[18]

CONCLUSION

Complex diplomatic initiatives rarely work out quite the way their authors anticipate. Mid-course corrections are part of the normal negotiating process. For American presidents in particular, the intrusion of domestic political considerations is also part of the game. In light of these realities,

18. These letters from Khalil can be found in *White Paper on Treaty of Peace between Egypt and Israel*, pp. 155–77.

one cannot judge results by the standard of initial designs or theoretical abstractions.

Instead, one must look at the Egyptian-Israeli peace treaty in its political context. What more might have been achieved, given the very real constraints operating on all the parties? Could positive aspects of the agreement have been enhanced? Could the negative ones have been minimized? Perhaps, but not without great effort.

Egyptians and Israelis will have their own reasons for wishing that the peace process had taken at times a different turn. No one has been entirely satisfied with the results. But Egypt and Israel have remained at peace, despite some difficult moments. And few Egyptians or Israelis seem to quarrel with the basic ingredients of the bilateral peace treaty.

For Americans, the question remains whether the Egyptian-Israeli treaty could have been followed by successful negotiations involving Jordan and the Palestinians with Israel. That such negotiations did not take place in the years immediately after the Egyptian-Israeli peace treaty is part of the historical record. And at least one of the reasons, it would seem, was that Begin succeeded in defining the Camp David Accords in narrow terms. Neither Sadat nor Carter had the will or the power to challenge Begin's interpretation with a more generous one of his own. As a result, the part of the accords that concerned the West Bank and Gaza has remained a dead letter.

Why was Carter unable to make headway on the West Bank and Gaza? Why did he seem to care less about those areas than he did about Sinai? First, Egypt and Israel were talking to each other and were ready to make decisions. The other Arabs were either opposed to the process or were sitting on the sidelines to see what would be offered them. Carter felt more of an obligation to Sadat because Sadat had taken risks for peace.

Second, the chance for a successful negotiation between Egypt and Israel was much greater than between Israel and any of the other Arab parties. Two disengagement agreements had already been signed in 1974 and 1975. Direct talks between the parties had shown that the distance between them on bilateral issues was not large. Carter's involvement could plausibly help bridge the remaining gap.

Third, Egypt was the most powerful Arab country. Peace between Egypt and Israel would not make war impossible in the Middle East, but it would dramatically change its nature. The danger of U.S.-Soviet confrontation would be reduced as well. On these grounds even a separate peace had immense strategic value for the United States.

Finally, one must frankly admit, the American political system makes it difficult for a president to tackle a problem like that of the Palestinians. Presidential authority in foreign affairs is theoretically extensive, but in practice it is circumscribed by political realities. And the Palestinian question has proved to be so controversial that most presidents have been reluctant to get deeply involved in it. Sadat, who was genuinely popular with the American public, was, in Carter's view, worth a fight with Begin. But the Palestinians had no domestic constituency, and when Sadat seemed less concerned about their fate than about Sinai, Carter found it impossible to be more demanding than the leader of the largest Arab country.

Begin, of all the participants in the negotiations, seemed to have understood the constraints on Carter best. He knew when he could afford to stand up to the president and when it was best to yield. He had an uncanny sense for timing, realizing better than most that the longer the negotiations went on, the less appetite Carter would have for a confrontation with Israel over the Palestinian issue. This consideration, it would seem, helped to dictate Begin's rigid position in the fall of 1978, convincing him that by the following spring the realities of the coming election year would make themselves felt and Carter would do little to push Israel for concessions in the talks on the West Bank and Gaza.

Signing the peace treaty in March 1979 instead of October 1978 was determined not so much by the content of the document as by the political calendar. The earlier date would have left Carter some time to devote to the autonomy talks on the West Bank and Gaza; the later date did not. And Begin certainly did not want Carter involved in those negotiations, knowing as he did the depth of the U.S.-Israeli disagreement on how the Camp David Accords should be interpreted and carried out.

Of the three chief participants in the negotiations, Begin did best by his own criteria. Admittedly, he had to relinquish the Sinai to secure Eretz Israel, but according to his values and ideology this was a good bargain. Begin thought in strategic terms; he understood the uses of power in negotiations; he was prepared to threaten and bluff; and he knew that time mattered. His legalistic concentration on language served him well, even if it was sometimes a mask for his broader purposes. I personally felt his vision of Israel's place in the Middle East was profoundly flawed, anchored more in the past than directed to the future. Nonetheless, I thought he was the most able of the Camp David negotiators and a remarkable politician as well.

Sadat came from a different mold. He believed in the politics of the grand gesture, the bold stroke, and he was not very interested in details. He saw much of the conflict with Israel as psychological. If he could break down the barriers of distrust, he seemed to believe, the Israelis should be prepared to return Arab territory and allow the Palestinians to enjoy some of their rights. When Begin resisted, Sadat tried to use the power of the United States to force a change in the Israeli position. But his reading of U.S. politics was less accurate than Begin's. Carter had no stomach for a confrontation with Israel.

Carter's reluctance to pressure Begin for concessions on the Palestinian question meant that Sadat had to settle for a thinly disguised bilateral peace with Israel. Objectively, this was not such a bad outcome. Egypt recovered its territory and its oil fields and was handsomely rewarded with arms and aid by the United States. But to many Egyptians, Sadat seemed to be paying too high a price, especially in terms of Egypt's relations with other Arab countries. Egypt was spared the danger of future wars, but the damage to Egyptian self-esteem was high. Sadat had certainly hoped for more when he set off for Jerusalem in November 1977, but in time he had come to realize that Begin was tougher than he had thought and that Carter could do little to alter that fact.

Carter came to the negotiations with the least knowledge of the issues and with the greatest capacity to evolve in his understanding. The Middle East was important in his view, but he did not have fixed ideas on exactly how the problems should be solved. The engineer in him seemed to want the grand design of a comprehensive peace; left to his own devices, he might have remained wedded to that appealing notion. But he could not build the edifice alone, and so he began to concentrate on the part that was most feasible. He was slow to understand that the rest of the design would probably be lost if he concentrated exclusively on the Egyptian-Israeli part.

The idealist in Carter also played a role. The president deeply believed that men of good will could resolve problems by talking to one another. At Camp David he initially thought he would need only to get Sadat and Begin together and help them to overcome their mutual dislike. The agreement itself would then be worked out by the two leaders in a spirit of compromise and accommodation. The depth of their distrust, even hatred, was hard for him to understand. Begin's fixation on Judea and Samaria was especially hard for him to grasp. Finally, it was Carter who was forced to reexamine his assumptions and change his approach in the face of Begin's intransigence and Sadat's apparent willingness to settle for a bilateral deal.

The politician in Carter was slow to make his entry into the negotiations. For most of the first year, domestic politics rarely seemed to concern the president as he tackled the Middle East problem. He was sometimes reckless in his disregard for public opinion, and probably would have done better to have engaged in less controversy with Israel in public in the first months of his term. In retrospect, his behavior gained him little on the Arab side and may have helped marginally in Begin's rise to power. As time wore on, Carter, and especially his advisers, came to believe that he was paying a heavy price for his involvement in the Arab-Israeli imbroglio. They also saw the Egyptian-Israeli peace treaty as one of the few potential successes that could boost the president's prestige at home and abroad.[19] By early 1979 politics had come to the fore in the decisions leading to the final push for peace. Soon after the peace treaty was signed, Carter turned over the next phase of Middle East diplomacy to Robert Strauss, fully expecting him to help cover the president's political flanks as the campaign for reelection got under way.

Carter, Sadat, and Begin each brought something special to the achievement of peace between Egypt and Israel. Carter contributed his determination and his positive vision of peace. It is hard to imagine the treaty being achieved without his efforts. Sadat added a dramatic sense of history, a willingness to step outside the normal limits set by his own society. This was both a strength and, ultimately, a weakness. But in November 1977, in one bold stroke, Sadat made Israelis believe that peace with an Arab state was possible. Finally, Begin's vision of peace with Egypt as the key step toward consolidating Israel's hold on the whole of Eretz Israel meant that he was prepared to meet most of Sadat's demands on bilateral matters, while strenuously rejecting Sadat's pleas for gestures to the Palestinians. And Begin was a strong enough leader to bring virtually his entire country with him in support of the peace with Egypt.

In the end, the peace treaty between Egypt and Israel was much more than just an agreement worked out by Carter, Sadat, and Begin. Carter's role in particular reflected more than just his own beliefs and ambitions. He was, after all, the president of the United States, a man with incredible resources at his disposal. But he was also operating within the special

19. Ironically, according to public opinion polls, Carter gained very little as a result of the peace treaty. See Powell, *Other Side of the Story*, p. 102.

confines of a political system that was never designed to make the conduct of foreign policy easy. In light of those realities, it is perhaps surprising that the American role was as effective as it was in helping to bring peace between Egypt and Israel.

The lesson from the Camp David negotiations seems to be that the president can tackle complex foreign policy problems with some chance of success. The system is not hopelessly loaded against him. But the effort required is likely to be much greater than the president might expect at the outset, and in the end he will probably have to settle for less than he sought. And perhaps most important, any president will have to do much of the hard work early in his term, for time begins to run out for political reasons as the election year approaches. These are not, of course, immutable realities. But the Camp David negotiations suggest they cannot be ignored.

CHAPTER TWELVE

Conclusion

Jimmy Carter was unique among American presidents in the depth of his concern to find a peaceful resolution of the conflict between Israel and its Arab neighbors. More than any other foreign policy issue, the Middle East occupied his time and energies.

At the beginning of his administration, he knew little about the intricacies of the problem. But he felt the challenge of tackling an issue that had eluded solutions in the past. And he no doubt felt that American interests would be well served if peace could be brought to the Middle East.

As time went on, Carter came to know many of the leaders in the Middle East, and he turned his extraordinary capacity for mastering detail to the negotiations between Egypt and Israel. He pored over maps of Sinai to identify lines for the interim withdrawal. He personally drafted the first version of the Egyptian-Israeli framework agreement at Camp David. And twice he put his political reputation on the line by engaging in summit negotiations that could easily have failed.

In the end, Carter was able to preside over the signing of the Egyptian-Israeli peace treaty, perhaps the most noteworthy foreign policy achievement of his administration. Yet he gained little in domestic political terms for these efforts, and some would argue that he even weakened his political base.

It does nothing to diminish Carter's achievement in the Middle East to acknowledge that he built on firm foundations laid by Presidents Richard Nixon and Gerald Ford, and especially the remarkable diplomatic efforts of Henry Kissinger in brokering three Arab-Israeli agreements during 1974–75. Carter was also ably served by his secretary of state, Cyrus Vance, who deserves much of the credit for patiently shaping the Camp David Accords and the text of the peace treaty.

Carter's initiatives would have come to naught had the leaders of Egypt and Israel been unwilling to accept American mediation and to make peace between their two countries. At no point did Carter forcefully impose American views on either side, though often he was able to change the positions of either Prime Minister Begin or President Sadat, especially Sadat. American leadership was certainly a necessary condition for the success of the negotiations, but it was not sufficient. The parties to the conflict had to be ready for agreement.

Unfortunately, in the course of working for the Egyptian-Israeli peace, the negotiators lost the objective of a broader Middle East settlement. Lebanon, for example, slid even more deeply into conflict after Camp David, culminating in the Israeli invasion of 1982. Many observers, including Egyptians, have argued that the war in Lebanon would never have happened on the scale it did if Egypt and Israel had not been at peace. The assault on Lebanon, after all, was a "war of choice" for Israel, and it would probably not have launched such an operation if it had still been obliged to keep a good part of its army on the Egyptian front. The Israelis were so confident that the treaty with Egypt would hold that they never fully mobilized for the war in Lebanon. All this suggests that many Lebanese and Palestinians, as well as many Israelis, may have paid a high price for the peace between Egypt and Israel.

Lebanon, however, was never the central concern of the Camp David negotiations. The Palestinian question was. And on that score the record shows that Camp David did little to bring about a settlement.

Camp David alone cannot be blamed for the lack of peace between Israel and the Palestinians. The intractability of the conflict is such that no formula has been found to bring the parties toward mutual recognition and some reconciliation of their competing national claims. Nonetheless, Carter's efforts to resolve the Palestinian problem were stymied by more than the intrinsic complexity of the issues and the unwillingness of the parties to talk directly with one another.

Carter dealt extensively with Sadat and Begin and often took their advice on how to address the Palestinian issue. Carter's reliance on the views of his Camp David partners no doubt led to many misperceptions, such as his belief that King Hussein would eventually join the Camp David process. Carter had a hard time understanding the Palestinian-Israeli conflict in its full complexity, in part because he had few opportunities to talk with Palestinians or with Israelis who did not share the views of Begin and his colleagues on how the conflict should be resolved. Not until he visited the West Bank as a private citizen in 1983 did Carter become aware of many of the realities of the situation.[1]

Besides understanding the Palestinian issue less well than the Egyptian-

1. See Jimmy Carter, *The Blood of Abraham*, pp. 115–29. See also his interview with Helena Cobban, *At-Tadamoun* (in Arabic), June 29–July 5, 1985, pp. 9–14.

Israeli dispute, Carter also found that the constraints of the American political system came into play whenever he tried to deal with the Palestinian question. Even to refer to Palestinian rights or to a Palestinian homeland could set off shock waves within the American Jewish community. These would be instantly felt in Congress and relayed back to the White House. Before long Carter learned to say less in public, thereby giving the impression that he was backing down under domestic pressure.

Finally, when Carter turned his attention from the Middle East after the signing of the Egyptian-Israeli peace treaty, both Arabs and Israelis knew that American attitudes and priorities had changed. However talented his special negotiators might have been, they had little chance of succeeding once Carter no longer seemed to be personally involved in the negotiations.

CAMP DAVID AND THE PALESTINIAN QUESTION

Throughout the Egyptian-Israeli peace negotiations, Sadat maintained he needed to demonstrate that he had achieved something for the Palestinians. He repeatedly said he was not prepared for a "separate peace." What he wanted from Begin was a simple statement that Israel was willing to return Arab territory captured in the 1967 war in exchange for peace, recognition, and security from the Arabs. Also, he hoped for some form of commitment from Israel to Palestinian rights, including the right of self-determination. This commitment, of course, Begin would not give.

Because of Begin's refusal to give Sadat the cover he wanted, the Americans became involved in the much more cumbersome exercise of trying to blend elements of the Israeli proposal for self-rule in the West Bank and Gaza with Sadat's desire for a set of general principles to settle the Arab-Israeli conflict. The result was an elaborate agreement at Camp David on three stages of negotiations. First Egypt would launch the process by reaching agreement with Israel on a transitional period. Then Jordan would be invited to join the talks, and toward the end of the transitional period the Palestinians would also be included in the negotiations to determine the final status of the West Bank and Gaza.

In retrospect, it is clear that Sadat and Carter both overestimated the role that Egypt could play in laying the groundwork for a negotiated settlement of the Palestinian issue. Both misread the attitudes of King Hussein and the Palestinian leaders. Both misjudged the part that the Saudis might be willing to take in the negotiations. Neither took Syria sufficiently into account.

Even with these errors, it might have been possible to carry out the provisions of the Camp David Accords if the idea of self-government for the Palestinians in the West Bank and Gaza could have been given real content. For example, if Carter had succeeded in getting Begin's agreement to a freeze on settlement activity; if the self-governing authority had been given control over land and water resources; if genuinely free elections, including the right to vote for Palestinians living in East Jerusalem, had been promised; and if the military occupation authority had been abolished, then it might have been possible to attract Palestinians into the negotiating process.

But none of these measures proved feasible while Begin was prime minister, and thus the concept of autonomy was devalued in the eyes of those who were most crucial in determining its viability. When Begin refused to budge on these matters, neither Sadat nor Carter could find a way to persuade him to change his mind.

Carter was slow to recognize the depth of Begin's attachment to the West Bank and Gaza.[2] He was also slow to understand the linkage issue.[3] Once Egypt and Israel were at peace, Begin had few remaining incentives to deal constructively with the Palestinian question. Sadat did feel strongly about the need for linkage, and for many months he tried to establish some explicit connection between what would happen in bilateral Egyptian-Israeli relations and the Palestinian negotiations. But when put under pressure by Carter, in the face of Begin's intransigence, and when confronted with hostility from other Arab leaders, Sadat resigned himself to the separate agreement that he had hoped to avoid when he first set off for Jerusalem in November 1977.

2. In an interview with me on May 22, 1985, Carter referred to the cyclical nature of his relationship with Begin. On some occasions Begin would take a very hard-line position, and then later would appear to have softened. In retrospect, Carter believed that Begin never changed his basic commitments, but he would sometimes give an impression of flexibility, often by simply remaining silent. Carter felt Begin did make some genuine concessions at Camp David, but ran into a "firestorm" when he returned to Israel. As a result, he pulled back from the concessions he had made. Only then did Carter begin to conclude that Begin would never budge on the Palestinian question.

3. Carter later showed that he understood the linkage issue quite well. In *Blood of Abraham*, p. 45, he wrote: "From Begin's point of view, the peace agreement with Egypt was the significant act for Israel; the references to the West Bank and Palestinians were to be finessed. With the bilateral treaty, he removed Egypt's considerable strength from the military equation of the Middle East and thus gave the Israelis renewed freedom to pursue their goals of fortifying and settling the occupied territories and removing perceived threats by preemptive military strikes against some of their neighbors."

ASSESSING CARTER'S ROLE

No one can ever be sure whether Carter could have done more to build the foundations for a broadly based Middle East peace. Hindsight opens vistas that were not so apparent at the time. Still, having participated in the negotiations and having subsequently reflected on them, I think there were avoidable mistakes made along the way.

A judgment on Camp David must begin with what Sadat and Begin, given their views and political constraints, might have been persuaded to accept. And from an American perspective one must ask how well the results served U.S. interests.

Gains for Egypt and Israel

By these standards the Egyptian-Israeli peace treaty looks very good. Egypt recovered its territory and oil fields, and was able to turn some of its energies from the planning of war to the challenge of development. The minor territorial dispute over Taba, a tiny spot of Sinai that the Israelis sought to hold onto, does little to cloud the total achievement.

For Israel, too, the treaty has been valuable. On the strategic level Egypt today poses no military danger. This means that most of Israel's formidable arsenal can be aimed at deterring Syrian threats. A one-front war is a much less alarming prospect for Israel than a two-front war.

Israel has also been able to meet its oil needs by purchasing Egyptian oil, though in the soft oil markets of the mid-1980s that is only a marginal advantage, since ample supplies exist at comparable prices. Elsewhere on the economic side there has been little exchange between the two countries. This lack, as well as the paucity of contact at the human level and the cool state of diplomatic relations, has disappointed many Israelis who had hoped for a warm peace with Egypt. Still, few Israelis would choose to return to a belligerent relationship with Egypt.

U.S. Interests

From the U.S. perspective, peace between Egypt and Israel has been a major achievement. The relations of the United States with both countries have expanded. Compared with the ten years from 1965 to 1975, when U.S. interests suffered from Arab-Israeli tensions and the attendant superpower rivalry, the subsequent ten years, during which Egypt and Israel have been involved in negotiations or formally at peace, have been considerably better for Americans in the Middle East.

But the question still arises of how durable the Egyptian-Israeli treaty will prove to be and whether even more might have been achieved. And that in turn raises the question whether Jordan and the Palestinians might have been brought into the Camp David process as Carter had originally hoped. Few would question that a broader peace, especially one that included the Palestinians, would have been an important buttress for a lasting Egyptian-Israeli peace.

Many would say that nothing more could have been done to open the way for accommodation between Israel and its neighbors to the east. After all, Begin was adamant about never yielding the West Bank and East Jerusalem to anyone under any circumstances. And he had the Israeli cabinet and Knesset fully behind him. As for Sadat, with the best will in the world he could not speak for the Palestinians or make binding commitments on their behalf. He was a staunch advocate of general principles in a situation in which details mattered mightily to the Israelis— and to the Palestinians.

Finally, Carter was also unable to do much for the peace process after the signing of the Egyptian-Israeli treaty. He felt obliged to turn his attention to other unfinished business, and in 1980 the hostage crisis in Iran closed in on him, and he lost his bid for reelection. Carter almost certainly had hoped to work on the Palestinian question in a second term, but he never had the chance.

Avoidable Mistakes

Despite these sobering realities, some significant mistakes could have been avoided and a serious bid for Jordanian and Palestinian involvement in the peace process might have been made in 1978. Their rejection of Camp David had not been immediate, total, or inevitable.

To have improved the prospects for a broader peace, Carter and his aides would have needed to keep their eyes carefully on the political clock. If real headway was to be made, especially after the false starts of 1977 (many of them instructive but politically costly), it had to take place in 1978, the sooner the better. Presidents simply run out of time if they get well into their third year without a big head of steam behind their foreign policy initiatives.

Carter wasted several precious months in 1978, one could argue, with the arms package for Saudi Arabia, Israel, and Egypt. Although he won the fight in Congress, it was a costly and time-consuming battle. The Saudis could have been told in early 1978 that their request was being placed on hold, along with those of Egypt and Israel, until the United States had achieved a breakthrough in the peace negotiations. In retrospect, there is no reason to believe the Saudis would have reacted strongly to such news. And in any event, the sale did not result in their active support for Camp David, nor could it have been expected to do so.

Carter also spent several more months in 1978 on a sterile exercise in diplomacy by questionnaire—which produced little more than a sense of frustration. It probably would have been more useful if Secretary Vance had made one or two trips to the Middle East in the spring of 1978 to explore with the Egyptians and Israelis various formulations for dealing with the West Bank and Gaza. Sadat was ready to work closely with the United States after February 1978, but he needed to remain in almost constant touch with Carter or Vance or he would fly off in new, and often unproductive, directions.

Once Carter had Sadat and Begin with him at Camp David, he should have aimed for a simpler, cleaner document on the issues of the West Bank and Gaza. By following Begin into endless legalistic formulations, Carter and Sadat lost sight of the intended audience, the Palestinians and the Jordanians. For them the details did not disguise the fact that the Camp David Accords avoided all reference to eventual Israeli withdrawal from the West Bank, self-determination, or a freeze on settlements. Instead, the details made it seem as if everything had already been worked out before Jordan and the Palestinians were even invited to join the negotiations. A more general and open-ended set of formulations, followed by serious consultations by Carter and Sadat with King Hussein and with Palestinian leaders, might have had a better chance of success.

No doubt Begin would have resisted any clear-cut statement on Israeli withdrawal from the West Bank and Gaza and self-determination for the Palestinians. But the Americans might have been able to convince Begin to agree that negotiations over the future of the West Bank and Gaza would take place as soon as possible among Israel, Jordan, and representatives of the Palestinians, the only precondition being an acceptance of all the principles of U.N. Resolution 242 and respect for the rights of all the other parties to the negotiations.

Having little more than a formula of this sort, Egypt and Israel, with help from the United States, could have undertaken to develop guidelines for a transitional period for the West Bank and Gaza. The key elements could have been to end the Israeli military government; to hold elections for a Palestinian self-governing authority whose initial powers and responsibilities would be generally defined; and to get an Israeli agreement not to build more settlements in the West Bank and Gaza during the period set for completing negotiations between Egypt and Israel to establish the Palestinian self-government, namely one year from the time of signing the agreement.

None of these elements would have been out of the question for Begin. He would have continued to interpret U.N. Resolution 242 as he always did, but Carter, Sadat, and perhaps eventually Begin's successor could have upheld the conventional interpretation of "territory for peace" on all fronts. Begin would have been reluctant to agree to a freeze on settlements, but he had already accepted a de facto freeze for most of 1978, and it would not have been a great hardship for him to accept a freeze for one more year. In his Saturday night talk with Carter at Camp David, Begin saw his choices as a permanent freeze on Israeli settlements in the West Bank or a three-month freeze. No one tried to obtain a one-year freeze, tied to what became the target date for Egypt and Israel to complete negotiations for establishing the transitional period in the West Bank and Gaza. It might have been worth the effort to do so.

Begin's concern, after all, was that Jews should have the right to live anywhere in Eretz Israel, not that a given number of settlements be established each year. During the interim period, and even beyond, Israel would have been able to hold out for a continuation of some Jewish settlements in the West Bank and Gaza. Even PLO leaders seemed to understand that it was impossible to insist on all Jews leaving the West Bank and Gaza.[4]

Had such a set of guidelines been included in the Camp David Accords, and had Carter and Sadat both made a serious effort to win Jordanian and Palestinian support, a broader peace process might have been launched. But it must be recognized that in 1978 Jordan and the PLO were not on good terms and that Syria would have been strongly opposed to the entire process. So the alternative approach described here would have been a gamble. Still, the odds would have been less daunting than they were for the actual Camp David Accords.

DEVELOPMENTS SINCE CAMP DAVID

Since the signing of the Camp David Accords in September 1978, much has happened to change the prospects for eventual accommodation between Israel and the Palestinians. Some trends lead to the pessimistic conclusion

---

4. See Helena Cobban, *The Palestinian Liberation Organization*, p. 18, where she quotes Khalid al-Hassan of Fatah as saying that some Israeli settlements in the West Bank and Gaza could remain after Palestinians established their authority.

that a negotiated settlement is impossible. Others suggest that a slim opportunity still exists.

By 1985 all the architects of the Camp David Accords had passed from the scene. Israel was governed by a coalition led by Shimon Peres, a man who had spoken openly of the possibility of a "territorial compromise" that would return at least some of the West Bank and Gaza to Jordanian-Palestinian authority.[5] His coalition partners, however, included the Likud, whose leaders were still wedded to the idea that Judea and Samaria must remain permanently under Israeli control.

Egypt, too, had changed leaders, and President Husni Mubarak made it clear that he had no desire to negotiate an autonomy agreement for the West Bank and Gaza with Israel. Instead, he favored bringing Jordan and the Palestinians directly into a dialogue with the United States and eventually with Israel. Egypt was prepared to assume the part of impresario, but preferred not to be at center stage when the play began.

Somewhat ironically, those who shunned Camp David in 1978 were still in positions of authority in the mid-1980s. King Hussein, PLO Chairman Yasir Arafat, and Syrian President Hafiz al-Asad were all part of the diplomatic scene and remained as opposed as ever to Camp David. Jordan and the Palestinians, however, had moved closer to agreement on the idea of a joint role in any future negotiations, and both favored an eventual confederation of Jordan and a Palestinian state. But any negotiations would have to be based on the principle of "territory for peace," not autonomy.

Syria, with a major political victory to its credit in Lebanon in 1983–84, was determined to block any negotiations over the Palestinian issue that did not have the prior approval of Damascus. Asad had declared Arafat persona non grata in Syria after 1984, and the PLO seemed deeply split between the factions allied to Syria and the Fatah leadership of Yasir Arafat and his colleagues. From most indications the Palestinians in the West Bank and Gaza were largely behind Arafat in this debate, but above all were looking for someone who could help bring the Israeli occupation to an end.

American policy, too, had evolved since 1978. After the trauma of the Israeli invasion of Lebanon and the evacuation of the PLO from Beirut, President Reagan made a speech on September 1, 1982, that followed

5. The prospects for "territorial compromise" were clouded by the fact that by 1985 some 40,000 Israelis lived in settlements in the West Bank and Gaza. In addition, over 80,000 lived in what had been Arab Jerusalem before 1967. See Meron Benvenisti, *The West Bank Data Project*; and Usamah Halabi, Aron Turner, and Meron Benvenisti, "Land Alienation in the West Bank."

the broad lines of Camp David, but with some notable additions. In his initiative Reagan emphasized the "territory for peace" formula and the need to bring Jordan and the Palestinians into the negotiating process. In subsequent clarifications Reagan implied that the transitional period of autonomy could be short, and that negotiations on the final status of the West Bank and Gaza could begin immediately. Furthermore, the president undertook to get Israeli agreement to a freeze on settlements if Jordan and the Palestinians would enter negotiations. American views on autonomy also became more precise. The U.S. position was that during the interim period of autonomy for the West Bank and Gaza, the Palestinians should be given substantial control over land and water, and the Palestinians in East Jerusalem should be allowed to vote for the self-governing authority.

None of these developments during the Reagan administration was inconsistent with Camp David, but each had the virtue in Arab eyes of coming with a new label. Unfortunately, the creativity shown by Reagan in repackaging Camp David did not extend to figuring out how to press the peace process forward. By mid-1983 the Reagan initiative seemed to have succumbed, at least for the moment, to the mounting violence in Lebanon. During much of 1985 another round of talks took place involving the Reagan administration and Arab and Israeli leaders, but with little prospect for a breakthrough.

CAMP DAVID: MODEL OR OBSTACLE?

Whatever one may think of the Camp David Accords and the Egyptian-Israeli peace treaty, few would deny that they changed the course of events in the Middle East. With Israel and the largest and most powerful Arab country at peace, the Arab-Israeli conflict and the Palestinian issue took on a fundamentally different character.

Until Sadat's trip to Jerusalem in November 1977, most Arab leaders would have accepted the proposition that there could be no war or peace with Israel without Egypt. In return for their acceptance of Egypt's leadership in the conflict with Israel, other Arab countries expected Egypt not to break ranks and make a separate agreement with Israel.

The leaders of Jordan, Syria, and the Palestinians feared that a separate Egyptian-Israeli accord would leave the Arab side so weak that it could never negotiate successfully with Israel, or mount a credible military threat. The prospect of such a separate deal aroused Arab anxiety when the Camp David Accords were first published. The details of the arrangements for autonomy on the West Bank and Gaza added to the concern, but it was Egypt's final defection from an Arab consensus that was most alarming.

For most Israelis, by contrast, the idea of separating Egypt from the other Arabs was a long-held objective. Without Egypt as a belligerent, Israel could manage to cope with threats from other Arab states. Some Israelis also hoped that Egypt's move toward peace would have a sobering effect on other Arab leaders, convincing them that the best course of action would be to seek their own bilateral accommodation with Israel.

Those on the American side who were most optimistic about Camp David genuinely believed it could be a model for future negotiations between Israel and its other Arab neighbors. First, Camp David proved that negotiations under American auspices could produce an agreement based on the "territory for peace" formula. Second, some thought that peace between Egypt and Israel would gradually reduce Israeli fears and security concerns, thus opening the way for more flexible positions in negotiations with other Arab parties. Third, Carter felt that moderate Arab leaders would see they had no choice but to negotiate with Israel once Egypt had concluded a peace treaty.

Given enough time, some of these assumptions might still be shown to have merit. It is still conceivable, though not likely, that negotiations between Israel and its neighbors may take place and that some elements of the Egyptian-Israeli agreement could be reflected in future peace treaties. If this were to happen, Camp David could be seen as something of a model for Arab-Israeli peace negotiations. American and Egyptian officials have tended to speak of Camp David in those terms.

Other, less optimistic Americans maintained that Camp David would reduce the chances of ever achieving a comprehensive Middle East peace settlement. With Egypt at peace, Israel would have little incentive to make further territorial concessions. Without return of territory, other Arab leaders would have no incentive to make peace with Israel.

One can also argue that Sadat set a very high standard by which other Arab negotiators will be judged. He recovered all of Sinai, with the insignificant exception of Taba. No other Arab leader is likely to be able to recover all the territory his country lost to Israel in the 1967 war. And as time goes on, the amount of territory that Israel might return as the price for peace will diminish. Since the signing of the Camp David Accords, Israel has formally annexed East Jerusalem, extended Israeli law to the Golan Heights, and increased its civilian presence in the West Bank and Gaza. None of these actions will be easy to reverse.

Nor is it easy to imagine other Arab leaders following Sadat's example of dramatically offering Israel peace and fully aligning themselves with the United States. The relatively weak positions of other Arab leaders makes such a course of action risky. In the Arab world Egypt is almost alone in being fairly immune to pressure from other Arab countries. Jordan is much more vulnerable. King Hussein must therefore be much more careful in his dealings with Israel than Sadat was.

This analysis suggests that the Camp David Accords do not provide a model that can be easily copied in future negotiations. The legacy is more complicated. By removing Egypt from the military conflict with Israel, Camp David greatly strengthened Israel's bargaining position vis-à-vis Jordan, Syria, and the Palestinians. So for the foreseeable future, no Arab leader can expect to gain as much from negotiations as Sadat did. This result is precisely what Begin hoped to achieve with Camp David.

Nonetheless, to hold the Camp David Accords primarily responsible for this imbalance between Israel and the Arabs is a mistake. From 1974 on, Sadat had clearly demonstrated that he would not be bound by an Arab consensus. He was moving toward a negotiated agreement with Israel, and it was always an open question whether other Arab leaders would follow in his footsteps. Syria did follow the Egyptian lead with the Syrian-Israeli disengagement agreement of May 1974. But Egypt's leadership in the Arab world was on the wane.

Camp David formalized an existing reality: Egypt, under Sadat's leadership, was not prepared to sacrifice its own national interests for the sake of the other Arabs. Despite a change in style and rhetoric, Sadat's successor has continued the same policy.

If one acknowledges that Egypt is unlikely to revert to the pan-Arab policies of the 1950s, and if the Egyptian-Israeli treaty holds, Jordan, Syria, and the Palestinians will not be able to count the weight of Egypt in the scales of the Arab-Israeli conflict. This weakens the Arab position. But does it make negotiations with Israel impossible?

The answer, it would seem, is that any future negotiations between Israel and an Arab partner will be even more difficult than those that resulted in the Egyptian-Israeli treaty. The balance of power between Israel and the other Arabs indicates that the outcome of negotiations will be heavily to Israel's advantage. Nonetheless, the Camp David experience holds out some hope. Negotiations do create a new political dynamic, sometimes opening avenues that are not apparent at the beginning; the American role can help to tip the balance toward a "territory for peace" outcome; and skill, an adroit sense of timing, and a strategic perspective are important, besides the more objective balance of power, in determining the outcome of negotiations. The cards one is dealt do matter, but so does the talent of the player.

In brief, from the perspective of the mid-1980s, it is too simple to label Camp David as either a model for, or an obstacle to, further Arab-Israeli peace negotiations. One can say, however, that the easiest part of the Arab-Israeli conflict was resolved with the Egyptian-Israeli peace treaty. The rest will be more difficult, perhaps impossible. If and when those negotiations are attempted, some parts of the Camp David approach will be found to be of value, while others will be irrelevant or in need of revision.

A REALISTIC APPROACH TO PEACE

Certain elements of both Camp David and the Reagan initiative are likely to have enduring influence on any future negotiations. For example, the idea of aiming first for an interim agreement is realistic, given the enormous gap between the parties over the possible terms of a final settlement. At the same time an interim agreement needs to be placed within a framework of some basic principles that will govern a final settlement. At a minimum, the "territory for peace" equation of U.N. Resolution 242 and the right of the Palestinians to self-determination within the framework of a Jordanian-Palestinian confederation will have a part in any ultimate agreement. In return, the Jordanians and Palestinians will have to accept specific security arrangements and explicit recognition of Israel.

Jordan and the Palestinians will have to assume the primary responsibility for the details of any negotiation with Israel on the future of the West Bank and Gaza. Egyptian support will help, but Egypt alone cannot go beyond articulating general principles. Somehow Syria's opposition will have to be dealt with. At the least, the Syrians should understand that the future of the Golan Heights could also be addressed in negotiations—though this does not appear to be the highest priority of the regime in Damascus. But to grant the Syrians a veto over negotiations on the Palestinian question would vastly complicate matters and lead to an impasse.

If negotiations between Israel and a Jordanian-Palestinian delegation over the West Bank and Gaza are to have a chance of success, there will have to be some blending of the ideas of "territory for peace" and genuine self-government during a transitional period. Emphasis will have to be given to ending the Israeli military occupation as part of the interim agreement, while at the same time providing for legitimate Israeli security concerns. Cosmetic changes will not be enough to attract Palestinian support. And during both the negotiations and the interim agreement, limits must be placed on Israeli settlements.

As for the Arabs, they will have to recognize that certain objectives are not attainable. Full Israeli withdrawal to the 1967 lines is not a realistic goal; a physical division of Jerusalem is not acceptable to any Israelis; and the dismantling of all existing settlements is not possible. In brief, Jordan and the Palestinians cannot hope to achieve as much as Egypt did. Consequently, many Arabs will feel that negotiations are a trap best avoided.

The only way to bridge the gap between the Israeli and Palestinian positions will be with creative political ideas for which no clear precedents exist. Classical concepts of sovereignty will have to be modified if there is to be a negotiated agreement. Ideas of shared authority, overlapping sovereignty, and mixed regimes will be needed. Citizens of each party will have rights and claims within the other's political systems. Borders will almost certainly have to remain open to the movement of goods and people. The key to finding solutions to these problems will lie with the Israelis, the Palestinians, and their Jordanian partners. With or without a formal agreement, they are fated to live with one another.

If most Israelis or Palestinians are opposed to a peace settlement along these lines, no outside power is likely to be effective in promoting negotiations. But if both communities are divided between "rejectionists" and "moderates," then the role of outsiders, especially the United States, could help to tip the balance one way or the other. It is for this reason that the American role is worth examining, not because the United States can design and impose a blueprint of its own.

THE AMERICAN ROLE

Can the United States still play a part in helping to solve the Palestinian conflict? Many would argue that it cannot and that a posture of benign neglect would be best for all concerned. Most Americans, in any case, do not see a clear link between their national interests and the Palestinian question. What would change if the problem was solved?

The Question of National Interests

In the past the answer to the question of how the United States would benefit from a peace agreement seemed obvious. Without progress toward an Arab-Israeli settlement, there would probably be another round of war between Israel and a group of Arab states. In one way or another, the wars of 1948–49, 1956, 1967, 1973, and 1982 all grew out of the unresolved Palestinian question. The last four involved some degree of U.S.- Soviet confrontation. In each instance, moderate Arab regimes felt on the defensive and were moved to curtail their relations with Washington, if only briefly. In 1973 the Arabs used oil as a political weapon, as an adjunct to the war, and the economic consequences were enormous.

In the mid-1980s, however, the only Arab-Israeli war on the horizon involves Syria, and few think that a step-by-step approach to solving the Palestinian question will lessen the dangers of that war. Moreover, the oil weapon is no longer credible. And the Soviets seem to be having little success in turning the frustrations of the Palestinians to their advantage within the region. As a result, few Americans see much reason to spend time and energy on finding a diplomatic solution to the Palestinian question.

To find a compelling reason for American leadership requires a longer perspective than most American administrations seem to have. For example, one has to look at the consequences for the Egyptian-Israeli-American triangular relationship if there is no further movement toward peace. At a minimum, the Egyptian-Israeli relationship would remain cool, which would make it difficult for the United States to maintain close ties to Egypt. Among other things, Congress would see little reason to be generous to Egypt unless the promise of peace with Israel was being fulfilled. If at some point Egypt and Israel reverted to a position of belligerency, the United States would see its substantial investment in Egypt quickly dry up. At stake is not only peace in the Middle East and the risk of U.S.-Soviet confrontation there, but also the strategic advantages that the United States has gained from access to Egyptian territory and facilities as it seeks to protect interests elsewhere in the region.

Another concern for Americans should be the growth of political extremism in the Middle East. This phenomenon is not exclusively Shiite, though the most impressive political successes of Muslim militancy have come in Iran and Lebanon among the Shia. But in Saudi Arabia and Egypt, Sunni Muslim extremists have also challenged the prevailing political order. Insofar as the current regimes appear to have failed to deliver on their promises of development, social justice, and an equitable settlement of the Palestinian question, they become vulnerable to domestic criticism. A solution to the Palestinian question will not guarantee a moderate political order in the Arab world, but it could be a positive development.

Finally, short-term realities with respect to oil and Soviet influence should not blind Americans to longer-term dangers. By the mid-1990s oil from the Gulf could again be in great demand. And even sooner, under their new leadership the Soviets might begin to regain influence in the region by playing on genuine Arab grievances associated with the Palestinian question and the conflict with Israel.

Admittedly, this line of reasoning rests on many assumptions. There is no way to prove that American interests will or will not be well served by seeking a solution to the Palestinian question. Diplomats are not allowed the luxury of such certainties. So unless the sense of crisis becomes compelling, no president will find it easy to explain to the American public why he is spending time and resources on this problem.

Credibility on the Line

There is, however, an intangible consideration that should be taken into account in assessing the consequences for the United States of doing nothing to settle the Palestinian question. The reputation of the United States, its credibility, is involved because of the promise it made in the Camp David Accords to be a full partner in seeking a fair solution to the Palestinian question. Needless to say, great and small powers ignore such promises regularly, but a price can be paid for doing so. After the disasters for American policy in Iran in 1979 and Lebanon in 1983, the United States badly needs to refurbish its credentials in the Middle East. Walking away from the Palestinian question will simply reinforce the impression of American weakness and inconsistency, the legacy of recent debacles.

Middle East realities, of course, combined with the facts of American politics, make it difficult for any president to play a positive role in resolving the Palestinian-Israeli conflict. But the United States is inevitably involved in the region because of the more than $5 billion in economic and military aid that flows to Egypt and Israel each year, in addition to vast quantities of military equipment. Americans cannot be bystanders. They can try to buttress, and sometimes change, the status quo in the region by their policies. They can also try to resolve some of the outstanding sources of tension in the region. But they cannot maintain that they are uninterested and without any means of influence.

Lessons from Camp David

If progress can still be made on the Palestinian question, clearly the American role will be important. But the parties to the conflict will themselves have to assume a major burden in any negotiations. This is one lesson of Camp David. The key decisions are not made in Washington. The Americans can, however, help to make it easier for those decisions to be made. The record shows that direct negotiations, without American involvement, have had little success.

A second lesson of Camp David is that only the president and the secretary of state have much clout with the Middle East parties. Special envoys rarely produce results. No one in the Middle East will show his cards to anyone on the American side other than the highest authority. Kissinger and Carter may have spoiled Middle Easterners by lavishing attention on them. Now nothing less seems to produce results. If the Americans are to get involved, it cannot be halfheartedly or without full presidential attention.

Jimmy Carter has shown that commitment, tenacity, and sincerity can count for much in the diplomacy of the Middle East. These are qualities that will have to be brought to bear in any future negotiations if the American role is to be played well.

One can draw other conclusions from Carter's experience. For instance, a president must look after his domestic political constituency. If he loses support in Congress and in public opinion, he cannot be an effective mediator in complex foreign policy issues. No president has unchallenged authority in foreign affairs, but the room for maneuver can be affected by the skill with which the president tends to his political base. Carter was generally inattentive to that base, and in the end was unable to win reelection. Even before that, however, his authority had been badly eroded, and he was unable to pursue the Camp David Accords with full vigor.

A third lesson of Camp David is that negotiations require strategic thinking. Much more is involved than simply encouraging reluctant parties to talk to one another. Real influence has to be wielded in order to get Arabs and Israelis to modify their positions. Power is at the core of negotiations. A skillful blending of inducements and pressures is central to playing the role of mediator. Timing is of the essence.

Carter was not a particularly good strategist. He had trouble setting priorities. If something needed doing, he wanted to get directly involved immediately. He did not always recognize the connections among issues. He was overambitious at the start of his presidency; he took on too many problems; and he had trouble delegating authority. He was also impatient for results, which was understandable given his political calendar, but consequently he showed his hand too readily and was too quick to shift gears if one approach was not working. His moves were therefore sometimes poorly planned. His diplomacy had an improvised quality, especially in the first year.

The Problem of Time

For any president a structural problem grows out of the cycles of the American political system. Since time is short to produce results, priority is often given to immediate problems, to the appearance of rapid progress. It is difficult for an activist president to accept the advice that the time is not ripe for a new initiative, that the parties are not ready. This impatience to show results is often a diplomatic liability, one that weakens the hand of a president who must constantly be able to justify his policies before a critical Congress and public opinion. Foreign leaders who are less constrained by the political calendar, who can afford to be more patient, or who have steadier nerves can exploit this feature of the president's position to their advantage.

The president needs to combine a realistic appreciation of the limited time available, to create a proper sense of urgency, while simultaneously appearing to be steady and patient, as if time did not matter so much after all. Carter could not find this balance, and that reduced his effectiveness as a mediator, especially in dealing with the Israelis, for whom time was not such a problem. When he felt that the entire Egyptian-Israeli peace treaty could be negotiated within two weeks, he said so. Begin, for one, would not be rushed. He realized that Carter's impatience signaled a willingness to pay a high price to reach an agreement, including added pressure on Egypt for concessions if that proved to be the only way to clinch the treaty.

Carter's impatience seemed to stem from his beliefs that conflicts were the result of misunderstandings and that the solution lay in building trust more than wielding power. He had a hard time accepting the fact that some issues could not be resolved through reason and compromise. He had seen a massive social change take place in the American south in his own lifetime, and he was unwilling to believe that comparable change could not take place in the Middle East. It was an appealing vision, but it made him feel frustrated when things moved slowly. At such moments he would talk as if he were ready to abandon his involvement in Middle East diplomacy. The result was mixed signals: sometimes Carter conveyed a sense of immediacy; on other occasions he seemed to have little time for the complexities of the Middle East.

Carter's experience in office confirms the point that time is short for a president to make his mark on Middle East diplomacy. Because of the workings of the American political system, the first two years of a presidential term are about the only period when complex initiatives can be launched. By the third year pressure is mounting on the president to turn his attention to domestic issues and to bring foreign policy efforts to a conclusion one way or the other. Inevitably, this undermines the president's leadership in foreign policy in the last part of his term.

Qualities of Leadership

In summary, then, an American president, if he is to tackle the Arab-Israeli conflict with hope for success, must combine some remarkable qualities. Carter brought the necessary sense of dedication, determination, and decency, and he achieved impressive results. His willingness to become personally involved in the negotiations was important to the outcome.

President Nixon, with Henry Kissinger's assistance, brought to the task a strategic perspective that Carter often lacked. Although some serious mistakes were made, especially in the 1969–71 period, after the October 1973 war this strategic perspective, coupled with skillful negotiating technique, launched the process that ultimately yielded the Egyptian-Israeli peace treaty.

But Carter and Nixon, in quite different ways, were both flawed as politicians, and their careers were cut short as a result. Unless a president can preserve his domestic base, unless he can explain his policies to the American people, and unless he can bring Congress with him, his dedication, his strategic insight, and his knowledge of the issues will count for little. It is in this area of communicating to the American public and maintaining popular support that Ronald Reagan has proved himself a master.

Presidents do matter, and they can leave their mark on history, including the tangled history of the Middle East. But to do so in the future, given the intractability of the issues, they will have to combine qualities of leadership that rarely come together in one person. And if

Americans aspire to play a major role in the world, they will have to choose leaders with vision, political skill, and a sense of diplomatic strategy. Without all three qualities, the president will be unable to overcome the constraints imposed by both the American political system and the realities of Middle East politics. Foreign policy will then most likely be reactive, lacking in consistency, disjointed, and geared to the immediate rather than the important. This would ensure, among other things, that the promise of the Camp David Accords would remain a dead letter.

APPENDIX A

U.N. Resolutions 242 and 338

U.N. RESOLUTION 242, NOVEMBER 22, 1967

The Security Council,

Expressing its continuing concern with the grave situation in the Middle East,

Emphasizing the inadmissibility of the acquisition of territory by war and the need to work for a just and lasting peace in which every State in the area can live in security,

Emphasizing further that all Member States in their acceptance of the Charter of the United Nations have undertaken a commitment to act in accordance with Article 2 of the Charter.

1. *Affirms* that the fulfillment of Charter principles requires the establishment of a just and lasting peace in the Middle East which should include the application of both the following principles:

(i) Withdrawal of Israeli armed forces from territories occupied in the recent conflict;

(ii) Termination of all claims or states of belligerency and respect for and acknowledgement of the sovereignty, territorial integrity and political independence of every State in the area and their right to live in peace within secure and recognized boundaries free from threats or acts of force;

2. *Affirms further* the necessity:

(a) For guaranteeing freedom of navigation through international waterways in the area;

(b) For achieving a just settlement of the refugee problem;

(c) For guaranteeing the territorial inviolability and political independence of every State in the area, through measures including the establishment of demilitarized zones;

3. *Requests* the Secretary-General to designate a Special Representative to proceed to the Middle East to establish and maintain contacts with the States concerned in order to promote agreement and assist efforts to

achieve a peaceful and accepted settlement in accordance with the provisions and principles of this resolution;

4. *Requests* the Secretary-General to report to the Security Council on the progress of the efforts of the Special Representative as soon as possible.

U.N. RESOLUTION 338, OCTOBER 22, 1973

The Security Council

1. *Calls upon* all parties to the present fighting to cease all firing and terminate all military activity immediately, no later than 12 hours after the moment of the adoption of this decision, in the positions they now occupy;

2. *Calls upon* the parties concerned to start immediately after the cease-fire the implementation of Security Council Resolution 242 (1967) in all of its parts;

3. *Decides that*, immediately and concurrently with the cease-fire, negotiations shall start between the parties concerned under appropriate auspices aimed at establishing a just and durable peace in the Middle East.

Joint Communiqué by the Governments of the United States and the Union of Soviet Socialist Republics, October 1, 1977

Having exchanged views regarding the unsafe situation which remains in the Middle East, U.S. Secretary of State Cyrus Vance and Member of the Politbureau of the Central Committee of the CPSU, Minister for Foreign Affairs of the U.S.S.R. A.A. Gromyko have the following statement to make on behalf of their countries, which are cochairmen of the Geneva Peace Conference on the Middle East:

1. Both governments are convinced that vital interests of the peoples of this area, as well as the interests of strengthening peace and international security in general, urgently dictate the necessity of achieving, as soon as possible, a just and lasting settlement of the Arab-Israeli conflict. This settlement should be comprehensive, incorporating all parties concerned and all questions.

The United States and the Soviet Union believe that, within the framework of a comprehensive settlement of the Middle East problem, all specific questions of the settlement should be resolved, including such key issues as withdrawal of Israeli Armed Forces from territories occupied in the 1967 conflict; the resolution of the Palestinian question, including insuring the legitimate rights of the Palestinian people; termination of the state of war and establishment of normal peaceful relations on the basis of mutual recognition of the principles of sovereignty, territorial integrity, and political independence.

The two governments believe that, in addition to such measures for insuring the security of the borders between Israel and the neighboring Arab states as the establishment of demilitarized zones and the agreed stationing in them of U.N. troops or observers, international guarantees of such borders as well as of the observance of the terms of the settlement can also be established should the contracting parties so desire. The

---

The text comes from "U.S., U.S.S.R. Issue Statement on the Middle East," *Department of State Bulletin*, vol. 77 (November 7, 1977), pp. 639–40. The statement was issued in New York City.

United States and the Soviet Union are ready to participate in these guarantees, subject to their constitutional processes.

2. The United States and the Soviet Union believe that the only right and effective way for achieving a fundamental solution to all aspects of the Middle East problem in its entirety is negotiations within the framework of the Geneva peace conference, specially convened for these purposes, with participation in its work of the representatives of all the parties involved in the conflict including those of the Palestinian people, and legal and contractual formalization of the decisions reached at the conference.

In their capacity as cochairmen of the Geneva conference, the United States and the U.S.S.R. affirm their intention, through joint efforts and in their contacts with the parties concerned, to facilitate in every way the resumption of the work of the conference not later than December 1977. The cochairmen note that there still exist several questions of a procedural and organizational nature which remain to be agreed upon by the participants to the conference.

3. Guided by the goal of achieving a just political settlement in the Middle East and of eliminating the explosive situation in this area of the world, the United States and the U.S.S.R. appeal to all the parties in the conflict to understand the necessity for careful consideration of each other's legitimate rights and interests and to demonstrate mutual readiness to act accordingly.

President Anwar Sadat's Address
to the Israeli Knesset, November 20, 1977

In the name of God, Mr. Speaker of the Knesset, ladies and gentlemen, allow me first to thank deeply the Speaker of the Knesset for affording me this opportunity to address you. . . .

I come to you today on solid ground to shape a new life and to establish peace. We all love this land, the land of God, we all, Moslems, Christians and Jews, all worship God. . . .

I do not blame all those who received my decision when I announced it to the entire world before the Egyptian People's Assembly. I do not blame all those who received my decision with surprise and even with amazement, some gripped even by violent surprise. Still others interpreted it as political, to camouflage my intentions of launching a new war.

I would go so far as to tell you that one of my aides at the presidential office contacted me at a late hour following my return home from the People's Assembly and sounded worried as he asked me: "Mr. President, what would be our reaction if Israel actually extended an invitation to you?"

I replied calmly: "I would accept it immediately. I have declared that I would go to the end of the earth. I would go to Israel, for I want to put before the people of Israel all the facts. . . ." No one could have ever conceived that the president of the biggest Arab state, which bears the heaviest burden and the main responsibility pertaining to the cause of war and peace in the Middle East, should declare his readiness to go to the land of the adversary while we were still in a state of war.

We all still bear the consequences of four fierce wars waged within 30 years. All this at the time when the families of the 1973 October war are still mourning under the cruel pain of bereavement of father, son, husband and brother.

As I have already declared, I have not consulted as far as this decision

The text has been slightly edited from the version published in the *New York Times*, November 21, 1977.

is concerned with any of my colleagues or brothers, the Arab heads of state or the confrontation states.

Most of those who contacted me following the declaration of this decision expressed their objection because of the feeling of utter suspicion and absolute lack of confidence between the Arab states and the Palestine people on the one hand and Israel on the other that still surges in us all.

Many months in which peace could have been brought about have been wasted over differences and fruitless discussions on the procedure of convening the Geneva conference. All have shared suspicion and absolute lack of confidence.

But to be absolutely frank with you, I took this decision after long thought, knowing that it constitutes a great risk, for God Almighty has made it my fate to assume responsibility on behalf of the Egyptian people, to share in the responsibility of the Arab nation, the main duty of which, dictated by responsibility, is to exploit all and every means in a bid to save my Egyptian Arab people and the pan-Arab nation from the horrors of new suffering and destructive wars, the dimensions of which are foreseen only by God Himself.

After long thinking, I was convinced that the obligation of responsibility before God and before the people make it incumbent upon me that I should go to the far corners of the world, even to Jerusalem to address members of the Knesset and acquaint them with all the facts surging in me, then I would let you decide for yourselves. . . .

Ladies and gentlemen, there are moments in the lives of nations and peoples when it is incumbent upon those known for their wisdom and clarity of vision to survey the problem, with all its complexities and vain memories, in a bold drive towards new horizons.

Those who like us are shouldering the same responsibilities entrusted to us are the first who should have the courage to make determining decisions that are consonant with the magnitude of the circumstances. We must all rise above all forms of obsolete theories of superiority, and the most important thing is never to forget that infallibility is the prerogative of God alone.

If I said that I wanted to avert from all the Arab people the horrors of shocking and destructive wars I must sincerely declare before you that I have the same feelings and bear the same responsibility towards all and every man on earth, and certainly towards the Israeli people.

Any life that is lost in war is a human life be it that of an Arab or an

Israeli. A wife who becomes a widow is a human being entitled to a happy family life, whether she be an Arab or an Israeli.

Innocent children who are deprived of the care and compassion of their parents are ours. They are ours, be they living on Arab or Israeli land.

They command our full responsibility to afford them a comfortable life today and tomorrow.

For the sake of them all, for the sake of the lives of all our sons and brothers, for the sake of affording our communities the opportunity to work for the progress and happiness of man, feeling secure and with the right to a dignified life, for the generations to come, for a smile on the face of every child born in our land, for all that I have taken my decision to come to you, despite all the hazards, to deliver my address.

I have shouldered the prerequisites of the historic responsibility and therefore I declared on Feb. 4, 1971, that I was willing to sign a peace agreement with Israel. This was the first declaration made by a responsible Arab official since the outbreak of the Arab-Israeli conflict. Motivated by all these factors dictated by the responsibilities of leadership, on Oct. 16, 1973, before the Egyptian People's Assembly, I called for an international conference to establish permanent peace based on justice. I was not heard.

I was in the position of a man pleading for peace or asking for a cease-fire. Motivated by the duties of history and leadership, I signed the first disengagement agreement, followed by the second disengagement agreement at Sinai.

Then we proceeded, trying both open and closed doors in a bid to find a certain road leading to a durable and just peace.

We opened our heart to the peoples of the entire world to make them understand our motivations and objectives and actually to convince them of the fact that we are advocates of justice and peacemakers. Motivated by all these factors, I also decided to come to you with an open mind and an open heart and with a conscious determination so that we might establish permanent peace based on justice. . . .

Ladies and gentlemen, let us be frank with each other. Using straightforward words and a clear conception with no ambiguity, let us be frank with each other today while the entire world, both East and West, follows these unparalleled moments, which could prove to be a radical turning point in the history of this part of the world if not in the history of the world as a whole.

Let us be frank with each other, let us be frank with each other as we answer this important question.

How can we achieve permanent peace based on justice? Well, I have come to you carrying my clear and frank answer to this big question, so that the people in Israel as well as the entire world may hear it. . . .

Before I proclaim my answer, I wish to assure you that in my clear and frank answer I am availing myself of a number of facts that no one can deny.

The first fact is that no one can build his happiness at the expense of the misery of others.

The second fact: never have I spoken, nor will I ever speak, with two tongues; never have I adopted, nor will I ever adopt, two policies. I never deal with anyone except in one tongue, one policy and with one face.

The third fact: direct confrontation is the nearest and most successful method to reach a clear objective.

The fourth fact: the call for permanent and just peace based on respect for United Nations resolutions has now become the call of the entire world. It has become the expression of the will of the international community, whether in official capitals where policies are made and decisions taken, or at the level of the world public opinion, which influences policymaking and decision-taking.

The fifth fact, and this is probably the clearest and most prominent, is that the Arab nation, in its drive for permanent peace based on justice, does not proceed from a position of weakness. On the contrary, it has the power and stability for a sincere will for peace.

The Arab declared intention stems from an awareness prompted by a heritage of civilization, that to avoid an inevitable disaster that will befall us, you and the whole world, there is no alternative to the establishment of permanent peace based on justice, peace that is not swayed by suspicion or jeopardized by ill intentions.

In the light of these facts, which I meant to place before you the way I see them, I would also wish to warn you, in all sincerity I warn you, against some thoughts that could cross your minds.

Frankness makes it incumbent upon me to tell you the following:

First, I have not come here for a separate agreement between Egypt and Israel. This is not part of the policy of Egypt. The problem is not that of Egypt and Israel.

An interim peace between Egypt and Israel, or between any Arab confrontation state and Israel, will not bring permanent peace based on justice in the entire region.

Rather, even if peace between all the confrontation states and Israel were achieved in the absence of a just solution of the Palestinian problem, never will there be that durable and just peace upon which the entire world insists.

Second, I have not come to you to seek a partial peace, namely to terminate the state of belligerency at this stage and put off the entire problem to a subsequent stage. This is not the radical solution that would steer us to permanent peace.

Equally, I have not come to you for a third disengagement agreement in Sinai or in Golan or the West Bank.

For this would mean that we are merely delaying the ignition of the fuse. It would also mean that we are lacking the courage to face peace, that we are too weak to shoulder the burdens and responsibilities of a durable peace based upon justice.

I have come to you so that together we should build a durable peace based on justice to avoid the shedding of one single drop of blood by both sides. It is for this reason that I have proclaimed my readiness to go to the farthest corner of the earth.

Here I would go back to the big question.

How can we achieve a durable peace based on justice? In my opinion, and I declare it to the whole world, from this forum, the answer is neither difficult nor is it impossible despite long years of feuds, blood, faction, strife, hatreds and deep-rooted animosity. . . .

You want to live with us, in this part of the world.

In all sincerity I tell you we welcome you among us with full security and safety. This in itself is a tremendous turning point, one of the landmarks of a decisive historical change. We used to reject you. We had our reasons and our fears, yes.

We refused to meet with you, anywhere, yes.

We were together in international conferences and organizations and our representatives did not, and still do not, exchange greetings with you. Yes. This has happened and is still happening.

It is also true that we used to set as a precondition for any negotiations with you a mediator who would meet separately with each party.

Yes. Through this procedure the talks of the first and second disengagement agreements took place.

Our delegates met in the first Geneva conference without exchanging a direct word, yes, this has happened.

Yet today I tell you, and I declare it to the whole world, that we accept to live with you in permanent peace based on justice. We do not want to encircle you or be encircled ourselves by destructive missiles ready for launching, nor by the shells of grudges and hatreds.

I have announced on more than one occasion that Israel has become a fait accompli, recognized by the world, and that the two superpowers have undertaken the responsibility for its security and the defense of its existence. As we really and truly seek peace we really and truly welcome you to live among us in peace and security.

There was a huge wall between us that you tried to build up over a quarter of a century but it was destroyed in 1973. It was the wall of an implacable and escalating psychological warfare.

It was a wall of the fear of the force that could sweep the entire Arab nation. It was a wall of propaganda that we were a nation reduced to immobility. Some of you have gone as far as to say that even for 50 years to come, the Arabs will not regain their strength. It was a wall that always threatened with a long arm that could reach and strike anywhere. It was a wall that warned us of extermination and annihilation if we tried to use our legitimate rights to liberate the occupied territories.

Together we have to admit that that wall fell and collapsed in 1973. Yet, there remains another wall. This wall constitutes a psychological barrier between us, a barrier of suspicion, a barrier of rejection; a barrier of fear, of deception, a barrier of hallucination without any action, deed or decision.

A barrier of distorted and eroded interpretation of every event and statement. It is this psychological barrier that I described in official statements as constituting 70 percent of the whole problem.

Today, through my visit to you, I ask why don't we stretch out our hands with faith and sincerity so that together we might destroy this barrier? Why shouldn't our and your will meet with faith and sincerity so that together we might remove all suspicion of fear, betrayal and bad intentions?

Why don't we stand together with the courage of men and the boldness of heroes who dedicate themselves to a sublime aim? Why don't we stand together with the same courage and daring to erect a huge edifice of peace?

An edifice that builds and does not destroy. An edifice that serves as a beacon for generations to come with the human message for construction, development and the dignity of man.

Ladies and gentlemen, to tell you the truth, peace cannot be worth its name unless it is based on justice and not on the occupation of the land of others. It would not be right for you to demand for yourselves what you deny to others. With all frankness and in the spirit that has prompted me to come to you today, I tell you you have to give up once and for all the dreams of conquest and give up the belief that force is the best method for dealing with the Arabs.

You should clearly understand the lesson of confrontation between you and us. Expansion does not pay. To speak frankly, our land does not yield itself to bargaining, it is not even open to argument. . . .

We cannot accept any attempt to take away or accept to seek one inch of it nor can we accept the principle of debating or bargaining over it.

I sincerely tell you also that before us today lies the appropriate chance for peace. If we are really serious in our endeavor for peace, it is a chance that may never come again. It is a chance that if lost or wasted, the resulting slaughter would bear the curse of humanity and of history.

What is peace for Israel? It means that Israel lives in the region with her Arab neighbors in security and safety. Is that logical? I say yes. It means that Israel lives within its borders, secure against any aggression. Is that logical? And I say yes. It means that Israel obtains all kinds of guarantees that will ensure these two factors. To this demand, I say yes.

Beyond that we declare that we accept all the international guarantees you envisage and accept. We declare that we accept all the guarantees you want from the two superpowers or from either of them or from the Big Five or from some of them. Once again, I declare clearly and unequivocally that we agree to any guarantees you accept, because in return we shall receive the same guarantees.

In short then, when we ask what is peace for Israel, the answer would be that Israel lives within her borders, among her Arab neighbors in safety and security, within the framework of all the guarantees she accepts and that are offered to her.

But, how can this be achieved? How can we reach this conclusion that would lead us to permanent peace based on justice? There are facts that should be faced with courage and clarity. There are Arab territories that Israel has occupied and still occupies by force. We insist on complete withdrawal from these territories, including Arab Jerusalem.

I have come to Jerusalem, the city of peace, which will always remain as a living embodiment of coexistence among believers of the three religions. It is inadmissible that anyone should conceive the special status of the city of Jerusalem within the framework of annexation or expansionism. It should be a free and open city for all believers.

Above all, this city should not be severed from those who have made it their abode for centuries. Instead of reviving the precedent of the Crusades, we should revive the spirit of Omar Ibn al-Khattab and Saladin, namely the spirit of tolerance and respect for right.

The holy shrines of Islam and Christianity are not only places of worship but a living testimony of our interrupted presence here. Politically, spiritually and intellectually, here let us make no mistake about the importance and reverence we Christians and Moslems attach to Jerusalem.

Let me tell you without the slightest hesitation that I have not come to you under this roof to make a request that your troops evacuate the occupied territories. Complete withdrawal from the Arab territories occupied after 1967 is a logical and undisputed fact. Nobody should plead for that. Any talk about permanent peace based on justice and any move to ensure our coexistence in peace and security in this part of the world would become meaningless while you occupy Arab territories by force of arms.

For there is no peace that could be built on the occupation of the land of others, otherwise it would not be a serious peace. Yet this is a foregone conclusion that is not open to the passion of debate if intentions are sincere or if endeavors to establish a just and durable peace for our and for your generations to come are genuine.

As for the Palestine cause, nobody could deny that it is the crux of the entire problem. Nobody in the world could accept today slogans propagated here in Israel, ignoring the existence of a Palestinian people and questioning even their whereabouts. Because the Palestine people and their legitimate rights are no longer denied today by anybody; that is nobody who has the ability of judgment can deny or ignore it. It is an acknowledged fact, perceived by the world community, both in the East and in the West, with support and recognition in international documents and official statements. It is of no use to anybody to turn deaf ears to its resounding voice, which is being heard day and night, or to overlook its historical reality.

Even the United States of America, your first ally, which is absolutely committed to safeguard Israel's security and existence and which offered and still offers Israel every moral, material and military support. I say, even the United States has opted to face up to reality and admit that the

Palestinian people are entitled to legitimate rights and that the Palestine problem is the cause and essence of the conflict and that so long as it continues to be unresolved, the conflict will continue to aggravate, reaching new dimensions.

In all sincerity I tell you that there can be no peace without the Palestinians. It is a grave error of unpredictable consequences to overlook or brush aside this cause.

I shall not indulge in past events such as the Balfour Declaration 60 years ago. You are well acquainted with the relevant text. If you have found the moral and legal justification to set up a national home on a land that did not all belong to you, it is incumbent upon you to show understanding of the insistence of the people of Palestine for establishment once again of a state on their land. When some extremists ask the Palestinians to give up the sublime objective, this in fact means asking them to renounce their identity and every hope for the future.

I hail the Israeli voices that called for the recognition of the Palestinian people's right to achieve and safeguard peace.

Here I tell you, ladies and gentlemen, that it is no use to refrain from recognizing the Palestinian people and their right to statehood as their right of return. We, the Arabs, have faced this experience before with you. And with the reality of the Israeli existence, the struggle that took us from war to war, from victims to more victims, until you and we have today reached the edge of a horrible abyss and a terrifying disaster unless, together, we seize this opportunity today of a durable peace based on justice.

You have to face reality bravely, as I have done. There can never be any solution to a problem by evading it or turning a deaf ear to it. Peace cannot last if attempts are made to impose fantasy concepts on which the world has turned its back and announced its unanimous call for the respect of rights and facts. . . .

Direct confrontation and straightforwardness are the shortcuts and the most successful way to reach a clear objective. Direct confrontation concerning the Palestinian problem and tackling it in one single language with a view to achieving a durable and just peace lie in the establishment of that peace. With all the guarantees you demand, there should be no fear of a newly born state that needs the assistance of all countries of the world.

When the bells of peace ring there will be no hands to beat the drums of war. Even if they existed, they would be stilled.

Conceive with me a peace agreement in Geneva that we would herald to a world thirsting for peace. A peace agreement based on the following points:

—Ending the occupation of the Arab territories occupied in 1967.

—Achievement of the fundamental rights of the Palestinian people and their right to self-determination, including their right to establish their own state.

—The right of all states in the area to live in peace within their boundaries, their secure boundaries, which will be secured and guaranteed through procedures to be agreed upon, which will provide appropriate security to international boundaries in addition to appropriate international guarantees.

—Commitment of all states in the region to administer the relations among them in accordance with the objectives and principles of the United Nations Charter. Particularly the principles concerning the nonuse of force and a solution of differences among them by peaceful means.

—Ending the state of belligerence in the region.

Ladies and gentlemen, peace is not a mere endorsement of written lines. Rather it is a rewriting of history. Peace is not a game of calling for peace to defend certain whims or hide certain admissions. Peace in its essence is a dire struggle against all and every ambition and whim.

Perhaps the example taken and experienced, taken from ancient and modern history, teaches that missiles, warships and nuclear weapons cannot establish security. Instead they destroy what peace and security build.

For the sake of our peoples and for the sake of the civilization made by man, we have to defend man everywhere against rule by the force of arms so that we may endow the rule of humanity with all the power of the values and principles that further the sublime position of mankind.

Allow me to address my call from this rostrum to the people of Israel. I pledge myself with true and sincere words to every man, woman and child in Israel. I tell them, from the Egyptian people who bless this sacred mission of peace, I convey to you the message of peace of the Egyptian people, who do not harbor fanaticism and whose sons, Moslems, Christians and Jews, live together in a state of cordiality, love and tolerance.

This is Egypt, whose people have entrusted me with their sacred message. A message of security, safety and peace to every man, woman and child in Israel. I say, encourage your leadership to struggle for peace. Let all endeavors be channeled towards building a huge stronghold for peace instead of building destructive rockets.

Introduce to the entire world the image of the new man in this area so that he might set an example to the man of our age, the man of peace everywhere. Ring the bells for your sons. Tell them that those wars were the last of wars and the end of sorrows. Tell them that we are entering upon a new beginning, a new life, a life of love, prosperity, freedom and peace.

You, sorrowing mother, you, widowed wife, you, the son who lost a brother or a father, all the victims of wars, fill the air and space with recitals of peace, fill bosoms and hearts with the aspirations of peace. Make a reality that blossoms and lives. Make hope a code of conduct and endeavor. . . .

I have chosen to set aside all precedents and traditions known by warring countries. In spite of the fact that occupation of Arab territories is still there, the declaration of my readiness to proceed to Israel came as a great surprise that stirred many feelings and confounded many minds. Some of them even doubted its intent.

Despite all that, the decision was inspired by all the clarity and purity of belief and with all the true passions of my people's will and intentions, and I have chosen this road, considered by many to be the most difficult road.

I have chosen to come to you with an open heart and an open mind. I have chosen to give this great impetus to all international efforts exerted for peace. I have chosen to present to you, in your own home, the realities, devoid of any scheme or whim. Not to maneuver, or win a round, but for us to win together, the most dangerous of rounds embattled in modern history, the battle of permanent peace based on justice.

It is not my battle alone. Nor is it the battle of the leadership in Israel alone. It is the battle of all and every citizen in all our territories, whose right it is to live in peace. It is the commitment of conscience and responsibility in the hearts of millions.

When I put forward this initiative, many asked what is it that I conceived as possible to achieve during this visit and what my expectations were. And as I answer the questions, I announce before you that I have not thought of carrying out this initiative from the precepts of what could be achieved during this visit. And I have come here to deliver a message. I have delivered the message and may God be my witness. . . .

Egyptian Proposal at Camp David

FRAMEWORK FOR THE COMPREHENSIVE PEACE SETTLEMENT OF THE MIDDLE EAST PROBLEM

Following: The historic initiative of President SADAT which rekindled the hopes of all nations for a better future for mankind.

In view of the firm determination of the peoples of the Middle East, together with all peace-loving nations, to put an end to the unhappy past, spare this generation and the generations to come the scourge of War and open a new chapter in their history ushering in an era of mutual respect and understanding.

Desirous to make the Middle East, the cradle of civilization and the birthplace of all Divine missions, a shining model for coexistence and cooperation among nations.

Determined to revive the great tradition of tolerance and mutual acceptance free from prejudice and discrimination.

Determined to conduct their relations in accordance with the provisions of the Charter of the United Nations and the accepted norms of international law and legitimacy.

Committed to adhere to the letter and spirit of the Universal Declaration of Human Rights.

Desirous to develop between them good-neighborly relations in accordance with the Declaration of Principles of International Law Concerning Friendly Relations and Cooperation Among States in Accordance with the Charter of the United Nations.

Bearing in mind that the establishment of peace and good-neighborly relations should be founded upon legitimacy, justice, equality and respect for fundamental rights and that good neighbors should demonstrate, in their acts and claims, a strict adherence to the rule of law and a genuine

The complete Arabic text can be found in Muhammad Ibrahim Kamil, *The Lost Peace in the Camp David Accords*, pp. 629–34.

willingness to assume their mutual obligation to refrain from any infringement upon each other's sovereignty or territorial integrity.

Convinced that military occupation and/or the denial of other peoples' rights and legitimate aspirations to live and develop freely are incompatible with the spirit of peace.

Considering the vital interests of all the peoples of the Middle East as well as the universal interest that exists in strengthening World Peace and security.

Article 1

The Parties express their determination to reach a comprehensive settlement of the Middle East problem through the conclusion of peace treaties on the basis of the full implementation of Security Council Resolutions 242 and 338 in all their parts.

Article 2

The Parties agree that the establishment of a just and lasting peace among them requires the fulfillment of the following:

First: Withdrawal of Israel from the occupied territories in accordance with the principle of inadmissibility of the acquisition of territory by War.

In Sinai and the Golan, withdrawal shall take place to the international boundaries between mandated Palestine and Egypt and Syria respectively.

In the West Bank, Israel shall withdraw to the demarcation lines of the 1949 Armistice Agreement between Israel and Jordan with such insubstantial alterations as might be mutually accepted by the Parties concerned. It is to be understood that such alterations should not reflect the weight of conquest. Security measures shall be introduced in accordance with the provisions below mentioned with a view to meeting the Parties' legitimate concern for security and safeguarding the rights and aspirations of the Palestinian people.

Withdrawal from the Gaza Strip shall take place to the demarcation lines of the 1949 Armistice Agreement between Egypt and Israel.

Israeli withdrawal shall commence immediately after the signing of the peace treaties and shall be completed according to a time-table to be agreed upon within the period referred to in Article 6.

Second: Removal of the Israeli settlements in the occupied territories according to a time-table to be agreed upon within the period referred to in Article 6.

Third: Guaranteeing the security, sovereignty, territorial integrity and inviolability and the political independence of every State through the following measures:

(a) The establishment of demilitarized zones astride the borders.

(b) The establishment of limited armament zones astride the borders.

(c) The stationing of United Nations forces astride the borders.

(d) The stationing of early warning systems on the basis of reciprocity.

(e) Regulating the acquisition of arms by the Parties and the type of their armament and weapons systems.

(f) The adherence by all the Parties to the Treaty on the Non-Proliferation of nuclear weapons. The Parties undertake not to manufacture or acquire nuclear weapons or other nuclear explosive devices.

(g) Applying the principle of innocent passage to transit through the Straits of Tiran.

(h) The establishment of relations of peace and good-neighborly cooperation among the Parties.

Fourth: An undertaking by all the Parties not to resort to the threat or the use of force to settle disputes. Any disputes shall be settled by peaceful means in accordance with the provisions of Article 33 of the Charter of the United Nations.

The Parties also undertake to accept the compulsory jurisdiction of the International Court of Justice with respect to all disputes emanating from the application or the interpretation of their contractual arrangements.

Fifth: Upon the signing of the peace treaties, the Israeli military Government in the West Bank and Gaza shall be abolished and authority shall be transferred to the Arab side in an orderly and peaceful manner. There shall be a transitional period not to exceed five years from the date of the signing of the "Framework" during which Jordan shall supervise the administration of the West Bank and Egypt shall supervise the administration of the Gaza Strip.

Egypt and Jordan shall carry out their responsibility in cooperation with freely elected representatives of the Palestinian people who shall exercise direct authority over the administration of the West Bank and Gaza simultaneously with the abolition of the Israeli military government.

Six months before the end of the transitional period, the Palestinian people shall exercise their fundamental right to self-determination and shall be enabled to establish their national entity. Egypt and Jordan by virtue of their responsibility in the Gaza Strip and the West Bank, shall recommend that the entity be linked with Jordan as decided by their peoples.

Palestinian refugees and displaced persons shall be enabled to exercise the right to return or receive compensation in accordance with relevant United Nations resolutions.

Sixth: Israel shall withdraw from Jerusalem to the demarcation lines of the Armistice Agreement of 1949 in conformity with the Principle of the inadmissibility of the acquisition of territory by war. Arab sovereignty and administration shall be restored to the Arab sector.

A joint municipal council composed of an equal number of Palestinian and Israeli members shall be entrusted with regulating and supervising the following matters:

(a) Public utilities throughout the City.

(b) Public transportation and traffic.

(c) Postal and telephone services.

(d) Tourism.

The Parties undertake to ensure the free exercise of worship, the freedom of access, visit and transit to the holy places without distinction or discrimination.

Seventh: Synchronized with the implementation of the provisions related to withdrawal, the Parties shall proceed to establish among them relationships normal to States at peace with one another. To this end, they undertake to abide by all the provisions of the Charter of the United Nations. Steps taken in this respect include:

(a) Full recognition.

(b) Abolishing economic boycott.

(c) Ensuring the freedom of passage through the Suez Canal in accordance with the provisions of the Constantinople Convention of 1888 and the Declaration of the Egyptian Government of April 24, 1957.

(d) Guaranteeing that under their jurisdiction the citizens of the other Parties shall enjoy the protection of the due process of law.

Eighth: Israel undertakes to pay full and prompt compensation for the damage which resulted from the operations of its armed forces against the civilian population and installations, as well as its exploitation of natural resources in occupied territories.

Article 3

Upon the signing of this "Framework," which represents a comprehensive and balanced package embodying all the rights and obligations of the

Parties, other Parties concerned shall be invited to adhere to it under the Middle East Peace Conference in Geneva.

Article 4

The representatives of the Palestinian people shall take part in the peace talks to be held after the signing of the "Framework."

Article 5

The United States shall participate in the talks on matters related to the modalities of the implementation of the agreements and working out the time-table for the carrying out of the obligations of the Parties.

Article 6

Peace treaties shall be concluded within three months from the signing of this "Framework" by the Parties concerned, thus signalling the beginning of the peace process and setting in motion the dynamics of peace and co-existence.

Article 7

The Security Council shall be requested to endorse the Peace Treaties and ensure that their provisions shall not be violated. The Council shall also be requested to guarantee the boundaries between the Parties.

Article 8

The Permanent members of the Security Council shall be requested to underwrite the Peace Treaties and ensure respect for their provisions. They shall also be requested to conform their policies and actions with the undertakings contained in this Framework.

Article 9

The United States shall guarantee the implementation of this "Framework" and the peace treaties in full and in good faith.

First Draft of the American Proposal at Camp David, September 10, 1978

Muhammad Anwar al-Sadat, President of the Arab Republic of Egypt, and Menachem Begin, Prime Minister of Israel, met with Jimmy Carter, President of the United States of America, at Camp David from September 5 to —, 1978, and have agreed on the following framework for peace in the Middle East. They invite other parties to the Arab-Israeli conflict to adhere to it.

Preamble

The search for peace in the Middle East must be guided by the following:

—After four wars during thirty years, despite intensive human efforts, the Middle East, which is the cradle of civilization and the birthplace of three great religions, does not yet enjoy the blessings of peace. The people of the Middle East yearn for peace so that the vast human and natural resources of the region can be turned to the pursuits of peace and so that this area can become a model for coexistence and cooperation among nations.

—The historic initiative of President Sadat in visiting Jerusalem and the reciprocal visit of Prime Minister Begin to Ismailia, the constructive peace proposals made by both leaders, as well as the warm reception of these missions by the peoples of both countries, have created an unprec-

---

The first version of this negotiating draft was prepared by Harold H. Saunders on September 9, 1978, and was then reviewed by President Carter later in the day. The version presented here was shown to Carter at 2:00 p.m. on September 10 and included marginal notations indicating the likely reactions to specific points by the Egyptian and Israeli delegations. The footnotes here reflect those comments; the underlining was in the original document to highlight important phrases. In point 2c the word *minor* was removed before the draft was shown to the Israelis later in the afternoon. The Department of State declassified this document on October 28, 1985.

edented opportunity for peace which must not be lost if this generation and future generations are to be spared the tragedies of war.

—The provisions of the Charter of the United Nations and the other accepted norms of international law and legitimacy now provide accepted standards for the conduct of relations among all states.

—The only agreed basis for a peaceful settlement of the Arab-Israeli conflict is United Nations Security Council Resolution 242, supplemented by Resolution 338. Resolution 242 in its preamble emphasizes the obligation of Member States in the United Nations to act in accordance with Article 2 of the Charter. Article 2, among other points, calls for the settlement of disputes by peaceful means and for Members to refrain from the threat or use of force. Egypt and Israel in their agreement signed September 4, 1975, agreed: "The Parties hereby undertake not to resort to the threat or use of force or military blockade against each other." They have both also stated that there shall be no more war between them. In a relationship of peace, in the spirit of Article 2, negotiations between Israel and any neighbor prepared to negotiate peace and security with it should be based on all the provisions and principles of Resolution 242, including the inadmissibility of the acquisition of territory by war[1] and the need to work for a just and lasting peace in which every state in the area can live in security within secure and recognized borders. Negotiations based on these principles are necessary with respect to all fronts of the conflict[2]—the Sinai, the Golan Heights, the West Bank and Gaza, and Lebanon.

—Peace is more than the juridical end of the state of belligerency.[3] It should encompass the full range of normal relations between nations. Progress toward that goal can accelerate movement toward a new era of reconciliation in the Middle East marked by cooperation in promoting economic development, in maintaining stability, and in assuring security.

—Security is enhanced by a relationship of peace and by cooperation between nations which enjoy normal relations. In addition, under the terms of peace treaties, the sovereign parties can agree to special security arrangements such as demilitarized zones, limited armaments areas, early warning stations, special security forces, liaison, agreed measures for monitoring, and other arrangements that they agree are useful.

---

1. This was seen as language that would be very difficult for Begin to accept.

2. This was likely to trouble Begin because it implied to him full Israeli withdrawal from the West Bank and Golan.

3. Begin was expected to like this point.

Agreement

Taking these factors into account, Egypt and Israel are determined to reach a just, comprehensive, and durable settlement of the Middle East conflict through the conclusion of peace treaties on the basis of the full implementation of Security Council Resolutions 242 and 338 in all their parts.[4] Their purpose is to achieve peace and good neighborly relations. They recognize that, for peace to endure, it must involve all those who have been principal parties to the Arab-Israeli conflict; it must provide security; and it must give the peoples who have been most deeply affected by the conflict, including the Palestinians, a sense that they have been dealt with fairly in the peace agreement. They therefore agree that this Framework as appropriate is intended by them to constitute a basis for peace not only between Egypt and Israel, but also between Israel and each of its other neighbors which is prepared to negotiate peace with Israel on this basis. With that objective in mind, they have agreed to proceed as follows:

A. Egypt-Israel

1. Egypt and Israel undertake not to resort to the threat or the use of force to settle disputes. Any disputes shall be settled by peaceful means in accordance with the provisions of Article 33 of the Charter of the United Nations. In the event of disputes arising from the application or interpretation of their contractual agreements, the two parties will seek to reach a settlement by direct negotiations. Failing agreement, the parties accept the compulsory jurisdiction of the International Court of Justice with respect to all disputes emanating from the application or the interpretation of their contractual arrangements.

2. In order to achieve peace between them, they have agreed to negotiate without interruption with a goal of concluding within three months from the signing of this Framework a peace treaty between them,[5] while inviting the other parties to the conflict to proceed simultaneously to negotiate and conclude similar peace treaties with a view to achieving a comprehensive peace in the area. Israel has agreed to the restoration of the exercise of full Egyptian sovereignty in the Sinai up to the internationally recognized border between Egypt and Israel,[6] and Egypt has

---

4. The Israelis were expected to object that this implied full withdrawal because of the language in U.N. Resolution 242 on the "inadmissibility of the acquisition of territory by war."

5. This was seen as highly desirable from Israel's standpoint.

6. Egypt was thought to prefer language calling for Israeli withdrawal.

agreed to establish full peace and normal relations with Israel. Security arrangements, the timing of withdrawal of all Israeli forces from the Sinai, and the elements of a normal, peaceful relationship between them have been discussed and will be defined in the peace treaty.

3. Egypt and Israel agree that freedom of passage through the Suez Canal, the Strait of Tiran, and the Gulf of Suez should be assured for ships of all flags, including Israel.

B. West Bank and Gaza[7]

1. Egypt and Israel will participate in negotiations on resolution of the Palestinian problem in all its aspects.[8] The solution must recognize the legitimate rights of the Palestinian people and enable the Palestinians to participate in the determination of their own future.[9]

2. To this end, negotiations relating to the West Bank and Gaza should provide for links between these areas and Jordan and should proceed in three stages:

(a) Egypt and Israel hereby agree that the following should be the main elements of a settlement in the West Bank and Gaza: In order to ensure a peaceful and orderly transfer of authority, there should be transitional arrangements for the West Bank and Gaza for a period not exceeding five years. In order to provide full autonomy[10] to the inhabitants, under these arrangements the Israeli military government[11] and administration will be abolished and withdrawn as soon as a self-governing authority can be freely elected by the inhabitants of these areas to replace the existing military government. This transitional arrangement should derive its authority for self-government from Egypt and Israel, and Jordan, when Jordan joins the negotiations. To negotiate the details of a transitional arrangement, the Government of Jordan will be invited to join the negotiations on the basis of this Framework. These new arrangements should give due consideration both to the principle of self-

---

7. It was noted here that Sadat might raise the issue of the linkage between a Sinai agreement and a West Bank–Gaza agreement.

8. This phrase, plus reference to the "Palestinian people," was seen as difficult for Begin to accept.

9. This language, from Carter's Aswan declaration in January 1978, was thought to be acceptable to Sadat, though he would have preferred mention of "self-determination" for the Palestinians.

10. Some of the Egyptians disliked the word *autonomy*, but Sadat was not expected to object.

11. It was noted that Israel wanted to abolish only the military governor's administration—not his office—at least initially.

government by the inhabitants of these territories and to the legitimate security concerns of Egypt, Israel, Jordan, and the inhabitants of the West Bank and Gaza.

(b) Egypt, Israel, and Jordan will determine the modalities for establishing the elected self-governing authority in the West Bank and Gaza. The delegations may include Palestinians from the West Bank and Gaza. The parties will negotiate an agreement which will define the powers and responsibilities of the self-governing authority. The agreement will provide for the withdrawal of Israeli armed forces and the redeployment of some of them to limited and specified security points.[12] It will also include arrangements for assuring internal and external security and public order, including the respective roles of Israeli armed forces and local police.

(c) When the self-governing authority in the West Bank and Gaza is inaugurated, the transitional period will begin. Within three years[13] after the beginning of the transitional period, Egypt, Israel, Jordan and the self-governing authority in the West Bank and Gaza will undertake negotiations for a peace treaty which will settle the final status of the West Bank and Gaza after the transitional period and its relationship with its neighbors on the basis of all of the principles of UN Security Council Resolution 242, including the mutual obligations of peace, the necessity for security arrangements for all parties concerned following the transitional period, the withdrawal of Israeli forces,[14] a just settlement of the refugee problem, and the establishment of secure and recognized boundaries. The boundaries and security arrangements must both satisfy the aspirations of the Palestinians and meet Israel's security needs.[15] They may incorporate agreed minor modifications in the temporary armistice lines which existed between 1949 and 1967.[16] The peace treaty will define the rights of the citizens of each of the parties to do business, to work, to live, and to carry on other transactions in each other's territory on a reciprocal basis.[17]

3. All necessary measures will be taken and provisions made to assure

12. Israel was expected to insist that its forces could not be restricted to security points. It was thought Israel would have to change its position.

13. Israel was hoping to put this off for five years, but was likely to accept the three-year formulation.

14. Begin was expected to object to this phrase.

15. Some Egyptians disliked this language—the so-called Vienna declaration—but Sadat had said it was acceptable.

16. The word *minor* was of great importance to Sadat, and a red flag to most Israelis.

17. Sadat's advisers did not want to go into such detail, but Sadat would not object.

Israel's security during the transitional period and beyond. To assist in providing security during and beyond the transitional period:

(a) Egypt and Israel propose that Jordan and Egypt assign personnel to the police forces of the self-governing authority in the West Bank and Gaza, respectively.[18] They will also maintain continuing liaison on internal security matters with the designated Israeli authorities to ensure that no hostile threats or acts against Israel or its citizens originate from the West Bank or Gaza.[19] The numbers, equipment, and responsibilities of such Egyptian and Jordanian personnel will be defined by the agreement. By mutual agreement, United Nations forces or observers may also be introduced during the transitional period.[20]

(b) The nature of the Israeli security presence during the transitional period and beyond will be agreed in the negotiations described in paragraphs B2 (b) and (c) above.[21]

4. During the transitional period, the negotiating parties (Egypt, Israel, Jordan, the self-governing authority) will constitute a continuing committee to reach mutual agreements applicable during that period on:

(a) issues involving interpretation of the agreement or issues unforeseen during the negotiation of the agreement, if not resolvable by the self-governing authority;

(b) the return of agreed numbers of persons displaced from the West Bank in 1967 and of Palestinian refugees together with necessary measures in connection with their return to prevent disruption and disorder.[22]

5. Jerusalem, the city of peace, shall not be divided. It is a city holy to Jew, Muslim, and Christian and all peoples must have free access to it and enjoy the free exercise of worship and the right to visit and transit to the holy places without distinction or discrimination. The holy places of each faith will be under the administration of their representatives. For peace to endure, each community in Jerusalem must be able to express freely its cultural and religious values in an acceptable political framework.

18. Begin would object to troops from either Egypt or Jordan in the West Bank and Gaza.

19. Israel would favor this point.

20. Israel would oppose a U.N. force; Sadat was not enthusiastic about a U.N. force, but the Egyptian proposal did call for one.

21. This was an important point for Israel, but one that would cause Sadat difficulty in the Arab world, since it would look like a perpetuation of Israeli occupation.

22. Egypt was expected to ask for explicit reference to U.N. General Assembly Resolution 194, calling for the right of Palestinian refugees to return to their homes or receive compensation.

A representative municipal council shall supervise essential functions in the city. An agreement on relationships in Jerusalem should be reached in the negotiations dealing with the final status of the West Bank and Gaza.

6. Egypt and Israel agree to work with each other and with other interested parties to achieve a just and permanent solution of the problems of Palestinian and Jewish refugees.[23]

7. If Jordan is unable to join these negotiations, Egypt, Israel, and the inhabitants of the West Bank and Gaza will proceed to establish and administer the self-governing authority.[24]

C. Settlements

(Language to be inserted)

D. Associated Principles

1. Egypt and Israel believe that the principles and provisions described below should apply to peace treaties on all fronts.

2. Synchronized with the implementation of the provisions related to withdrawal, signatories shall proceed to establish among themselves relationships normal to states at peace with one another. To this end, they should undertake to abide by all the provisions of the Charter of the United Nations. Steps to be taken in this respect include:

(a) full recognition, including diplomatic,[25] economic and cultural relations;

(b) abolishing economic boycotts and barriers to the free movement of goods and people;

(c) guaranteeing that under their jurisdiction the citizens of the other parties shall enjoy the protection of the due process of law.

3. Signatories should agree to provide for the security and respect the sovereignty, territorial integrity and inviolability and the political independence of each state negotiating peace through measures such as the following:

(a) the establishment of demilitarized zones;

(b) the establishment of limited armament zones;

(c) the stationing of United Nations forces or observer groups as agreed;

(d) the stationing of early warning systems on the basis of reciprocity;

23. Israel would like the reference to Jewish refugees and Egypt would not.
24. Dayan was thought to favor this formulation; Begin's views were less certain.
25. Important for the Israelis, as was the next point on free movement of goods and people.

(e) regulating the size of their armed forces and the types of their armament and weapons systems.

4. Signatories should explore possibilities for regional economic development in the context of both traditional arrangements and final peace treaties, with the objective of contributing to the atmosphere of peace, cooperation and friendship which is their common goal.[26]

5. Claims Commissions may be established for the mutual settlement of all financial claims.

6. The United States shall be invited to participate in the talks on matters related to the modalities of the implementation of the agreements and working out the timetable for the carrying out of the obligations of the parties.

7. The United Nations Security Council shall be requested to endorse the peace treaties and ensure that their provisions shall not be violated. The permanent members of the Security Council shall be requested to underwrite the peace treaties and ensure respect for their provisions. They shall also be requested to conform their policies and actions with the undertakings contained in this Framework.

For the Government of the   For the Government of
Arab Republic of Egypt: Israel:

_____   _____

Witnessed by:

_____

Jimmy Carter, President of
the United States of America

26. This point was seen as good for the Israelis—and some U.S. senators—but it was noted that the Egyptians were not very enthusiastic about regional economic cooperation.

APPENDIX F

President Carter's First Draft of the Sinai Proposal

President Carter arrived at Camp David convinced that the essential points of an Egyptian-Israeli peace treaty could be agreed upon at the summit. On September 11, 1978, he personally wrote a draft entitled "Outline of a Settlement in Sinai." After some discussion with his advisers, he revised and expanded his first draft, calling the new version "Framework for a Settlement in Sinai."

This six-page version, reproduced here, was presented in typewritten form to President Sadat late on September 11, 1978. The next day, September 12, the document was discussed with Prime Minister Begin, who strongly objected to the language calling for the "withdrawal of Israeli personnel from Sinai."

Framework for a Settlement in Sinai

In order to achieve peace between them, Israel and Egypt agree to negotiate in good faith with a goal of concluding within three months of the signing of this framework a peace treaty between them. [~~There are no preconditions to the commencement of the negotiations.~~]

All of the principles of U.N. Resolution 242 will apply in this resolution of the dispute between Israel and Egypt.

PEACE TREATY

Unless otherwise mutually agreed, terms of the peace treaty will be implemented

between two and three years
after the peace treaty is
signed.

In the peace treaty ∧ the
issues of: a) the full exercise
of Egyptian sovereignty up to the
internationally recognized border
between Egypt and mandated Palestine; b) ∧ the time of
withdrawal of Israeli
personnel from the Sinai; c) the
~~civilian~~ use of airfields near [El
[El Arish] [Rafah] [Ras at Nagb] [Sharm el Sheikh
Arish, Etam, Etzion and Ofir,
d) for civilian purposes only;
the right of free passage by ∧ ships of Israel
and other nations through the Strait
of Tiran, the Gulf of Suez and
the Suez Canal; e) the construction
of an international highway

between the Sinai and Jordan
near Elat; and f) the ~~reduction~~ stationing
of military ~~threats~~ forces against
~~Israel and Egypt by the steps
listed before~~ (will be resolved by
~~negotiations~~ between the parties)
<u>Stationing of forces</u>
-- Within an area lying
approximately 50 kilometers (km)
east of the Gulf of Suez and
the Suez Canal, no more than
one division of Egyptian mechanized
or infantry armed forces will be
stationed. ~~No state~~

-- Only United Nations forces
and civil police equipped with light
weapons to perform normal police
functions will be stationed x lying West of

P 2 ↑

Typed page →

-- in the area not included above, border patrol units, not to exceed three battalions, will supplement the civil police in maintaining order

The exact demarcation of the above areas will be as mutually agreed during the peace negotiations.

Early warning stations may
exist
~~remain or be established~~ as mutually agreed to insure compliance with the terms of the agreement.

United Nations forces will
be stationed in the Sharm el
Sheikh area to insure freedom
of passage through the Straits of
I. Tiran, and will be removed
only if [both ~~nations agree and
after~~] such agreements is approved
by the Security Council of the
United Nations.

Normal relations will be
established between Egypt and
Israel, including: full recognition;
[diplomatic, economic ~~and cultural~~
relations;] termination of economic
boycotts [and ~~barriers to the free
movement of goods and people~~]; and
mutual protection of citizens by
the due process of law.

INTERIM WITHDRAWAL

Between three months and nine months after the signing of the peace treaty, all Israeli forces will withdraw to east of a line extending from a point [just] east of El Arish to Ras Muhammad, the exact location of this line to be determined by mutual agreement.

The Camp David Accords, September 17, 1978

A FRAMEWORK FOR PEACE IN THE MIDDLE EAST AGREED AT CAMP DAVID

Muhammad Anwar al-Sadat, President of the Arab Republic of Egypt, and Menachem Begin, Prime Minister of Israel, met with Jimmy Carter, President of the United States of America, at Camp David from September 5 to September 17, 1978, and have agreed on the following framework for peace in the Middle East. They invite other parties to the Arab-Israeli conflict to adhere to it.

Preamble

The search for peace in the Middle East must be guided by the following:

—The agreed basis for a peaceful settlement of the conflict between Israel and its neighbors is United Nations Security Council Resolution 242, in all its parts.

—After four wars during thirty years, despite intensive human efforts, the Middle East, which is the cradle of civilization and the birthplace of three great religions, does not yet enjoy the blessings of peace. The people of the Middle East yearn for peace so that the vast human and natural resources of the region can be turned to the pursuits of peace and so that this area can become a model for coexistence and cooperation among nations.

—The historic initiative of President Sadat in visiting Jerusalem and the reception accorded to him by the Parliament, government and people of Israel, and the reciprocal visit of Prime Minister Begin to Ismailia, the peace proposals made by both leaders, as well as the warm reception of these missions by the peoples of both countries, have created an unprecedented opportunity for peace which must not be lost if this generation and future generations are to be spared the tragedies of war.

The texts of the documents were released on September 18, 1978.

—The provisions of the Charter of the United Nations and the other accepted norms of international law and legitimacy now provide accepted standards for the conduct of relations among all states.

—To achieve a relationship of peace, in the spirit of Article 2 of the United Nations Charter, future negotiations between Israel and any neighbor prepared to negotiate peace and security with it, are necessary for the purpose of carrying out all the provisions and principles of Resolutions 242 and 338.

—Peace requires respect for the sovereignty, territorial integrity and political independence of every state in the area and their right to live in peace within secure and recognized boundaries free from threats or acts of force. Progress toward that goal can accelerate movement toward a new era of reconciliation in the Middle East marked by cooperation in promoting economic development, in maintaining stability, and in assuring security.

—Security is enhanced by a relationship of peace and by cooperation between nations which enjoy normal relations. In addition, under the terms of peace treaties, the parties can, on the basis of reciprocity, agree to special security arrangements such as demilitarized zones, limited armaments areas, early warning stations, the presence of international forces, liaison, agreed measures for monitoring, and other arrangements that they agree are useful.

Framework

Taking these factors into account, the parties are determined to reach a just, comprehensive, and durable settlement of the Middle East conflict through the conclusion of peace treaties based on Security Council Resolutions 242 and 338 in all their parts. Their purpose is to achieve peace and good neighborly relations. They recognize that, for peace to endure, it must involve all those who have been most deeply affected by the conflict. They therefore agree that this framework as appropriate is intended by them to constitute a basis for peace not only between Egypt and Israel, but also between Israel and each of its other neighbors which is prepared to negotiate peace with Israel on this basis. With that objective in mind, they have agreed to proceed as follows:

A. *West Bank and Gaza*

1. Egypt, Israel, Jordan and the representatives of the Palestinian people should participate in negotiations on the resolution of the Palestinian

problem in all its aspects. To achieve that objective, negotiations relating to the West Bank and Gaza should proceed in three stages:

(a) Egypt and Israel agree that, in order to ensure a peaceful and orderly transfer of authority, and taking into account the security concerns of all the parties, there should be transitional arrangements for the West Bank and Gaza for a period not exceeding five years. In order to provide full autonomy to the inhabitants, under these arrangements the Israeli military government and its civilian administration will be withdrawn as soon as a self-governing authority has been freely elected by the inhabitants of these areas to replace the existing military government. To negotiate the details of a transitional arrangement, the Government of Jordan will be invited to join the negotiations on the basis of this framework. These new arrangements should give due consideration both to the principle of self-government by the inhabitants of these territories and to the legitimate security concerns of the parties involved.

(b) Egypt, Israel, and Jordan will agree on the modalities for establishing the elected self-governing authority in the West Bank and Gaza. The delegations of Egypt and Jordan may include Palestinians from the West Bank and Gaza or other Palestinians as mutually agreed. The parties will negotiate an agreement which will define the powers and responsibilities of the self-governing authority to be exercised in the West Bank and Gaza. A withdrawal of Israeli armed forces will take place and there will be a redeployment of the remaining Israeli forces into specified security locations. The agreement will also include arrangements for assuring internal and external security and public order. A strong local police force will be established, which may include Jordanian citizens. In addition, Israeli and Jordanian forces will participate in joint patrols and in the manning of control posts to assure the security of the borders.

(c) When the self-governing authority (administrative council) in the West Bank and Gaza is established and inaugurated, the transitional period of five years will begin. As soon as possible, but not later than the third year after the beginning of the transitional period, negotiations will take place to determine the final status of the West Bank and Gaza and its relationship with its neighbors, and to conclude a peace treaty between Israel and Jordan by the end of the transitional period. These negotiations will be conducted among Egypt, Israel, Jordan, and the elected representatives of the inhabitants of the West Bank and Gaza. Two separate but related committees will be convened, one committee, consisting of representatives of the four parties which will negotiate and agree on the final status of the West Bank and Gaza, and its relationship with its neighbors, and the second committee, consisting of representatives of Israel and representatives of Jordan to be joined by the elected representatives of the inhabitants of the West Bank and Gaza, to negotiate the peace treaty between Israel and Jordan, taking into account the agreement reached on the final status of the West Bank and Gaza. The negotiations shall be based on all the provisions and principles of UN Security Council Resolution 242. The negotiations will resolve, among other matters, the location of the boundaries and the nature of the security arrangements. The solution from the negotiations must also recognize the legitimate rights of the Palestinian people and their just requirements. In this way, the Palestinians will participate in the determination of their own future through:

(1) The negotiations among Egypt, Israel, Jordan and the representatives of the inhabitants of the West Bank and Gaza to agree on the final status of the West Bank and Gaza and other outstanding issues by the end of the transitional period.

(2) Submitting their agreement to a vote by the elected representatives of the inhabitants of the West Bank and Gaza.

(3) Providing for the elected representatives of the inhabitants of the West Bank and Gaza to decide how they shall govern themselves consistent with the provisions of their agreement.

(4) Participating as stated above in the work of the committee negotiating the peace treaty between Israel and Jordan.

2. All necessary measures will be taken and provisions made to assure the security of Israel and its neighbors during the transitional period and beyond. To assist in providing such security, a strong local police force will be constituted by the self-governing authority. It will be composed of inhabitants of the West Bank and Gaza. The police will maintain continuing liaison on internal security matters with the designated Israeli, Jordanian, and Egyptian officers.

3. During the transitional period, representatives of Egypt, Israel, Jordan, and the self-governing authority will constitute a continuing committee to decide by agreement on the modalities of admission of persons displaced from the West Bank and Gaza in 1967, together with necessary measures to prevent disruption and disorder. Other matters of common concern may also be dealt with by this committee.

4. Egypt and Israel will work with each other and with other interested parties to establish agreed procedures for a prompt, just and permanent implementation of the resolution of the refugee problem.

B. Egypt-Israel

1. Egypt and Israel undertake not to resort to the threat or the use of force to settle disputes. Any disputes shall be settled by peaceful means in accordance with the provisions of Article 33 of the Charter of the United Nations.

2. In order to achieve peace between them, the parties agree to negotiate in good faith with a goal of concluding within three months from the signing of this Framework a peace treaty between them, while inviting the other parties to the conflict to proceed simultaneously to negotiate and conclude similar peace treaties with a view to achieving a comprehensive peace in the area. The Framework for the Conclusion of a Peace Treaty between Egypt and Israel will govern the peace negotiations between them. The parties will agree on the modalities and the timetable for the implementation of their obligations under the treaty.

C. Associated Principles

1. Egypt and Israel state that the principles and provisions described below should apply to peace treaties between Israel and each of its neighbors—Egypt, Jordan, Syria and Lebanon.

2. Signatories shall establish among themselves relationships normal to states at peace with one another. To this end, they should undertake to abide by all the provisions of the Charter of the United Nations. Steps to be taken in this respect include:

(a) full recognition;

(b) abolishing economic boycotts;

(c) guaranteeing that under their jurisdiction the citizens of the other parties shall enjoy the protection of the due process of law.

3. Signatories should explore possibilities for economic development in the context of final peace treaties, with the objective of contributing to the atmosphere of peace, cooperation and friendship which is their common goal.

4. Claims Commissions may be established for the mutual settlement of all financial claims.

5. The United States shall be invited to participate in the talks on matters related to the modalities of the implementation of the agreements

and working out the timetable for the carrying out of the obligations of the parties.

6. The United Nations Security Council shall be requested to endorse the peace treaties and ensure that their provisions shall not be violated. The permanent members of the Security Council shall be requested to underwrite the peace treaties and ensure respect for their provisions. They shall also be requested to conform their policies and actions with the undertakings contained in this Framework.

For the Government of the Arab Republic of Egypt:

A. Sadat

For the Government of Israel:

M. Begin

Witnessed by:

Jimmy Carter
Jimmy Carter, President of
the United States of America

FRAMEWORK FOR THE CONCLUSION OF A PEACE TREATY BETWEEN EGYPT AND ISRAEL

In order to achieve peace between them, Israel and Egypt agree to negotiate in good faith with a goal of concluding within three months of the signing of this framework a peace treaty between them.

It is agreed that:

The site of the negotiations will be under a United Nations flag at a location or locations to be mutually agreed.

All of the principles of UN Resolution 242 will apply in this resolution of the dispute between Israel and Egypt.

Unless otherwise mutually agreed, terms of the peace treaty will be implemented between two and three years after the peace treaty is signed.

The following matters are agreed between the parties:

(a) the full exercise of Egyptian sovereignty up to the internationally recognized border between Egypt and mandated Palestine;

(b) the withdrawal of Israeli armed forces from the Sinai;

(c) the use of airfields left by the Israelis near El Arish, Rafah, Ras en Naqb, and Sharm el Sheikh for civilian purposes only, including possible commercial use by all nations;

(d) the right of free passage by ships of Israel through the Gulf of Suez and the Suez Canal on the basis of the Constantinople Convention of 1888 applying to all nations; the Strait of Tiran and the Gulf of Aqaba are international waterways to be open to all nations for unimpeded and nonsuspendable freedom of navigation and overflight;

(e) the construction of a highway between the Sinai and Jordan near Elat with guaranteed free and peaceful passage by Egypt and Jordan; and

(f) the stationing of military forces listed below.

Stationing of Forces

A. No more than one division (mechanized or infantry) of Egyptian armed forces will be stationed within an area lying approximately 50 kilometers (km) east of the Gulf of Suez and the Suez Canal.

B. Only United Nations forces and civil police equipped with light weapons to perform normal police functions will be stationed within an area lying west of the international border and the Gulf of Aqaba, varying in width from 20 km to 40 km.

C. In the area within 3 km east of the international border there will be Israeli limited military forces not to exceed four infantry battalions and United Nations observers.

D. Border patrol units, not to exceed three battalions, will supplement the civil police in maintaining order in the area not included above.

The exact demarcation of the above areas will be as decided during the peace negotiations.

Early warning stations may exist to insure compliance with the terms of the agreement.

United Nations forces will be stationed: (a) in part of the area in the Sinai lying within about 20 km of the Mediterranean Sea and adjacent to the international border, and (b) in the Sharm el Sheikh area to ensure freedom of passage through the Strait of Tiran; and these forces will not be removed unless such removal is approved by the Security Council of the United Nations with a unanimous vote of the five permanent members.

After a peace treaty is signed, and after the interim withdrawal is complete, normal relations will be established between Egypt and Israel, including: full recognition, including diplomatic, economic and cultural relations; termination of economic boycotts and barriers to the free movement of goods and people; and mutual protection of citizens by the due process of law.

Interim Withdrawal

Between three months and nine months after the signing of the peace treaty, all Israeli forces will withdraw east of a line extending from a point east of El Arish to Ras Muhammad, the exact location of this line to be determined by mutual agreement.

For the Government of the Arab Republic of Egypt:

A. Sadat

For the Government of Israel:

M. Begin

Witnessed by:

Jimmy Carter
Jimmy Carter, President of
the United State of America

LETTER FROM ISRAELI PRIME MINISTER MENACHEM BEGIN TO PRESIDENT JIMMY CARTER, SEPTEMBER 17, 1978

Dear Mr. President:

I have the honor to inform you that during two weeks after my return home I will submit a motion before Israel's Parliament (the Knesset) to decide on the following question:

If during the negotiations to conclude a peace treaty between Israel and Egypt all outstanding issues are agreed upon, "are you in favor of the removal of the Israeli settlers from the northern and southern Sinai areas or are you in favor of keeping the aforementioned settlers in those areas?"

The vote, Mr. President, on this issue will be completely free from the usual Parliamentary Party discipline to the effect that although the coalition is being now supported by 70 members out of 120, every member of the Knesset, as I believe, both on the Government and the Opposition benches will be enabled to vote in accordance with his own conscience.

Sincerely yours,

Menachem Begin

LETTER FROM PRESIDENT JIMMY CARTER TO EGYPTIAN PRESIDENT ANWAR EL SADAT, SEPTEMBER 22, 1978

Dear Mr. President:

I transmit herewith a copy of a letter to me from Prime Minister Begin setting forth how he proposes to present the issue of the Sinai settlements to the Knesset for the latter's decision.

In this connection, I understand from your letter that Knesset approval to withdraw all Israeli settlers from Sinai according to a timetable within the period specified for the implementation of the peace treaty is a prerequisite to any negotiations on a peace treaty between Egypt and Israel.

Sincerely,

Jimmy Carter

Enclosure:
Letter from Prime Minister Begin

LETTER FROM EGYPTIAN PRESIDENT ANWAR EL SADAT TO PRESIDENT JIMMY CARTER, SEPTEMBER 17, 1978

Dear Mr. President:

In connection with the "Framework for a Settlement in Sinai" to be signed tonight, I would like to reaffirm the position of the Arab Republic of Egypt with respect to the settlements:

1. All Israeli settlers must be withdrawn from Sinai according to a timetable within the period specified for the implementation of the peace treaty.

2. Agreement by the Israeli Government and its constitutional institutions to this basic principle is therefore a prerequisite to starting peace negotiations for concluding a peace treaty.

3. If Israel fails to meet this commitment, the "Framework" shall be void and invalid.

Sincerely,

Mohamed Anwar El Sadat

LETTER FROM PRESIDENT JIMMY CARTER TO ISRAELI PRIME MINISTER MENACHEM BEGIN, SEPTEMBER 22, 1978

Dear Mr. Prime Minister:

I have received your letter of September 17, 1978, describing how you intend to place the question of the future of Israeli settlements in Sinai before the Knesset for its decision.

Enclosed is a copy of President Sadat's letter to me on this subject.

Sincerely,

Jimmy Carter

Enclosure:

Letter from President Sadat

LETTER FROM EGYPTIAN PRESIDENT ANWAR EL SADAT TO PRESIDENT JIMMY CARTER, SEPTEMBER 17, 1978

Dear Mr. President:

I am writing you to reaffirm the position of the Arab Republic of Egypt with respect to Jerusalem:

1. Arab Jerusalem is an integral part of the West Bank. Legal and historical Arab rights in the City must be respected and restored.

2. Arab Jerusalem should be under Arab sovereignty.

3. The Palestinian inhabitants of Arab Jerusalem are entitled to exercise their legitimate national rights, being part of the Palestinian People in the West Bank.

4. Relevant Security Council Resolutions, particularly Resolutions 242 and 267, must be applied with regard to Jerusalem. All the measures taken by Israel to alter the status of the City are null and void and should be rescinded.

5. All peoples must have free access to the City and enjoy the free exercise of worship and the right to visit and transit to the holy places without distinction or discrimination.

6. The holy places of each faith may be placed under the administration and control of their representatives.

7. Essential functions in the City should be undivided and a joint municipal council composed of an equal number of Arab and Israeli members can supervise the carrying out of these functions. In this way, the City shall be undivided.

Sincerely,

Mohamed Anwar El Sadat

LETTER FROM ISRAELI PRIME MINISTER MENACHEM BEGIN TO PRESIDENT JIMMY CARTER, SEPTEMBER 17, 1978

Dear Mr. President:

I have the honor to inform you, Mr. President, that on 28 June 1967—Israel's Parliament (The Knesset) promulgated and adopted a law to the effect: "the Government is empowered by a decree to apply the law, the jurisdiction and administration of the State to any part of Eretz Israel (land of Israel—Palestine), as stated in that decree."

On the basis of this law, the Government of Israel decreed in July 1967 that Jerusalem is one city indivisible, the Capital of the State of Israel.

Sincerely,

Menachem Begin

LETTER FROM PRESIDENT JIMMY CARTER TO EGYPTIAN PRESIDENT ANWAR EL SADAT, SEPTEMBER 22, 1978

Dear Mr. President:

I have received your letter of September 17, 1978, setting forth the Egyptian position on Jerusalem. I am transmitting a copy of that letter to Prime Minister Begin for his information.

The position of the United States on Jerusalem remains as stated by Ambassador Goldberg in the United Nations General Assembly on July 14, 1967, and subsequently by Ambassador Yost in the United Nations Security Council on July 1, 1969.

Sincerely,

Jimmy Carter

LETTER FROM EGYPTIAN PRESIDENT ANWAR EL SADAT TO PRESIDENT JIMMY CARTER, SEPTEMBER 17, 1978

Dear Mr. President:

In connection with the "Framework for Peace in the Middle East," I am writing you this letter to inform you of the position of the Arab Republic of Egypt, with respect to the implementation of the comprehensive settlement.

To ensure the implementation of the provisions related to the West Bank and Gaza and in order to safeguard the legitimate rights of the Palestinian people, Egypt will be prepared to assume the Arab role emanating from these provisions, following consultations with Jordan and the representatives of the Palestinian people.

Sincerely,

Mohamed Anwar El Sadat

LETTER FROM PRESIDENT JIMMY CARTER TO ISRAELI PRIME MINISTER MENACHEM BEGIN, SEPTEMBER 22, 1978

Dear Mr. Prime Minister:

I hereby acknowledge that you have informed me as follows:

A) In each paragraph of the Agreed Framework Document the expressions "Palestinians" or "Palestinian People" are being and will be construed and understood by you as "Palestinian Arabs."

B) In each paragraph in which the expression "West Bank" appears, it is being, and will be, understood by the Government of Israel as Judea and Samaria.

Sincerely,

Jimmy Carter

LETTER FROM SECRETARY OF DEFENSE HAROLD BROWN TO ISRAELI DEFENSE MINISTER EZER WEIZMAN, ACCOMPANYING THE DOCUMENTS AGREED TO AT CAMP DAVID, RELEASED SEPTEMBER 29, 1978

September 28, 1978

Dear Mr. Minister:

The U.S. understands that, in connection with carrying out the agreements reached at Camp David, Israel intends to build two military airbases at appropriate sites in the Negev to replace the airbases at Eitam and Etzion which will be evacuated by Israel in accordance with the peace treaty to be concluded between Egypt and Israel. We also understand the special urgency and priority which Israel attaches to preparing the new bases in light of its conviction that it cannot safely leave the Sinai airbases until the new ones are operational.

I suggest that our two governments consult on the scope and costs of the two new airbases as well as on related forms of assistance which the United States might appropriately provide in light of the special problems which may be presented by carrying out such a project on an urgent basis. The President is prepared to seek the necessary Congressional approvals for such assistance as may be agreed upon by the U.S. side as a result of such consultations.

Harold Brown

American Answers to Jordanian Questions, October 1978

1. *Does the United States intend to be a full partner in negotiations regarding the West Bank and Gaza and the Palestinian question in general? At what stage of the negotiations will the United States participate and in what role?*

Yes, the United States will be a full partner in all the Arab-Israeli peace negotiations, leading to the achievement of a just, lasting and comprehensive Middle East peace.

The United States will use its full influence to see that the negotiations are brought to a successful conclusion.

President Carter will continue to take an active personal part in the negotiations.

2. *What does the Framework agreement mean in its paragraph (A)1, where it refers to "the representatives of the Palestinian people?"*

No comprehensive definition is attempted. In some cases, the representatives of the inhabitants of the West Bank and Gaza are specified. In one case, it is clear that "other Palestinians as mutually agreed" refers to representatives from outside the West Bank and Gaza and need not be citizens of Egypt or Jordan. Palestinians who are citizens of Egypt or Jordan may, of course, be members of the negotiating teams representing those countries. In other cases, the self-governing authority itself is mentioned.

The United States interprets the phrase "the representatives of the Palestinian people" not in terms of any single group or organization as representing the Palestinian people, but as encompassing those elected or chosen for participation in negotiations. It is expected that they will accept the purposes of the negotiations as defined in United Nations Security Council Resolution 242, and in the framework of a settlement will be prepared to live in peace and good neighbourly relations with Israel.

From a typed copy made available by the Government of Jordan. The only point missing from this version is President Carter's signature at the bottom of the last page.

3. *Why has the duration of five years been chosen for the transition period in the West Bank and Gaza?*

The idea of a five-year transitional period for the West Bank and Gaza was an American suggestion which was first put to the parties in the summer of 1977. The key point is the concept of a transitional period— not the precise duration of five years which has been suggested and agreed.

We believe a transitional process of several years—at the outset of which the Israeli military government and its civilian administration will be withdrawn and a self-governing authority established for the West Bank and Gaza inhabitants—can demonstrate that the practical problems arising from a transition to peace can be satisfactorily resolved. We see the transitional period as essential to build confidence, gain momentum and bring about the changes in attitude that can assure a final settlement which realizes the legitimate rights of the Palestinian people while assuring the security of Israel and of the other parties.

4(A). *What is the geographical definition of the "West Bank" and of Gaza in the view of the United States Government? Is Arab Jerusalem and its surrounding Arab areas incorporated into Israel after June 1967 included in the definition of the "West Bank"?*

In the view of the United States the term "West Bank and Gaza" describes all of the area west of the Jordan River under Jordanian administration prior to the 1967 war and all of the area east of the western border of the British Mandate of Palestine which, prior to the 1967 war, was under Egyptian control and is known as the Gaza Strip.

With respect to negotiations envisaged in the Framework agreement, we believe a distinction must be made between Jerusalem and the rest of the West Bank because of the City's special status and circumstances. We would envisage, therefore, a negotiated solution for the final status of Jerusalem that could be different in character in some respects from that of the rest of the West Bank.

The final status of Jerusalem should not be prejudged by the unilateral actions undertaken in Jerusalem since the 1967 war. The full United States position on Jerusalem remains as stated by Ambassador Goldberg in his address to the United Nations General Assembly on 14 July 1967, and by Ambassador Yost to the Security Council on 1 July 1969.

4(B). *At the end of the five years of transitional arrangements, what would be the status of the West Bank and of Gaza from the point of view of sovereignty?*

The final status of the West Bank and Gaza, including the question of sovereignty, should be determined on the basis of Security Council Resolution 242 in all its parts in negotiations among Jordan, Egypt, Israel and the elected representatives of the inhabitants of the West Bank and Gaza, which should begin not later than the third year after the beginning of the transitional period. Under the terms of the Framework agreement, the outcome of those negotiations—including determining the issue of sovereignty—shall be submitted to a vote by the elected representatives of the inhabitants of the West Bank and Gaza for ratification or rejection.

Since the negotiation of the peace treaty between Israel and Jordan and the negotiations on the final status of the West Bank and Gaza are interrelated, the Framework provides that representatives of the inhabitants of the West Bank and Gaza should participate in both these negotiations.

Thus Palestinians will participate in each negotiation to resolve the final status of the West Bank and Gaza.

4(C). *What is the United States' position regarding these questions?*

The view of the United States on the geographical definition of the term "West Bank and Gaza" is stated in paragraph 4(A) above. The United States' position regarding the question of sovereignty in the West Bank and Gaza is expressed in paragraph 4(B) above.

4(D). *Will any Israeli forces remain in any part of the West Bank and of Gaza after the transitional period of five years? If so, by what right and with what justification?*

Security arrangements after the five-year interim period in the West Bank and Gaza, including the question of the possible retention of Israeli security personnel and the duration of any such presence, must be dealt with in the negotiations on the final status of the West Bank and Gaza that are to begin no later than the third year after the beginning of the transitional period.

4(E). *What is the United States' position regarding these questions?*

The United States believes that the agreement on the final status of the West Bank and Gaza must meet the legitimate aspirations of the Palestinian people and provide for Israel's security needs. The United States would not oppose, if agreed to by the parties, the stationing in the West Bank and Gaza of limited numbers of Israeli security personnel in specifically designated areas, and with a defined role, as one element in providing for the security of Israel.

5. *During the transitional period of self-government in the West Bank and Gaza, under what higher supervisory authority would the self-governing authority operate? Would it be a United Nations or a similar neutral international supervisory authority? What source would finance the budgetary needs of the self-governing authority? What would be the extent of its powers? What would constitute the limitations on its powers?*

The Framework provides that the parties, i.e., Egypt, Israel and Jordan, with Palestinians in the Egyptian and Jordanian delegations, "will negotiate an agreement which will define the powers and responsibilities of the self-governing authority to be exercised in the West Bank and Gaza." Thus the self-governing authority in the transitional period is established by an international agreement among the three parties. The agreement will define the powers of the self-governing authority and provide full autonomy for the inhabitants. Nothing in the Framework excludes the parties from deciding, should they so agree, to give a supervisory or other role to a United Nations or similar neutral international authority or to decide that there should be no supervisory authority. In addition, during the transitional period, representatives of Egypt, Israel, Jordan and the self-governing authority will constitute a continuing committee which may deal with matters of common concern. Methods of financing of the self-governing authority were not discussed at Camp David and remain to be set out in the agreement among the parties.

6(A). *Where the document refers to the self-governing authority which is to be constituted in the West Bank–Gaza area, does the jurisdiction of this authority extend to the part of Jerusalem which had been part of the West Bank when it fell under occupation as well as other annexed areas around it, both in terms of territory and people?*

As stated above, the issue of the status of Jerusalem was not resolved at Camp David and must be dealt with in subsequent negotiations. The questions of how the Arab inhabitants of East Jerusalem relate to the self-governing authority remains to be determined in the negotiations on the transitional arrangements.

6(B). *What is the United States' position on this question?*

In those negotiations the United States will support proposals that would permit Arab inhabitants of East Jerusalem who are not Israeli citizens to participate in the elections to constitute the self-governing authority and in the work of the self-governing authority itself. It is probably not realistic to expect that the full scope of the self-governing authority can be extended to East Jerusalem during the transitional period. Such an outcome would not, however, prejudge the final status of Jerusalem, which must be resolved in the negotiations that are to begin no later than the third year after the beginning of the transitional period.

7(A). *At the end of the five-year transitional period, what would be the status of occupied Arab Jerusalem?*

The status of the West Bank and Gaza, and their relationship with their neighbours, as well as peace between Israel and Jordan, will be determined in the negotiations referred to in paragraph A.1.(c) of the Framework. The United States believes that the status of that portion of Jerusalem which Israel occupied in 1967 should be resolved in those negotiations.[1] The Framework envisages that these negotiations will involve Egypt, Israel, Jordan and the elected representatives of the inhabitants of the West Bank and Gaza.

7(B). *What is the United States' position on this matter?*

The position of the United States on Jerusalem is stated in Paragraph 4(A) above. The final status of Jerusalem should not be prejudged by the unilateral actions undertaken in Jerusalem since the 1967 war. Whatever solution is agreed upon should preserve Jerusalem as a physically undivided city. It should provide for free access to the Jewish, Muslim, and Christian holy places without distinction or discrimination for the free exercise of worship. It should assure the basic rights of all the City's residents. The holy places of each faith should be under the full authority of their representatives.

8(A). *What would happen to the Israeli settlements in the occupied areas during and after the transitional period? What would happen to the properties acquired and construction made there and what would their status be?*

The Framework does not deal with the status of Israeli settlements in the occupied areas, nor with the properties acquired or construction made there. The powers and responsibilities of the self-governing authority, which will exercise full autonomy on the West Bank and Gaza during the transitional period, will be defined in an agreement to be negotiated between Egypt, Israel, Jordan and, as provided in the Framework,

---

1. Provisions regarding Jerusalem could be included in the agreements that emerge from either or both of these negotiations. (This note appears in the original text.)

Palestinians from the West Bank and Gaza or other Palestinians as mutually agreed to be on Egyptian and Jordanian national delegations. The question of the Israeli settlements in the West Bank and Gaza, and their relationship with the self-governing authority during the transitional period, will have to be dealt with in the course of those negotiations. The Framework also provides for a continuing committee, including representatives of Egypt, Israel, Jordan, and the self-governing authority, which may deal with outstanding matters of common concern during the transitional period.

The question of the Israeli settlements and their status after the transitional period would be a matter for discussion during the negotiations regarding the final status of the West Bank and Gaza referred to in paragraph A.1.(c).

8(B). *What will be Israel's obligation, during the coming period until the end of the transitional period, regarding the policy of settlement?*

It is the position of the United States that Israel should refrain from creating new settlements on the West Bank while negotiations are under way on the establishment of the self-governing authority. These negotiations will determine the question of existing settlements as well as any new settlement activity during the transitional period.

8(C). *What is the United States' position regarding both of the above questions?*

The United States' position is that settlements established during a military occupation are in violation of the Fourth Geneva Convention on the Protection of Persons in Time of War. However, in a relationship of peace, the parties to the peace should define the mutual rights of inhabitants to do business, to work, to live, and to carry on other transactions in each other's territory.

9(A). *Will the Israeli citizens who reside at present in the settlements be eligible for participation in the establishment of the self-governing authority and its subsequent activities?*

Israeli citizens residing in settlements on the West Bank and Gaza could participate in the establishment of the self-governing authority only as members of the Israeli negotiating delegation; there is no provision for their separate participation. Their participation, if any, in the self-governing authority must be determined in the negotiations for the transitional regime.

9(B). *What will be the status of the Israeli citizens residing in the West Bank and Gaza during the transitional period and will there be any, and if so what would their status be after the end of the transitional period?*

The negotiations under paragraph A.1.(b) defining the powers and responsibilities of the authority will deal with the status of Israeli settlements on the West Bank and Gaza and, accordingly, with the status of Israeli citizens residing in them. Whatever number that might remain beyond the transitional period, and their status, would presumably be agreed in the negotiations concerning the final status of the West Bank and Gaza envisaged under paragraph A.1.(c).

10(A). *At the end of the five-year transitional period, will the inhabitants of the West Bank and Gaza exercise in freedom the right of self-determination in order to decide their political future?*

The Framework provides for the elected representatives of the inhabitants of the West Bank and Gaza to participate fully in the negotiations that will determine the final status of the West Bank and Gaza and, in addition, for their elected representatives to ratify or reject the agreement reached in those negotiations. The Framework further provides that the solution from the negotiations must also recognize the legitimate rights of the Palestinian people and their just requirements. The wide acceptability of the results of this process is in the interest of all parties and is directly related to its being carried out "in freedom." In this respect, at the time the process described above is taking place, a strong local police force will exist and will be responsible to the self-governing authority to ensure that there is no interference in the political process that ensures these rights.

10(B). *What is the United States' position on this question?*

The United States supports the right of the Palestinians to participate in the determination of their own future, and believes that the Framework provides for such participation in all the important steps in determining the future of the West Bank and Gaza. The United States believes that paragraph A.1.(c) (2) does not preclude the holding of an election by the inhabitants of the West Bank and Gaza, after the conclusion of an agreement on the final status of the West Bank and Gaza, for the express purpose of electing representatives to whom that agreement will be submitted for a vote.

11(A). *What solution does the Framework Agreement envisage for the problem of the Palestinians living outside the occupied areas as refugees and for the restoration of their rights?*

Paragraph A.4. of the Framework provides that Egypt and Israel will work together with other interested parties to agree on a resolution of the refugee problem. Implementation of the procedures agreed upon is to be prompt, just and permanent.

Paragraph A.3. of the Framework provides for a continuing committee to decide on arrangements for the admission to the West Bank and Gaza of persons displaced from those areas in 1967.

In addition, as the political institutions of self-government take shape on the West Bank and Gaza through negotiations among the parties the relationship between those institutions and the Palestinians living outside the area would be addressed.

11(B). *What does the United States regard as the basis for the solution of this question? How does it define these rights?*

The United States believes that a resolution of the refugee problem should reflect applicable United Nations Resolutions. Any program for implementation must provide those refugees living outside the West Bank and Gaza a choice and opportunity in settling themselves permanently in the context of present-day realities and circumstances.

12. *What does the Framework Agreement envisage for the future of the rest of the occupied Arab territories? What is the United States Government's position on this question?*

The Framework states that it is intended to constitute a basis for peace between Israel and each of its other neighbors. It further states that the objective is a just, comprehensive, and durable peace and that each negotiation must carry out all the provisions and principles of United Nations Security Council Resolutions 242 and 338. Paragraph C.1. specifically states that the principles of the Framework should apply to treaties between Israel and Jordan, Syria, and Lebanon in addition to Egypt. Concerning the West Bank in particular, paragraph A.1.(c) requires negotiations based on all the provisions and principles of Resolution 242 which will resolve, among other matters, the location of boundaries. The United States continues to advocate a comprehensive peace involving all of Israel's neighbors. As regards the possibility of negotiations for a peaceful settlement between Israel and Syria, the United States will support the application of all the principles and provisions of Resolution 242 to such a settlement.

13. *In the definition of the security requirements in the area, does the United States Government endorse the principle of reciprocity on these requirements or does the United States Government regard these requirements to be one sided only?*

The United States fully endorses the principle of reciprocity as applied to security requirements in the context of Middle East peace negotiations. The preamble of the Framework specifically refers to reciprocity as the basis on which the parties can agree to special security arrangements. The Framework also refers to the security concerns "of all parties" and to the security of "Israel and its neighbors."

14. *As Security Council Resolution 242 is stated to be the basis of any negotiations for the settlement of the West Bank–Gaza and other aspects of the conflict, what would the United States Government do in the event of conflicting interpretations between the negotiating parties particularly in view of the United States Government's previous interpretations of Security Council Resolution 242 and commitments based thereon which were the basis of acceptance by Jordan of the said Resolution?*

The United States will, first, adhere to its own consistent interpretation of Resolution 242, and in particular to its interpretation that the withdrawal provision of that resolution applies on all fronts. In the event of conflicting interpretations among the negotiating parties, the United States will seek, as it did during the intensive negotiations at Camp David, to bring about a consensus among the parties and will make known its own interpretations as required to bring about resolution of the conflict. The interpretations of the United States remain those it has held since 1967.

Egyptian-Israeli Peace Treaty, March 26, 1979

TREATY OF PEACE BETWEEN THE ARAB REPUBLIC OF EGYPT
AND THE STATE OF ISRAEL

The Government of the Arab Republic of Egypt and the Government of the State of Israel:

Preamble

Convinced of the urgent necessity of the establishment of a just, comprehensive and lasting peace in the Middle East in accordance with Security Council Resolutions 242 and 338;

Reaffirming their adherence to the "Framework for Peace in the Middle East Agreed at Camp David," dated September 17, 1978;

Noting that the aforementioned Framework as appropriate is intended to constitute a basis for peace not only between Egypt and Israel but also between Israel and each of its other Arab neighbors which is prepared to negotiate peace with it on this basis;

Desiring to bring to an end the state of war between them and to establish a peace in which every state in the area can live in security;

Convinced that the conclusion of a Treaty of Peace between Egypt and Israel is an important step in the search for comprehensive peace in the area and for the attainment of the settlement of the Arab-Israeli conflict in all its aspects;

Inviting the other Arab parties to this dispute to join the peace process with Israel guided by and based on the principles of the aforementioned Framework;

Desiring as well to develop friendly relations and cooperation between themselves in accordance with the United Nations Charter and the principles of international law governing international relations in times of peace;

Agree to the following provisions in the free exercise of their sovereignty, in order to implement the "Framework for the Conclusion of a Peace Treaty Between Egypt and Israel:"

Article I

1. The state of war between the Parties will be terminated and peace will be established between them upon the exchange of instruments of ratification of this Treaty.

2. Israel will withdraw all its armed forces and civilians from the Sinai behind the international boundary between Egypt and mandated Palestine, as provided in the annexed protocol (Annex I), and Egypt will resume the exercise of its full sovereignty over the Sinai.

3. Upon completion of the interim withdrawal provided for in Annex I, the Parties will establish normal and friendly relations, in accordance with Article III(3).

Article II

The permanent boundary between Egypt and Israel is the recognized international boundary between Egypt and the former mandated territory of Palestine, as shown on the map at Annex II, without prejudice to the issue of the status of the Gaza Strip. The Parties recognize this boundary as inviolable. Each will respect the territorial integrity of the other, including their territorial waters and airspace.

Article III

1. The Parties will apply between them the provisions of the Charter of the United Nations and the principles of international law governing relations among states in times of peace. In particular:

a. They recognize and will respect each other's sovereignty, territorial integrity and political independence;

b. They recognize and will respect each other's right to live in peace within their secure and recognized boundaries;

c. They will refrain from the threat or use of force, directly or indirectly, against each other and will settle all disputes between them by peaceful means.

2. Each Party undertakes to ensure that acts or threats of belligerency, hostility, or violence do not originate from and are not committed from within its territory, or by any forces subject to its control or by any other forces stationed on its territory, against the population, citizens or property of the other Party. Each Party also undertakes to refrain from organizing, instigating, inciting, assisting or participating in acts or threats of belligerency, hostility, subversion or violence against the other Party,

anywhere, and undertakes to ensure that perpetrators of such acts are brought to justice.

3. The Parties agree that the normal relationship established between them will include full recognition, diplomatic, economic and cultural relations, termination of economic boycotts and discriminatory barriers to the free movement of people and goods, and will guarantee the mutual enjoyment by citizens of the due process of law. The process by which they undertake to achieve such a relationship parallel to the implementation of other provisions of this Treaty is set out in the annexed protocol (Annex III).

Article IV

1. In order to provide maximum security for both Parties on the basis of reciprocity, agreed security arrangements will be established including limited force zones in Egyptian and Israeli territory, and United Nations forces and observers, described in detail as to nature and timing in Annex I, and other security arrangements the Parties may agree upon.

2. The Parties agree to the stationing of United Nations personnel in areas described in Annex I. The Parties agree not to request withdrawal of the United Nations personnel and that these personnel will not be removed unless such removal is approved by the Security Council of the United Nations, with the affirmative vote of the five Permanent Members, unless the Parties otherwise agree.

3. A Joint Commission will be established to facilitate the implementation of the Treaty, as provided for in Annex I.

4. The security arrangements provided for in paragraphs 1 and 2 of this Article may at the request of either party be reviewed and amended by mutual agreement of the Parties.

Article V

1. Ships of Israel, and cargoes destined for or coming from Israel, shall enjoy the right of free passage through the Suez Canal and its approaches through the Gulf of Suez and the Mediterranean Sea on the basis of the Constantinople Convention of 1888, applying to all nations. Israeli nationals, vessels and cargoes, as well as persons, vessels and cargoes destined for or coming from Israel, shall be accorded non-discriminatory treatment in all matters connected with usage of the canal.

2. The Parties consider the Strait of Tiran and the Gulf of Aqaba to be international waterways open to all nations for unimpeded and non-

suspendable freedom of navigation and overflight. The Parties will respect each other's right to navigation and overflight for access to either country through the Strait of Tiran and the Gulf of Aqaba.

Article VI

1. This Treaty does not affect and shall not be interpreted as affecting in any way the rights and obligations of the Parties under the Charter of the United Nations.

2. The Parties undertake to fulfill in good faith their obligations under this Treaty, without regard to action or inaction of any other party and independently of any instrument external to this Treaty.

3. They further undertake to take all the necessary measures for the application in their relations of the provisions of the multilateral conventions to which they are parties, including the submission of appropriate notification to the Secretary General of the United Nations and other depositaries of such conventions.

4. The Parties undertake not to enter into any obligations in conflict with this Treaty.

5. Subject to Article 103 of the United Nations Charter, in the event of a conflict between the obligations of the Parties under the present Treaty and any of their other obligations, the obligations under this Treaty will be binding and implemented.

Article VII

1. Disputes arising out of the application or interpretation of this Treaty shall be resolved by negotiations.

2. Any such disputes which cannot be settled by negotiations shall be resolved by conciliation or submitted to arbitration.

Article VIII

The Parties agree to establish a claims commission for the mutual settlement of all financial claims.

Article IX

1. This Treaty shall enter into force upon exchange of instruments of ratification.

2. This Treaty supersedes the Agreement between Egypt and Israel of September, 1975.

3. All protocols, annexes, and maps attached to this Treaty shall be regarded as an integral part hereof.

4. The Treaty shall be communicated to the Secretary General of the United Nations for registration in accordance with the provisions of Article 102 of the Charter of the United Nations.

Done at Washington, D.C. this 26th day of March, 1979, in triplicate in the English, Arabic, and Hebrew languages, each text being equally authentic. In case of any divergence of interpretation, the English text shall prevail.

For the Government of the Arab Republic of Egypt:

A. Sadat

For the Government of Israel:

M. Begin

Witnessed by:

Jimmy Carter
Jimmy Carter, President of
the United States of America

AGREED MINUTES TO ARTICLES I, IV, V AND VI AND ANNEXES I AND III OF THE TREATY OF PEACE

Article I

Egypt's resumption of the exercise of full sovereignty over the Sinai provided for in paragraph 2 of Article I shall occur with regard to each area upon Israel's withdrawal from that area.

Article IV

It is agreed between the Parties that the review provided for in Article IV(4) will be undertaken when requested by either Party, commencing within three months of such a request, but that any amendment can be made only with the mutual agreement of both Parties.

Article V

The second sentence of paragraph 2 of Article V shall not be construed as limiting the first sentence of that paragraph. The foregoing is not to be construed as contravening the second sentence of paragraph 2 of Article V, which reads as follows:

"The Parties will respect each other's right to navigation and overflight for access to either country through the Strait of Tiran and the Gulf of Aqaba."

Article VI(2)

The provisions of Article VI shall not be construed in contradiction to the provisions of the framework for peace in the Middle East agreed at Camp David. The foregoing is not to be construed as contravening the provisions of Article VI(2) of the treaty, which reads as follows:

"The Parties undertake to fulfill in good faith their obligations under this Treaty, without regard to action or inaction of any other Party and independently of any instrument external to this Treaty."

Article VI(5)

It is agreed by the Parties that there is no assertion that this Treaty prevails over other Treaties or agreements or that other Treaties or agreements prevail over this Treaty. The foregoing is not to be construed as contravening the provisions of Article VI(5) of the Treaty, which reads as follows:

"Subject to Article 103 of the United Nations Charter, in the event of a conflict between the obligations of the Parties under the present Treaty and any of their other obligations, the obligations under this Treaty will be binding and implemented."

Annex I

Article VI, Paragraph 8, of Annex I provides as follows: "The Parties shall agree on the nations from which the United Nations force and observers will be drawn. They will be drawn from nations other than those which are permanent members of the United Nations Security Council." The Parties have agreed as follows:

"With respect to the provisions of paragraph 8, Article VI, of Annex I, if no agreement is reached between the Parties, they will accept or support a U.S. proposal concerning the composition of the United Nations force and observers."

Annex III

The Treaty of Peace and Annex III thereto provide for establishing normal economic relations between the Parties. In accordance therewith, it is agreed that such relations will include normal commercial sales of oil by Egypt to Israel, and that Israel shall be fully entitled to make bids for Egyptian-origin oil not needed for Egyptian domestic oil consumption, and Egypt and its oil concessionaires will entertain bids made by Israel on the same basis and terms as apply to other bidders for such oil.

Republic of Egypt:

A. Sadat

For the Government of Israel:

M. Begin

Witnessed by:

Jimmy Carter

Jimmy Carter, President
of the United States of America

LETTER FROM ISRAELI PRIME MINISTER MENACHEM BEGIN AND EGYPTIAN PRESIDENT ANWAR EL SADAT TO PRESIDENT JIMMY CARTER, MARCH 26, 1979

Dear Mr. President:

This letter confirms that Egypt and Israel have agreed as follows:

The Governments of Egypt and Israel recall that they concluded at Camp David and signed at the White House on September 17, 1978, the annexed documents entitled "A Framework for Peace in the Middle East Agreed at Camp David" and "Framework for the Conclusion of a Peace Treaty between Egypt and Israel."

For the purpose of achieving a comprehensive peace settlement in accordance with the above-mentioned Frameworks, Egypt and Israel will proceed with the implementation of those provisions relating to the West Bank and the Gaza Strip. They have agreed to start negotiations within a month after the exchange of the instruments of ratification of the Peace Treaty. In accordance with the "Framework for Peace in the Middle East," the Hashemite Kingdom of Jordan is invited to join the negotiations. The Delegations of Egypt and Jordan may include Palestinians from the West Bank and Gaza Strip or other Palestinians as mutually agreed. The purpose of the negotiation shall be to agree, prior to the elections, on the modalities for establishing the elected self-governing authority (administrative council), define its powers and responsibilities, and agreed upon other related issues. In the event Jordan decides not to take part in the negotiations, the negotiations will be held by Egypt and Israel.

The two Governments agree to negotiate continuously and in good faith to conclude these negotiations at the earliest possible date. They also agree that the objective of the negotiations is the establishment of the self-governing authority in the West Bank and Gaza in order to provide full autonomy to the inhabitants.

Egypt and Israel set for themselves the goal of completing the negotiations within one year so that elections will be held as expeditiously as possible after agreement has been reached between the parties. The self-governing authority referred to in the "Framework for Peace in the Middle East" will be established and inaugurated within one month after it has been elected, at which time the transitional period of five years will begin. The Israeli military government and its civilian administration will be withdrawn, to be replaced by the self-governing authority, as specified in the "Framework for Peace in the Middle East." A withdrawal of Israeli armed forces will then take place and there will be a redeployment of the remaining Israeli forces into specified security locations.

This letter also confirms our understanding that the United States Government will participate fully in all stages of negotiations.

Sincerely yours,

For the Government of Israel:

M. Begin
Menachem Begin

For the Government of the Arab Republic of Egypt:

A. Sadat
Mohamed Anwar El Sadat

NOTE: President Carter, upon receipt of the joint letter to him from President Sadat and Prime Minister Begin, added to the American and Israeli copies the notation:

"I have been informed that the expression 'West Bank' is understood by the Government of Israel to mean 'Judea and Samaria.' "

This notation is in accordance with similar procedures established at Camp David.[1]

---

1. Explanatory note with the original documents.

LETTER FROM PRESIDENT ANWAR EL SADAT TO PRESIDENT
JIMMY CARTER, MARCH 26, 1979

Dear Mr. President:

In response to your request, I can confirm that, within one month after
the completion of Israel's withdrawal to the interim line as provided for
in the Treaty of Peace between Egypt and Israel, Egypt will send a
resident ambassador to Israel and will receive a resident Israeli ambassador
in Egypt.

Sincerely,

A. Sadat
Mohamed Anwar El Sadat

LETTER FROM PRESIDENT JIMMY CARTER TO ISRAELI PRIME
MINISTER MENACHEM BEGIN, MARCH 26, 1979

Dear Mr. Prime Minister:

I have received a letter from President Sadat that, within one month after
Israel completes its withdrawal to the interim line in Sinai, as provided
for in the Treaty of Peace between Egypt and Israel, Egypt will send a
resident ambassador to Israel and will receive in Egypt a resident Israeli
ambassador.

I will be grateful if you will confirm that this procedure will be
agreeable to the Government of Israel.

Sincerely,

Jimmy Carter
Jimmy Carter

LETTER FROM ISRAELI PRIME MINISTER MENACHEM BEGIN
TO PRESIDENT JIMMY CARTER, MARCH 26, 1979

Dear Mr. President:

I am pleased to be able to confirm that the Government of Israel is
agreeable to the procedure set out in your letter of March 26, 1979 in
which you state:

"I have received a letter from President Sadat that, within one month
after Israel completes its withdrawal to the interim line in Sinai, as
provided for in the Treaty of Peace between Egypt and Israel, Egypt
will send a resident ambassador to Israel and will receive in Egypt a
resident Israeli ambassador."

Sincerely,

M. Begin
Menachem Begin

LETTERS FROM PRESIDENT JIMMY CARTER TO EGYPTIAN
PRESIDENT ANWAR EL SADAT AND ISRAELI PRIME MINISTER
MENACHEM BEGIN, MARCH 26, 1979[2]

Dear Mr. President: [Prime Minister]:

I wish to confirm to you that subject to United States Constitutional processes:

In the event of an actual or threatened violation of the Treaty of Peace between Egypt and Israel, the United States will, on request of one or both of the Parties, consult with the Parties with respect thereto and will take such other actions as it may deem appropriate and helpful to achieve compliance with the Treaty.

The United States will conduct aerial monitoring as requested by the Parties pursuant to Annex I of the Treaty.

The United States believes the Treaty provision for permanent stationing of United Nations personnel in the designated limited force zone can and should be implemented by the United Nations Security Council. The United States will exert its utmost efforts to obtain the requisite action by the Security Council. If the Security Council fails to establish and maintain the arrangements called for in the Treaty, the President will be prepared to take those steps necessary to ensure the establishment and maintenance of an acceptable alternative multinational force.

Sincerely,

Jimmy Carter
Jimmy Carter

2. Separate but identical letters were sent to President Sadat and Prime Minister Begin.

Chronology

1977

January 6	The Israeli government decides to hold early elections in May.
January 18–19	Riots occur in Cairo following the sudden food price increases.
February 4	The Policy Review Committee meets on the Middle East.
February 14	Secretary of State Cyrus Vance travels to the Middle East.
February 16	Vance meets with Prime Minister Yitzhak Rabin and Foreign Minister Yigal Allon in Jerusalem.
February 17	Vance meets with President Anwar Sadat in Egypt.
February 20	Vance meets with President Hafiz al-Asad in Syria.
February 23	The National Security Council meets on the Middle East.
March 7–8	President Jimmy Carter meets Israeli Prime Minister Rabin in Washington.
March 9	Carter makes a statement on the three key ingredients of a Middle East settlement: real peace, secure borders, Palestinian rights.
March 16	Carter speaks of a "homeland" for the Palestinians in a town meeting in Clinton, Massachusetts.
April 4–5	Carter meets Sadat in Washington.
April 19	The Policy Review Committee meets on the Middle East.
April 22	Carter meets Syrian Foreign Minister Abd al-Halim Khaddam in Washington
April 25–26	Carter meets Jordan's King Hussein in Washington.
May 9	Carter meets Syrian President Asad in Geneva.

May 11	Vance meets Israeli Foreign Minister Allon in London.
May 17	Israeli elections favor Likud bloc.
May 24–25	Carter meets Saudi Arabia's Crown Prince Fahd in Washington.
June 10	The Policy Review Committee meets on the Middle East.
June 17	Vice President Walter Mondale speaks on the Middle East at the World Affairs Council in San Francisco.
June 21	Menachem Begin becomes prime minister of Israel, with Moshe Dayan as his foreign minister.
June 25	The Policy Review Committee meets on the Middle East.
July 5	The Policy Review Committee meets on the Middle East.
July 12	The Policy Review Committee meets on the Middle East.
July 19–20	Carter meets Prime Minister Begin in Washington.
August 1–2	Vance meets Sadat in Alexandria.
August 4	Vance meets Asad in Damascus.
August 5	Vance meets King Hussein in Jordan.
August 9–10	Vance meets Begin in Jerusalem.
August 11	Vance meets Sadat near Alexandria.
August 22	Dayan meets secretly with King Hussein in London.
September 16	Dayan meets secretly in Morocco with Hassan Tuhamy, adviser to Sadat.
September 19	Carter meets with Dayan in Washington.
September 21	Carter meets with Egyptian Foreign Minister Ismail Fahmy in Washington.
September 28	Carter meets with Syrian Foreign Minister Khaddam and Jordanian Prime Minister Abd al-Hamid Sharaf in Washington.
October 1	The United States and the Soviet Union issue a joint communiqué on the Middle East.
October 4	Carter meets with Egyptian Foreign Minister Fahmy and Israeli Foreign Minister Dayan in New York.

October 21	Carter sends a handwritten letter to Sadat asking for help.
October 25–26	Carter meets with Saudi Foreign Minister Saud in Washington.
November 2	Carter speaks on the Middle East before the World Jewish Congress.
November 3	Carter receives Sadat's proposal for a conference in East Jerusalem.
November 9	Sadat announces his willingness to go to Jerusalem to speak before the Knesset.
November 19–20	Sadat meets with Begin and other Israeli political figures in Jerusalem.
December 10	Vance meets Sadat in Egypt.
December 11	Vance meets Begin in Jerusalem.
December 12	Vance meets King Hussein in Jordan.
December 15–17	Begin presents his "home rule" proposal to Carter in Washington.
December 25–26	Begin meets Sadat in Ismailiya, Egypt.
December 31	Carter leaves on trip that takes him to Iran, where he meets with King Hussein; he subsequently visits Saudi Arabia and Egypt.

1978

January 4	In Aswan Carter makes a statement on the Palestinians.
January 16–18	Vance joins the meeting of the Egyptian-Israeli "political committee" in Jerusalem.
January 20	Vance meets Sadat in Cairo.
February 3–4	Carter meets Sadat at Camp David.
February 16	Carter meets Dayan in Washington.
March 7	Americans receive Egyptian proposal for solving Palestinian question.
March 9	Vance meets Begin in Jerusalem.
March 11	The PLO attacks an Israeli bus; Israelis respond by launching Operation Litani, a military intervention in southern Lebanon.
March 21–22	Carter meets Begin in Washington.
April 26–27	Carter and Vance meet Dayan in Washington.

April 28	A Middle East aircraft package is sent to Congress.
May 1	Carter meets briefly with Begin in Washington. Americans receive the revised Egyptian proposal on the Palestinian question.
May 15	Americans receive further revisions to the Egyptian proposal on the Palestinian question. The Senate votes not to veto the Middle East aircraft package.
June 18	Israel sends its answers to Washington on how the question of sovereignty over the West Bank will be resolved.
July 2	Vice President Mondale arrives in Israel for talks with Begin.
July 3	Mondale meets with Sadat in Egypt.
July 17–19	Vance, Dayan, and Egyptian Foreign Minister Muhammad Ibrahim Kamil meet at Leeds Castle, England.
July 30	Carter decides to invite Sadat and Begin to summit meeting at Camp David.
August 6	Vance visits Jerusalem to invite Begin to Camp David.
August 7–8	Vance visits Alexandria to invite Sadat to Camp David.
September 1	Carter holds a National Security Council meeting to discuss the Camp David summit.
September 5–17	Carter, Sadat, and Begin meet at Camp David.
September 17	Sadat and Begin sign the Camp David Accords at the White House; Carter signs as witness.
September 25	Vance meets King Hussein in Jordan.
October 10	Carter meets Dayan in Washington.
October 11	Carter meets the Egyptian delegation led by Kamal Hassan Ali in Washington.
October 12	Blair House talks begin.
October 17	Carter meets with Egyptian and Israeli delegations.
November 2	Vance meets Begin in New York.
November 5	The Arab summit in Baghdad criticizes Camp David Accords.
November 11	Vance tries to complete the text of the Egyptian-Israeli treaty.

November 16	Carter meets Egyptian Vice President Husni Mubarak in Washington.
December 10–12	Vance meets Sadat in Egypt.
December 13–14	Vance meets Begin in Jerusalem.
December 14	Vance returns to Egypt for a meeting with Sadat.
December 23–24	Vance, Dayan, and Egyptian Prime Minister Mustafa Khalil meet in Brussels.

1979

January 15	The shah of Iran leaves his country.
January 23	The Policy Review Committee meets on the Middle East.
February 1	Ayatollah Khomeini returns to Iran.
February 21–22	Vance, Dayan, and Khalil meet at Camp David.
March 2–4	Carter meets with Begin in Washington.
March 6	Brzezinski meets with Sadat in Cairo to convey the new proposals.
March 7–13	Carter travels to Egypt and Israel to bring the negotiations to an end.
March 26	Sadat and Begin sign the Egyptian-Israeli peace treaty in Washington.

Bibliography

Bass, Peter. "The Anti-Politics of Presidential Leadership: Jimmy Carter and American Jews." Senior thesis presented to the faculty of the Woodrow Wilson School of International Affairs, Princeton University, April 12, 1985.

Bell, J. Bowyer. *Terror Out of Zion: Irgun Zvai Leumi, LEHI, and the Palestine Underground, 1929–1949*. New York: St. Martin's Press, 1977.

Benvenisti, Meron. *The West Bank Data Project: A Survey of Israel's Policies*. Washington, D.C.: American Enterprise Institute for Public Policy Research, 1984.

Benziman, Uzi. *Prime Minister under Siege* (in Hebrew). Jerusalem: Adam Publishers, 1981.

Brzezinski, Zbigniew. *Power and Principle: Memoirs of the National Security Adviser, 1977–1981*. New York: Farrar, Strauss, Giroux, 1983.

———, François Duchêne, and Kiichi Saeki. "Peace in an International Framework." *Foreign Policy*, no. 19 (Summer 1975), pp. 3–17.

Carter, Jimmy. *The Blood of Abraham*. Boston: Houghton Mifflin Company, 1985.

———. *Keeping Faith: Memoirs of a President*. New York: Bantam Books, 1982.

Carter, Rosalynn. *First Lady from Plains*. Boston: Houghton Mifflin Company, 1984.

Charney, Leon H. *Special Counsel*. New York: Philosophical Library, 1984.

Cobban, Helena. *The Palestinian Liberation Organization: People, Power and Politics*. New York: Cambridge University Press, 1984.

Dayan, Moshe. *Breakthrough: A Personal Account of the Egypt-Israel Peace Negotiations*. New York: Alfred A. Knopf, 1981.

Donovan, Hedley. *Roosevelt to Reagan: A Reporter's Encounters with Nine Presidents*. New York: Harper and Row, 1985.

The Egyptian Position in Negotiations Concerning the Establishment of Transitional Arrangements for the West Bank and Gaza. Cairo: Ministry of Foreign Affairs, 1980.

Eilts, Hermann Frederick. "Improve the Framework." *Foreign Policy*, no. 41 (Winter 1980–81), pp. 3–20.

Fahmy, Ismail. *Negotiating for Peace in the Middle East*. Baltimore: Johns Hopkins University Press, 1983.

Friedlander, Melvin A. *Sadat and Begin: The Domestic Politics of Peacemaking*. Boulder, Colo.: Westview, 1983.

Haber, Eitan, Ze'ev Schiff, and Ehud Ya'ari. *The Year of the Dove*. New York: Bantam Books, 1979.

Halabi, Usamah, Aron Turner, and Meron Benvenisti. "Land Alienation in the

West Bank: A Legal and Spatial Analysis." Jerusalem: The West Bank Data Base Project, April 1985.

Indyk, Martin. *"To the Ends of the Earth": Sadat's Jerusalem Initiative.* Cambridge, Mass.: Harvard University, Center for Middle Eastern Studies, 1984.

Jordan, Hamilton. *Crisis: The Last Year of the Carter Presidency.* New York: Putnam Publishing Group, 1982.

Kamil, Muhammad Ibrahim. *The Lost Peace in the Camp David Accords* (in Arabic). Jidda: Saudi Research and Marketing Company, 1984.

Kissinger, Henry A. *White House Years.* Boston: Little, Brown, 1979.

Medzini, Meron, ed. *Israel's Foreign Relations: Selected Documents, 1977–1979,* vols. 4 and 5. Jerusalem: Ministry for Foreign Affairs, 1981.

Powell, Jody. *The Other Side of the Story.* New York: William Morrow and Company, 1984.

Public Papers of the Presidents: Jimmy Carter, 1977, vol. 1. Washington, D.C.: Government Printing Office, 1977.

————, vol. 2. Washington, D.C.: Government Printing Office, 1978.

Public Papers of the Presidents: Jimmy Carter, 1978, vol. 1. Washington, D.C.: Government Printing Office, 1979.

Quandt, William B. *Decade of Decisions: American Policy Toward the Arab-Israeli Conflict, 1967–1976.* Berkeley: University of California Press, 1977.

————. "Reagan's Lebanon Policy: Trial and Error." *Middle East Journal,* vol. 38 (Spring 1984), pp. 237–54.

————. "U.S. Policy in the Jordan Crisis, 1970," in Barry M. Blechman and Stephen S. Kaplan, eds., *Force without War: U.S. Armed Forces as a Political Instrument.* Washington, D.C.: Brookings Institution, 1978.

Rabin, Yitzhak. *The Rabin Memoirs.* Boston: Little, Brown, 1979.

Rabinowicz, Oscar K. *Vladimir Jabotinsky's Conception of a Nation.* New York: Beechhurst Press, 1946.

Sadat, Anwar el-. *In Search of Identity: An Autobiography.* New York: Harper and Row, 1977.

————. *Those I Have Known.* New York: Continuum, 1984.

Schiff, Ze'ev, and Ehud Ya'ari. *Israel's Lebanon War.* New York: Simon and Schuster, 1984.

Sick, Gary. *All Fall Down: America's Tragic Encounter with Iran.* New York: Random House, 1985.

Silver, Eric. *Begin: The Haunted Prophet.* New York: Random House, 1984.

Spiegel, Steven L. *The Other Arab-Israeli Conflict: Making America's Middle East Policy, from Truman to Reagan.* Chicago: University of Chicago Press, 1985.

Toward Peace in the Middle East. Report of a Study Group. Washington, D.C.: Brookings Institution, 1975.

Vance, Cyrus. *Hard Choices: Critical Years in America's Foreign Policy.* New York: Simon and Schuster, 1983.

Weizman, Ezer. *The Battle for Peace.* New York: Bantam Books, 1981.

White Paper on Treaty of Peace between Egypt and Israel. Cairo: Ministry of Foreign Affairs, 1979.

Zartman, I. William, and Maureen R. Berman. *The Practical Negotiator.* New Haven: Yale University Press, 1982.

Index

Aaron, David, 194
Abd al-Magid, Ismat, 159
Afghanistan, 24, 26
Aid programs, U.S., 335. *See also* Arms sales, U.S.
  bilateral commitments, 294
  Egypt, 314
  Israel, 7, 38–39, 71, 83, 312–313
  Saudi Arabia, 271
  settlements and, 280, 296
  Sinai withdrawal and, 279–82
Airborne warning and control system, 19
Aircraft. *See* Arms sales, U.S.
Airfields
  Camp David Accords on, 255
  Israeli withdrawal, 227, 236–37
  Negev, 241, 277
  Sinai, 223, 236–37, 240–41, 298
  U.S. buffer, 242
  U.S.-Israeli, 264, 267, 313–14
Al-Arish, 198
  Israeli withdrawal, 200, 202, 273
Algerian National Liberation Front, 46
Ali, Kamal Hassan, 270, 281
  Carter and, 273
Allon, Yigal, 41
Ambassadors, exchange of, 51, 210, 232, 237, 257, 269, 273–74, 281–82, 286–88, 294–96, 305, 309, 313
American Israel Public Affairs Committee, 69. *See also* Jews, American
Arab(s). *See also* Palestinians; *names of specific countries, rulers*
  Arab League, 88, 124, 276, 280
  Arafat and, 101–02
  Baghdad summit, 260, 273, 275, 279–80
  break with Egypt, 153
  Camp David Accords and, 260, 262, 328
  Egyptian defense pacts, 269
  Geneva conference and, 42–43, 74, 79–80, 90, 93, 112–15, 117, 122, 126
  Iran revolution and, 291
  as Israeli citizens, 156
  moderate coalitions, 1, 37, 67, 72, 83

Muslim militancy, 334
  nationalism, 57
  peace treaty and, 291, 312, 329–30
  recognition of Israel, 63, 69
  regional economic development, 58
  as trustees, 70, 89, 94, 101
  United States and, 33, 125, 267, 302, 328–29, 332–39
  U.S.-Israeli Working Paper and, 129–30, 138, 142, 152–53
Arabi, Nabil al-, 222n
Arab-Israeli wars, 4, 79. *See also names of wars, regions*
  Arab territory seized, 209
  Carter on, 58–59
  cease-fire, 20, 104
  electoral cycles and, 8
  June *1967*, 17, 32
  October *1973*, 32, 76
  Operation Litani, 183
  post-treaty, 328–32
  U.S. policy, 32–33, 63
Arab League, 88, 124
  headquarters, 280
  treaty and, 276
Arafat, Yasir. *See also* Palestine Liberation Organization
  Carter and, 48
  Geneva and, 124–25
  opposition to Camp David Accords, 328
  Palestinian state and, 85–86
  Sadat and, 52, 135
  Saudis and, 91
  superconference and, 144
  U.N. Resolution *242* and, 93–94, 100–03
Arms Export Control Act (*1976*), 103
Arms sales, U.S., 18, 26, 41, 325
  debate, 75, 188
  Ecuador, 39, 42
  Egypt, 52, 55, 70–71, 170
  Israel, 70–71, 83, 176, 179, 193
  Lebanon war and, 103
  peace treaty and, 313–14
  Saudi Arabia, 70–71, 160, 176, 179

Asad, Hafiz al-, 34. *See also* Syria
  Carter and, 56–58
  Crown Prince Fahd and, 67
  Geneva conference and, 61, 90, 135–36
  opposition to Camp David Accords, 328
  Sadat and, 52, 97, 142, 154, 197
Aswan Declaration, 160–61, 179, 192, 194,
    213–14
  as compromise, 216–17
Atherton, Alfred L., Jr., 119–20
  as ambassador-at-large, 188
  on borders, 76
  in Cairo, 181
  Fahmy and, 121
  Sadat and, 202
  secret planning group, 194–96
  summit strategy, 212–14
  treaty role, 294–95

Baghdad summit, 260, 273, 275, 279–80
Balfour Declaration, 146
Barak, Aharon, 184, 193
  at Camp David, 224, 230, 232–33
  in Egypt, 158–60
  on freeze, 249, 264
  post-summit role, 271
  Sadat-Gamasy talks, 188
  on West Bank–Gaza plan, 243–44, 274
Bass, Peter Evan, 39n
Baz, Usama al-, 111n, 159, 262, 271, 278
  post-summit role, 270, 276
  security concerns, 199–200
  summit role, 231–33, 253
  treaty negotiations by, 285
Begin, Menachem, 2, 37. *See also* Israel
  American Jews and, 62
  Arab leaders and, 108
  background, 64–67
  Carter and, 47
  domestic problems, 261
  in Egypt, 159–60
  election, 62–63
  home rule plan, 150–58, 168, 178
  Nobel peace prize, 277
  on plebiscite, 186
  PLO and, 93
  resignation, 2
  Sadat and, 5, 162–63
  "six noes" of, 182–86
  Soviets and, 120
  at summit, 219–58
  U.S. politics and, 14, 78
  Vance and, 207
  Washington, D.C. visits, 68, 77–84, 155–
    58, 184, 298
  withdrawal position, 153, 192

Bell, J. Bowyer, 66n
Ben-Gurion, David, 64, 66
Benvenisti, Meron, 328n
Benziman, Uzi, 113n
Berman, Maureen R., 40n
Blair House talks, 268–75
Blechman, Barry M., 20n
Bolling, Landrum, 101–02
Borders. *See also* United Nations, Security
    Council Resolution *242*
  Arab agreement on, 63
  Begin on, 82n
  cease-fire lines, 106
  defensible, 44, 47
  in draft treaty, 105
  Egyptian, 51, 120, 232, 256
  international, 155, 226, 268–69
  Israeli policy, 39, 41, 213–14
  Jordanian, 7, 106
  minor modifications, 228–29
  1947 partition lines, 68n
  1949 Armistice Demarcation Lines, 105,
    231
  1967 lines, 39, 46, 59, 74, 76, 85, 92, 96,
    119, 127, 129, 154, 199, 227
  open, 227, 333
  West Bank, 88
Boutros Ghali, Boutros
  Carter and, 273
  on linkage, 281
  treaty negotiations, 270–71
Brezhnev, Leonid I., 144
Brown, Harold, 38, 72, 75
  on airfields, 267
  Geneva summit and, 54
  Iran crisis, 296
  Middle East trip, 294
  on military aid, 179, 313
  National Security Council and, 217
Brzezinski, Zbigniew, 15, 34, 55n, 69, 114n,
    127n, 202n, 239n, 265n, 273n. *See also*
    Policy Review Committee
  background, 35
  Begin and, 62, 66
  Begin-Sadat plan, 149–50
  bilateral treaty study, 177
  Bolling and, 101–02
  Camp David initiative, 165–66, 170–72
  on Geneva plan, 61–62
  on home rule, 156–57
  Katz and, 69
  on linkage, 285
  Marei and, 176–77n
  Middle East strategy, 105–106
  National Security Council memo to, 187–
    88n

on PLO, 43
Sadat and, 53, 301–02
Saudis and, 312
secret planning group, 194–96
summit strategy, 163, 207–20, 229, 233
on superconference, 144–45
treaty concerns, 295
Trilateral Commission, 31
Bunche, Ralph, 104
Byrd, Robert, 284

Cairo conference, 149–50
Israel's position, 153
Camp David, February 1978, Sadat-Carter at, 172–78
Camp David summit, 167. *See also* Sinai Peninsula; West Bank–Gaza proposals
Accords, 3, 252–58
Arab opposition, 243, 260, 264–65, 282
Baghdad summit and, 279–80
Begin-Sadat encounter, 223–24
briefing books, 209–19
Carter role, 29, 201–02, 257–58
diplomatic relations, 286
draft proposals, 224–29
Egyptian role, 215–16, 245–47, 254–55
final days, 237–58
first days, 220–36
Hussein and, 265–66
impasse, 233–36, 242
interpretations of Camp David Accords, 225–26, 259–90
Israeli role, 245–47, 255–57
mistakes, 296–97
as model, 330–31
Palestinian linkage issue, 271–72
Sadat's threat, 238–40
timetable, 175, 218
U.S. strategy, 206–20
Camp David II, 295–98
Carter, Amy, 45n
Carter, Gloria, 31
Carter, Jimmy, 2. *See also names of adminis-tration personnel*
on Arab leaders, 49–58
on arms sales, 41–42
Aswan Declaration, 160–61, 179, 213–17
background, 30–32
Begin and, 77–84, 103, 184–86
Camp David initiative, 29, 165–66
Carter Doctrine, 295
contributions, 5, 324–27, 336–37
credibility, 98
Dayan and, 112
domestic pressures on, 62, 69, 125–31, 136, 145, 169, 174, 204, 258, 295

draft version of Sinai settlement, 232
failure speech, 240–41
first year, 18, 30
Geneva commitment, 137–43
Iran crisis, 14, 24, 26, 296, 325, 335
Israeli pressures on, 125–31
Jewish support, 286
malaise speech, 24
Middle East team, 70, 285, 306–11
Middle East trips, 151, 274, 276, 302–11
misjudgments, 131–34
Mubarak and, 283
National Security Council and, 218
on Palestinian linkage issue, 323n
PLO and, 46, 110–11
policies of, 9–10, 76, 86–87, 293
pre-Geneva strategy, 38–40, 96–134
Rabin and, 43–49
reassessment by, 63–64
reelection, 3, 239, 292, 325
Sadat and, 139–42, 239
second year, 21, 163
Sharaf and, 121–22
Sinai–West Bank linkage, 212–14
at summit, 219–58
summit strategy, 137–67, 197–98, 209–19
on superconference, 145
third year, 23–24
treaty and, 317–20
U.N. speech, 32n, 125–26
Carter, Rosalynn, 26n, 145n
Carter Doctrine, 295
Ceauşescu, Nicolae, 109–10
on Begin, 144
Chamberlain, Neville, 91
China, normalization of relations, 270, 289
Clymer, Adam, 3n
Cohen, Geulah, 308
Congress
arms sales debate, 188, 190–91
Begin-Carter appearance, 265n
Carter and, 129, 187
elections, 20
Lebanon and, 8
Middle East Policy, 7–8, 15
Panama Canal treaty, 171, 174, 188
pro-Israel stance, 7, 160
presidency and, 338
Senate Foreign Relations Committee, 16
Cyprus agreement, 34

Dayan, Moshe, 82n, 92n. *See also* Israel
Camp David II, 297–98
Carter and, 126–31, 134–36, 180–81
in Egypt, 158–60

on Geneva procedures, 142–43
Hassan and, 109
Hussein and, 108
Leeds Castle talks, 198–201
Mondale and, 196
National Security Council on, 193
secret Moroccan trip, 109–10
on settlements, 161, 236, 238, 248–49
on Sinai, 232
at summit, 221–24, 230, 232–33
treaty negotiations, 179, 211, 217, 273, 277–79, 309–13
Vance and, 93, 180, 309–10
in Washington, D.C., 111–14
on West Bank–Gaza plan, 243–44
on withdrawal, 84
Deir Yassin, 64
Demilitarized zones, 39, 48, 185–86. *See also* Borders
early warning stations, 59
Department of Defense, 207
Department of Interior, 43–44
Dinitz, Simcha, 84
Dobrynin, Anatoly, 119
Donovan, Hedley, 31n
Duchêne, François, 34n

East Bank, 210
East Jerusalem
Holy Places, 58
Israeli annexation, 330
Israeli occupation, 32, 193, 209–11
Israeli withdrawal, 55
Palestinian elections, 272, 275, 323, 329
self-governing authority, 266
superconference plan, 144
U.S. policy, 252
Ecuador, aircraft sales to, 39, 42
Egypt. *See also* Egyptian-Israeli peace treaty; Gaza; Sadat, Anwar; Sinai Peninsula
Begin visit, 158–60
borders, 51, 120, 232, 256, 269
Carter in, 160–61, 302–03, 310–11
concessions of, 50–52
draft peace treaty, 90, 93
food riots, 36
Gaza transfer to, 222
on Geneva, 88
Israeli disengagement agreements, 33, 108–09
Israeli military mission in, 201
Israeli occupation, 32, 84, 89
Israeli war, 32, 76
Palestinian plan, 182, 322–24
nine-point plan, 195
oil sales, 198

pan-Arab policies, 1, 331
on PLO in Geneva, 115
post-summit strategy, 259–68, 270
priority of obligations, 274, 276, 281, 283–84, 292–93, 298–300, 304–05
recognition of Israel, 227
return of territory, 53
Rogers Plan, 17
settlements and, 215, 217
Sinai II, 23
Soviet threat, 18
Suez Canal agreement, 21–22, 26, 272
summit concessions, 22
superconference plan, 144
Syria and, 136
U.S. arms sales to, 52, 55, 70–71, 170
U.S. interests in, 7, 302, 334
U.S. summit draft, 231
Egyptian-Israeli peace treaty, 2, 24, 115. *See also* Camp David summit
annexes, 270, 313
Carter and, 5, 29, 150, 176–78, 324–27, 336–37
declaration of principles, 181
diplomatic relations, 269, 273, 281–82
drafts, 120, 164–65, 195, 268–72, 281n
Egyptian revisions, 284–85
exchange of ambassadors, 51, 210, 232, 237, 257, 269, 273–74, 281–82, 286–88, 294–96, 305, 309, 313
final agreement, 302–11, 324
future treaties, 330
impasses, 137–43, 163n, 181–82, 289–92, 306–11
Jordan's role, 325
as model, 211
nine-point plan, 171–72
National Security Council strategy, 191–94
Palestinian linkage, 178, 182, 207–08, 211–12, 261, 270, 290, 322–25
political context, 315–19
post-summit negotiations, 259–90
priority of obligations issue, 269, 274, 276, 281, 283–84, 287, 292–93, 298–300, 304–05
settlements issue, 247–51
signing, 313
Sinai in, 193, 204, 216, 270, 276
Syria and, 116–17
territorial concessions, 330
time frame, 232, 273, 289
United States and, 136–37, 194–96, 306–13, 324–25
unresolved issues, 315–19
West Bank–Gaza formula, 218–19, 271

Egyptian National Assembly, 144, 146, 152
Eilts, Hermann F., 33n, 146, 227, 265n, 296
  Byrd-Sadat talks, 284
  Fahmy and, 144
  on Israelis, 202
  Sadat and, 142, 148, 159, 166, 198, 215, 220, 276n
  on settlements freeze, 251n
  summit plans, 217
  treaty role, 283
Eisenhower, Dwight D., 8, 13
  Suez crisis, 26
Eizenstat, Stuart, 69
Elections
  Carter reelection, 292, 325
  electoral cycles, 8–9, 14–15, 22, 33, 337–38
  Israeli, 60, 62–63
  peace treaty and, 260
  West Bank–Gaza, 269, 277–79, 283–84, 299–301
  window of opportunity and, 15
Energy programs, 32, 53. *See also* Oil
  security plan, 68
Eretz Israel. *See also* West Bank–Gaza proposals
  Arabs of, 94
  Begin's commitment, 153, 164
  Camp David Accords, 256
  Sinai trade, 316
  territory, 64–66
Eritrea, 79
Ethiopian war, 79
Etzion airfield, 227

Fahd, Crown Prince, 58, 303n
  peace treaty and, 312
  U.S. visit, 67–69
Fahmy, Ismail, 88, 106n, 137n
  Carter and, 125–26, 138
  Dayan on, 113
  draft peace treaty, 90n
  in Jerusalem, 148
  resignation, 147, 262
  Sadat and, 110
  superconference plan, 144
  Vance and, 89, 92
  in Washington, D.C., 114–16, 124
Fatah organization, 86. *See also* Arafat, Yasir; Palestine Liberation Organization
Ford, Gerald R., 13
  aid to Israel, 38–39
  election-year agenda, 26
  Middle East role, 23
  on Palestinians, 60

  promises to Israel, 201, 220
  Sinai II and, 33, 59n
  transition papers, 36
Foreign Relations Committee, Senate, 16

Gamasy, Abd al-Ghani al-, 148, 162
  replacement, 270
Gaza. *See also* Borders; West Bank–Gaza proposals
  autonomy plan, 1, 276, 283, 288, 308
  cultural autonomy plan, 92, 94
  Dayan on, 127–28
  demilitarized, 185–86
  Egyptian claim, 126 175, 242, 244, 275–76, 278, 281, 284, 288
  Egyptian liaison officers, 287, 304–05, 308–10
  enlargement of, 149
  interim regime plans, 23, 105, 150, 167, 174, 182, 326
  Israeli occupation, 32, 64, 82, 255
  Israeli withdrawal, 73–74, 155–58, 222, 230
  new settlements in, 330
  referendum plan, 54, 112
  security, 187
  trusteeship, 70, 89, 94, 101
  U.S. summit plan, 171–72, 212–14
Geneva Conference proposal
  Begin plan, 79
  Brzezinski on, 40
  Palestinian representation, 86, 91, 101–02, 105–06, 112, 119, 124–28, 138
  planning for, 18, 36, 49–58, 61, 70, 76, 102
  PLO role, 46, 116, 142
  procedures, 117–34
  Sadat on, 51
  Soviet role, 56
  Syrian representation, 135
  unified Arab delegation, 43, 45, 79–80, 87–88, 90, 93, 112–15, 117, 122, 126
  U.S.-Israeli Working Paper, 129–130, 138, 142, 152–53
  U.S.-Soviet communiqué, 119–125, 130, 133, 135
  Vance on, 40
  West Bank mayors, 128
Geneva Convention (*1949*), 252
Ghorbal, Ashraf, 143
Giddi pass, 228
Golan Heights
  Ford on, 59n
  Israelis in, 32, 45, 82, 129, 215, 330
  Israeli withdrawal, 73–74, 181
  Sadat on, 88

Syrian-Israeli agreement, 21, 33, 212
Goldberg, Arthur J., 104, 252
Gromyko, Andrei, 120
Gush Emunim movement, 162n
Gwertzman, Bernard, 44n, 100n, 190n

Haber, Eitan, 109n, 160n
Habib, Philip, 21
Haig, Alexander M., Jr., 18, 21
Halabi, Usamah, 328n
Hansell, Herbert J., 270–71, 294–95
Hassan, King, 109
Hitler, Adolf, 65, 91
Holocaust, 65
Home rule
    Begin plan, 150–59, 163, 182–90, 195–96
    interim regime, 213
    Jordan on, 192
    U.N. Resolution *242* and, 168–69
    U.S. plan, 171–72
Horn of Africa, 52
Hostage crisis. *See* Iran, hostage crisis
House, Karen Elliott, 15n
Hua Guofeng, 144
Hussein I, King, 24n. *See also* Jordan
    Begin and, 274–75
    Camp David Accords and, 251, 256, 260, 265–66, 328
    Carter and, 55–56, 160
    Gaza agreement and, 283
    Geneva role, 113, 127
    on home rule, 192, 253n
    Israeli talks with, 108
    peace treaty and, 203, 234, 271, 274–76, 312
    PLO and, 20
    Sadat and, 97, 150, 153, 197
    West Bank and, 88

Indyk, Martin, 111n, 118–19n, 124n
Iran
    hostage crisis, 14, 26, 325, 335
    Muslim militancy, 334
    oil crisis and, 68, 299
    revolution, 24, 284, 290–92, 296, 298n, 307, 311
Iraq, 302. *See also* Arabs
Irgun movement, 64–65, 275
Irrigation plan, 198
Ismailiya. *See* Egypt
Israel. *See also* Arab-Israeli wars; Egyptian-Israeli peace treaty; Jews, American; Knesset; Settlements, Israeli; Sinai Peninsula
    Arab boycott, 38
    arms embargo, 23
    Army Planning Branch, 230

Carter in, 303–10
Carter pressure on, 182–90
current policy, 330–31
disengagement agreements, 21, 33, 109
draft peace treaty, 90, 93, 105–07, 112
Ecuador and, 42
Egyptian military mission, 201
elections, 36–37, 45
Eretz Israel, 64–66, 94, 153, 164, 256, 316
Foreign Affairs and Security Committee, 308
Geneva procedures, 126–31
Golan Heights agreement, 21
Herut party, 64, 261
home rule plan, 155–58, 175
Irgun movement, 64–65, 275
Labor party, 2, 64, 84
in Lebanon, 2, 19, 21, 41, 99–100, 104, 112, 183, 268, 321, 329
Likud bloc, 2, 36, 62–63, 65, 69, 328
1967 borders, 39, 46, 59, 74, 76, 85, 92, 96, 119, 127, 129, 154, 178, 199, 213–14, 227
PLO and, 20, 43, 103
political cycles, 49
post-summit strategy, 259–68, 271
Rogers Plan, 17
Romania and, 109–10
Sadat and, 109, 147
security concerns, 199–200, 207, 217
Sinai II, 23, 33, 51n, 59n, 76, 201, 262
Soviet threat, 18, 120
statehood, 65–66
summit strategy, 225–26
as trustee, 94, 101
U.S. military aid, 7, 38–39, 71, 75, 83, 312–13
U.S. policy, 26, 99
U.S.-Soviet communiqué, 127
war damage compensation, 222
withdrawal plans, 73–74, 80, 123, 254–55, 273–74

Jabotinsky, Vladimir Ze'ev, 65, 83, 155n
Jackson, Henry, 157
Javits, Jacob, 73n
Jerusalem. *See also* East Jerusalem
    Arab role, 232, 243, 328
    Camp David Accords and, 251, 255
    Egyptian concessions, 222
    Holy Places, 58, 222
    Israeli control, 2, 193
    legal status, 7
    Mondale speech, 196
    political committee at, 162–65
    post-summit status, 283

Sadat visit, 61, 114, 136–37, 142–52, 329
summit drafts, 246
treaty talks, 303–11
U.S. position, 252, 275
Vance in, 91–92
West Bank autonomy and, 246
Jews, American, 12, 43, 116, 167
American Israel Public Affairs Committee, 69
Carter and, 62, 129, 131, 134, 286, 295, 322
Carter's liaison to, 49n
Israeli leaders and, 64, 66
PLO and, 57
Reagan speech, 21
Saudi arms sales and, 195, 204
Johnson, Lyndon B., 34
Joint Chiefs of Staff, 294
Jones, David C., 294
Jordan, Hamilton, 26n, 38, 49n, 69, 182, 245, 279, 285, 300
Israelis and, 114
secret planning group, 194
strategy debate, 197
Jordan. *See also* Hussein; Jordanian-Palestinian relationship
Geneva, 113, 127
hijacking, 20
Israeli occupation, 2, 32
opposition to Camp David Accords, 264–65
peace negotiations, 244–45
PLO and, 327
summit role, 220
transitional regime and, 200
treaty and, 33, 105, 180–81, 196, 280, 303
as trustee, 94, 101
U.S. strategy, 25, 192
Vance in, 91
West Bank and, 88, 183, 197, 222, 243–44, 299
Jordan River, 77
Israeli security and, 106
Jordanian-Palestinian relationship, 41, 45, 79, 158, 180, 184, 328, 332
Asad on, 57
Sadat on, 51
treaty linkage, 76
U.S. position, 74
Judea. *See* West Bank

Kadishai, Yehiel, 155
Kamil, Muhammad Ibrahim, 159, 174–77n, 189–90n, 195n, 202n, 221n, 225n, 238, 239–40n
at Leeds Castle, 198–201

political committee and, 164–65
resignation, 262, 270
summit drafts, 231
on treaty, 178
Kaplan, Stephen S., 20n
Karawan, Ibrahim, 142n
Katz, Shmuel, 69, 79
Kennedy, Edward M., 24, 27
Khaddam, Abd al-Halim, 55, 94
Carter and, 116
PLO and, 102
treaty role, 314
Khalid, King, 145. *See also* Saudi Arabia
Carter visit, 160
Khalil, Mustafa, 270
Camp David II, 297–98
Dayan-Vance talks, 292
treaty negotiations, 276n, 285, 294
King David Hotel, bombing, 64
Kissinger, Henry A., 34
disengagement agreement, 88
Israeli commitment, 85
Middle East role, 17–18, 20–21, 39, 90, 336–37
Rabin on, 47
Sadat and, 50
shuttle diplomacy, 4, 33, 96, 174
Sinai II and, 23
on Suez Canal, 22n
Knesset
Begin in, 64
Camp David Accords vote, 245, 266, 283
Carter address, 308
draft treaty approval, 277
Sadat speech, 144, 146–47
Sinai settlements vote, 263
treaty vote, 283, 304
U.S. proposals and, 301
on withdrawal, 281

Lauterpacht, Hersch, 92
Lawrence, Richard, 270–71
Lebanon war, 19, 21, 103, 267–68
Begin on, 79
cease-fire, 104, 268
Congress and, 8
Israeli invasion, 2, 112, 183, 321, 328–39
Marine barracks bombing, 25
Maronites, 217, 268
Muslim majority, 268, 334
PLO in, 92, 99–100
Rabin on, 41
Reagan and, 14
Syria and, 26, 57, 328
U.N. forces in, 94
U.N. Resolution, 183
U.S. policy, 25, 335

Leeds Castle meeting, 198–201
Lewis, Samuel W., 79, 146, 296
  Begin and, 264, 294
  Dayan and, 194
  at Leeds Castle, 199
  summit plans, 217
Linowitz, Sol, 24
Loan programs. *See* Aid programs, U.S.
Lobbyists, pro-Israeli, 12

Maale Adumim, 161
Maher, Ahmed, 177n, 222n
Mapai Plan, 81
Marei, Sayyid, 176n
Marshall Plan, 68
Medzini, Meron, 83n, 196n
Meir, Golda, 64
  Sadat and, 147, 215
Mitla pass, 228
Mondale, Walter F., 24, 38, 69
  arms sales and, 204
  Begin on, 162
  Dayan and, 112
  Israeli trust of, 218
  Middle East policy, 66, 70–71, 195–97
  strategy debate, 197
  summit drafts, 229
Mt. Sinai, 198
Mubarak, Husni. *See also* Egypt
  as president, 328
  treaty role, 283

Nasser, Gamal Abd al-, 17
National Press Club, 173
National Security Council. *See also* Quandt,
  William B.
  position papers, 36
  reassessment memo, 191–94
  summit plans, 207–20
  Vance report, 42–43
Navigation rights, 269
Negev
  airfields in, 241, 264, 267, 277, 313–14
  Nile water for irrigation, 198
Newsom, David, 194
Nile River, 198
Nixon, Richard M., 8
  Kissinger and, 17–18
  Middle East policy, 20–21, 26, 338
  on Palestinians, 60
  third year, 22–23
  Watergate crisis, 17, 20
  window of opportunity, 15
Nobel peace prize, 277
North Yemen, 292
Nuclear weapons ban, 222

O'Neill, Thomas P., 46
Oberdorfer, Don, 186n
Oil
  Begin-Sadat agreement, 307–08, 314
  compensation, 222
  crisis, 24, 32, 294, 301
  energy security plan, 68
  Iranian crisis and, 284, 290–92, 299
  Israeli withdrawal and, 254–55
  Sinai, 238, 270
  treaty and, 53–54, 281
  U.S. guarantees, 305, 312
  as weapon, 334
Operation Litani, 183

Palestine
  Balfour Declaration, 146
  claim to, 64
  mandated borders, 232, 256, 268–69
  Western, 69
Palestine Liberation Organization (PLO)
  attack on Israel, 183
  Begin and, 85
  Camp David Accords and, 265
  Carter on, 48
  Central Committee, 100
  charter, 91
  factions, 86, 328
  Geneva role, 41, 74, 79, 85
  Hussein and, 20
  Israeli recognition, 42, 76n
  in Lebanon, 21, 99–100, 328
  National Congress meeting, 48
  as Palestinian representative, 181
  Sadat on, 88
  U.N. Resolution *242* and, 41, 54, 57, 60,
    67–68, 74–75, 89, 116, 132–33
  U.S. policy, 60, 85–86, 101–02, 169
  West Bank negotiations, 70, 327
Palestinian(s). *See also* Jordanian-Palestinian
  relationship; Palestine; Palestine Lib-
  eration Organization; Palestinian state
  Aswan formula, 179, 213–14
  autonomy, 23, 26, 94, 261
  Begin on, 84
  Camp David Accords and, 259
  Carter and, 29, 31, 60
  Egyptian plans for, 97, 182, 190–91, 211,
    292, 322–24
  Geneva representation, 42, 74, 91, 101–
    02, 105–06, 112, 119, 124–28, 138
  history, 79
  home rule, 153–54, 159, 189, 209, 213,
    217, 295
  inter-Arab divisions, 37
  interim regime, 213

Israel and, 62, 100, 150–51, 196, 327–28
legitimate rights, 120, 124, 245–46, 251,
    255, 275, 322
massacre of, 64
plebiscite, 182, 185–87, 200, 240
Rabin-Vance meeting, 40–41
referendum, 112, 121, 180, 185
self-determination for, 55, 80, 94, 98, 156,
    160–61, 183, 217, 222, 237, 255, 326,
    332
treaty linkage issue, 178, 211–12, 261,
    270, 280, 290, 321
trusteeship, 74
U.S. role, 333–38
Palestinian state, 67, 71, 76–77, 79, 102,
    124, 129, 181, 187, 246, 261. *See also*
    Jordanian-Palestinian relationship
Arafat on, 85, 102
Asad and, 128
Aswan Declaration, 160–61, 179, 192,
    194, 213–14, 216–17
Carter and, 60, 183
Gaza, 149
Israel on, 80–81, 127
right to, 68
trusteeship, 81
United States on, 73–74
Panama Canal treaties
political costs, 204
Senate vote, 171, 174, 188
Parker, Richard, 268
Peres, Shimon, 37, 215, 328
Rabin and, 53
Sadat and, 198, 203
West Bank and, 2
Persian Gulf, 335
Carter Doctrine, 295
oil crisis, 292
security in, 294–95
PLO. *See* Palestine Liberation Organization
Policy Review Committee. *See also* Vance,
    Cyrus R.
agenda, 38–40
arms sales, 71–72
on Begin visit, 70
Geneva and, 54–55, 74–76
Iranian crisis, 294
Powell, Jody, 254, 310
Presidency. *See also names of presidents*
domestic constituency, 336
electoral cycles, 13, 19–27
leadership and, 338–39
power base, 10

Quandt, William B., 8n, 20n, 33n, 54n, 76n,
    99–100n, 108n, 122n, 163n, 187–88n

National Security Council reassessment,
    191–94
secret planning group, 194–96
summit and, 212–14, 224, 227–30, 234,
    249, 251
treaty negotiations, 295–97

Rabin, Yitzhak, 37
Carter and, 62, 78
in Morocco, 109
PLO and, 79
resignation, 53
U.S. visit, 43–49, 81
Vance and, 40–41
Rabinowicz, Oscar K., 155n
Rafah, 149, 227
Rafshoon, Gerald, 254
Ras Muhammad, 200
Reagan, Ronald, 8n, 13
electoral cycle and, 18–19, 21, 25, 27
Lebanon and, 14
Middle East initiative, 328–29, 332
Referendum, Palestinian, 70, 180, 185
Refugees, 54, 63, 86. *See also* Palestinians;
    United Nations, Security Council Res-
    olution *242*
claims of, 114
compensation for, 222
Dayan on, 112
homeland for, 60, 102
rights of, 182
summit draft and, 245
Rhodes talks, 45, 104, 124
Rogers, William P., 17, 20, 41
Rogers Plan, 17–18, 41, 54
Romania
Israel and, 109–10
Sadat's visit, 144
Rosenne, Meir, 271
Rostow, Eugene, 274

Sadat, Anwar. *See also* Egypt; Egyptian-
    Israeli peace treaty
advisers, 231
Arab support, 97, 234, 302
Asad and, 34
assassination, 2
Begin and, 5, 72, 81, 162–63
Carter and, 14, 50–55, 115, 170–71, 258
concessions, 219
on Dayan, 148
doubts of, 87, 204
Fahd and, 67
Geneva procedures and, 61, 75, 138–40
on Israel, 96–97, 178

Jerusalem visit, 2, 18, 61, 114, 124, 136–139
Mondale talks, 197
Nixon and, 22
Nobel peace prize, 277
Palestinians and, 118, 190–91
political committee and, 165, 169
Soviets and, 26, 152
at summit, 219–58
summit strategy, 152, 213–14, 218, 220–23, 237–38
trilateral agreement, 208
U.S.-Soviet communiqué and, 123–25
Vance and, 87–90, 92–93
Saeki, Kiichi, 34n
SALT. *See* Strategic arms limitation talks
Samaria. *See* West Bank
Saud bin Faisal, Prince, 142
Saudi Arabia
aid to Egypt, 271
arms sales to, 19, 49n, 183, 190, 195, 204
Camp David Accords and, 212, 264
Carter and, 143, 160
oil, 37, 67, 292
as peacemaker, 34
post-summit role, 275, 283
Sadat and, 37, 197
Soviet threat, 18, 298
summit plans, 215, 231
treaty role, 297, 302–03
U.S. relations, 33
Vance and, 91, 160
Saunders, Harold H., 188, 194
Begin and, 276
summit drafts, 226–27
West Bank–Gaza plan, 201–02
Saxon, Wolfgang, 73n
Schiff, Ze'ev, 21n, 109n, 160n
Schlesinger, Arthur, Jr., 13n
Schlesinger, James R., 68
Self-rule proposal. *See* Home rule
Senate. *See also* Congress
Foreign Relations Committee, 16
Panama Canal treaty, 171, 174, 188
Settlements, Israeli, 45, 79, 153. *See also* names of specific places
freeze, 210–11, 217, 223, 226, 231, 247–53, 262–63, 323, 327, 329
Israeli policy, 69, 99, 113, 168, 238–54
legal status, 83
Mapai Plan, 81
post-summit, 161–62, 173, 276, 280
Sinai, 164, 210–11, 220, 225, 229, 231, 234, 236–37, 284, 293
summit disagreements, 100, 223–54, 263–64
U.N. resolution, 120

U.S.-Soviet communiqué, 119
Sharaf, Abd al-Hamid, 121–22
Sharm al-Sheikh, 44, 112
Sharon, Ariel
anti-Americanism, 288–89
on settlements, 111, 161n, 241–42, 257
treaty role, 309
on U.S. pressure, 197
Shia Muslims, 334
Shiloh, 162n
Shultz, George P., 21
Lebanon and, 25
Sick, Gary, 291n
Siegal, Mark, 49n, 182
Silver, Eric, 65n
Sinai Peninsula, 32. *See also* Settlements, Sinai
airfields, 223, 227–28, 236–37, 241
armament zones, 227
Egyptian-Israeli agreement, 254–57
Egypt's claim, 33, 66, 149, 155, 192, 232
impasse on, 217
Israeli withdrawal plans, 44, 73–74, 82, 110, 153, 155, 196, 200, 229, 234, 236, 245, 252, 256–57, 279–80, 282, 284, 286, 293
limited force zones, 273
oil fields, 238, 254–55, 281, 299, 302
permanent force limits, 276
Rogers Plan, 17–18, 41, 54
Sadat on, 88
secret agreements, 189
security arrangements, 173, 270
summit agreement, 227, 237–38, 241, 252–54
treaty negotiations, 266–68
U.N. peace forces, 312
U.S.-Israeli airfields, 298
U.S. summit plan, 212–14, 230–32, 234
Sinai II agreement, 23, 33, 51n, 59n, 201
Egyptian violations, 76
Ford's promise, 220
Sadat and, 262
Soviet Union
Afghanistan invasion, 24, 26
Geneva role, 36, 61–62, 86–87, 95, 98–99
Lebanon cease-fire and, 268
Middle East role, 18, 80–81, 298
Nixon and, 17
Sadat on, 88
U.S. joint communiqué, 18, 119–25, 130, 133, 135
U.S. policy, 8, 16, 334
State Department. *See also* Policy Review Committee; Vance, Cyrus R.
Lebanon options, 268

Middle East role, 12, 73–74, 95
Policy Planning Staff, 35
position papers, 36
Sadat memo, 170
summit plans, 207–20
Strait of Tiran, 112
Strategic arms limitation talks (SALT)
negotiations, 174
SALT II, 270
treaties, 26, 270
Strauss, Robert S., 24, 318
Sudan, 292
Suez Canal
Israeli transit through, 272
United States and, 21–22, 26
Sunni Muslims, 334
Syria. *See also* Asad, Hafiz al-; Golan Heights
Baath party, 146n, 152
bilateral treaty and, 180–81
break with Egypt, 149
Camp David Accords and, 128
cease-fire line, 106
diplomatic positions, 107
draft Israeli treaty, 105
Geneva role, 75, 116–17
Israeli agreements, 21, 33, 212
Israeli occupation, 32
Lebanon victory, 328
PLO and, 20, 102–03, 107, 328
treaty role, 137–38, 305
Sadat and, 90, 123
Sinai II and, 118
U.S.-PLO dialogue, 102–03
Vance in, 91
Sytenko, Mikhail, 120

Taba, 330
Tamir, Avraham, 230
Tel Aviv, 65
"Territory for peace" formula, 62–63, 327,
329, 332. *See also* United Nations, Se-
curity Council Resolution *242*
Transjordan, 64
Treaties. *See specific names, countries*
Trilateral Commission, 31
Tuhamy, Hassan, 148, 153
Dayan and, 109–11
Turner, Aron, 328n
Turner, Stansfield, 217

United Arab Kingdom, 88
United Nations
Carter speech to, 125–26
interim regime and, 182, 191, 228
Lebanon Resolution, 183, 267–68
Palestine mandate, 68n
Secretary General, 143

Security Council, 144
settlements and, 120
Truce Supervision Organization, 94, 112,
183, 242–43
United Nations, Security Council Resolu-
tion *242*. *See also* Borders
Camp David Accords and, 235, 243–44,
255–56
home rule and, 168–69
Israeli position, 33, 64, 72–77, 79, 84,
180, 210, 221, 228–29, 233–35, 327
Jordanian-Israeli treaty and, 245
PLO and, 46, 85–86, 89, 91, 98
Sadat on, 177
Soviets on, 119
treaty and, 80, 246
U.S. position, 59–60, 75, 107, 156, 172,
179, 193, 195–96, 216
withdrawal principles, 73, 184, 216, 240
United Nations, Security Council Resolution *338*, 33
Israeli position, 79
negotiations on, 80
U.S. support, 60, 75
United States. *See also specific agencies, depart-
ments, persons, programs*
credibility, 335–37
foreign policy, 3–4, 6–29, 333–39
Israeli defense pact, 59, 71, 126, 217–18,
242
in Lebanon, 25, 27
post-summit strategy, 259–68, 279
Reagan initiative, 328–29, 332
secret planning group, 194–96
Soviet communiqué, 119–25, 130, 133,
135
Strategic Petroleum Reserve, 68
summit preparations, 206–20
Working Paper for Geneva, 129–30, 138,
142, 152–53

Vance, Cyrus R., 15n. *See also* Policy Review
Committee; State Department
on arms sales, 179
background, 34–35
Begin and, 79–81, 153, 281–82, 287–89
Camp David Accords and, 4, 167, 257
Camp David II, 297–98
Dayan and, 111–12, 120–21, 188–90
on foreign policy, 14–15, 149–50, 197–98
Geneva plans, 61–62, 104–06
on home rule, 156–57
Hussein and, 153–54
Middle East trips, 39–40, 89–94, 151,
264–65, 286–89, 326
nine-point proposal, 172n
post-summit role, 270

priority of obligations and, 269
Sadat and, 53, 207, 286–87
summit strategy, 175, 207–20, 223–24, 229
treaty signing, 313
trusteeship, 94n
Venezuela, 68
Vietnam War, 8
Paris talks, 34

War Powers Act, 7
Watergate crisis, 17, 20
Weinberger, Caspar W., 19
Weizman, Ezer, 148, 161n, 189n, 202n
in Egypt, 158–60
Gamasy and, 162, 188
military committee and, 165
Mubarak and, 283
post-summit role, 211, 271, 277
resignation threat, 309
Sadat and, 192, 198, 203, 215, 238
settlements and, 236
at summit, 221, 223–27, 230–32, 241
Vance and, 288
in Washington, D.C., 183
West, John C., 303n
West Bank. *See also* Jerusalem; Palestinians; Settlements, Israeli; West Bank–Gaza proposals
Arab Jerusalem, 232
Begin on, 193–94, 323
Carter visit, 321
Israeli claim, 32, 64–65, 82, 84, 104, 200, 203, 209, 225, 227, 264, 305, 328
Jordanian claim, 126, 230
land sales, 200
mayors, 113
Syria and, 136
West Bank–Gaza proposals, 228–54. *See also* Jordanian-Palestinian relationship
Administrative Council, 246
autonomy talks, 1, 240, 248–49, 251, 256, 261, 316

Begin and, 193–94, 251–52, 260–61, 299, 323
cultural autonomy, 92, 94
Dayan on, 127–28
demilitarized, 185–86
elections, 283–84, 301
Egyptian policy, 171, 175, 200, 272, 280, 283
interim regime plan, 23, 55, 105, 150, 167, 172, 174, 182, 230–31, 240, 242, 326
Israeli concessions, 55, 73–74, 155–58, 216, 242–43
Jordan and, 114, 222, 242, 299, 332–33
mistakes, 325–27
Mubarak and, 328
Palestinian linkage, 243, 257, 277
peace treaty link, 218–19, 274, 312–14
Reagan on, 329
referendum, 54, 180
Sadat and, 287
secret agreements, 189
security concerns, 181–82, 187, 217–18
self-governing authority, 263, 269, 278, 282, 285–86
settlements, 231, 234, 247–51, 255–56, 263–64, 277, 330
signing, 254
sovereignty, 106, 210, 227
stages of negotiation, 226
territorial compromise, 45
trusteeship, 70, 89, 94, 101
U.N. control, 149
U.S. policy, 171–72, 212–14, 281, 329

Ya'ari, Ehud, 21n, 109n, 160n
Yadin, Yigal, 309
Yale University, 274
Yamit, 149, 153, 227, 257
Yost, Charles, 252
Zartman, I. William, 40n
Zionism, 31, 83. *See also* Jews, American
Betar wing, 65